Rabbinic Tales of Destruction

Rabbinic Tales of Destruction

Gender, Sex, and Disability in the Ruins of Jerusalem

JULIA WATTS BELSER

OXFORD
UNIVERSITY PRESS

OXFORD

UNIVERSITY PRESS

Oxford University Press is a department of the University of Oxford. It furthers
the University's objective of excellence in research, scholarship, and education
by publishing worldwide. Oxford is a registered trade mark of Oxford University
Press in the UK and certain other countries.

Published in the United States of America by Oxford University Press
198 Madison Avenue, New York, NY 10016, United States of America.

Library of Congress Cataloging-in-Publication Data
Names: Belser, Julia Watts, 1978– author.
Title: Rabbinic tales of destruction : gender, sex, and disability in the
ruins of Jerusalem / Julia Watts Belser.
Description: New York : Oxford University Press, [2018] |
Includes bibliographical references and index. |
Identifiers: LCCN 2017028642 (print) | LCCN 2017030893 (ebook) |
ISBN 9780190600488 (updf) | ISBN 9780190600495 (online content) |
ISBN 9780190853259 (epub) | ISBN 9780190600471 (cloth) |
ISBN 9780197536414 (paperback)
Subjects: LCSH: Women in rabbinical literature. | Sex in rabbinical
literature. | Sex crimes.
Classification: LCC BM509.W7 (ebook) | LCC BM509.W7 .B45 2018 (print) |
DDC 296.1/25306—dc23
LC record available at https://lccn.loc.gov/2017028642

Contents

Acknowledgements

MANY FRIENDS AND colleagues have been generous conversation partners over the course of writing this book, and I am grateful beyond measure for the rich exchange of ideas and questions that have helped bring these words into the world. I thank Ilana Szobel for an early conversation that catalyzed my thinking about violence and survival, as well as for friendship across disciplines. Bernadette Brooten has been a generous intellectual companion throughout the writing of this book, and I am grateful for her friendship and wise counsel. Daniel Boyarin, Krista Dalton, Gwynn Kessler, Lennart Lehmhaus, and Devorah Schoenfeld all shared perceptive comments that helped shape my thinking and hone my analysis. I'm grateful for a vibrant scholarly community in Disability Studies that has embraced my work and proven willing to venture with me beyond the modern moment. I thank Riva Lehrer, for a brilliant conversation about disability aesthetics and ruins, and Rosemarie Garland-Thomson, for thinking with me at the intersection of disability, literature, and ethics. Jeff Brune, Jonathan Hsy, Robert McRuer, David Mitchell, and Sharon Snyder offered comments and suggestions that helped transform a pivotal chapter, while a conversation with Alison Kafer helped crystalize its final form.

I had the pleasure of sharing this work in progress with many colleagues through seminars and invited lectures, all of which helped hone my arguments and often sparked new lines of inquiry. Thank you to the Yale Ancient Judaism Workshop, especially to Chris Hayes and Pratima Gopalakrishnan; the Frankel Center for Judaic Studies at the University of Michigan, especially to Rachel Neis and Jeffrey Veidlinger; Haverford College Gender and Sexuality Studies and the Department of Religion, especially to Anne Balay; the University of Aberdeen, especially to John Swinton and Aileen Barclay for amazing hospitality; and the University of Glasgow, especially to Hannah Tweed. I had the opportunity to teach texts from this book at the Maimonides Centre for Advanced Studies Summer School on Skepticism at the University of Hamburg; many thanks to Racheli Haliva for the invitation, and to the rabbinics cohort for incisive conversation. Profound gratitude goes the Institute for Research on Women and Gender at the University of Michigan, especially to Heidi Bennett, for the generous support of a Feminist Research Seminar, "Talmud Interrupted." In particular, I thank Rachel Neis and Max Strassfeld, my fellow seminar organizers and co-conspirators, who have been brilliant partners with whom to explore new modes of doing rabbinics, as well as to the scholars who dove so deeply into creative conversation with us: Cynthia Baker, Beth Berkowitz, Charlotte Fonrobert, Chaya Halberstam, Gwynn Kessler, Gil Klein, Sarra Lev, and Jennie Rosenfeld.

I began this book during a transformative year as a faculty fellow in Women's Studies in Religion at Harvard Divinity School. Profound thanks are due Ann Braude for creating such a fruitful crucible for innovative scholarship, as well as to Rachel Adelman, Azza Basarudin, Hauwa Ibrahim, and Michelle Wolfe, my fellow WSRP colleagues, for intellectual insights and encouragement while this book was in its earliest stages. I thank Jack Llewellyn and Victor Matthews for facilitating my leave from Missouri State University, and John Strong, for conversations about gender, violence, and the Hebrew Prophets after I returned. Thanks also to Jane Terry, administrative assistant at Missouri State, and Jacob Rhoads, WSRP administrator, for helping to manage the myriad details.

I wrote most of this book while at Georgetown University, and I am grateful to colleagues in the Theology Department for their warm welcome to a wonderful scholarly home. Department chairs Chris Steck and Fran Cho, as well as Graduate Director Jonathan Ray, have been generous in their support of my research. I am profoundly grateful to Georgetown for granting me Summer Faculty Research Grants, as well as a Junior Faculty Research Fellowship that provided me the gift of time to complete the manuscript. My graduate research assistant, Ray Kim, provided exceptional bibliographic assistance and offered an insightful reading of the entire manuscript. Many of my students read portions of this book and engaged in conversations that have helped shape my thinking about these ideas. I thank, in particular, the members of my 2016 Religion and Gender seminar, Nick Acosta, Danielle Clausnitzer, Ray Kim, Nathan Lean, and Shelton Nalley, whose perceptive comments and insightful questions helped me finalize the manuscript. Carole Sargent in the Office of Scholarly Publications once again provided invaluable support in navigating the waters of scholarly publishing. Amy Phillips at Georgetown's Woodstock Theological Library has been a tireless advocate for Judaica resources and continues to secure critical tools for my research.

Two chapters of this book first appeared elsewhere in earlier forms. Chapter two was first published as "Sex in the Shadow of Rome: Sexual Violence and Theological Lament in Talmudic Disaster Tales," in the *Journal of Feminist Studies in Religion*, and chapter seven first appeared as "Opulence and Oblivion:

Talmudic Feasting, Famine, and the Social Politics of Disaster" in the *AJS Review*. I thank both journals for permission to revise and include the chapters in this book.

It has been a tremendous pleasure working with Oxford University Press. As an editor, Cynthia Read championed this project from the very first and guided the manuscript expertly and expeditiously toward publication. Many thanks to the fantastic team that has worked to bring my book into the world: Drew Anderla, for all manner of editorial and production assistance, as well as for helping to secure such a beautiful cover image; Alyssa Russell, for marketing and promotion; Sivaranjani C., for managing the book's production; and Katherine Eirene Ulrich, for exceptional copyediting. I am grateful to Nancy Zibman for preparing a beautiful index; her meticulous attention to detail has saved me from error, even at the final hour.

Finally, my deepest gratitude to Devorah Greenstein, who has read these chapters many times and lingered with me over every word; to Sofia Betancourt, for probing with me the contours of violence and liberation; to Ibrahim Farajajé, z"l, who dared me to live into the deepest intersections of passionate scholarship and ethical commitment; to my parents, who have taught me so much and given so generously; and to Josh Johnson, for love and partnership, and for spiriting me away to wild places, so that the words stay true.

Thank you.

Introduction

THE DESTRUCTION OF the Jerusalem Temple by the Romans in 70 CE is argu-
ably the most over-narrated event in pre-modern Jewish history. A watershed
moment for the early Jewish community, the destruction radically reoriented
Jewish religious life and ushered in a new era of Roman political dominance over
Judea. Seth Schwartz gives a provocative assessment of the impact of the destruction. In the face of theological and political cataclysm, he asserts, Judaism "shattered."[1] While rabbinic Judaism eventually rises from the ashes of political defeat
to refashion Jewish identity and culture, the destruction of the temple remains a
foundational catastrophe in the Jewish religious imagination. Frequently elided
with the Babylonian destruction of the Solomonic temple half a millennium
before, these two disasters have long been imagined as the formative tragedies
of the Jewish people, a primal wound that both recalls and anticipates the sto-
ried misfortunes of the Jewish experience. In Jewish religious practice, the loss
of the temple encodes the ache of exile, an absence and estrangement that shapes
the contours of Jewish prayer and piety. Yet if the destruction stands as a potent
means of narrating the past, it also serves as an evocative articulation of catastrophe and resilience in the Jewish present. A powerful interpretive hermeneutic
for grappling with formative events of twentieth-century Jewish experience—the
cataclysm of the Holocaust, the advent of Zionism, and the emergence of the
modern state of Israel—the destruction has been used to seam together myriad

---

1. Seth Schwartz, *Imperialism and Jewish Society, 200 B.C.E. to 640 C.E.* (Princeton: Princeton
University Press, 2001). Schwartz's work has prompted substantial discussion in the literature;
for a substantial and important response, see Fergus Millar, "Transformations of Judaism under
Graeco-Roman Rule: Responses to Seth Schwartz's 'Imperialism and Jewish Society,'" *Journal
of Jewish Studies* 57, no. 1 (Spring 2006): 139–158. Schwartz's own retrospective reflection on his
work has been particularly important for my thinking. Seth Schwartz, "Was There a 'Common
Judaism' after the Destruction?," in *Envisioning Judaism: Studies in Honor of Peter Schäfer on
the Occasion of His Seventieth Birthday*, ed. Ra'anan S. Boustan, Klaus Herrmann, Reimund
Leicht, Annette Y. Reed, and Giuseppe Veltri, with the collaboration of Alex Ramos, vol. 1
(Tubingen: Mohr Siebeck, 2003).

stories of Jewish grief and Jewish survivals. It is a narrative inextricably entangled with the politics of loss and longing, a tale already overburdened with memory.

Why then another book about the destruction of the temple? This book makes two primary interventions. First, I center attention on the material and corporeal dimensions of rabbinic disaster narratives, to showcase catastrophe as a crisis of the flesh. *Rabbinic Tales of Destruction* offers a literary and cultural analysis of Bavli Gittin 55b–58a, the Babylonian Talmud's longest sustained account of the Roman conquest of Jerusalem. The Talmud's account begins with the famous story of Qamtsa and Bar Qamtsa, a tale that attributes the fall of the Second Temple to an act of grievous inhospitality at an ill-fated banquet and that culminates in Rabbi Yoḥanan ben Zakkai's daring escape from besieged Jerusalem. The passage has exercised a powerful hold on the Jewish imagination for centuries. While that cluster of stories has been the subject of considerable scholarly attention, the rest of Bavli Gittin's narrative has received scant critical attention.[2] I focus on this neglected corpus. In this book, I read Bavli Gittin's account of Roman conquest from the perspective of the wounded body and the scarred land. Bavli Gittin's stories are saturated with sexual violence, slavery, and the brutal corporeal costs of Roman imperial ambition. In these accounts, Roman dominance is etched on Jewish flesh and inscribed in rabbinic memory as an assault on the body and a violation of the land.

Our literary paradigms for thinking through the destruction have not yet grappled sufficiently with the consequences disaster has for ancient Jewish bodies. In this book, I analyze the effect of the brutal body costs of Roman domination— the material realities of sexual violence, enslavement, and disability—on rabbinic

---

2. In his influential treatment of the first portion of this complex story cycle, Jeffrey Rubenstein emphasizes that these tales were the subject of intricate, intentional redaction as a literary unit—and notes that "a comprehensive literary analysis" of the entire narrative remains "a desideratum." Jeffrey Rubenstein, *Talmudic Stories: Narrative Art, Composition, and Culture* (Baltimore: Johns Hopkins University Press, 1999), 140. The literature on Bavli Gittin 55b–56b is vast. See Jacob Neusner, *Development of a Legend: Studies on the Traditions Concerning Yohanan ben Zakkai* (Binghamton: Global Publications, 1960); Jacob Neusner, *A Life of Rabban Yohanan Ben Zakkai, ca. 1–80 CE* (Leiden: Brill, 1962); Anthony J. Saldarini, "Johanan ben Zakkai's Escape from Jerusalem: Origin and Development of a Rabbinic Story," *Journal for the Study of Judaism* 6 (1975): 189–220; Gedalia Alon, "Rabban Joḥanan B. Zakkai's Removal to Jabneh," in *Jews, Judaism, and the Classical World*, trans. Israel Abrahams (Jerusalem: Magnes Press, 1977), 269–313; Peter Schäfer, "Die Flucht Yoḥanan b. Zakkais aus Jerusalem und die Gründung des 'Lehrhauses' in Jabne," *Aufstieg und Niedergang der römischen Welt* 2.19.2 (1979): 43–101; David Kraemer, *Responses to Suffering in Classical Rabbinic Literature* (New York: Oxford University Press, 1995), 179–183; Anat Yisraeli-Taran, *Aggadot ha-Ḥurban* (Tel Aviv: Hakibbutz Hame'uḥad, 1997); Amram Tropper, "Yohanan ben Zakkai, *Amicus Caesaris*: A Jewish Hero in Rabbinic Eyes," *Jewish Studies, an Internet Journal* 4 (2005): 133–149; Sonja K. Pilz, *Food and Fear: Metaphors of Bodies and Spaces in the Stories of Destruction* (Würzburg: Ergon Verlag, 2016).

consciousness and rabbinic texts. In addition to the physical impact of catastrophe on tangible human bodies, I argue that corporeal risk profoundly shapes rabbinic narrative. To understand the material impact of destruction on rabbinic culture, I draw upon the rich theoretical resources of disability studies, gender and sexuality studies, as well as new materialist ecological criticism. Through such approaches, I illuminate the complex gender and sexual politics expressed in Bavli Gittin's accounts of rape and sexual captivity, its narratives of beautiful Jewish men and women assailed and desired by the powerful and decadent empire. I parse the Bavli's accounts of Jewish bodies undone by Roman violence, of the dismembered corpses that haunt the ruined places of Judea, of the blood and flesh that linger in its memories of the land. Catastrophe, I argue, textures the intimate interconnections rabbinic narratives draw between land and body, between bone and blood, river and stone. And when Bavli Gittin imagines God's ultimate triumph over imperial Rome? Here too, I show, divine power emerges victorious over the bodies of the enemy in strikingly corporeal terms. Through images of bodily rupture and physical suffering, the imperial body is revealed as porous and permeable: a body open to divine incursion, subject to torture and transformation.

Alongside this renewed attention to the material dimensions of catastrophe, I also make a second intervention. I argue that the theological frame we most frequently use to explain the meaning of destruction for ancient Jews does not accurately represent the full diversity of rabbinic responses to disaster.[3] Ancient Jewish writers commonly explain catastrophe in covenantal terms. According to this framework, disaster is inextricably linked with disobedience. Destruction and exile are the result of Jewish sin, and God will chastise a wayward Jewish community with the harsh rod of foreign domination, before ultimately restoring

---

3. On rabbinic responses to the destruction, see Jacob Neusner, "Judaism in a Time of Crisis: Four Responses to the Destruction of the Second Temple," *Judaism* 21 (1972): 313–327; Michael Stone, "Reactions to Destructions of the Second Temple," *Journal for the Study of Judaism* 12 (1981): 195–204; Anthony J. Saldarini, "Varieties of Rabbinic Response to the Destruction of the Temple," *Society of Biblical Literature Seminar Papers* 21 (1982): 437–458; Shaye J. D. Cohen, "The Destruction: From Scripture to Midrash," *Prooftexts* 2, no. 1 (1982): 18–39; Norman J. Cohen, "'Shekhinta ba-Galuta': A Midrashic Response to Destruction and Persecution," *Journal for the Study of Judaism* 13 (1982): 147–159; Robert Goldenberg, "Early Rabbinic Explanations of the Destruction of Jerusalem," *Journal of Jewish Studies* 33 (1982): 517–525; Baruch Bokser, "Rabbinic Responses to Catastrophe: From Continuity to Discontinuity," *Proceedings of the American Academy for Jewish Research* 50 (1983): 37–61; Robert Kirschner, "Apocalyptic and Rabbinic Responses to the Destruction of 70," *Harvard Theological Review* 78, no. 1–2 (1985): 27–46; David Kraemer, *Responses to Suffering in Rabbinic Literature*; Galit Hasan-Roken, *Web of Life: Folklore and Midrash in Rabbinic Literature* (Stanford: Stanford University Press, 2000); Kenneth R. Jones, *Jewish Reactions to the Destruction of Jerusalem in A.D. 70: Apocalypses and Related Pseudepigrapha* (Leiden: Brill, 2011).

their fortunes and turning back to them with love. These narratives offer an
account of pathos steeped in the poetics of self-recrimination, articulating a
theology of communal culpability that has been rejected by virtually all Jewish
thinkers writing in the post-Holocaust era. Yet as Alan Mintz and Jonathan
Klawans have argued, this idea had powerful theological utility in late antiquity.[4]
It affirms Jewish trust that the covenant remains intact, that sin can be expiated,
that their return to God's favor will come in God's own time. Such claims have
a long history in Jewish thought. Articulated already in the prophetic books of
Isaiah and Jeremiah, this frame for reading catastrophe shapes the writings of the
first-century Jewish historian Josephus.[5] It drives the theological discourse of the
Palestinian midrash collection Lamentations Rabbah, as well as the destruction
of Jerusalem and Judea in Yerushalmi Ta'anit.[6] It appears in Babylonian sources as
well, perhaps most famously in Bavli Yoma's claim that the temple was destroyed
on account of baseless hatred (*sinat ḥinam*).[7]

Yet something different happens in the fifth chapter of Bavli Gittin, the
Babylonian Talmud's longest account of the destruction of the Jerusalem Temple
and the devastation of Judea. Bavli Gittin has very little to say about Jewish sin.
While parallel narratives in the Palestinian sources emphasize collective transgression, Bavli Gittin's telling gives little voice to the trope of communal wrongdoing. Its few stories that feature Jewish sin focus on the aberrant behavior of
individuals, not the community as a whole. It also studiously avoids framing the
destruction as an act of divine chastisement. While Bavli Gittin does, at times,
imagine God as the ultimate architect of Jewish catastrophe, its portrayal of
the destruction does not highlight divine anger, but instead emphasizes God's
self-sacrificial empathy for individual Jews who have been wronged. Building on
David Kraemer's trenchant insight that Bavli Gittin's destruction narrative offers

4. Jonathan Klawans, "Josephus, the Rabbis, and Responses to Catastrophes Ancient
and Modern," *Jewish Quarterly Review* 100, no. 2 (Spring 2010): 278–309; Alan Mintz,
Ḥurban: Responses to Catastrophe in Hebrew Literature (New York: Columbia University
Press, 1984).

5. Jonathan Klawans, *Josephus and the Theologies of Ancient Judaism* (New York: Oxford
University Press, 2012).

6. On the reasons for destruction in Lamentations Rabbah, see S. Cohen, "The Destruction."
On the difference in emphasis between Bavli Gittin and Lamentations Rabbah, see Kraemer,
Responses to Suffering in Rabbinic Literature, 140–143, 179–183. On the role of complaint against
divine (in)justice in Lamentations Rabbah, see David Stern, *Parables in Midrash: Narrative
and Exegesis in Rabbinic Literature* (Cambridge: Harvard University Press, 1991), 134.

7. Bavli Yoma 9b.

"a strikingly naturalistic account of catastrophe,"[8] I argue that this theological reorientation offers an important and understudied voice amidst the diversity of rabbinic Jewish responses to the destruction. While Bavli Gittin ultimately affirms God's capacity to bring judgment upon the empire and reaffirms God's role as the ultimate architect of Jewish catastrophe, the bulk of the narrative focuses not on divine power, but on Roman might. Rome replaces God as the force to be reckoned with, the agent and arbiter of Jewish suffering.

At first glance, these two interests might strike the reader as distinct. But in this book, I argue that Bavli Gittin's corporeal and theological interests operate in tandem. Its stories are profoundly concerned with suffering, with the imprint that Roman violence leaves upon skin and soil and bone, with the loss of bodily sovereignty, with enslavement, with rape, with dismemberment, with pain. Bavli Gittin's alternative assessment of God's relationship to catastrophe—its avoidance of the trope of sin and punishment, its reticence to lay out strong claims about communal transgression of the covenant, its framing of sexual violation as the consequence but not the cause of destruction—go hand in hand with its narrative attention to Roman violence, its interest in the bodies that bear the impact of Roman imperial dominance. The rabbis, I argue, grapple with theology in and through the flesh. The victimized, vulnerable body becomes the ground out of which Bavli Gittin articulates an alternative theology of destruction, a theology in which God's presence is aligned not with the ascendant bodies of the victorious Roman conquerors, but with suffering Jewish flesh.

Rabbis, Romans, and Sassanians: Reading the Bavli between Empires

Rabbinic Judaism is a culture that emerges in the shadow of imperial power.[9] While scholars have increasingly come to agree that grappling with the impact

---

8. Kraemer, *Responses to Suffering in Rabbinic Literature*, 181.

9. In thinking about the relationship between the ancient and modern uses of the terms empire, imperialism, and colonialism, I am indebted to Mattingly's assessment of the Roman empire as an enterprise that shares many key characteristics with the empires of the nineteenth century and the present day, while also differing in certain significant respects from these modern and postmodern colonial practices. Following Mattingly's definitions, I use "imperialism" to refer to the cultural attitudes and geopolitical practices that allow a state to extend its reach beyond its own core territory, to exercise power and suasion over the populations of peripheral territories. "Colonialism" I take to refer to the system of rule by which a state exercises sovereignty over another people at a distance, often through the installation of settlements or other apparatuses of power within a conquered territory. David J. Mattingly, *Imperialism, Power, and Identity: Experiencing the Roman Empire* (Princeton: Princeton University Press, 2011), 5–10.

of the Roman Empire is foundational for understanding late antique Jewish culture, we can nonetheless note key differences in the way scholars approach the rabbis' relationship to Rome. Seth Schwartz has famously argued that the rabbis were a marginal force in the context of Roman society, positioning them as a largely closed group on the fringes of the Roman city.[10] More recently, Hayim Lapin has urged us to read the Palestinian rabbis as Roman provincials, as sub-elites who were not only profoundly affected by Romanization, but who engaged and deployed Roman norms of law and governance to create a place for themselves within the Roman political economy and the Roman provincial system.[11] My own work treats both paradigms as valuable frames for illuminating different dimensions of rabbinic culture, which I view as simultaneously marked by the experience of political and cultural marginality, as well as by accommodation and embrace. Such a dual perspective, I maintain, can help illuminate the ways in which rabbinic culture adopts a self-conscious posture of distinction and difference even as the rabbis are themselves embedded within Roman (and Sassanian) cultures. It allows us to better reckon with the multivalent nature of rabbinic agency: the way the rabbis operate under the constraints of empire, even as they actively craft a place for themselves within it. Such a frame highlights the complexity of rabbinic power, recognizing the rabbis as subject to imperial power, even as they engage in crafting a legal-cultural system that affords them elite status over their own marginalized others.

Consider my parenthetical insertion of Sassanian, another invitation to further complicate the imperial politics of rabbinic culture. While the relationship between rabbis and Romans has long been recognized as an important dimension of Jewish culture in late antiquity, scholars have only recently begun to consider the dynamic interplay between Babylonian rabbinic and Sassanian cultures, including the significant parallels that exist between rabbinic literature

---

10. Schwartz, *Imperialism and Jewish Society*.

11. Hayim Lapin, *Rabbis as Romans: The Rabbinic Movement in Palestine, 100–400 CE* (New York: Oxford University Press, 2012). Bernie Hodkin argues that Lapin's view does not fully take into account "the conscious ideological resistance of the rabbis . . . One is reminded of Homi Bhabha's argument that to be Anglicized is definitively not to be English; as such, to be Romanized is definitely not to be Roman." Bernie Hodkin, "Repression and Romanization: Postcolonial Studies in Ancient Judaism," *Ancient Jew Review*, November 26, 2014. For an assessment of Lapin's claims about Romanization, see Ishay Rosen-Zvi, "In What Sense Were the Rabbis Roman?," *Marginalia*, August 13, 2015. On mimicry and identity in colonial contexts, see Homi K. Bhabha, *The Location of Culture* (New York: Routledge, 1994), 85–92.

and Pahlavi sources.[12] In this book, I do not aim to make a definitive claim that the Bavli's Persian context plays a determinative role in shaping Bavli Gittin's portrayal of Rome. Such a reading, it seems to me, risks reducing complex cultural narratives to a simplistic interpretation of historical context. Yet, at various points, I will speculate about the ways in which the Bavli's cultural context may shape its narrative interests or its political aims. In considering this question, let me be clear: I do not pursue the question of whether Pahlavi sources influenced Bavli Gittin's portrayal of the destruction. Scholars have often framed the question of cultural influence in terms of concrete textual effects, using parallel sources to trace the significant impact that Zoroastrian religio-legal concepts have upon the development of rabbinic law and narrative.[13] The cumulative effect of such research has had a profound impact on my thinking about rabbinic culture, underscoring the degree to which Babylonian rabbinic literature is deeply embedded within Sassanian culture. My own work, however, approaches the question from a different tack. Rather than seek out narrative parallels, I wonder, instead, how the cultural and political position of Babylonian rabbinic Jews within the Sassanian Empire shapes rabbinic portrayals of Rome. In this way, I suggest, recognizing Babylonian rabbinic Jews as subjects of Rome's great imperial rival might inform our analysis of the cultural and political effects of rabbinic narrative.

Babylonian rabbinic Jewish culture emerges in a complex and contested borderland between the Sassanian and Roman empires. Rather than imagining a distinct boundary between these cultural regions, my own thinking is indebted to approaches that recognize the porous, fluid nature of cultural exchange. Richard Kalmin and Daniel Boyarin both situate rabbinic Babylonia within a shared cultural world that draws upon the intellectual currents of Roman Hellenism, Syriac Christianity, and Sassanian Zoroastrianism.[14] Kalmin argues that Roman

---

12. For an important discussion of legal parallels, see Yaakov Elman, "'Up to the Ears' in Horses' Necks (B.M. 108a): On Sasanian Agricultural Policy and Private 'Eminent Domain,'" *Jewish Studies, an Internet Journal* 3 (2004): 95–149. On recontextualizing the Bavli in the context of the Sassanian empire, see Shai Secunda, *The Iranian Talmud: Reading the Bavli in Its Sassanian Context* (Philadelphia: University of Pennsylvania Press, 2013) and Jason Sion Mokhtarian, *Rabbis, Sorcerers, Kings, and Priests: The Culture of the Talmud in Ancient Iran* (Berkeley: University of California Press, 2015).

13. Yaakov Elman has pioneered critical research on the relationship between early Iranian legal texts and rabbinic tradition. For a helpful introduction, see Elman, "Middle Persian Culture and Babylonian Sages: Accommodation and Resistance in the Shaping of Rabbinic Legal Tradition," in *Cambridge Companion to Rabbinic Literature*, ed. Charlotte Elisheva Fonrobert and Martin S. Jaffe (New York: Cambridge University Press, 2007), 165–197.

14. Daniel Boyarin, "Hellenism in Jewish Babylonia," in *Cambridge Companion to The Talmud and Rabbinic Literature*, ed. Charlotte E. Fonrobert and Martin S. Jaffee

culture had a significant reach within the eastern parts of the Sassanian Empire. Palestinian influences, he claims, shaped Babylonian rabbinic thought in the fourth century and beyond.[15] Syriac Christianity also has a significant impact on the development of Babylonian rabbinic culture, as Michal Bar-Asher Siegal has shown.[16] Following Bar-Asher Siegal, I agree that the interaction between Syriac Christianity and rabbinic Judaism should not solely be framed through the lens of polemic. Let us hold open an imaginative space to consider a wide range of interactions between and among these communities. Yet we must also recognize that the medium of cultural mixity in late antiquity was often intertwined with war and conquest, with the corporeal costs of imperial ambitions. During the centuries of the Bavli's composition and redaction, the two rival empires engaged in significant military conflict. After a series of victories along the border, the Sassanian king Shapur I (r. 239/240–272) made several advances into the eastern Roman Empire in which he captured and deported large numbers of people and resettled them within western Persian border provinces. A mainstay of Sassanian military practice, wartime population transfer brought a significant influx of Roman culture and learning into the Sassanian Empire, helping to fuel the development of Syriac Christianity and the Christian school at Nisibis.[17]

When we read Bavli Gittin's destruction narratives, we must consider the political salience of telling these tales in Sassanian Babylonia. In such a context, I suggest, rabbinic repudiation of Rome has a complex, multivalent significance. It surely reinforces a familiar articulation of Jewish difference that imagines the rabbinic in contrast to the Roman, a well-known trope that runs throughout late antique Jewish literature. Of course, the Bavli's vehemence against Rome may well function as a veiled polemic of Sassanian power. But I wonder: Might

(Cambridge: Cambridge University Press, 2007), 336–363; Daniel Boyarin, *Socrates and the Fat Rabbis* (Chicago: University of Chicago Press, 2009); and Richard Kalmin, *Jewish Babylonia between Persia and Roman Palestine* (New York: Oxford University Press, 2006).

15. Emphasizing that Palestinian traditions had long circulated in Babylonia, Kalmin argues that the fourth century marks an increase and intensification of the amount of Palestinian influence. Kalmin, *Jewish Babylonia*, 3–8, 174.

16. Michal Bar-Asher Siegal, *Early Christian Monastic Literature and the Babylonian Talmud* (New York: Cambridge University Press, 2013).

17. Erich Kettenhofen, "Deportations," *Encyclopedia Iranica* 7, no. 3 (2014): 297–312; Richard Frye, *History of Ancient Iran* (Munich: Beck, 1984), 296–303; Matthew P. Canepa, *The Two Eyes of the Earth: Art and Ritual of Kinship between Rome and Sasanian Iran* (Berkeley: University of California Press, 2009), 27–29; and Josef Wiesehöfer, *Ancient Persia from 550 BC to 650 AD* (London: Tauris, 1996), 201. On the School of Nisibis, see Adam Becker, *Fear of God and the Beginning of Wisdom: The School of Nisibis and Christian Scholastic Culture in Late Antique Mesopotamia* (Philadelphia: University of Pennsylvania Press, 2006).

the Bavli's anti-Roman posture also serve as a positive means of affiliation, a way through which rabbinic Jews might align themselves with Sassanian imperial ambition? Might these stories offer a means of signaling Jewish allegiance to the Sassanian political project, a way of articulating Jewish resistance to Rome as a quasi-"patriotic" gesture? Such a frame affords us a different lens through which to consider the significance of the Bavli's claims vis-à-vis Christianity. When the Bavli gives voice to anti-Christian polemic, those narratives need not be read only as expressions of "religious" difference, narrowly construed. In a context where Christianity is increasingly intertwined with the politics of the Roman Empire, rabbinic expressions of anti-Christian sentiment may well lodge a protest against Christian imperium, a protest that rejects and mocks the great rival of the Sassanian Empire. While this book leaves such questions of authorial intent ultimately unresolved, I hope that in gesturing toward these possibilities, my work opens up alternative modes of conceptualizing the cultural and political salience of rabbinic narrative.

Reconsidering Resistance: Subversion and Surrender in Rabbinic Literature

Postcolonial analysis of rabbinic literature has been deeply influenced by James C. Scott's idea of the "hidden transcript," the discourse of a subjugated people that exists beyond the gaze of the dominant power. While subordinate groups often collude with colonial powers in public, Scott argues that they simultaneously cultivate spaces for articulating alternative responses to dominant power. Meant to remain outside the view of the dominant gaze, such hidden transcripts offer marginalized communities a shared, subterranean means of mocking and subverting the claims of their rulers.[18] Scholars of rabbinics have made frequent use of Scott's theory. Daniel Boyarin has underscored the ways in which rabbinic narratives of gender and sexuality, martyrdom and heresy reveal a complex interplay of accommodation and resistance to Roman power.[19] Beth Berkowitz shows

---

18. James C. Scott, *Domination and the Arts of Resistance: Hidden Transcripts* (New Haven: Yale University Press, 1990). For an assessment of the significance of Scott's work for late antiquity, albeit focusing particularly on early Christianity, see Richard Horsley, ed., *Hidden Transcripts and the Arts of Resistance: Applying the Work of James C. Scott to Jesus and Paul* (Atlanta: Society of Biblical Literature, 2004).

19. Daniel Boyarin, *Dying for God: Martyrdom and the Making of Christianity and Judaism* (Stanford: Stanford University Press, 1999), 46–49; Daniel Boyarin, *Unheroic Conduct: The Rise of Heterosexuality and the Invention of the Jewish Man* (Berkeley: University of California Press, 1997), 240–241. Daniel Boyarin, *Carnal Israel: Reading Sex in Talmudic Culture* (Berkeley: University of California Press, 1993), 16–18.

how substantially rabbinic rituals of capital punishment have been inflected by the rabbis' experience as colonial subjects. Rabbinic portrayals of execution, she argues, utilize Roman norms in order to bolster rabbinic authority—and reappropriate them to critique Roman power and assert the primacy of Torah.[20] Ra'anan Boustan has also argued that rabbinic narratives of post-mortem punishment of the wicked and divine revenge upon Roman emperors become a means of resisting Christian Roman imperial claims, a perspective which will be particularly important for this study.[21]

When I began this book project, the twin motifs of resistance and subversion were my primary hermeneutical tools for grappling with these stories, for making meaning out of rabbinic accounts of conquest and catastrophe. Such frameworks offer a compelling way to highlight rabbinic agency, revealing the capacity of story to speak back to the grammar of empire, to snatch victory from the midst of political and somatic defeat. I still find Scott's theory an illuminating means of drawing forth a particular form of rabbinic response to Roman imperium, particularly the ways in which the Bavli flips the script of imperial power. Yet I also want to mark my own discomfort with this frame, my increasing distrust of the way I have, at times, used resistance to avoid a stark grappling with defeat, with the imprint that loss and incursion leave upon rabbinic narrative. Thinking with Ilana Szobel, who argues that American and Israeli interpreters have too often framed narratives of trauma and woundedness in terms of "recovery," I have grown skeptical of my own desire to find within these narratives a story of resilience and redemption.[22] In a retrospective response to critics of *Imperialism and Jewish Society*, Seth Schwartz asks similar questions. Considering the widespread opposition to his claim that the Jews who survived successive Roman assaults "simply exhausted their capacity to resist," Schwartz suggests that his conclusion was challenged in part because of its "apparent

---

20. Beth Berkowitz, *Execution and Invention: Death Penalty Discourse in Early Rabbinic and Christian Cultures* (New York: Oxford University Press, 2006), 154.

21. Ra'anan Boustan, "Immolating Emperors: Spectacles of Imperial Suffering and the Making of a Jewish Minority Culture in Late Antiquity," *Biblical Interpretation* 17 (2009): 207–238. My thinking has also been shaped by the work of Peter Schäfer, *Jesus in the Talmud* (Princeton: Princeton University Press, 2007) and Israel Yuval, *Two Nations in Your Womb: Perceptions of Jews and Christians in Late Antiquity and the Middle Ages* (Berkeley: University of California Press, 2008).

22. I am indebted to Ilana Szobel for an early conversation about this work that helped me articulate the importance of focusing on victimhood and counter-redemptive narrative. See Ilana Szobel, *A Poetics of Trauma: The Work of Dahlia Ravikovitch* (Waltham: Brandeis University Press, 2013).

antiromanticism," its refusal to imagine ancient Jews through the lens of heroic resistance.[23]

In this book, I take seriously both possibilities. I highlight moments in which Bavli Gittin's destruction narratives express resistance to Roman regimes, the way in which the Bavli's discourse mocks and subverts Roman power. But I also pause to interrogate my own readings, to ask how my desire to read resistance within rabbinic texts might obscure other dimensions of these tales: defeat, incursion, loss, and conquest. Thus, I aim to read in two directions: revealing rabbinic subversion, even as I also show how rabbinic story acquiesces to empire, how it surrenders to the material and metaphysical realities of Roman dominance. Such an act is both a literary and an ethical intervention. "Whatever else happened in the wake of the Destruction and the Bar Kokhba Revolt," Schwartz cautions, "the fact that great numbers of people were killed and enslaved must not be elided. Disasters are disasters, and there are no silver linings for their victims."[24] As readers, I believe, we must deepen our capacity to witness catastrophe. In his reading of Lamentations, Tod Linafelt observes that classical and contemporary readers of the biblical book have often sought to recuperate the raw emotions of the text, lifting up the rare expressions of comfort and professing these to be "the theological core" of the text.[25] Such an act, it seems to me, is its own kind of violence. Bavli Gittin's text is not oriented toward triumph or redemption; its tales give vivid voice to brutality, to violation, to death. Following Linafelt's counsel, I will ask us to linger with the fact of human suffering, with the dead and the dismembered. I tarry with pain, refusing the temptation to alchemize it into comfort and consolation. Even in narratives that articulate God's eventual triumph over Roman imperium, I argue, the visceral reality of physical pain and bodily rupture makes redemption a thing of guts and blood, an eschatology in extremis.

Rabbinics and New Materialism: Thinking Disaster Through Flesh, Blood, and Dirt

Rabbinic Tales of Destruction: Gender, Sex, and Disability in the Ruins of Jerusalem probes the literary remains of catastrophe, approaching these texts from a decidedly materialist bent. I examine the intertwined effects of Roman conquest on rabbinic accounts of body and land, asking how the rabbinic narrative grapples

---

23. Schwartz, " 'Common Judaism' After the Destruction," 16.

24. Schwartz, " 'Common Judaism' After the Destruction," 4.

25. Tod Linafelt, *Surviving Lamentations: Catastrophe, Lament, and Protest in the Afterlife of a Biblical Book.* (Chicago: University of Chicago Press, 2000), 2–4.

with the history of imperial violence, how the text wrestles with a past that is littered with the remains of ruined flesh. To do so, I turn to new materialist feminist theorist Stacy Alaimo's conception of transcorporeality, which tracks "the interconnections, interchanges, and transits between human bodies and nonhuman natures."[26] It is hardly a significant innovation to observe that war and conquest pose a crisis for the body and for the land. Yet, as Alaimo argues, modern notions of the self as a sovereign subject have often led us to imagine the body as separate from its environment, sealed off from meaningful encounter with its non-human surroundings. Such a tidy distinction is belied by Bavli Gittin's account of catastrophe, in which brutalized bodies bleed over into the soil, run into the rivers, and seep into the sea. A transcorporeal reading of rabbinic disaster narratives can help us better attend to the relationship between these two dimensions of material experience, to understand the visceral imprint empire leaves on the porous boundaries between blood, flesh, and stone. Through such striking interconnections, the land itself becomes a repository for the materiality of rabbinic memory, retaining the tangible remains of a catastrophe that has bled into the very earth.

But if land matters in these rabbinic destruction narratives, we must also account for the Bavli's distance from the epicenter of Roman conquest, its remove from the physical terrain of Judea. In this book, I draw upon postcolonial environmental theorists to shift the way we think about the impact of conquest and destruction, in order to better account for its diffuse temporal and geographic effects. Following Ann Laura Stoler's trenchant call, I aim to trace "the toxic corrosions and violent accruals of colonial aftermaths," focusing on way imperial violence shapes flesh, mind, earth, and memory.[27] Rabbinic Babylonia, I argue, is a fruitful site through which to grapple with Roman conquest precisely because it foregrounds the question of distance, because it challenges our tendency to circumscribe colonial effects by confining them to a narrowly bounded historical moment and geographical place. Violence lingers. Its effects persist, long after and long farther than such frames allow. Tracing the long arc of environmental and colonial devastation, Rob Nixon argues that conventional notions of violence most frequently focus on spectacle, registering primarily the immediate, direct impact of conquest and catastrophe. Such a frame obscures what he calls "slow violence," the incremental and diffuse effects that war and conquest have upon bodies, minds, and lands, the way violence continues to play out over

---

26. Stacy Alaimo, *Bodily Natures: Science, Environment, and the Material Self* (Bloomington: Indiana University Press, 2010), 2.

27. Ann Laura Stoler, ed., introduction to *Imperial Debris: On Ruins and Ruination* (Durham: Duke University Press, 2013), 2.

centuries. Nixon draws our attention to "attritional catastrophes that overspill clear boundaries in time and space," catastrophes that are "marked above all by displacements—temporal, geographical, rhetorical."[28] If we recognize the Roman conquest of Judea as an attritional catastrophe, a catastrophe shaped by temporal and geographical displacements, we become more attuned to the complex significance that Rome has within the Babylonian rabbinic imagination. As Stoler observes, colonial power is not "bounded by the formal legalities of imperial sovereignty over persons, places, and things."[29] Imperial presence extends beyond the formal jurisdiction of Roman law and legal authority, stretching past the specific confines of time and territory, shaping the terrain of rabbinic mind and body and memory even beyond the boundaries of empire.

Sex, Slavery, and Violence: Rabbinic Gender Politics and Colonial Conquest

While imperial presence surely has many consequences for rabbinic culture and consciousness, this book foregrounds the impact of conquest on rabbinic notions of gender and sexuality. In an illuminating postcolonial analysis of early Christian discourse, Davina Lopez argues that Roman imperial conquest was suffused with the imagery of sexual dominance, that the Romans conceptualized military victory as the rape and subjugation of nubile, feminized nations.[30] Building upon Lopez's claim that Paul's writings resist this imagery of Roman victory as sexual dominance, I argue that Bavli Gittin likewise subverts these gendered power ideologies and resists Roman triumphalism. While these discursive dimensions of violence are critical for parsing the gender and sexual politics of rabbinic disaster narratives, I emphasize that the impact of sexual violence extends beyond metaphor. Bavli Gittin's narratives expose the sexual risk and bodily vulnerability that Jewish men and women faced during Roman conquest, particularly in situations of forced prostitution and enslavement. My thinking about the intersection of sexual violence and slavery is indebted to the work of Bernadette Brooten, who emphasizes the profound role that slavery plays in shaping Jewish, Christian, and Muslim conceptions of gender, body, and personhood.[31]

---

28. Rob Nixon, *Slow Violence and the Environmentalism of the Poor* (Cambridge: Harvard University Press, 2011), 7.

29. Stoler, *Imperial Debris*, 2.

30. Davina Lopez, *Apostle to the Conquered: Reimagining Paul's Mission* (Minneapolis: Fortress Press, 2008).

31. Bernadette Brooten, ed., *Beyond Slavery: Overcoming Its Religious and Sexual Legacies* (New York: Palgrave Macmillan, 2010).

In *Rabbinic Tales of Destruction*, I argue that enslavement contours the rabbis' responses to conquest and catastrophe. Scholarship on slavery in rabbinic texts has focused primarily on the treatment of enslaved persons under rabbinic law. Catherine Hezser's pioneering study of Jewish slavery in late antiquity focuses almost entirely on ancient Jews as slaveholders.[32] Gail Labovitz's recent work on slavery and gender in rabbinic texts reveals the way in which the rabbis' sexual access to enslaved women threatens to undo their masculine virtue and destabilize the sexual morality of the rabbinic household.[33] My approach shifts our attention toward different questions. In Bavli Gittin, tales of conquest and its aftermath give voice to Jewish experiences of enslavement, portraying Jews as vulnerable to corporeal degradation and the sexual advances of their Roman masters. In ancient Rome, as Kyle Harper has shown, slavery was suffused with sex.[34] In an important study, Jennifer Glancy has argued that the material realities of slavery shape and constrain gender, body, and personhood in early Christian religious thought and social practice.[35] Similarly, I ask how enslavement as a real or remembered risk shapes the rabbis' own self-understanding, how the threat of enslavement bleeds into narrative, how it contours the after-images of destruction.

What consequence does conquest have for the rabbis' understanding of sex and gender? Daniel Boyarin has famously argued that Roman conquest profoundly shapes rabbinic masculinity, that while Roman culture celebrated the valorized virility of the Roman warrior as a model of ideal manhood, rabbinic culture affirmed a softer, more feminized man—the "sissy-boy" of the study house.[36] In a still influential assessment, Boyarin presented rabbinic masculinity

---

32. Catherine Hezser, *Jewish Slavery in Antiquity* (New York: Oxford University Press, 2006).

33. Gail Labovitz, "More Slave Women, More Lewdness: Freedom and Honor in Rabbinic Constructions of Female Sexuality," *Journal of Feminist Studies in Religion* 28 (2012): 69–87; Gail Labovitz, "The Purchase of His Money: Slavery and the Ethics of Jewish Marriage," in Brooten, *Beyond Slavery*, 91–106. My thinking on the way systems of enslavement shape late antique experiences of corporeality, gender, and sexuality within household space has also been influenced by Chris de Wet, *Preaching Bondage: John Chrysostom and the Discourse of Slavery in Early Christianity* (Berkeley: University of California Press, 2015).

34. Kyle Harper, *Slavery in the Late Roman World, AD 275–425* (Cambridge: Cambridge University Press, 2011); see also Craig Arthur Williams, *Roman Homosexuality: Ideologies of Masculinity in Classical Antiquity* (New York: Oxford University Press, 1999).

35. Jennifer Glancy, *Slavery in Early Christianity* (Minneapolis: Fortress Press, 2006).

36. On the gender implications of imperial power and colonial dominance in rabbinic contexts, see D. Boyarin, *Unheroic Conduct*; D. Boyarin, *Dying for God*; and Jonathan and Daniel Boyarin, *Powers of Diaspora: Two Essays on the Relevance of Jewish Culture* (Minneapolis: University of Minnesota Press, 2002).

as the countertype of Roman social norms, the inverse and opposite of Roman masculinity. As Ishay Rosen-Zvi has observed, rabbinic conceptions of masculinity are surely more complex than such a sharp dichotomy allows.[37] Rather than encoding a straightforward resistance to Roman gender norms, rabbinic culture also marks masculine virility through the register of combat within the agonistic world of the study house, a space that Jeffrey Rubenstein has shown to be suffused with the metaphors (and perhaps also embodied expressions) of violence.[38] More recently, Boyarin has moved away from the idea of a sharp dichotomy between the rabbinic and the Roman, recognizing instead the degree to which rabbinic culture is always already conditioned by the Roman and Sassanian cultures in which it is embedded.[39]

In my own work, I build upon Boyarin's insight that Roman conquest matters for rabbinic masculinity, without aiming to articulate an essential difference between rabbinic and Roman manhood. Where Boyarin has primarily focused attention on the ways in which the rabbis' status as colonial subjects shapes their experience of masculinity, I ask about the significance of Roman conquest for the rabbis' portrayal of Jewish women. I argue that the rabbis' experience on the underside of Roman imperium shapes their gender politics in significant ways. Foundational feminist scholarship focused on the rabbis as authoritative jurists, parsing the gender implications of rabbinic responses to sexual violence. Scholarship by Judith Hauptman, Rachel Biale, Ronit Irshai, and Aviva Richman has shed critical light on the complex ways rabbinic legal texts address sexual violence.[40] Such approaches have, understandably, treated the rabbis as legal authorities who *respond* to sexual violence. My work, by contrast, considers rabbinic vulnerability to sexual threat. By focusing particularly on narratives that make explicit reference to Roman conquest, I foreground the

---

37. Ishay Rosen-Zvi, "The Rise and Fall of Rabbinic Masculinity," *Jewish Studies, an Internet Journal* 12 (2013): 1–22.

38. Jeffrey Rubenstein, *The Culture of the Babylonian Talmud* (Baltimore: Johns Hopkins University Press, 2003), 54–66.

39. Daniel Boyarin, "Friends Without Benefits: Or, Academic Love," in *Sex in Antiquity: Exploring Gender and Sexuality in the Ancient World*, ed. Mark Masterson, Nancy Sorkin Rabinowitz, and James Robson (New York: Routledge, 2015), 517–535.

40. Rachel Biale, *Women and Jewish Law: An Exploration of Women's Issues in Halakhic Sources* (New York: Schocken Books, 1984); Judith Hauptman, *Rereading the Rabbis: A Woman's Voice* (Boulder: Westview Press, 1988); Ronit Irshai, "Rape in Jewish Law," paper presented at the Society for Jewish Ethics Annual Meeting, Washington, DC, January 7, 2012; Aviva Richman, "Sexual Coercion and Consent and the Development of Legal Subjectivity in Rabbinic Literature" paper presented at the Society for Jewish Ethics Annual Meeting, Toronto, January 8, 2016.

ways in which imperial violence forces the rabbis to grapple with men's sexual vulnerability and bodily risk. In these contexts, Bavli Gittin's narratives reveal a striking sensitivity to women's sexual risk. Where conventional rabbinic texts frequently portray women's beauty as an incitement to male sexual desire in ways that make women responsible for men's sexual interest, Bavli Gittin's stories make plain the way that Jewish women and men alike are vulnerable to the lust and avarice of the conqueror. These narratives recognize the sexual culpability of the aggressor, reconfiguring conventional rabbinic notions of beauty and danger.

Bavli Gittin's tales also depart from familiar tropes of women's sexual sin as an explanation for catastrophe. Within the Hebrew Bible, the prophets commonly deploy female infidelity as an explanatory metaphor for the national defeat of Israel and Judah. Prophetic rhetoric frames the Israelites' betrayal of the covenant as a sexual transgression that provokes divine violence. These metaphors of female infidelity are particularly prominent in prophetic narratives that respond to national catastrophe; exile becomes understood as a consequence of the feminized nation's sexual sin. Biblical scholars have documented how prophetic religious critique commonly uses pornographic portrayals of the female body to signal punishment and revulsion, figuring whoredom as justification for divine violence and abandonment. In the Bavli's narratives of destruction, however, sexual violence occupies a different rhetorical place. Furthering Michael Satlow's insight that Babylonian rabbinic culture often expresses discomfort with the prophetic "marriage metaphor," I argue that Bavli Gittin's destruction narratives avoid evoking the prophetic motif of national and religious catastrophe as divine response to women's sexual sin.[41] Instead, images of woman as whore are figured in these narratives *as the consequence, but not the cause* of destruction. In striking contrast to the prophetic image of the wayward wife, several Bavli narratives situate *male* sexual and ethical transgression as a key cause of destruction. In keeping with Ishay Rosen-Zvi's insight that the Bavli is often particularly interested in accentuating the sexual responsibility of rabbinic men, Bavli Gittin's stories also suggest that masculine virtue might persevere in the midst of disaster—and become an antidote to the violence and violation experienced by the Jewish body, the Jewish land, and the Jewish God.[42]

41. Michael Satlow, *Jewish Marriage in Antiquity* (Princeton: Princeton University Press, 2001), 56.

42. Ishay Rosen-Zvi, *Demonic Desires: "Yetzer Hara" and the Problem of Evil in Late Antiquity* (Philadelphia: University of Pennsylvania Press, 2011).

Disability Studies and Rabbinic Destruction Narratives

In tandem with my critical interest in sexuality and gender, I also apply disability studies theory to rabbinic literature, probing the cultural significance of disability and impairment in rabbinic law and narrative.[43] For religious studies scholars, disability studies offers a theoretical framework for interrogating the way in which religious texts and cultural systems construct ideals of bodily perfection and demarcate certain kinds of bodies as different or deviant. Disability studies "denaturalizes" disability. It treats disability as a social fact, not a straightforward bio-physical condition. Disability studies theorists stress that disability is produced through stigma and other social processes: stares and lingering looks that single out bodies that deviate from society's expectations, architectural and technological choices that privilege certain kinds of moving and being in the world, and conceptions of rationality and behavior that permit narrow expressions of appropriate cognition and emotion.[44] Rosemarie Garland-Thomson has coined the term "normate" to politicize the notion of a normal body and to call attention to its inverse—"the figure outlined by the array of deviant others whose marked bodies shore up the normate's boundaries."[45] Probing the cultural construction of these categories affords us critical insight into the way a given culture structures normalcy and deviance, the way it idealizes certain body forms, as well as the way it polices the boundaries of the human. As Candida Moss has argued, when

---

43. See Julia Watts Belser, "Reading Talmudic Bodies: Disability, Narrative, and the Gaze in Rabbinic Judaism," in *Disability in Judaism, Christianity and Islam: Sacred Texts, Historical Traditions and Social Analysis*, ed. Darla Schumm and Michael Stolzfus (New York: Palgrave Macmillan, 2011), 5–28; Julia Watts Belser, "Brides and Blemishes: Queering Women's Disability in Rabbinic Marriage Law," *Journal of the American Academy of Religion* 84, no. 2 (2016): 401–429; Julia Watts Belser, "Disability, Animality, and Enslavement in Rabbinic Narratives of Bodily Restoration and Resurrection" *Journal of Late Antiquity* 8, no. 2 (2015): 288–305.

44. For foundational discussion of the "social" model of disability, see Lennard Davis, *Enforcing Normalcy: Disability, Deafness, and the Body* (New York: Verso, 1995). My thinking on these issues has been particularly shaped by scholars working at the intersection of disability studies and feminist and queer theory, including Rosemarie Garland-Thomson, "Integrating Disability, Transforming Feminist Theory," *National Women's Studies Association Journal* 14, no. 3 (2002): 1–32; Alison Kafer, *Feminist, Crip, Queer* (Bloomington: Indiana University Press, 2013) and Robert McRuer, *Crip Theory: Cultural Signs of Queerness and Disability* (New York: New York University Press, 2006).

45. Rosemarie Garland-Thomson, *Extraordinary Bodies: Figuring Physical Disability in American Culture and Literature* (New York: Columbia University Press, 1997), 8.

historians and scholars of religion take disability for granted, we miss something vital about ancient perceptions of embodiment.[46]

How shall we define disability? Because the notion of disability is inseparably intertwined with culture, the category itself has no fixed, stable meaning. Neither biblical nor rabbinic texts have a single term that encompasses the modern concept of disability. Perhaps the closest term is *mum* (blemish), which biblical and rabbinic authors use to categorize a variety of physical and sensory impairments. In its biblical context, however, the term *mum* includes certain physical characteristics (such as a broken arm) that most moderns do not consider a disability, while excluding others (such as deafness) that are commonly included in modern definitions. Despite the differences between the biblical category of the *mum* and contemporary concepts of impairment, I find the modern scholarly conception of disability to be a useful frame for analyzing corporeal difference in rabbinic contexts. Rather than using the term disability to designate a stable, unified category of somatic or mental impairments, I use the terminology of disability to signal the way diverse bodily conditions operate within a given culture to generate a marked, stigmatized difference. Rabbinic sources do use certain disabilities as identity categories, most notably singling out individuals who are blind (*ʿivver*), lame (*piseaḥ*), deaf-mute (*ḥeresh*), and mentally disabled (*shoteh*); they also use a common triad of "the deaf-mute, the mentally disabled, and the young person" to identify individuals who are exempt from the performance of certain religious obligation. Such categories, I argue, evoke an implicit category of disability, a recognized and stigmatized identity constructed through a perceived physical or sensory impairment.[47]

In *Rabbinic Tales of Destruction*, I probe the significance of disability within rabbinic narrative, aiming to parse the meanings scripted onto disabled bodies, as well as the way that disability affords the rabbis a symbolic discourse with which to think through the ruin of Jerusalem. My work rests on the recognition that literary representations of disability perform potent cultural work. Disability studies scholars David Mitchell and Sharon Snyder have coined the term "narrative prosthesis" to describe literature's "perpetual discursive dependency upon

---

46. Candida R. Moss, "Heavenly Healing: Eschatological Cleansing and the Resurrection of the Dead in the Early Church," *Journal of the American Academy of Religion* 79. no. 4 (2011): 991–1017.

47. See Julia Watts Belser, "Judaism and Disability," in *World Religions and Disability,* ed. Darla Schumm and Michael Stolzfus (Waco: Baylor University Press, 2016), 93–113; Julia Watts Belser and Lennart Lehmhaus, "Disability in Rabbinic Judaism," in *Disability in Antiquity*, ed. Christian Laes (New York: Routledge University Press, 2016), 434–452.

disability."[48] Within the Western literary canon, they argue, disability is a "contrivance upon which so many of our cultural and literary narratives rely."[49] Disability imagery is not primarily about the physicality of particular bodies. Instead, literary evocations of disability are freighted with symbolic significance. Authors commonly make instrumental use of disability to convey character, express metaphor, and propel plot. Biblical narrative, Jeremy Schipper has shown, evinces a similar dependence on disability, using disability imagery to express, condense, and convey complex ideas about bodies and beauty, suffering and meaning, valor and heroism.[50] In his foundational work on disability in the accounts of the Davidic monarchy, Schipper argues that biblical writers use disability imagery to express complex and at times contradicting ideological positions related to national identity and Davidic kingship.[51]

My work also considers the role that disability plays in narrating national identity. In the cultural grammar of conquest, I argue, defeat disables the nation. While scholars increasingly recognize the effect that Roman conquest has on social experiences of gender and sexuality, the relationship between imperialism and disability has received less attention.[52] Alongside my interest in parsing the effects of imperial conquest on the social experience of gender and sexuality, I argue that the symbolic discourse of defeat at the hands of Rome shapes rabbinic perceptions of ability and capacity. In this book, I approach the project of reading for disability in two ways. First, I examine narratives that feature characters who might register "as disabled" according to either rabbinic or modern schemas of disablement. Such tales are obvious candidates for disability studies analysis. But I maintain that the tools of disability studies need not be confined to narratives that feature conventionally disabled characters. Instead, I apply a disability studies lens more broadly to tales of conquest and resilience, interrogating the ways

48. David T. Mitchell and Sharon L. Snyder, *Narrative Prosthesis: Disability and the Dependencies of Discourse* (Ann Arbor: University of Michigan Press, 2000), 47.

49. Mitchell and Synder, *Narrative Prosthesis*, 51.

50. Jeremy Schipper, *Disability and Isaiah's Suffering Servant* (New York: Oxford University Press, 2011); Jeremy Schipper, *Disability Studies and the Hebrew Bible: Figuring Mephibosheth in the David Story* (New York: T & T Clark, 2006).

51. Schipper, *Disability Studies and the Hebrew Bible*.

52. On the relationship between disabled bodies and Roman imperial conquest in early Christian narrative, see Warren Carter, "'The blind, lame and paralyzed' (John 5:3): John's Gospel, Disability Studies, and Postcolonial Perspectives," in *Disability Studies and Biblical Literature*, ed. Candida R. Moss and Jeremy Schipper (New York: Palgrave Macmillan, 2011), 129–150, and Sharon V. Betcher, *Spirit and the Politics of Disablement* (Minneapolis: Fortress Press, 2007), 128.

these narratives figure the relationship between physical capacity and corporeal power, as well as the narrative significance they afford to bodily integrity and rupture.

The disabled body, I suggest, frequently functions as a powerful, expressive symbol of disaster.[53] Using disabled bodies to stand in for conquered Jerusalem affords certain rabbinic narratives a powerful symbolic discourse for expressing the visceral incursions of imperial power. Disability studies theorists have, however, emphasized the importance of critiquing cultural discourses that tie disability inexorably with tragedy and suffering.[54] Even as I parse the way in which disablement expresses trauma and violation, I also probe for ways in which disabled figures flip the conventional script of loss and vulnerability. At the same time that subjugated bodies bear the material costs of opposition to the imperial project, these very bodies can also become potent sites of resistance, sites through which communities can critique Roman power and dominance—and also articulate the subversive potency of the unruly, dissident body that refuses to perform as desired beneath the imperial regime.

Structure of the Book

I have chosen to organize *Rabbinic Tales of Destruction* thematically, rather than following the narrative sequence of Bavli Gittin's text. Within individual chapters, my readings of specific sections of Bavli Gittin aim to preserve the flow and sequence of the original narrative, but the book itself does not move sequentially through the talmudic text. Each chapter examines key literary motifs and cultural dynamics of Bavli Gittin's narratives in comparison with parallel rabbinic accounts of the destruction, primarily drawn from Lamentations Rabbah and Yerushalmi Taʿanit. I frequently return to narratives I have already discussed, situating them anew in a different analytical context, inviting the reader to encounter them again. Such choices may startle readers expecting a more conventional literary analysis, in which character development, plot, and moral meaning unfold and deepen over the course of narrative's arc. Yet Bavli Gittin's account of the destruction does not take the form of a singular, over-arching narrative. A few

---

53. Julia Watts Belser, "Disability and the Social Politics of 'Natural' Disaster: Toward A Jewish Feminist Ethics of Disaster Tales," *Worldviews: Global Religions, Culture, and Ecology* 19, no. 1 (2015): 51–68.

54. This critique is foundational in disability studies scholarship; I cite here two recent works that have been particularly influential for my thinking: Alison Kafer, *Feminist, Queer, Crip*; Rosemarie Garland-Thomson, "The Case for Conserving Disability," *Journal of Bioethical Inquiry* 9, no. 3 (September 2012): 339–355.

sections of Bavli Gittin's text have been carefully crafted as literary units. In his masterful analysis of the opening tale sequence in Bavli Gittin 55b–56b, Jeffrey Rubenstein has demonstrated that the redactors integrated disparate elements into a unified story, imposing an intentional temporal sequence on the narrative and underscoring key themes through recurring motifs and repeated words that link the individual stories together.[55] Other passages, such as Bavli Gittin's account of Titus's destruction of the temple and God's eventual recompense, show similar signs of literary craft. Yet taken as a whole, Bavli Gittin's account of the destruction has a largely anthological character.[56] Eli Yassif coined the term "story cycle" to describe this unit, which is composed of twenty-seven stories about the destruction.[57] In order to most cogently illuminate these tales, I eschew examining them in strict narrative sequence, focusing instead on recurring themes in order to best illuminate the distinctive dimensions of Bavli Gittin's portrayal of the destruction and probe its cultural significance.

The first chapter examines the nexus of gender, sex, and sin in early Jewish narrative, arguing that Bavli Gittin's account of catastrophe reveals a strikingly different portrayal of sexual sin. I begin by examining the motif of women's sexual transgression as a source of national danger in the Hebrew Prophets and in Palestinian rabbinic traditions. Biblical narrative frequently uses graphic portrayals of the female body to convey God's punishment of Israel, figuring women's "whoredom" as justification for divine violence and abandonment. The Palestinian midrash collection Lamentations Rabbah amplifies and intensifies such dynamics, coupling the motif of women's sexual infidelity with the notion of women's sexual treachery to produce a narrative account of Jerusalem's fall that figures sexual violation and bodily brutality as the fitting consequence of women's brazenness. Bavli Gittin, by contrast, studiously avoids associating destruction with women's sexual sin. Instead, its tales emphasize the consequences of men's

---

55. Rubenstein, *Talmudic Stories*, 144–147.

56. On the creative dimensions of the anthology as a genre, see David Stern, ed. *The Anthology in Jewish Literature* (New York: Oxford University Press, 2004). Eliezer Segal suggests that much of the Talmud should be understood in anthological terms; he also stresses the dynamic and constructive elements of the redactors' role in crafting an anthology. Eliezer Segal, "Anthological Dimensions of the Babylonian Talmud," in Stern, ed., *Anthology in Jewish Literature*, 84.

57. Eli Yassif, "The Cycle of Tales in Rabbinic Literature [Hebrew]," *Jerusalem Studies in Hebrew Literature* 12 (1990): 103–146; Eli Yassif, *The Hebrew Folktale: History, Genre, Meaning* (Bloomington: Indiana University Press, 1999), 209–244. Abraham Weiss calls these tales "the aggadot of destruction" and considers them a self-contained source inserted into the Bavli with only minor editing. Abraham Weiss, *Studies in the Literature of the Amoraim* [Hebrew] (New York: Horeb, 1962), 261–263.

sexual transgressions. But even as its narratives draw attention to male sexual sin, Bavli Gittin also portrays conquered men's compromised bodies as stunning sites of sexual virtue, suggesting that men's sexual piety might serve as an antidote to the violence and violation of the Jewish body amidst Roman conquest.

The second chapter examines the theological significance of sexual violence in the aftermath of Roman conquest. Rabbinic accounts of sexual violence, enslavement, and forced prostitution intertwine theological lament with the brutal body costs of Roman domination. Talmudic narratives mimic pervasive Roman symbolism of imperial dominance as a form of "sexual conquest," using that symbolism to express rabbinic lament and violation at the hands of Rome. These stories articulate of rabbinic resistance to imperial violence, emphasizing Jewish resilience even in the midst of intense suffering. In contrast to the biblical motif of women's whoredom as provoking divine punishment, the rabbinic narratives instead position God and woman alike as violated by Rome. While the move to align Jewish and divine suffering reveals an important cultural shift, I argue that these stories make instrumental use of rape as a way to give voice to divine woundedness and rabbinic lament. Ultimately, the symbolic and theological significance afforded to rape largely reinscribes the vulnerability of women and enslaved people—and draws attention away from the embodied experience of those most likely to bear the brunt of sexual violence.

The third chapter examines a particular feature of the Bavli's tales of men and women taken captive by Rome: their focus on the spectacular beauty of the captured Jewish body. In these stories, I contend, beauty performs potent cultural work, highlighting both the vulnerability of Jewish flesh and the covetousness of the conqueror. Through sexualized narratives that portray the captive Jew as victim of Roman greed, Bavli Gittin makes use of a common Roman moral trope: concern for *luxuria*, an insatiable desire for luxury that is also expressed in lust and licentiousness. The Bavli's beauty tales forge a potent critique of elite Roman decadence and moral degradation. Perhaps even more significantly, I argue, these tales reveal a striking departure from the conventional beauty politics of rabbinic culture. The Babylonian Talmud frequently figures women's beauty as a source of spiritual danger to rabbinic men and imposes limits on women's visibility and voice to curb the threat that beauty poses. By contrast, these narratives offer a strikingly different assessment. They portray the beautiful woman as a victim, not a threat. Amidst situations of overt Roman violence, Bavli Gittin affirms the moral innocence of violated men and women who are subjected to the conqueror's lust. In this respect, Bavli Gittin's stories articulate a strikingly egalitarian response to sexual danger. Beauty becomes a shared risk, a body burden borne by women and men alike.

The fourth chapter uses disability studies theory to analyze the political and cultural significations of the body amidst Roman conquest. Extending the insights of scholars who have examined how Roman colonial dominance reshapes Jewish gender discourse, this chapter argues that imperial violence similarly restructures the way rabbinic narrative portrays the body. My analysis centers on the figure of Rabbi Tsadok, a celebrated priest who fasted for forty years in an attempt to avert the destruction of Jerusalem. Examining the Rabbi Tsadok tales in Bavli Gittin and Lamentations Rabbah, I argue that Rabbi Tsadok's body is used to mark the visceral impact of Roman conquest—and to stage the possibility of rabbinic resistance to Roman domination. In contrast to Bavli Gittin's beauty tales, the Rabbi Tsadok traditions in Lamentations Rabbah chronicle the enduring scar that catastrophe leaves upon the flesh. Yet even as these stories use disability to make visible the tremendous loss that destruction brings, they also resignify the cultural logic of imperial victory, emphasizing the subversive power of disabled Jewish flesh.

The fifth chapter reads Bavli Gittin's destruction narratives through the lens of ecological materialist criticism, tracing the trail of blood and other fleshy residues of the body that run through Bavli Gittin's account of the devastation of Betar. Where the third chapter emphasized the beauty and integrity of the captive Jewish body, these tales imagine the body dismembered, undone by the conqueror's violence. Filled with transcorporeal images of blood and brain seeping into the land, these tales blur the boundaries between human bodies and the rest of the material world. The rocks and rivers of Judea bear the blood and viscera of murdered thousands, retaining some physical trace of the nameless dead. But even as Bavli Gittin's narratives mark and memorialize the lingering presence of body and blood in the land, the tales betray an anxious instability: the tangible remains of Jewish death are all too easily washed away, rendered ephemeral. In this chapter, I trace tensions over materiality and memory, permanence and erasure, heroism and defeat in the tales of the boiling blood of the slain prophet Zechariah and the martyrdom of the mother of seven sons, parsing the Bavli's complex discourse of ruin and redemption.

The sixth chapter grapples with rabbinic fantasies of revenge and recompense, focusing primarily on the lengthy rabbinic tale of Titus's downfall after his destruction of the temple. I analyze the Titus narrative through the framework of rabbinic eschatology, demonstrating how the tale critiques the arrogance and hubris of the conqueror, imagines the downfall of the wicked, and undercuts the triumphalist assertions of Roman imperial power. I argue that these rabbinic eschatological fantasies are expressed in striking corporeal terms: through images of bodily rupture and physical pain, as well as the humiliation and degradation of flesh that accompany the unmaking of the imperial body. Through striking images of the body as a porous and permeable space, these narratives challenge the notion of Roman-Christian power as sealed and sovereign—imagining the imperial body as vulnerable to divine incursion, open to divine touch.

The seventh chapter builds upon the critique of hubris begun in the previous chapter, but turns its attention to Bavli Gittin's self-critical assessment of the ethical failings of the rabbis and other Jewish elites. Through tales of feasting in the shadow of catastrophe, Bavli Gittin articulates striking concerns about the collateral costs of opulent wealth, calling attention to the way that extravagant luxury isolates and insulates those who dine at the fanciest tables from the gritty realities of violence and danger. Key moments in Bavli Gittin's narrative center around food: the shame of Bar Qamtsa at a feast sparks his eventual betrayal of the Jews, the tale of Marta bat Boethus recounts the starvation of the wealthiest woman in Jerusalem, and Caesar destroys Tur Malka in retaliation for an opulent banquet. This chapter contextualizes Bavli Gittin's feast tales in the context of Roman and Sassanian banquet culture, parsing the intersections of gender, class, and social status present in these rabbinic food narratives. Through its critical representation of high-class oblivion, these tales underscore the physical and moral dangers of social privilege. Throughout the book, I have argued that Bavli Gittin's narratives turn away from the familiar link between sin and disaster. Yet Bavli Gittin's account of the destruction is not unconcerned with ethics. This chapter argues that stories of luxurious eating serve as a powerful source of rabbinic social critique, illuminating the way that corrosive concerns about status and shame lead elites to protect their private interests by sacrificing the well-being of the broader community. Through these feasting narratives, Bavli Gittin crafts its account of the destruction as a potent call for self-critical reflection about the way wealth, luxury, and social privilege distance elites from the awareness of suffering in their midst.

I

The Sexual Politics of Destruction

GENDER, SEX, AND SIN IN BAVLI GITTIN

IN THE BABYLONIAN Talmud's longest and most elaborate account of the Roman conquest of Judea, the fifth chapter of the tractate Bavli Gittin blames the destruction of the Jerusalem Temple on a case of mistaken identity at a disastrous late antique dinner party—on the shame and betrayal sparked by a banquet gone wrong. One of the best-known episodes in the Babylonian Talmud, the story of Qamtsa and Bar Qamtsa initiates a chain of tales that culminates in the daring escape of Rabbi Yoḥanan ben Zakkai from the besieged city of Jerusalem, where the rabbinic hero negotiates with the Roman general Vespasian and secures the right to found the rabbinic academy of Yavneh. Brimming over with drama and pathos, tragedy and resilience, these stories have attracted an enormous amount of attention, both in scholarly and popular literature.[1] My interest lies elsewhere. I am drawn instead to the stories that come after—stories that recount the ruination of Judea and the devastating losses at Betar, stories that belie the redemptive arc of Rabbi Yoḥanan's famous flight. Taking up where most interpreters leave off, I focus on the rest of Bavli Gittin's narrative, which recounts in excruciating detail the bloodshed, brutality, enslavement, and sexual violation that follows in the wake of Roman conquest. These are stories that grapple with defeat and dismemberment, stories of desperation and despair. These are stories saturated with sexual violence, with colonial incursion and corporeal loss.

Bavli Gittin's narratives portray conquest and destruction as a crisis of the body, a crisis intertwined with sex and slavery, with a loss of sovereignty that

---

1. My thinking about these texts is indebted to Rubenstein, *Talmudic Stories*, 139–175. An important recent treatment of these narratives can be found in Pilz, *Food and Fear*. For a more comprehensive acknowledgment of the literature, see the introduction.

not only reorients Jewish relationships with land, but also with the flesh. Bavli Gittin frames the destruction of Judea as a *corporeal* violation. From a tale that depicts Titus's conquest of the temple through an act of rape on the altar to a story that imagines the sexual misuse of another man's wife as the catalyst that sparks the ruin of Jerusalem, sexual violence runs through Bavli Gittin's account of catastrophe.

When I first began this project, I expected the Bavli's tales to amplify the familiar motif of women's sexuality as a central cause of national calamity, to imagine "wayward women" as a risk to the security and sovereignty of the nation. Such links between sex and disaster have a long history in ancient Jewish literature. In the Hebrew Bible, the prophets commonly deploy female infidelity as an explanatory metaphor for the national defeat of Israel and Judah. The prophetic books of Hosea, Ezekiel, Jeremiah, and Judges frequently frame the Israelites' betrayal of the covenant as a sexual transgression that provokes divine violence. Military defeat and national catastrophe are often understood as a consequence of the feminized nation's sexual sin. Biblical scholars have documented how prophetic religious critique commonly uses pornographic portrayals of the female body to signal punishment and revulsion, figuring whoredom as justification for divine violence and abandonment.[2] Beyond the Bible, such rhetoric also holds a powerful place in rabbinic discourse. A lengthy story in the Palestinian midrash collection Lamentations Rabbah, for example, couples the motif of women's sexual infidelity with the notion of women's sexual treachery to produce a narrative account of Jerusalem's fall that figures sexual violation and bodily brutality as the fitting consequence of women's brazenness.

Because sexual violence plays such a significant role in Bavli Gittin's account of the destruction, I assumed its stories would reiterate—if not intensify—this familiar link between gender, sex, and sin. But as I probed the gender implications of these tales more deeply, I came to a surprising conclusion: Bavli Gittin reconfigures the sexual politics of destruction. It avoids evoking the prophetic motif of national and religious catastrophe as divine response to women's sexual sin. Instead, sexual violence occupies a strikingly different rhetorical place. While Bavli Gittin frequently depicts women in sexual danger, it steadfastly refuses to blame women for their own violation. It does not deploy the motif of the wayward wife or brazen daughter. When sexual sin *does* surface in the narrative, Bavli Gittin's destruction narratives focus instead on *men's* sexual transgression, highlighting the bitter consequences of male sexual indiscretions. Yet alongside this

2. While the literature on this subject is significant, I am particularly indebted to the work of Renita J. Weems, *Battered Love: Marriage, Sex, and Violence in the Hebrew Prophets* (Minneapolis: Fortress Press, 1995).

interest in masculinity in crisis, Bavli Gittin's narratives also open up a counter-discourse that portrays conquered men's compromised bodies as stunning sites of sexual virtue. In these tales, masculine virtue becomes a powerful force that might yet persevere in the midst of crisis—and serve as an antidote to violence and violation.

Accounting for Destruction: Sin, Punishment, and the Gendered Rhetoric of Covenant

The first and second centuries of the Common Era were a tumultuous time for the Judean community. A series of failed Jewish revolts led to tremendous destruction and a profound political reorientation of Judean life. The Romans destroyed the Second Temple in Jerusalem in 70 CE, setting fire to the sanctuary and razing the symbolic center of the Jewish community. They annexed the province of Judea, bringing it under direct Roman political control, and permanently stationed a full imperial legion in Jerusalem.[3] The Roman conquest had devastating consequences. Even beyond the massive casualties and loss of life, the war brought about land seizures, increased taxation, and economic repression.[4] The Bar Kokhba uprising in 132–135 CE, brutally suppressed by Rome, deepened the privations and losses that marked life in Judea after the first revolt.[5] Roman dominance refashioned the material and sacred geographies of the land. Describing the consequences of conquest, the Roman historian Cassius Dio writes, "At

---

3. Seth Schwartz, "Political, Social, and Economic Life in the Land of Israel, 66–c.235," in *The Cambridge History of Judaism, Volume 4*, ed. Steven T. Katz (New York: Cambridge University Press, 2006), 25; Schwartz, *Imperialism and Jewish Society*.

4. Cassius Dio's history portrays the tremendous loss of life and destruction of the war itself, claiming that the Romans destroyed 50 significant fortifications and 985 villages, killing 580,000 soldiers. While such accounts cannot, of course, be taken as a straightforward assessment of the consequences and casualties of the war, Fergus Millar suggests that they are suggestive of "the exceptional scale and ferocity of the conflict." Millar, "Transformations of Judaism," 145. Millar argues that the siege of Jerusalem in 70 CE was a substantial Roman military action, lasting five months and requiring more soldiers than the Romans assembled for the conquest of Britain. Fergus Millar, "Last Year in Jerusalem: The Commemoration of the Jewish War in Rome," in *Flavius Josephus and Flavian Rome*, ed. J. Edmondson, S. Mason, and J. Rives (Oxford: Oxford University Press, 2005), 101.

5. Assessing the Roman response to the Bar Kokhba revolt, Werner Eck concludes that "the Roman high command realized that it was facing a situation fraught with danger, a situation which called for tapping all possible resources and the new deployment of its military forces; it justified taking extraordinary measures to prevent the crisis from getting out of hand." Werner Eck, "The Bar Kokhba Revolt: The Roman Point of View," *Journal of Roman Studies* 89 (1999): 81–82. See also Peter Schäfer, *Der Bar-Kokhba-Aufstand: Studien zum zweiten jüdischen Krieg gegen Rom* (Tübingen: Mohr Siebeck, 1981).

Jerusalem, Hadrian founded a city in place of the one which had been razed to the ground, naming it Aelia Capitolina, and on the site of the temple of the god he raised a new temple to Jupiter."[6] Jews were forbidden residence within the city, even as the emerging architectural forms monumentalized Roman triumph.[7] Through the deliberate erasures and reconstructions of colonial dominance, Jerusalem was refashioned as a site of Roman military victory.

The Roman conquest, tied inextricably in Jewish imagination to the memory of the first destruction of Jerusalem by the Babylonians in 587 BCE, reverberates in Jewish thought as a catastrophe of devastating proportions. In his influential study of catastrophe in Jewish life and literature, Alan Mintz argues that an event becomes catastrophic not because of the scale or scope of physical and material devastation, but because of the existential challenge it poses to "shared assumptions about the destiny of the Jewish people in the world." In responding to catastrophe, Mintz maintains, interpreters face an urgent task: "to reconstruct, replace, or redraw the threatened paradigm of meaning, and thereby make creative survival possible."[8] Drawing on theological explanations that animate the writings of many biblical prophets, ancient Jewish writers most commonly explain catastrophe in covenantal terms.[9] According to this framework, disaster is inextricably linked with disobedience. When the Jewish people fail to fulfill their sacred and social obligations, God orchestrates political or military disaster, using the armies of the foreign conqueror to chastise and rebuke the Jewish community. Modern readers may well recoil from such theology, hearing in such formulations a justification for abuse and violence, an intimation that communal sin is repaid through collective suffering. Yet for ancient interpreters, this theological frame had tremendous potency. It made Jewish defeat comprehensible, without calling God's power or presence into question. It preserved the terms of the covenant, emphasizing that Jewish loyalty and fidelity to God would ultimately be

---

6. Cassius Dio, *Roman History*, trans. Earnest Cary, Loeb Classical Library (Cambridge: Harvard University Press, 1925), 69.12.1. On Aelia Capitolina and the refounding of other existing places as Greek cities, see Nicole Belayche, *Iudaea-Palaestina: The Pagan Cults in Roman Palestine (Second to Fourth Century)* (Tübingen: Mohr Siebeck, 2001).

7. On the role of architecture in articulating empire, see Laura Nasrallah, *Christian Responses to Roman Art and Architecture: The Second-Century Church Amid the Spaces of Empire* (New York: Cambridge University Press, 2010).

8. Mintz, *Ḥurban*, 2.

9. My thinking about early Jewish responses to the destruction has been particularly shaped by Cohen, "The Destruction"; Goldenberg, "Early Rabbinic Explanations"; Hasan-Rokem, *Web of Life*; Kirschner, "Apocalyptic and Rabbinic Responses"; Jonathan Klawans, *Josephus and the Theologies of Ancient*; Kraemer, *Suffering*; and Mintz, *Ḥurban*. Further acknowledgment of the vast literature on rabbinic responses to the destruction can be found in the introduction.

rewarded. It positioned Jewish political subjugation as a temporary condition, not a permanent and enduring reality. And it left intact God's eventual promise to restore Jewish fortunes and bring recompense to Israel's conquerors.[10]

Narratives grappling with the fall of the Second Temple appear in a variety of rabbinic sources, as well as in the chronicles of the ancient Jewish historian Josephus.[11] Within rabbinic literature, Lamentations Rabbah represents the longest and most elaborate collection of destruction narratives, framed through commentary and exegesis on the book of Lamentations.[12] Targum Lamentations, an Aramaic translation of the biblical book, likewise preserves commentary that aims to elucidate the biblical narrative in light of more recent disasters.[13] A substantial collection of disaster tales also appears in the fourth chapter of Yerushalmi Taʿanit, as the Palestinian Talmud discusses the fast days of the Seventeenth of Tammuz and the Ninth of Av, two days that commemorate disastrous occurrences in Jewish history. Scholars speculate that these traditions and tales had wide currency in early Jewish communities, particularly because the observance of these two holy days tied the recitation and exposition of the book of Lamentations into the regular rhythms of Jewish religious life and practice.[14] Many shared traditions appear across these diverse accounts, similarities that likely attest to the wide circulation of oral traditions and folk narratives about the

---

10. Jonathan Klawans, "Josephus, the Rabbis, and Responses," 278–309.

11. In an important assessment of the relationship between Josephus' account of the destruction and rabbinic traditions in Lamentations Rabbah, Holger Zellentin argues that Josephus' reception by early Christian thinkers and his influence upon Patristic literature is a decisive factor for understanding the relationship between Josephus and rabbinic literature. Holger M. Zellentin, "Jerusalem Fell after Betar: The Christian Josephus and Rabbinic Memory," in Boustan et al., eds., *Envisioning Judaism*.

12. On the textual history of Lamentations Rabbah, see Paul Mandel, "Between Byzantium and Islam: The Transmission of a Jewish Book in the Byzantine and Early Islamic Periods," in *Transmitting Jewish Traditions: Orality, Textuality, and Cultural Diffusion*, ed. Yaakov Elman and Israel Gershoni (New Haven: Yale University Press, 2000), 74–106. Paul Mandel, "Midrash Lamentations Rabbati: Prolegomenon, and a Critical Edition to the Third Parasha" [Hebrew] (Ph.D. diss., Hebrew University, 1997); Paul Mandel, "The Story in Midrash Eichah: Text and Style" [Hebrew] (M.A. thesis, Hebrew University, 1983). For a literary and folkloristic analysis, see Hasan-Rokem, *Web of Life*.

13. Christian M. M. Brady, *The Rabbinic Targum of Lamentations: Vindicating God* (Leiden: Brill, 2003); Philip S. Alexander, *The Targum of Lamentations* (Collegeville: Liturgical Press, 2007).

14. On the role of orality in the transmission and formation of Lamentations Rabbah and other rabbinic texts, see Mandel, "Between Byzantium and Islam." Strack and Stemberger suggest that similarities between Lamentations Rabbah and Bavli Gittin attest to the role these stories played in commemorating the destruction on Tisha b'Av, rather than direct dependence or literary influence. Hermann L. Strack and Günter Stemberger, *Introduction to the Talmud and Midrash*, trans. Markus Bockmuehl (Edinburgh: T & T Clark, 1991), 310.

fall of Jerusalem. Yet there are significant differences between these Palestinian rabbinic collections and the Babylonian Talmud's account. As Peter Schäfer has demonstrated, Lamentations Rabbah and Yerushalmi Taʿanit exhibit striking parallels with regard to their treatment of the destruction of the Second Temple and their portrayal of the Bar Kokhba revolt.[15] While the Babylonian Talmud's account draws on this shared core of material, Bavli Gittin includes a number of tales that have no parallel in either Palestinian collection; its redactors have also reworked familiar Palestinian sources, recasting those traditions in ways that give a different portrait of catastrophe.

One of the most striking dimensions of Bavli Gittin's account of the destruction is its hesitance to frame catastrophe in covenantal terms, its refusal to account for disaster by enumerating the community's transgressions and thereby justify the magnitude of the loss. Bavli Gittin's destruction narrative opens with a striking claim: the three great disasters of the first and second centuries are sparked not by Jewish moral failings, but by a series of improbable happenings that lead to disaster. Jerusalem falls, Bavli Gittin claims, after a servant invites the wrong man to a sumptuous feast. When the man is thrown out and shamed before his fellows, he turns traitor and manufactures a situation whereby the rabbis are faced with a pernicious choice: sacrifice a blemished animal and violate the law or refuse the sacrifice and risk imperial ire. Tur Malka and Betar, two sites the rabbis associate with the failed Bar Kokhba revolt, are likewise destroyed through bizarre mischance: a troop of soldiers seize a rooster and a hen that are instrumental to a local Jewish wedding custom, while in the case of Betar, they cut the branches of a symbolic tree to repair the litter of Caesar's daughter. When the locals react to such insult with violence, the hapless Roman soldiers misinterpret the facts on the ground and report to Caesar that the Jews are rebelling.[16]

In eschewing the conventional narrative of sin and punishment in favor of a human political frame, Bavli Gittin's narrative offers an unconventional accounting of catastrophe. Most rabbinic recollections of the destruction of Jerusalem give potent voice to the narrative of communal wrongdoing, understanding the disaster as a consequence of Jewish sin. The rabbis draw from a rich palette of transgressions to frame their account of Jerusalem's fall. An oft-cited tradition in Bavli Yoma 9b attributes the destruction of the Second Temple to causeless hatred (*sinat ḥinam*), while other passages blame the catastrophe on neglect

15. For extensive analysis of the narrative parallels, see Schäfer, "Der Bethar-Komplex in der rabbinischen Literatur," in *Der Bar-Kokhba-Aufstand*, 136–193.

16. In a later chapter, I assess the significance of these narratives in terms of their critique of the Roman empire and the limits of colonial knowledge.

of Torah or the failure to keep Shabbat.[17] According to one rabbinic tradition, Jerusalem was destroyed on account of strict legal punctiliousness and refusal to act beyond the letter of the law; other passages attribute disaster to small sins that no one would credit.[18] It is important to note that Bavli Gittin's response to disaster is not entirely unprecedented. As Shaye Cohen observes, some passages in Lamentations Rabbah evoke themes of Roman ignorance of Jewish custom or attribute the destruction to the Romans' irrational hatred of the Jews. That Lamentations Rabbah includes such tales serves as an important caution against treating Bavli Gittin's narrative as entirely innovative. Yet the motif of Roman fault, Cohen notes, "remains undeveloped" in Lamentations Rabbah; Jewish sin and divine chastisement remain its dominant means of accounting for catastrophe.[19]

Bavli Gittin's narrative thoroughly reorients the theological frame. In this chapter, I argue that this shift has striking implications—not just for theology, but for rabbinic conceptions of sex and gender. Why? Because the covenantal framework that undergirds the more conventional rabbinic account of sin and disaster rests upon a potent gendered metaphor: the biblical symbolism of covenant as a "marriage" between God and Israel. As Michael Satlow has shown, rabbinic traditions rarely make explicit appeal to the marriage metaphor as a framework for conceptualizing the covenantal understanding of God's relationship with the Jewish people. The rabbis, Satlow argues, largely rejected marriage as an explanatory metaphor for articulating God's bond to the nation, recognizing perhaps the theological threat of divorce. Especially at a time when ascendant Christian communities were proclaiming themselves the heirs of the covenant and the favored people of God, the rabbis, it seems, grasped the fragility of imagining covenant as a bond that could be undone by a "husband" who might all too easily embrace

---

17. Bavli Yoma 9b, recounting a tradition attributed to the mid-second-century Rabbi Yoḥanan ben Torta, reads as follows: "The first Temple was destroyed on account of idolatry, fornication, and bloodshed. But the second Temple was a place of Torah, commandments, and lovingkindness: why was it destroyed?" The text attributes the destruction to "causeless hatred," which it regards as equivalent to the abovementioned transgressions. See also Yerushalmi Yoma 1:1 38c, Tosefta Menaḥot 13:22. On early Jewish responses to the destruction, see Robert Goldenberg, "The Destruction of the Jerusalem Temple: Its Meaning and Consequences," in Katz, *The Cambridge History of Judaism, Volume 4*; Goldenberg, "Early Rabbinic Explanations."

18. The tradition that Jerusalem was destroyed due to refusal to go beyond the letter of the law appears in Bavli Baba Metsia 30b. On the role of small sins in rabbinic notions of divine accounting, see Jonathan Schofer, "Protest or Pedagogy? Trivial Sin and Divine Justice in Rabbinic Narrative," *Hebrew Union College Annual* 74 (2003): 243–278.

19. S. Cohen, "The Destruction," 25.

a new wife.[20] Yet despite the rabbis' disinclination to frame their own covenant with God in terms of a marriage bond, the other half of the metaphor remains intact: the idea that divine anger is provoked and justified by women's sexual sin.

Adultery as Provocation: Justified Violence in the Hebrew Bible's Marriage Metaphor

"I will betroth you for eternity," the prophet Hosea declaims, using the vows of a husband to his wife to express God's promises to the people of Israel. "I will betroth you with righteousness and justice, with love and compassion; I will betroth you with faithfulness and you will know the Lord."[21] In words exchanged by lovers and scripted on marriage contracts or engraved on wedding rings, words still recited during the daily morning devotional practice of donning of tefillin, the prayer amulets that give material expression to the tie between God and Jew, Hosea uses the language of betrothal to evoke a powerful bond between the human and the Holy.[22] Through the metaphor of marriage, the prophet voices the promise of covenantal loyalty and fidelity. The vows of betrothal express an aspiration to an eternal and enduring connection, to relations of faithfulness and honor, love and trust. Yet the language of marriage also summons forth the specter of infidelity and adultery, of promises broken and faith betrayed. In the verses that precede Hosea's betrothal vows, Hosea portrays God as castigating and rebuking the nation as a woman who has played Him false. God strips her

---

20. Michael Satlow, *Jewish Marriage in Antiquity*, 56.

21. Hosea 2:21. Unless otherwise noted, all biblical citations follow the Masoretic Text. Translations of biblical verses are drawn from the Jewish Publication Society translation (1985), though I have sometimes adapted translations to clarify rabbinic readings of biblical verses for English readers.

22. While Hosea is the first prophet to make explicit use of this metaphor, Isaiah, Ezekiel, and Jeremiah also frame the relationship between God and Israel as a marriage and frequently characterize idolatry as a form of adultery. Marriage and covenant imagery in the biblical prophets has drawn extensive attention among scholars. My own thinking has been particularly shaped by the work of Carole R. Fontaine, "Hosea" and "A Response to Hosea" in *Feminist Companion to the Later Prophets*, ed. Athalya Brenner (Philadelphia: Sheffield Academic Press, 1995), 40–59 and 60–69; Tamar Kamionkowski, *Gender Reversal and Cosmic Chaos: A Study in the Book of Ezekiel* (New York: Sheffield Academic Press, 2003); Christl M. Maier, *Daughter Zion, Mother Zion: Gender, Space, and the Sacred in Ancient Israel* (Minneapolis: Fortress Press, 2008); Judith Plaskow, "Preaching Against the Text," in *The Coming of Lilith: Essays on Feminism, Judaism, and Sexual Ethics, 1972–2003*, ed. Donna Berman (Boston: Beacon Press, 2005), 152–156; Satlow, *Jewish Marriage in Antiquity*; T. Drorah Setel, "Prophets and Pornography: Female Sexual Imagery in Hosea," in *Feminist Interpretation of the Bible*, ed. Letty M. Russell (Philadelphia: Westminster John Knox Press, 1985), 86–95; Weems, *Battered Love*.

naked, abandons her in the wilderness, and lets her die of thirst. Even her children pay for their mother's wayward ways; they are a harlot's brood, conceived through their mother's shame, and they will be disowned.[23]

In the book of Hosea, God commands the prophet to reenact the tumultuous marriage between God and Israel through his own intimate relationship. Obedient to the divine command, Hosea gets himself "a wife of whoredom," sires a whore's children, and then sends his wife away. Through these actions, Hosea's own family comes to mirror the sexual transgressions of the nation. His sons and daughter are named, at God's instruction, to mark the brutal violence that will come upon the house of Jehu and the house of Israel. Divine anger is expressed both rhetorically and corporeally through the body of the spurned wife. As Renita Weems has argued, such marital imagery is repeatedly used to justify and sanction violence—and to portray violence as the dominant party's necessary and just response to a subordinate partner's wrongdoing. "God," Weems writes, parsing the powerful logic of the biblical metaphor, "is not a harsh, cruel, vindictive husband who threatens and beats his wife simply because he has the power to do so. He is himself a victim, because he has been driven to extreme measures by a wife who has again and again dishonored him and disregarded the norms governing marriage relations."[24] By scripting an otherwise unseen divine-human drama through the visceral emotional relationship between husband and wife, the marriage metaphor lays claim to a powerful set of theological and ideological frameworks. By naturalizing God's response as the justified reactions of a scorned and dishonored husband, the metaphor renders divine brutality as a recognizable and comprehensible reaction to sexual transgression.[25] Through the powerful script of domestic catastrophe, destruction becomes a necessary reaction to disloyalty—one that leaves the tangible bodies of God's people vulnerable to intimate violence.

---

23. Hosea 2:4–2:7. Earlier biblical sources also describe idolatry in sexual terms; both Exodus 34:16 and Deuteronomy 21:16 describe Israel as "lusting after" or "playing the harlot" with foreign gods. The idea that sexual sin is passed down to children via a genealogical transfer is also present within the levitical texts, where the sexual transgressions of a priest's daughter disqualify her children from the priestly line. See Christine Hayes, *Gentile Impurities and Jewish Identities: Intermarriage and Conversion from the Bible to the Talmud* (New York: Oxford University Press, 2002), 40–43; Naomi Koltun-Fromm, *Hermeneutics of Holiness: Ancient Jewish and Christian Notions of Sexuality and Religious Community* (New York: Oxford University Press, 2010), 48–49.

24. Weems, *Battered Love*, 19.

25. On the significance of metaphor for structuring the cultural grammar of marriage, see Gail Labovitz, *Marriage and Metaphor: Constructions of Gender in Rabbinic Literature* (Lanham: Lexington Books, 2009).

Despite its significance within the prophetic tradition, the notion of God and Israel as husband and wife appears only rarely within rabbinic literature. Early rabbinic sources generally avoid marriage as a model for divine-human relations, preferring instead to deploy metaphors that imagine the relationship between God and Israel through the motif of father and son.[26] The marriage metaphor remains within the rabbinic repertoire, surfacing with some prominence in late rabbinic collections. David Stern has drawn attention to a parable in Lamentations Rabbah that likens Israel to an abandoned wife, comforted only in her husband's absence by her ketubah (marriage contract) and the promise of eventual return that it implies. Stern argues that while this parable ultimately underscores God's fidelity to Israel, the motif of divorce and marital abandonment allows the rabbis to voice a protest against God's apparent irrational and unfair treatment of Zion.[27] Even in the midrashic collections, rabbinic traditions only rarely make explicit appeal to the metaphor of God and Israel as husband and wife. Surveying a corpus of nearly a thousand rabbinic king parables, Ofra Meir finds only ten talmudic-era parables that liken God to a husband.[28] Rather than evoke the symbolism of divine marriage and its implied possibility of divorce, the rabbis commonly appeal to the social institution of paternity to posit a fundamental unbreakable connection between God and nation. Following a path hewn by Ben Sira and other Hellenistic Jewish writers, rabbinic sources often redirect the force of biblical marriage metaphors, applying prophetic marriage imagery to the realm of human social relations.[29] Yet this shift does not defang the gender politics of the wayward wife. Though the reconfigured metaphor means that women's sexual autonomy no longer threatens to

---

26. Michael Satlow argues that this shift may well reflect a privileging of the Greco-Roman notion that the aim of marriage is to form an *oikos*, a household. While the God-Israel marriage metaphor privileges the relationship of husband and wife, the *oikos* ideology privileges the relationship between parents and children. Satlow, *Jewish Marriage in Antiquity*, 46–47.

27. David Stern, *Parables in Midrash*, 99–101. A similar motif appears in Bavli Taʿanit 20a. See discussion in Julia Watts Belser, *Power, Ethics, and Ecology in Jewish Late Antiquity: Rabbinic Responses to Drought and Disaster* (New York: Cambridge University Press, 2015).

28. Ofra Meir, "The Subject of the Wedding in the Kin Parables in the Tales of the Sages" [Hebrew], in *Studies in Marriage Customs*, ed. Issachar Ben-Ami and Dov Noy (Jerusalem: Magnes Press, 1974), 9–51.

29. See Ben Sira 26:10–1. When Ben Sira glosses Ezekiel 16:25, a verse that frames Israel's betrayal of God as the act of an adulterous woman, he applies the biblical image of whoring Israel to the actions of a human woman. A similar process happens in the rabbinic targum to Hosea, which "completely obliterates its key metaphor." Eliminating reference to the marriage metaphor, the targum translates Hosea 2:18 as "And at that time, says the Lord, you shall eagerly follow my worship, and no more shall you worship idols." Satlow, *Jewish Marriage in Antiquity*, 47.

dishonor a cuckolded God, the adulterous woman remains powerful symbol of social disorder.[30] Beyond the risks that women's sexual autonomy poses for men's domestic honor, women's sexual treachery also serves as a powerful symbol of national danger.

Aligning God Against the Nation: Women's Sexual Sin in Lamentations Rabbah

Rabbinic discourse often figures female sexuality as a source of risk, a danger that imperils not only the virtue of individual men who might be "lured" into sin, but also the stability of the broader social order. In a number of rabbinic accounts of the destruction of Jerusalem, female sexuality serves as a provocation to catastrophe, a moral crisis that sparks national disaster. Let us begin by examining a narrative tradition from the Palestinian midrash collection Lamentations Rabbah 4:18,[31] which asserts a powerful causative link between women's brazen sexual behavior and the destruction of Jerusalem. Because the midrash is quite lengthy, I will examine it in three parts:

> *"Away! Impure!" the people shouted . . .* (Lamentations 4:15)
> Rabbi Ḥanina opened:
> It is written of the daughters of Zion:
> *God said, "Because the daughters of Zion are haughty* (Isaiah 3:16) . . ."
>> They would accentuate their height and walk about with pride.
> *"and go about with necks outstretched . . .*
>> When one of them would wear her finery,
>>> she would turn her neck one way and the other
>>> to display her jewels.

---

30. Claudia Camp analyzes gender discourse within Ben Sira, underscoring the risk that female sexuality poses to the honor of men and the nation. Probing the transformation of the biblical motif of the "strange woman" in Ben Sira's writing, Camp argues that Ben Sira emphasizes not simply the danger of the foreign woman or the harlot, but the dangers of ordinary wives and daughters—the threat of women within. In addition to stressing the obligation of a male householder to control the women within his domain, she argues that Ben Sira also evinces a striking concern with male sexual self-control. Claudia V. Camp, *Ben Sira and the Men Who Handle Books: Gender and the Rise of Canon-Consciousness* (Sheffield: Sheffield Phoenix Press, 2013).

31. I have translated Lamentations Rabbah 4:18 according to the Midrash Rabbah edition; the text appears also in the Buber edition. A parallel text appears in Pesikta deRav Kahana, Piska 17:6, Braude edition pg. 416–418. Bavli Shabbat 62b includes a similar exegesis of Isaiah 3:16, but the Bavli's account differs from the Palestinian tradition in important ways, as I will discuss below.

*"and roving (mesaqrot)*³² *eyes . . .*

Rabbi 'Asi of Caesaria said:

They would paint (*mesaqrot*) their eyes with red pigment.

Rabbi Shimon ben Laqish said: With red dye.

"and walk with mincing steps . . .

If one of them was tall, she would bring two short ones with her

and so appear to float above them.

If one of them was short, she would wear high shoes to appear tall.

*"with anklets tinkling on their feet."*³³

Rabbi Yose said: The image of a serpent was on her shoes.

The sages said: She brought a gullet of a rooster and filled it with balsam

and placed it between her heel and her shoe,

and when she saw a group of young men,

she would press her heel upon it so the scent would spread among them

like the venom of a snake.

The opening section of Lamentations Rabbah 4:18 centers on the exegesis of Isaiah 3:16, a biblical verse that links the destruction of Jerusalem with the brazenness of Jerusalem's women. The prophet Isaiah narrates destruction through the bodies of Jerusalem's women, using the motif of female beauty to paint a vivid portrait of the moral wrongdoing that calls forth God's punishment and to portray the material consequences of divine judgment.³⁴ Consider the biblical passage on which this midrash is based, Isaiah 3:16–4:1:

God said: "Because the daughters of Zion are haughty

and go about with necks outstretched

and roving (*mesaqrot*) eyes

and walk with mincing steps,

with anklets tinkling on their feet," —

---

32. The word *mesaqrot*, translated here as "roving," is a *hapax legomenon*, appearing only once in the Hebrew Bible. While some modern scholars follow the midrashic interpretation and translate it as "paint their eyes," most favor a translation that indicates a particular type of looking—either ogling or winking. Hugh Williamson, *Isaiah 1–5: A Critical and Exegetical Commentary* (New York: T & T Clark, 2006), 274.

33. Through a midrashic etymology, Rabbi Yosi links the term *ta'akasnah* to *'akas*, snake venom.

34. The link between beauty and judgment is made explicit in Targum Yonatan to Isaiah 3:24–5, which reads "This retribution shall be made on them because of [their] going astray due to their beauty. The beauty of your young men shall be killed by the sword." See Marvin Sweeney, *Isaiah 1–4 and the Post-exilic Understanding of the Isaianic Tradition* (Berlin: Walter de Gruyter, 1988), 154.

My Lord will bare the heads of Zion's daughters;
God will uncover their heads.

In that day, my Lord will strip off their finery:
　　the anklets, the fillets, the crescents,
　　the eardrops, the bracelets, and the veils;
　　the turbans and the amulets;
　　the signet rings and the nose rings;
　　the festive robes, the mantles, the shawls, the purses,
　　the lace gowns and the linen vests,
　　the kerchiefs and the capes.

And then:
　　Instead of perfume, rot.
　　Instead of an apron, a rope.
　　Instead of a diadem, a shorn head.
　　Instead of a rich robe, a girding of sackcloth.
A burn instead of beauty.

Her men shall fall by the sword,
　　her fighting manhood in battle.
Her gates shall lament and mourn,
　　and she shall be emptied
　　and shall sit on the ground.

On that day, seven women shall take hold of one man, saying:
　　"We will eat our own food and wear our own clothes.
　　Only let us be called by your name—
　　Take away our disgrace!"

Isaiah 3:16 opens by condemning the daughters of Zion for vanity, castigating Jerusalem's women for their cultivation of sexual allure. Isaiah frames female beauty as a deliberate modification and ornamentation of the female body, a form of self-fashioning. As the oracle unfolds, the adornments are stripped away and the "artifice" of female beauty is undone. Isaiah 3:18–23 describes how God will remove their jewelry and necklaces, their scarves and perfumes, their signet rings and fine robes. Isaiah 3:24 narrates the profound transformation that befalls Jerusalem's women: stench, decay, and the accoutrements of mourning replace their beautiful adornments.[35]

---

35. While scholars have often treated Isaiah 3:16–24 as an independent unit, Marvin Sweeney argues for a close textual connection between this passage and 3:25–4:1, the

In this passage, the destruction of women's beauty stands as a metonymy for Jerusalem's devastation, while the visible disgrace of the human woman serves as a tangible, corporeal sign of the nation's fall.[36] The prophet deploys a familiar motif of the city as woman, interposing a portrait of women's devastation with the lament of Jerusalem. Isaiah 3:25–26 links the judgment against Zion's women with the death of Jerusalem's men in battle, with the emptiness of the city and its terrible mourning. The final lines of the passage complete the oracle of destruction by emphasizing the eradication of the women's haughty pride. In Isaiah 4:1, the desperate would-be wives offer to provide their own food and clothing, asking nothing of their man but the dignity of his name. The original picture of confident and sexually autonomous women has been replaced by a vision of women's utter dependence. In Oswalt's words, "Wealthy women, secure in their luxury and their allure, are reduced to scabrous hags begging to belong to someone."[37] The prophet couples the physical reduction of Jerusalem's male population with the psychic devastation of Jerusalem's women. The slaughter has left so few men in Jerusalem that seven women cling to a single man. Where Jerusalem's women once sought to snag a man's eye through glamour and glitter, they now beg for his attention—renouncing marital support and the protections of wifehood for the mere promise of his name.

---

prophetic announcement of the punishment that will befall Jerusalem. Sweeney argues that the concluding verse of 3:24, "for instead of beauty" is grammatically incomplete as it stands and should be linked to 3:25, "her men shall fall by the sword." Marvin Sweeney, *Isaiah 1–4 and the Post-Exilic Understanding of the Isaianic Tradition.* (Berlin: Walter de Gruyter, 1988), 154. Hugh Williamson disagrees, arguing that this phrase is an independent and self-contained clause, reading the initial *ki* not as a conjunction, but as a noun formed from the root *kivah*, to burn, so that the verse reads, "branding in place of beauty." Hugh Williamson, *Isaiah 1–5: A Critical and Exegetical Commentary.* (New York: T&T Clark, 2006), 285.

36. On the metaphor of the city as woman, see Maier, *Daughter Zion.* The city as woman motif finds powerful expression in the Judaea Capta coins, Roman coins that commemorated the capture of Jerusalem through the iconic image of a woman sitting beneath a palm tree, her body bent forward in a posture of dejection. As Davina Lopez notes, the image expressed through this coin "constitutes a tiny, everyday portrait of imperial power relations . . . using gendered bodies both to show the differences between the conquerors and conquered and to communicate social superiority and inferiority" (123). Davina C. Lopez, "Before Your Very Eyes: Roman Imperial Ideology, Gender Constructs and Paul's Inter-Nationalism," in *Mapping Gender in Ancient Religious Discourses*, ed. Todd Penner and Caroline Vander Stichele (Leiden: Brill, 2007), 115–162.

37. John Oswalt, *The Book of Isaiah, Chapters 1–39* (Grand Rapids: William B. Eerdmans Publishing Company, 1986), 140.

Lamentations Rabbah 4:18 builds upon Isaiah's portrait, intensifying the claim that Jerusalem's women are culpable for the destruction to come. The first section of the midrash provides an extensive explanation of Isaiah 3:16, glossing each of the difficult Hebrew phrases with an example that highlights the artifice of Jerusalem's women. The midrash literalizes Isaiah's opening critique of the daughters' pride, taking it as a critique of the women's efforts to accentuate their height. In the hands of the midrashist, the biblical motif of the outstretched neck becomes a site not just for displaying her jewels, but for an act of intentional bodily exhibition: she turns her neck this way and that to catch the light, to showcase the sparkle. Her eyes are painted, adorned with dye to draw the gaze. Even her progress through the city is manufactured to present her body to best effect: tall women go about with short ones in train to set off their willowy beauty, while women of smaller stature wear shoes that add to their height, deliberately shaping a figure designed to appeal to the male eye. The midrash critiques Jerusalem's daughters not so much for the fact of their beauty, but for its deliberate cultivation. In the midrash, women's beauty is a crafted thing, an artifice of paint and careful staging. The final lines of this section intensify the critique by imagining the sexual entrapment of Jerusalem's men through a sinister, material manipulation. The rabbis imagine Zion's daughters fashioning sacks of scent and secreting them within their shoes, in order to pierce them with their heels when they draw near a group of eligible men. The midrash portrays the daughters as active agents who ensnare the vulnerable. With craft and guile, they fashion technologies of seduction that infect helpless men with the poison of desire.

In the next section, Lamentations Rabbah 4:18 describes an exchange between Zion's wayward daughters and the prophet Jeremiah, himself a survivor of the Babylonian destruction of Jerusalem in 587 BCE. While Jeremiah urges them to repent, the daughters assert that they will benefit from the coming of the conquerors. The midrash continues:

And Jeremiah said to them: "Repent, lest the enemies arrive!"
They said to him:
  "Even if the enemies come upon us, what can they do to us?"
Thus it is written:
They say: "Let God make haste, let Him speed His work
  that we may see it,
Let the plan of the Holy One of Israel hasten to fulfillment,
  that we may know it." (Isaiah 5:19)
"A Roman officer will see me and take me
  and seat me with him in his carriage!"

They said to Jeremiah:
    "We know whose will endure—this one or that one!"
When sins caused (*keivan shĕgarmu 'avonot*) their enemies to come,
    they went and adorned themselves
    and went toward them like harlots (*kezonot*).
An officer saw her and took her
    and seated her with him in his carriage.
A commander saw her and took her
    and seated her with him in his carriage.

This portion of Lamentations Rabbah 4:18 intensifies its critique of Zion's daughters by portraying the women as deliberately mocking God. In response to Jeremiah's rebuke, the midrash imagines the women speaking the words of Isaiah 5:19, in which the people scoff at the notion of divine judgment and call upon God to act so they can see the fulfillment of the divine plan. In its biblical context, the quoted verse appears in a prophetic oracle that promises woe to those who "haul sin with cords of falsehood and iniquity as with cart ropes"[38] The deft rhetoric of the verse targets those whose conduct causes divine anger as inevitably "as the wagon follows the ropes with which it is fastened to the draught oxen."[39] The people's words are strikingly ambiguous. Were the request spoken in a different manner, a call for God to bring the divine design to fulfillment might be taken as an expression of piety and devotion. Some commentators have read the biblical words as a condemnation of the people's moral ignorance. Transgressors call for God to fulfill the divine plan, unaware of the brutal punishment they will suffer when God answers their call.[40] Other interpreters read these words less charitably, imagining the speakers as daring God to act.[41] The transgressors deliberately mock divine power. "Do your worst," they taunt. "Bring your judgment, that we may see."

Within the context of Lamentations Rabbah, the verse clearly takes on the second valence. When Jeremiah warns the daughters that the enemies will come if they do not change their ways, the women embrace the promise of a foreign conqueror. In a striking reversal of the frequent wartime practice in which the soldiers of the victorious army pillage the stricken city and rape local women in the aftermath of battle, Lamentations Rabbah 4:18 imagines the women of Jerusalem

---

38. Isaiah 5:20.

39. Otto Kaiser, *Isaiah 1–12: A Commentary* (Philadelphia: Westminster John Knox Press, 1981), 102.

40. Walter Bruggeman, *Isaiah: 1–39* (Philadelphia: Westminster John Knox Press, 1998), 54.

41. Brevard S. Childs, *Isaiah* (Louisville: Westminster John Knox Press, 2001), 47.

eagerly awaiting the enemy generals—longing to be seized, taken, and settled in the carriages of the conquerors. The women adorn themselves and approach them as whores, and they are indeed lifted up as they had planned. The officers and commanders take what is offered; the midrash uses a verb with clear sexual connotations, one which can also be used to indicate marriage. By contrasting the plan of the wayward daughters with the plan of God, Lamentations Rabbah 4:18 imagines the two parties locked in a competition over the fulfillment of their desires. The women's sin has, in the language of the midrash, brought their scheme to fulfillment. By embracing conquest as an advance for their own personal status, by inviting and embracing the sexual degradation that has been meant as divine chastisement, the women claim it is their plan that will endure.

The final lines of the midrash narrate God's outrage—not simply because of the women's deeds, but because the women have countermanded God's plan and threaten to supplant it with their own. Lamentations Rabbah 4:18 concludes:

The Holy Blessed One said: "Mine will not stand, but theirs will stand?!"
What did He do?
YHVH will bare (věsipaḥ) the heads of the daughters of Zion . . . (Isaiah 3:17)
Rabbi Elazar said: He will punish them with skin disease (*tsaraʿat*)
    for it states [in a biblical passage dealing with skin afflictions]:
        for swellings, for rashes (ulasapaḥat), or for discolorations . . .
        (Leviticus 15:4)
Rabbi Yosi the son of Rabbi Ḥanina said:
    He brought upon their heads swarms and swarms of lice.
Rabbi Ḥiyya bar ʾAba said:
    He made them servant-women.
        What does it mean? Enslaved servant-women.
Rabbi Berekhiya and Ḥilfi bar Zevid said in the name of Rabbi ʾIssi:
    What is *věsipaḥ?*
    It is like *věshipʿa*—He will cause [their blood] to flow
        in order to guard the holy seed [of Israel]
        that they should not mix with the people of the land.
    For the Holy Blessed One said: I know that the nations of the world
        do not keep themselves apart from those with skin disease (*tsaraʿat*).
    What did He do?
        . . . YHVH will uncover their hidden parts.[42] (Isaiah 3:17)

---

42. I have translated the verse in keeping with the midrashic reading. Many translations render this word as "forehead," a reading supported by Akkadian parallels. See Oswalt, *Book of Isaiah,* 139. See also Williamson, *Isaiah 1–5,* 277.

He gestured to their source and blood came forth
    until it filled the entire carriage
and that officer stabbed her with a spear
    and threw her down before the carriage
and the carriage ran her over and split her apart.
And this is what Jeremiah said:
    "Away! Impure!" the people shouted . . . (Lamentations 4:15)
Rabbi 'Aba said:
    In the language of the Greeks, this means: "Despicable one!"

In this final section, Lamentations Rabbah affirms the primacy of God's plan and details the brutal corporeal punishment that God brings against the daughters. The first two rabbinic voices imagine God afflicting the women with vermin and skin disease, deploying familiar biblical tropes of plague and punishment. The next speaker portrays their comeuppance through the loss of their exalted status, imagining the daughters turned into slave-women for their new masters. But it is the final rabbinic opinion that brings home the extent of the midrashist's brutality. In this account, God plans a novel and graphic demise for the women who challenged the divine plan. At God's gesture, a flow of blood comes forth from their bodies, a flow so immense that it fills the carriages in a grotesque parody of menstruation. By interjecting unexpected and uncontrolled menstrual blood into the carriages that the women had designated as signs of their new status as the chosen partners of Roman officers, the midrashist marks the carriage with the vivid symbolism of impurity and forbidden sexuality. With chilling logic, Lamentations Rabbah figures the blood bath as an act of protection of Israel, lest the "holy seed" be profaned through illicit sexual congress.[43] For the midrashist's God, skin disease is insufficient to keep the Roman generals at bay. The nations of the world will hardly contain desire for the sake of such trifles; it will take an outpouring of blood to chill Roman lust. Indeed, the blood proves to be a potent prophylactic. At the sight of the blood, the Roman officers are provoked to rage. Each stabs his woman with a spear, a scene that evokes sexual encounter, but turns the woman's penetration into an act of brutality. He throws her down, a bitter reversal of the woman's desire to be raised up. In a final denouement, the carriage—the original symbol of her triumph—runs her over and splits her in two, an act of dismemberment that unmakes the very body that was the site of sin.

---

43. Naomi Koltun-Fromm argues that Second Temple Jewish writers frequently join the notion of "holy seed," articulated with particular distinction in the biblical book of Ezra, with the prophetic conception of idolatry as an act of religious prostitution (*Hermeneutics of Holiness*, 54–59). As Christine Hayes has shown, the ideology of Israel as a "holy seed" gives particular force to the notion of intermarriage as an act of defilement (*Gentile Impurities*, 68–91).

Lamentations Rabbah 4:18 thus gives powerful expression to the notion of women's sexual transgression as a risk to the nation. Not only does the midrash mark God as the explicit architect of the daughters' deaths, it aims to justify divine violence through the rhetoric of protection. For the good of Israel, for the preservation of the nation's purity, the divine hand brings about these women's end. Drawing upon familiar biblical tropes that associate women's sexuality with transgression and danger, Lamentations Rabbah 4:18 situates women's sexual agency as a threat to Israel's moral virtue and material security.

The midrash explicitly frames women's desires as counter to the divine will, imagining the haughty daughters challenging—and nearly neutralizing—God's intended plan. God and the daughters struggle against one another, agonist and antagonist. In the moral landscape of the midrash, Jeremiah frames the daughters' actions as summoning forth divine response. Israel's enemies come upon them as an act of divine rebuke, a chastisement demanded by the daughters' deeds. Within the text itself, God and the daughters work at cross-purposes. God's triumph requires the daughters' defeat; their dismembered bodies testify to the unassailable force of divine power.

Sex and Gender as Catastrophic Cause: Bavli Gittin and the Palestinian Sources

The association between women and sexual danger is a familiar trope in rabbinic literature. Scholars have drawn particular attention to the way in which Palestinian and Babylonian narratives commonly portray women as sites of sexual temptation, frequently establishing rabbinic men's virtue through their capacity to keep themselves separate from women.[44] In other contexts, the Babylonian Talmud makes frequent reference to women as a source of sexual and social danger. Bavli Shabbat 62b offers a reading of Isaiah 3:16 quite similar to the first portion of Lamentations Rabbah 4:18, narrating how the daughters of Zion held their heads high and painted their eyes, deliberately altering their gait and establishing a retinue to draw the eye. The Bavli's version preserves the scent and the shoes, imagining these women infecting men with the venom of passionate desire. As it narrates their

---

44. On the rabbinic practice of gender separation and its use as an effort to regulate sexual temptation, see Hauptman, *Rereading the Rabbis*, 30–59; Miriam Peskowitz, *Spinning Fantasies: Rabbis, Gender, and History* (Berkeley: University of California Press, 1997), 49–76. On the perception of women as a source of sexual danger for men, see Boyarin, *Carnal Israel*, 61–76; Gail Labovitz, "Heruta's Ruse: What We Mean When We Talk About Desire," in *The Passionate Torah: Sex and Judaism*, ed. Danya Ruttenberg (New York: New York University Press, 2009), 229–244. On the significance that the Bavli attributes to men's struggles against the sexual impulse, see Rosen-Zvi, *Demonic Desires*, 102–119.

punishment, Bavli Shabbat 62b details a series of physical reversals: sores instead of perfume, baldness instead of carefully coiffed hair, sackcloth instead of finery, ulcers instead of beauty. This tradition likewise imagines the women afflicted with skin disease, even evoking the symbolism of Israel "poured out" and emptied. But Bavli Shabbat 62b lacks the elaborate blood scene of Lamentations Rabbah 4:18. Unlike the vivid particularism that grounds the Lamentations Rabbah tradition, the Bavli's account has no clear historical anchor. There are no women lusting after conquerors, no Roman officers with carriages who might raise up Israel's beautiful whores. The Bavli's tale lacks the rivalry between the women and God, the taunt and dare over whose plan will endure. While it treats the daughters of Zion as exemplars of sexual sin, Bavli Shabbat 62b makes only an oblique connection between these women and communal disaster.

Strikingly, Bavli Gittin's account of the destruction of Jerusalem avoids even this intimation of women's sexual sin as a spark to collective catastrophe. It never deploys the motif of the whoring wife to characterize the transgressions of Israel, and it does not portray women's sexual sin as a cause of the destruction. Rather than using women's sexuality to illustrate Israel's misdeeds, Bavli Gittin shifts the rhetorical emphasis toward women's violation. While female sexuality still remains a central part of the narrative, the valence has changed. Rather than narrate the cause of destruction through women's sexual sin, Bavli Gittin chronicles the consequence of crisis through the wounding of women's bodies. The later narrative choice is hardly unique to the Bavli. The motif of the suffering nation embodied through a violated and brutalized woman is well known from the book of Lamentations and recurs in many rabbinic narratives. Yet because Bavli Gittin remains strikingly circumspect on the matter of women's culpability for disaster—because it refrains from sounding the familiar notes of women's sexual autonomy as cause for a justifiable punishment—its tales of women in distress take on a different narrative tone. Without harlots and brazen women to take the fall in the familiar set-piece of sexual sin, Bavli Gittin's narratives of women in distress do not aim to "justify" Jewish suffering. Instead, as the next chapter will show, these tales protest sexual violence and use the example of women's violation to evoke the pathos of the nation.

To examine in more detail the difference in how Bavli Gittin positions gender and sexuality in its account of catastrophe, let us consider a narrative that has parallels in both Bavli Gittin and the Palestinian sources. The tradition concerns the destruction of Jerusalem and the devastation of the settlements of King's Mountain, contrasting the tremendous population of these sites before their destruction with their current desolation. The Palestinian versions exemplify a tendency to make a strong causal connection between destruction and sin, making frequent appeal to gendered or sexualized transgressions. Yerushalmi Ta'anit 4:5 69a reads:

Two cedars stood upon the Mount of Olives
  and beneath one of them were four stalls
  that sold pure things [for use in the temple].
One of them brought forth forty weights of doves each and every month,
  and from these, they had enough to provide bird offerings for all Israel.
Tur Shimon used to provide three hundred measures of bread
  to the poor every Sabbath eve.
Then why was it destroyed?
  There are those who say, "Because of fornication (*zenut*)."
  There are those who say, "Because of playing ball."

Ten thousand villages were on King's Mountain
  and R. Eleazar b. Harsom owned a thousand of them,
  and for each of the thousand, a ship upon the sea—
  and all of them were destroyed.
There were three cities [that were so large]
  that their census records were brought up to Jerusalem in a cart!
They were Kabul, Shiḥin, and Migdol Ṣebayya.
All three were destroyed:
  Kabul, because of contention (*maḥloqet*),
  Shihin, because of witchcraft (*keshafim*),
  Migdol Ṣebayya, because of fornication (*zenut*).

In this narrative, Yerushalmi Taʿanit accounts for destruction through a rich palette of transgression. Different accounts link the devastation of the cities to sexual sin, excessive argumentation, witchcraft, and even inappropriate idleness. While the Yerushalmi itself provides no definitive explanation for the sin of "playing ball," a parallel passage in Lamentations Rabbah (examined below) specifies that the community is condemned for ball play on the Sabbath. It is important to note that this Palestinian tradition does not assert an exclusive connection between women and disaster. Even so, its accounting of sin has significant gender connotations. Following a common notion in the ancient world, the rabbis frequently assume that witchcraft is the particular province of women.[45] Likewise, fornication is a sharply gendered crime. While rabbinic sources surely imagine that *zenut*

---

45. On the association between witchcraft and women in rabbinic and other ancient sources see Kimberly Stratton, *Naming the Witch: Magic, Ideology, and Stereotype in the Ancient World* (New York: Columbia University Press, 2007); Rebecca Lesses, "Exc(o)rcising Power: Women as Sorceresses, Exorcists, and Demonesses in Babylonian Jewish Society in Late Antiquity," *Journal of the American Academy of Religion* 69 (2003): 343–375; Michael D. Swartz, "Jewish Magic in Late Antiquity," in *Cambridge History of Judaism, Volume 4*, ed. Steven T. Katz (New York: Cambridge University Press, 2006), 705.

is an act that involves a woman and a man, the term is close kin to the Hebrew word for harlot or whore.

The association between *zenut* and women is particularly apparent in Lamentations Rabbah 2:4, a close parallel to the Yerushalmi passage. In the Lamentations Rabbah account, the midrashist raises and rejects the idea that the Mount of Olives was destroyed because of sexual sin:

> Why was it destroyed?
> If you say it was because of fornication—
>   there was only one young woman,
>   and they sent her away from there!
> Rabbi Huna said: Because they played ball on the Sabbath.

Though Lamentations Rabbah 2:4 here rejects the idea that destruction can be attributed to women's sexual transgressions, it goes on to echo the Yerushalmi's claim that two of the three other cities were destroyed because of witchcraft and fornication. Furthermore, the very way in which the midrash rejects the charges of sexual immorality reveals the tight link between women and sexual sin. How do we know the Mount of Olives did not suffer on account of sexual transgression? Because it was a region almost entirely without women! Despite the vast population of the mountain, with its many markets and stalls, only a single girl was found among them—and she was driven out. Whether she was sent away on account of a sexual incident or in order to avoid one, the logic of the midrashist is clear. Sexual sin is inconceivable without a woman's presence. The simplest way to ensure sexual morality is to fashion a world without women. Like the cloud of fragrant scent wafting up from the shoes of the haughty daughters of Zion, forbidden sexuality is evoked through the female body. Harlotry attaches to women. Without a woman on the scene, sexual sin cannot be there.

In Bavli Gittin's telling, the narration of catastrophe is quite different. The Bavli's version begins with the mention of the once abundant inhabitations of King's Mountain. The beginning of the passage again emphasizes the vast size and scope of the settlements on King's Mountain. Bavli Gittin 57a recounts:

> King Yannai had sixty myriad cities on King's Mountain.
> Each and every one was the size of the exodus from Egypt,
>   except for three which were double the size of the exodus from Egypt.

Like the Palestinian accounts of Tur Shimon, Bavli Gittin recounts a tale of destruction that befalls an apparently virtuous city. But while the Palestinian accounts enumerate the sins that caused the destruction and laid low these once mighty habitations, Bavli Gittin has no such narrative. Instead, the Bavli's telling centers upon the destruction of the village of Sekhania, as three rabbis sit together to recall and discuss its fate. Bavli Gittin's narrative is structured as a challenge, calling anyone who has "heard something" about the city to recount its faults and issue reproof. As we will see, the rabbis tell several stories of sexual danger, including episodes of sexual compulsion and transgression. With such evocative tales, the Bavli's narrators could have easily built a compelling case for Sekhania's destruction due to sexual sin. But in Bavli Gittin, such sexual condemnation remains a road not taken. Instead, the Bavli constructs an elaborate account of the virtue present in the city before its fall, using its stories to praise the ethics and efficacy of men's sexual and judicial righteousness in a world rife with sin.

Sexual Violence and Virtue: Heroic Masculinity in Bavli Gittin's First Tale of Sekhania

In the middle section of Bavli Gittin's tripartite account of the devastation of Judea, as the Bavli details the destruction of Tur Malka, it recounts three stories about the city of Sekhania that center on sexual violence or compulsion. The passage opens with a conversation between three rabbis, who ask each other for episodes that might explain the destruction of Sekhania. Each of the rabbis relates a tale of troubled or troubling sexuality—and asserts that the men of Sekhania respond righteously, either by demonstrating a heroic refusal to participate in sexual wrongdoing or by using proactive judicial authority to punish sexual offenders. In order to address the stories in depth, I will treat them each in turn. Bavli Gittin 57a begins:

> Rav Menimin[46] bar Ḥelqiah, Rav Ḥelqiah bar Tuvia,
>   and Rav Huna bar Ḥiyya were sitting together and said:
> If anyone has heard something [blameworthy]
>   about the village of Sekhania of Egypt,[47]
>   let him speak.

---

46. The spelling of this sage's name varies somewhat in the manuscripts. I have followed the version that appears in Munich 95, Vatican 140, JTS Rab. 1718.93–100 and JTS Rab. 1729.64–67. I have relied upon the Sol and Evelyn Henkind Talmud Text Databank from the Saul Lieberman Institute (http://eng.liebermaninstitute.org/fyz/) to examine manuscripts. When quoting talmudic texts, I acknowledge significant manuscript variants in the notes. For an overview of the extant manuscripts of the Talmud, see Michael Krupp, "Manuscripts of the Babylonian Talmud," in *The Literature of the Sages. Vol. 1: Oral Tora, Halakha, Mishna, Tosefta, Talmud, External Tractates*, ed. Shmuel Safrai. (Philadelphia: Fortress Press, 1987), 346–66.

47. The place name is difficult. Kefar Sekhania, the name of the place referenced in this tale, also appears in Bavli Avodah Zarah 27b, where it is identified as the home of Jacob, a disciple of

One of them began:

A betrothed man and woman were taken captive among the nations,[48]
   and [their captors] married them to each other.

She said to him:
   "I beg of you, do not touch me
   for I have no ketubah (marriage contract) from you."

And he did not touch her, even until his dying day.

When he died, she said to them:
   "Mourn[49] for this one, who controlled his desire more than Joseph.

For Joseph [withstood temptation with Potiphar's wife]
   for but a single hour,
     while this man did so each and every day.

Joseph did not [lie beside her] in a single bed,
   while this man [lay beside her] in a single bed.

And in Joseph's case, she was not his wife,
   while in this case, she was his wife."

In the first story of Sekhania, captivity becomes the site for profound sexual vulnerability—as well as the performance of extraordinary sexual virtue. This tale evokes a common motif in captivity stories in which a captured man and woman who have a prior relationship come unaccountably into renewed contact with each other. In the well-known Lamentations Rabbah tale of the two children of the high priest Tsadok, or in Bavli Gittin's tale of the two children of Rabbi Yishmael ben Elisha, two enslaved siblings are brought together by their captors for sexual purposes—and eventually come to recognize each other as brother and sister.[50] In a later chapter, I will examine that story in more detail to show how beauty, lament, and forbidden desire operate within the charged context of colonized sexuality. At present, I highlight this

---

Jesus, thus likely in the Galilee. This passage, however, indicates that the place is associated with Egypt (Mitsrayim), which strains geographical likelihood. Rabbinic accounts also refer to the Galilean town of Sakhnin, sometimes vocalized as Sikhnin, which was associated with Rabbi Hananya ben Tradyon and Rabbi Joshua. Ben-Zion Rosenfeld argues that associating Kefar Sekhania (and other similarly named and difficult to identify towns) with Sakhnin "is problematic, despite the similarity in names," but comes to no final conclusions about the identification of these places. See Ben-Zion Rosenfeld, *Torah Centers and Rabbinic Activity in Palestine, 70–400 CE: History and Geographic Distribution* (Leiden: Brill, 2010), 132–133.

48. The Vilna edition reads, "among idolaters."

49. JTS Rab. 1718.93–100 and JTS Rab. 1729.64–67 have "Weep for this one."

50. For an analysis of this tale within Lamentations Rabbah, see Hasan-Roken, *Web of Life*, 16–38. On Jewish use of the Greco-Roman motif of the tragic romance, see David Stern, "The

familiar narrative context to illustrate an important variation in the Sekhania narrative: the social identity of the captives as betrothed. Rabbinic stories of captive brothers and sisters dramatize a barely averted moment of incest, a near violation of a near-universal sexual taboo. In the Sekhania tale, by contrast, the violation is different. The pair are already pledged to one another, but according to rabbinic law, they are not yet allowed to consummate their marriage. By imagining the captive couple as already betrothed, Bavli Gittin highlights the exemplary virtue of a man whose allegiance to rabbinic sexual ethics is so great that it will keep him from touching the woman once intended as his wife.

In rabbinic marriage law, betrothal forges a powerful bond between the intended parties, effecting a formal change in their social status and designating the woman as the eventual sexual partner of this particular man. In certain respects, the sexual and economic strictures of marriage already apply to the woman. Because she has been set apart for her betrothed, rabbinic law forbids intimacy between a betrothed woman and another man. Sexual contact with a betrothed woman is recognized as adultery, a violation of her husband's right to sexual exclusivity. But the betrothed couple is also forbidden sexual contact with each other; rabbinic law expects them to exercise sexual restraint with one another until they are formally married. The notion of the betrothed woman as lacking her ketubah is actually at some variance with rabbinic legal norms. Rabbinic law considers a betrothed woman already entitled to her ketubah— that is, to a stipulated sum of money—if the relationship is dissolved. [51] Our narrative, however, treats the ketubah not as simply as an economic agreement, but a material, tangible possession of a true rabbinic wife. As a document that encodes the social and economic obligations of the husband to his wife, rabbinic tradition imagines the ketubah as a document that serves as both material and symbolic testimony to a husband's obligations to care and provide for her.[52] The ketubah thus stands as a powerful symbol of rabbinic marriage. Without a ketubah, a woman is unrecognizable as a rabbinic wife. Yet within the context of captivity and enslavement, the betrothed man cannot make a marriage; he cannot take on the social role of husband, nor provide the protection,

Captive Woman: Hellenization, Greco-Roman Erotic Narrative, and Rabbinic Literature," *Poetics Today* 19, no. 1 (1998): 91–127.

51. On the institution of betrothal in rabbinic law, see Satlow, *Jewish Marriage in Antiquity*, 68–84.

52. On the midrashic image of the ketubah as the property of the wife, see Stern, *Parables in Midrash*, 56–62.

provision, and honor a wife is due.[53] Captivity breaks the link that should have bound the couple. The captors bring the betrothed parties together in body, thrusting them back into a marriage they were denied. But the Bavli's narrative refuses the validity of a marriage fashioned according to the captors' desires. Enslavement has shattered the possibility of licit sexuality, denied them the capacity to consummate a rabbinic union. For lack of a ketubah, the woman begs her betrothed not to touch her. They lie together each night on a single bed, pressed against the body of their betrothed—estranged only and always by the gulf of captivity.

The first tale of Sekhania situates the captive man as an exemplar of heroic masculinity. When the betrothed woman eulogizes him after his death, she lauds his sexual self-control, praising the captive man's restraint as greater than that of Joseph, who withstood temptation in Potiphar's house. The biblical narrative of Joseph and Potiphar's wife is an important locus for rabbinic conceptions of male sexual virtue.[54] Like the biblical Joseph, our unnamed protagonist struggles against desire and subdues it, demonstrating his capacity to withstand temptation and to preserve Jewish virtue in the midst of captivity. Yet if the Bavli's appeal to the Joseph motif aligns well with the situation of a Jewish man taken captive and thrust into a situation of sexual danger, the biblical trope works less well to evoke the situation of the captive wife. As Ishay Rosen-Zvi observes, the Bavli's tale fashions the female captive as Potiphar's wife—a powerful, beautiful woman who desires Joseph and commands him to fulfill her sexual desires.[55] By figuring her betrothed as Joseph, the Bavli's captive woman positions herself as a sexual temptress who must be resisted at all costs. This appeal to the biblical trope silences the woman's own struggles, subordinating her own virtue for the sake of accentuating her betrothed's righteousness. In this, Bavli Gittin once again reveals its characteristic interest in the performance of male sexual virtue. As Rosen-Zvi has shown, the Bavli presents the struggle against the *yetzer* (the sexual impulse)

53. Rabbinic sources also state that an enslaved woman cannot be party to a legally binding marriage. Noting the particular sexual vulnerabilities of enslavement, Labovitz writes, "She is no more entitled to this protection than she is to the right to claim a sexual assault as rape or coercion." Labovitz, "More Slave Women, More Lewdness," 82.

54. On the treatment of this tale in rabbinic literature, see James L. Kugel, *In Potifar's House: The Interpretive Life of Biblical Texts* (Cambridge: Harvard University Press, 1994); on Joseph and Potiphar's wife in earlier Jewish literature, see Erich Gruen, *Heritage and Hellenism: The Reinvention of Jewish Tradition* (Berkeley: University of California Press, 1998).

55. Rosen-Zvi, *Demonic Desires*, 124.

as a quintessentially masculine task. While the Bavli recognizes the presence of female passion, it offers no tales of women's heroic struggles to master or subdue sexual arousal.[56] Women are sources of temptation, not agents of sexual resistance. Yet even though the Bavli's tale centers on the betrothed man's heroic self-mastery, it also gives voice to an even more unexpected agency. The first tale of Sekhania features a captive woman successfully negotiating the sexually charged space of captivity. Though rabbinic legal texts make the assumption that a woman was subjected to sex during her captivity, the Sekhania tale portrays a woman preserving sovereignty over her body.[57] Not only does she navigate the dangers of captivity, she exercises sexual agency within marriage—successfully calling upon a man to restrain his own desire.

To understand the potent charge of the tale, we must recognize the degree to which the social spaces of captivity and enslavement are thoroughly associated in rabbinic sources with sexual risk. Through stories of Jews taken captive, the rabbis grapple with and give voice to the loss of body sovereignty that enslavement entails. In the ancient world, the widespread practice of taking captives rendered the people of a defeated nation vulnerable to their new masters' whim. Ancient systems of slavery afford the master control over the physical body and sexual capacities of the enslaved person.[58] In the Roman context, slaves were sexually available to their purchaser, his family members, and his associates. As Gail Labovitz notes, "the bodily boundaries of the slave may be invaded by the free, not only through

---

56. Rosen-Zvi, *Demonic Desires*, 120–126.

57. The figure of the chaste captive woman runs counter to the intense sexualization of male and female slaves in the Roman world. Analyzing the relationship between gender, sexuality, and Christian belonging in early Christian narratives, Bernadette Brooten has argued that the distinction between slave and free profoundly shaped the capacity of women to participate in early Christian discourses of sexual virtue. In a forthcoming work, Brooten analyzes the *Passion of Andrew*, in which the pious Christian woman Maximilla enlists her slave-woman Euklia into having sex with her pagan husband so that she can keep her body pure for Christ. She argues that free Christian women's capacity to exercise sexual autonomy and practice chastity was frequently accomplished through the sexual surrogacy of their female slaves. Bernadette Brooten, "Sexual Surrogacy Enables Holy Celibacy: Euklia, Iphidama, and Maximilla in the Passion of Andrew." Harvard Women's Studies in Religion Program Colloquium, Cambridge, MA, March 28, 2012.

58. On enslavement in rabbinic culture and within the Roman world, see Hezser, *Jewish Slavery in Antiquity*; Diane Kriger, *Sex Rewarded, Sex Punished: A Study of the Status of "Female Slave" in Early Jewish Law* (Boston: Academic Studies Press, 2011); Dale B. Martin, "Slavery and the Ancient Jewish Family" in *The Jewish Family in Antiquity*, ed. Shaye Cohen (Atlanta: Scholars Press, 1993), 113–129; Harper, *Slavery in the Late Roman World*; Glancy, *Slavery in Early Christianity*; de Wet, *Preaching Bondage*.

forced labor but also by physical violence and/or sexual assault; the slave has at best severely restricted rights of self-protection."[59] Beyond the fulfillment of the master's own desires, enslaved women were valuable commodities in a slave economy, because they could produce through their own bodies the next generation of enslaved labor. Enslaved men were likewise conscripted into a system of reproduction in which their sexual energies were directed according to the master's will, not their own.[60] As Jennifer Glancy has shown, enslavement threatened key dimensions of late antique masculinity.[61] In a world where manhood was bound up with capacity for self-control and self-determination, slavery could unmake men.

In such a context, Bavli Gittin's tale of sexual abstention in captivity takes on a profound resistance to the brutal logic of enslavement. Yet it is important not to overstate the nature of the resistance. Along with other narratives in Bavli Gittin's account, this tale voices rabbinic lament for the captivity and enslavement of Jews—but its protest is not indicative of broader rabbinic resistance to slavery as a social practice. Rabbinic Jewish culture inherited a legal legacy of slaveholding from the Hebrew Bible and operated within the slaveholding cultures of Greco-Roman and Sassanian society. Rabbinic texts routinely discuss slaves and slaveholding, suggesting that the realities of enslavement were deeply embedded in early Jewish culture and daily life. As Gail Labovitz has observed, "rabbinic texts legislate for a slave society." While rabbinic law often aims to regulate the violence of enslavement, "no rabbinic text ever considers the notion that slavery should be abolished or even addresses slavery as a particular evil."[62] These narratives express rabbinic resistance not to the institution of slavery itself, but to the horror of becoming a slave, to the loss of corporeal sovereignty that followed in the wake of conquest and capture. In this story, our captive man's sexual restraint allows him to simultaneously reclaim the bodily self-control that enslavement would ordinarily deny him—and to refuse to participate in the corporeal reproduction of slavery as a social institution. The sexual politics of his abstinence are bound up with a social politics of resistance, with Bavli Gittin's refusal to fashion the rabbinic body as the tidy subject of imperial dominance.

---

59. Labovitz, "More Slave Women," 75. It was not only enslaved women who were sexually violable. In Roman culture, free Romans frequently made sexual use of enslaved men. Williams, *Roman Homosexuality*, 30–31.

60. Chris de Wet emphasizes the degree to which freeborn Roman masculinity was constructed over and against that of the slave—and highlights how thoroughly slavery as a discursive idea and a bodily practice shaped Roman Christian social life, especially sexuality. De Wet, *Preaching Bondage*.

61. Glancy, *Slavery in Early Christianity*, 25, 98.

62. Labovitz, "More Slave Women," 71; Gail Labovitz, "Purchase of His Money," 92.

Negotiating Sexual Transgression: The Heroism of Male Judicial Virtue

In the first Sekhania story, Bavli Gittin imagines the now-destroyed city as the site of a heroic man's struggle to preserve sexual virtue amidst the bitter constraints of captivity. The Bavli's tale deploys familiar tropes of male sexual restraint, imagining the hero displaying his righteousness despite a tragic and challenging trial. The betrothed man and woman demonstrate their fidelity to rabbinic law in the midst of their captivity, affirming their allegiance to rabbinic principles through their refusal to consummate their marriage at their captors' demand. By insisting on the need for a rabbinic ketubah, by refusing marital sex in the absence of rabbinic sanction, the couple gives corporeal testimony to the integrity of rabbinic law. In the final two tales of the Sekhania cycle, the Bavli's narration of masculine virtue becomes considerably more complex. While the first story situated the Jewish man and his betrothed as preserving their sexual virtue in a non-Jewish context, the next two tales dramatize situations of serious sexual immorality that occur within Jewish communities. Though these stories recount the egregious sexual sins of particular Jewish men, Bavli Gittin ultimately maintains its insistence upon the righteousness and virtue of the citizens of Sekhania. Refusing to pursue the claim that sexual sin served as the grounds for Sekhania's destruction, the Bavli uses these cases of sexual transgression to affirm the moral excellence of the majority of the community.

The final two Sekhania tales affirm the potent power of law. As Bavli Gittin narrates the judicial and punitive actions of the court, its stories recount the triumph of a particular mode of masculine righteousness. The court has the capacity to uncover sexual secrets and unravel sexual schemes, to interpose order in the face of subversive social danger and thereby safeguard the virtue of a compromised community. As it narrates the last two rabbinic accounts of Sekhania, Bavli Gittin 57a continues:

Another began:
The price stood at 40 *modiyot* [a Roman measure] for a *dinar* [a coin].
When the price went down by one *modius*,
    they investigated and found that a father and his son
    had intercourse[63] with a betrothed maiden on the Day of Atonement.
They brought them before the court and they stoned them,
    and the price returned to what it was before.

---

63. The Vilna edition reads *ba'u*, while the manuscripts use the verb *ba'alu*.

Another began:

An account: A certain man desired to divorce his wife,
    but she had a large ketubah.
What did he do?
He went and invited the groomsmen from his wedding
    and he provided them with food and drink.
He got them drunk and laid them out on a single bed
    and poured the white of an egg between them.
He brought witnesses to see them and went before the court.
There was an elder there, named Baba ben Buta,
    who had been a student of Shammai the Elder.
The elder said to them:
    Thus I have received from Shammai the Elder:
        "The white of an egg hardens in the light,
        while an emission of semen becomes thin in the light."
They checked and found that it was according to the elder's word,
    so they brought the husband to the court and flogged him
    and forced him to pay her ketubah.

Abaye said to Rav Yosef:
    "Since all of them were so righteous,
        for what reason were they punished?"
He said to him:
    "On account of the fact that they did not mourn for Jerusalem,"
    as it is written:
        Rejoice with Jerusalem and be glad for her, all you who love her!
        Join in her jubilation, all you who mourned over her. (Isaiah 66:10)

At the outset of this passage, the second of three rabbis recounts a dramatic drop in the price of produce, a misfortune that the town correctly attributes as evidence of some wrongdoing. "They investigated," our narrative recounts, "and found that a father and his son had intercourse with a betrothed maiden on the Day of Atonement." With this charge, Bavli Gittin evokes the grand trifecta of rabbinic sexual sin: father and son alike commit adultery with a woman who is betrothed to another man, profaning the most solemn sacred occasion of the Jewish year, when even licit sex is forbidden. In rabbinic texts, this charge appears frequently as the epitome of sexual immorality, a crime frequently used to characterize the ultimate sexual criminal.[64] The imagined sexual collusion between father and son suggests a

---

64. A similar charge appears in Bavli Baba Metsia 83b, where it likewise serves as evidence of an extraordinary degree of moral depravity on the part of the accused.

form of incest, as both father and son have illicit relations with the same woman. By situating the sex on Yom Kippur, the Bavli fashions the man into a transgressor who profanes the very day that could bring him atonement.

In this story, the women's identity as a betrothed woman is particularly significant, for her betrothal establishes clear and certain grounds for sexual crime. The act of sexual relations with a betrothed woman is itself forbidden, for any man who has sex with a betrothed woman violates her husband's rights by making sexual use of his bride. Bavli Gittin's story gives us no indication of the woman's response to their sexual advances. For the Bavli, this question is irrelevant. Yet for a modern reader, one significant aspect of the charge remains ambiguous: whether the man is also a rapist. By presenting both father and son as sexual actors and by placing the encounter on Yom Kippur, our narrative suggests an act of forced or coerced sex; the context is hardly suggestive of female desire. But by framing the crime as an assault upon a betrothed woman, Bavli Gittin further veils the woman's own subjectivity from the reader's eye. Regardless of the woman's wishes, the liaison is an act of sexual aggression against her husband, a violation of the sexual rights of another man.

Despite the clear potential to narrate this tale as an act that might evoke divine outrage or justify divine punishment, Bavli Gittin steadfastly refuses to make such a claim. Our story does acknowledge that the deed has certain consequences. The crime causes a momentary decline in market price. But this evidence of economic misfortune simply serves as the narrative springboard for the court's judicious action. The price fall is no disaster, but a cautionary red flag that alerts the town to a moral misdeed in their midst. The decline in price is quickly remedied through deliberate judicial action. "They brought them before the court and they stoned them," Bavli Gittin concludes, "and the price returned to what it was before." The logic of the tale frames the fallen price as a divine sign, an expression of divine dissatisfaction with an act of sexual transgression. Yet due to the court's swift response, our rabbinic narrator marshals the account as evidence not of Sekhania's transgression, but as testimony to the people's righteousness. The decisive action of the court successfully neutralizes divine judgment. By emphasizing the social effectiveness of the court's prosecution of sexual crime, the rabbinic story lauds the power of a human court to enact divine justice. The Sekhania story highlights the validity—and the virility—of the court's management of sexual crime. Their robust response to sexual transgression reveals their virtue, their acute responsiveness to God's own sensitivity to sexual sin.[65]

---

65. As Chaya Halberstam has observed, the relationship between the human court and divine judgment is a central concern in rabbinic sources. While rabbinic sources idealize a harmony between divine and human jurisprudence, Halberstam underscores the way in

The final tale continues the theme of sexual crime and punishment, detailing an elaborate ruse concocted by a man who wishes to divorce his wife without paying her ketubah. Because rabbinic law allows a man to divorce his wife without paying her marriage settlement under certain conditions, the conniving husband aims to convince the rabbinic court that she had committed adultery. Bavli Gittin's tale presents his scheme as an egregious moral violation. By invoking key elements of the original celebration of the marriage banquet, the story figures the husband's fraudulent feast as a perverse inversion of the celebration that first bound the couple together. The husband reassembles his groomsmen, the very men who witnessed and affirmed the sanctity of their marriage. He conspires to get them drunk and then arranges them in a compromising position, so he can accuse them of sexual immorality with his wife. Echoing a central motif of the first Sekhania tale, this final story also turns on the drama of a single shared bed. Yet in this case, the woman's husband incites sexual transgression, not restraint. The bed has lost its heroic charge. Slumbering and unconscious with drink, no one engages in resistance. Instead, masculine virtue arises from the court of law—through an elder associated with one of the earliest voices of rabbinic authority. Baba ben Buta uses rabbinic knowledge to uncover the fraud and expose the husband's ruse. His careful investigation empowers the court to issue a proper ruling. Through the exercise of bold judicial agency, the court intercedes in matters usually reserved for the husband alone.[66] They force him to pay her ketubah and grant her a divorce, thus intervening on the woman's behalf in order to reestablish justice in the world.

By centering on the righteousness of the rabbinic court to unearth and properly adjudicate sexual sin, the final Sekhania stories evoke a rabbinic judicial fantasy. The ideal society the rabbis imagine is not a society in which there is no sexual crime, nor a society in which men always exercise sexual restraint. Instead, Bavli Gittin portrays Sekhania as a righteous place because the city is

---

which rabbinic narratives reveal gaps and disjunctures between the human and divine execution of justice. Chaya T. Halberstam, *Law and Truth in Biblical and Rabbinic Literature* (Bloomington: Indiana University Press, 2010).

66. Rabbinic law affords the husband unilateral right of divorce and does not allow a wife to initiate the dissolution of the marriage. While contemporary halakhic authorities generally assert that the court cannot compel a divorce in the case of a recalcitrant husband, rabbinic sources do record situations which the court is figured as forcing a husband to grant his wife a divorce. Mishnah Ketubot 7:10 rules that if a husband develops a significant bodily blemish over the course of their marriage, the court can force him to divorce his wife. See Samuel Greengus, *Laws in the Bible and in Early Rabbinic Collections: The Legal Legacy of the Ancient Near East* (Eugene: Wipf and Stock Publishers, 2011), 35–48. On Mishnah Ketubot 7:10 and its parallel traditions in the Tosefta, see Judith Hauptman, *Rereading the Mishnah: A New Approach to Ancient Jewish Texts* (Tübingen: Mohr Siebeck, 2005), 36–40.

a site of demonstrated legal justice and appropriate punishment. Yet the tale must still grapple with the fact of Sekhania's destruction. After the three rabbis have told their three tales to establish Sekhania's goodness, Abaye asks why the city was destroyed. Bavli Gittin attributes the destruction to a failure to remember Jerusalem, asserting that their failure to mourn Jerusalem's loss led to their doom. This passage represents Bavli Gittin's only explicit post-biblical claim that catastrophe is driven by collective transgression. But even here, I argue, Bavli Gittin equivocates. In contrast to the Palestinian traditions, which begin with an assertion that the cities were virtuous but then focus on revealing their sins, the Bavli's tales have a different rhetorical emphasis. Even in the final stories, where Bavli Gittin might easily have castigated the cities for sexual sin, the stories focus not on enumerating transgression, but on affirming the court as a powerful site for the practice of justice and the restoration of moral order.

But let us tarry for a moment with Abaye's claim. Through the assertion that Sekhania was destroyed on account of its inhabitants' failure to remember Jerusalem, Bavli Gittin situates the responsibility to remember and lament the loss of Jerusalem as the central moral responsibility of the exilic age. Taken at face value, the tradition is suggestive of an important raison d'être of Bavli Gittin's own elaborate narratives that recount and mourn the catastrophe. But shifted into a different register, perhaps Abaye's question exposes a crack in Bavli Gittin's vision of masculine heroics. If Jerusalem stands not for a physical place but for the ideal social reality, if it stands in for the utopian imaginary of a world redeemed, then Abaye's question might serve to reveal a subversive disjuncture between the ideal society and the city the rabbis have described. Sekhania's tales give potent voice to the pervasive presence of violence and brutality—not only beyond Jewish borders, not just in places of captivity that represent the moral outlands of the rabbinic imagination, but also within Jewish communal bounds. While the bitter fact of profound injustice provides exemplary men with the opportunity to demonstrate their virtue through heroic sexual asceticism or through courtroom diligence, the people of Sekhania aren't all righteous—they simply punish well. In a suggestive reading of the first chapter of Bavli Gittin, Aryeh Cohen has argued that its legal poetics call the reader to recognize and confront the violence of the law, particularly the legal violence expressed and channeled through patriarchal control over marriage and divorce.[67] The stories of Sekhania likewise suggest the danger of celebrating too securely the advent of rabbinic power, the ascendance of law in exile. Perhaps the prospect of judicial righteousness becomes

---

67. Aryeh Cohen, "Beginning Gittin/Mapping Exile," in *Beginning/Again: Toward a Hermeneutics of Jewish Texts*, ed. Aryeh Cohen and Shaul Magid (New York: Seven Bridges Press, 2002), 69–112.

seductive in its own right, leading the men of Sekhania to forsake the dream of a different order. In a world scarred by violence and violent desire, they let go of even a longing for Jerusalem.

Sexual Violence and Catastrophe in the Bavli: Desire, Disaster, and Men's Sexual Sin

Despite a rich biblical repertoire that imagines Israel as a wayward wife or willful whore, despite the vivid associations in Palestinian rabbinic texts that link national catastrophe with the brazenness of Zion's daughters and their treacherous schemes, Bavli Gittin's destruction narrative resists the familiar trope that explains Israel's disaster through the symbolism of women's sexual sin. Though it frequently tells stories of sexual violence and violation, Bavli Gittin steadfastly refuses the trope of women's sexual perfidy as a cause of national catastrophe. To illuminate the significance of this choice, I turn to the final narrative in Bavli Gittin's story-cycle, a tale that, on its face, most closely connects the destruction with sexual sin. In this tale, a carpenter's apprentice desires his master's wife and conspires to convince the master to divorce her so that the apprentice can marry her himself. Even here, though the tale is rife with moments that might ordinarily prompt rabbinic ruminations on female sexuality as a source of social and moral danger, Bavli Gittin refrains from attributing destruction to a woman's sexual indiscretion. Instead, the story condemns the apprentice's betrayal and his sexual misconduct—and highlights God's empathy for the (male) victim of corrosive male desire. Bavli Gittin 58a reads:

> Rav Yehudah said Rav said: What is it that is written?
>   *They oppress a man and his house,*
>   *a person and his ancestral land.* (Micah 2:2)
> An account:
> A certain man who was a carpenter's apprentice
>   set his eyes upon the wife of his master.
> One time, his master needed [money] from him.
> The apprentice said to him:
>   "Send your wife to me and I will receive her [and lend her the money].
> The master sent his wife to him
>   and waited three days for her to return.
> Then the master went to him and said:
>   "Where is my wife, who I sent to you?"
> The apprentice said to him:

"I sent her back right away!
But I heard that young men abused her sexually on the road."
The master said to him: "What shall I do?"
The apprentice said to him:
"If you would heed my counsel, divorce her."
The master said to him: "Her ketubah is large."
He said to him:
"I will receive you and give you the money for her ketubah."
So he divorced her, and the other married her.
When the time arrived and the master was not able to pay him,
the apprentice said to him, "Come and work off your debt for me."
The apprentice and his new wife used to sit and eat and drink,
while the master would stand and serve them drinks
and the tears would flow from his eyes and fall into their cups—
and at that very hour, the decree of judgment was sealed.
And some say, it was for two wicks in a single candle-lamp.

In this story, Bavli Gittin links the devastation of Judea with the pain experienced by a duped husband who was tricked by his scheming apprentice into divorcing his wife. The opening pericope from the second chapter of Micah, from which the verse that begins our tale is drawn, castigates those who "plan iniquity (*ḥoshvei-'aven*)" by coveting and seizing other men's fields and houses, "oppressing the man and his house (*ʿashqu gever ubeito*)." The verses emphasize that covetousness leads these men to devise evil schemes, to oppress and expropriate the property of others. In condemning these acts, the prophet reveals how oppression and exploitation threaten the foundational institutions of society: "homesteads, families, fields, little communities rooted in the soil" are swept away through robbery and violence.[68] But the violence that Micah condemns is not primarily the brute exercise of physical force. Instead, the verse frames these acts as violence of the heart, a violation of the commandment against "coveting your neighbor's house."[69] The rabbinic narrative reconfigures the prophetic notion of "covetousness" as the cause of destruction. Following a common rabbinic interpretive

---

68. William McKane, *The Book of Micah: Introduction and Commentary* (Edinburgh: T & T Clark, 1998), 61.

69. Andersen and Freedman include an extended discussion of the relationship between this verse and the verses of the Decalogue. Francis I. Andersen and David Noel Freedman, *Micah: A New Translation with Introduction and Commentary*, Anchor Yale Bible Commentaries, vol. 24 (New York: Doubleday, 2000), 270–273. See also James Luther Mays, *Micah: A Commentary* (Philadelphia: Westminster John Knox Press, 1976), 63.

practice that understands a man's "house" as a veiled reference to his wife, Bavli Gittin uses the biblical verse as a springboard to recount a tale of a marriage torn apart by another man's greed.

In this narrative, Bavli Gittin dramatizes the corrosive nature of illicit male desire. The apprentice's inappropriate desire for his master's wife drives the tale, and his deft manipulation of sexual threat propels the plot. In an unusual inversion of expected social dynamics, the apprentice appears to have more financial resources than the master. Because he desires his master's wife, he maneuvers his master into a position of dependence. When the master needs money, he follows his apprentice's counsel and sends his wife to receive it. The master confronts his apprentice three days later, when his wife has still not returned home. The apprentice concocts a tale of sexual violation, suggesting that she was assaulted by young men on the road. The apprentice tells a recognizable story, a story that plays upon the familiar cultural trope that a woman's decision to "go out" alone makes her vulnerable to sexual danger.[70] Had our hapless husband responded differently—had he affirmed his loyalty to his wife in the face of sexual violation—our story would have a very different ending. Instead, he turns to the conniving apprentice for advice. When the apprentice suggests divorce, the husband's only protest is economic.[71] Again, we might imagine a host of different responses. The husband might have registered outrage at his wife's abuse or expressed concern for her well-being. But his focus remains on financial matters: her large ketubah and his own poverty. The apprentice offers to lend him the funds so that he can accomplish the divorce. When the husband proves unable to repay the loan, he ends up a servant in his erstwhile apprentice's household, serving at the table before the new master and his own ex-wife.

Through the motif of the husband's tears, the Bavli makes plain the devastation that comes about through men's illicit sexual desire. As Bavli Gittin imagines the first husband's servitude, it showcases his tears as a vivid symbol of suffering

---

70. In rabbinic discourse, the discussion of women's "going out" often centers on the biblical narrative of Dinah—and the suggestion in Genesis Rabbah 34:1 that women who go out, go out to seduce. See Lori Hope Lefkowitz, *In Scripture: The First Stories of Jewish Sexual Identities* (Lanham: Rowman & Littlefield, 2010), 113. For a discussion of Dinah in rabbinic narrative, see Mary Anna Bader, *Tracing the Evidence: Dinah in Post-Hebrew Bible Literature* (New York: Peter Lang Publishing, 2008).

71. For a critique of this tale and the Sekhania narratives in terms of their portrayal of sexual violence in intimate relationships and men's manipulation of women for their own ends, see Bonna Devora Haberman, "Divorcing Ba'al: The Sex of Ownership in Jewish Marriage," in *The Passionate Torah: Sex and Judaism*, ed. Danya Ruttenberg (New York: New York University Press, 2009), 36–57, esp. 38–40.

and distress.[72] Through the narrative detail of the husband's tears, the reader comes to understand the devastation that the scheming apprentice has brought to his master: the ruin of his marriage and the loss of his own sovereignty as a free man. Once a master craftsman with an apprentice of his own, the distraught husband is now a servant in his erstwhile subordinate's house. The tears also signal his feeling for his now-divorced wife, evoking a vivid portrait of lament, perhaps even regret. For all that this rabbinic husband fails his wife in her moment of pain, for all that he fails to empathize with her suffering or to affirm his steadfast loyalty to her regardless of her violation, our story *does* imagine the husband as emotionally involved with his wife. He weeps when he sees her sitting with another man; he weeps, and God responds to the pathos, the depth of his loss.

Bavli Gittin's tale affords the reader a powerful glimpse of the corrosive power of unchecked male desire. The conclusion of the tale imagines that the destruction comes about in response to the wronged husband's tears, a motif to which I will return at the end of this book. But an alternative opinion speculates that the destruction comes about because of sexual transgression, what the Bavli evocatively terms, "two wicks in a single candle-lamp." As Galit Hasan-Rokem has observed, rabbinic texts often use the candle-lamp as a metaphor for sexual intercourse. Because ancient candle-lamps consisted of a long bowl filled with oil, the act of "inserting a wick" serves the rabbis as a symbolic representation of sexual intercourse.[73] According to this etiology, destruction follows from sexual sin, when one woman serves as a sexual vessel for two men's desires. But even this scenario, for all its misogynist assumptions, refrains from castigating *the woman* for her role in this plot. The absence of blame is something of a mixed blessing, bound up as it is with the woman's utter lack of agency. As Bonna Devora Haberman observes, the woman moves through the tale like a puppet; she is an object of two men's desire, manipulated only for the purposes of accomplishing men's aims.[74] Yet though we can clearly recognize the Bavli's tale as counter-feminist discourse, it is important to parse the particulars of its gender implications. Even here, amidst a tale whose characters take for granted the appropriateness of divorcing a woman in the aftermath of sexual assault, Bavli Gittin avoids portraying sexual violation as a sign of women's moral transgression. Bavli Gittin's condemnation falls upon the apprentice, not the woman who "went out" in response

---

72. On the significance of men's tears as a poignant symbol of suffering in the Bavli, see Shulamit Valler, *Sorrow and Distress in the Babylonian Talmud* (Boston: Academic Studies Press, 2011).

73. Galit Hasan-Rokem, "Rabbi Meir, the Illuminated and the Illuminating," in *Two Trends in the Study of Midrash*, ed. Carol Bakhtos (Leiden: Brill, 2006), 227–244, esp. 236.

74. Haberman, "Divorcing Ba'al," 40.

to her husband's instruction. If the temple falls because of sexual sin, as this tradition suggests, it is *men's* sexual schemes and *men's* covetous desires that bring chaos and catastrophe into the world.

Over the course of this chapter, I have argued that Bavli Gittin's treatment of sexual transgression and sexual violence avoids a number of tropes prominent in earlier Jewish narratives. Refusing the familiar prophetic motif that frames destruction through the metaphor of a wife's infidelity and adultery, Bavli Gittin does not portray Israel as a sexually promiscuous woman, nor does it frame stories of women's sexual desire as the cause of national catastrophe. Bavli Gittin instead draws attention to men's sexual transgression, revealing the depravity of unbridled male sexual desire even as it also upholds the striking possibilities of men's sexual virtue and sexual restraint.

But what does this shift mean for women? Even as Bavli Gittin avoids framing women's sexuality as a catastrophic force that provokes divine destruction, its narratives silence women's experiences of sexual violence. As the tale of the carpenter's apprentice makes plain, Bavli Gittin highlights divine empathy for the wronged husband, but pays little heed to the pain of the wife. The rabbinic story affords her virtually no agency. It offers readers no insight into how she experiences divorce or remarriage. The Bavli affords her no voice. She sits silent at another man's side. She never speaks; she never weeps. In the next chapter, I argue that Bavli Gittin's destruction narratives frequently use sexual violence as a symbol of Israel's suffering. Within these narratives, women's bodies take on a powerful symbolic currency to demonstrate the depths of Israel's degradation, to signal the brutality of conquest. Within the broader symbolic landscape of Bavli Gittin, Aryeh Cohen suggests that these accounts of sexual violence give voice to the particular risk that exile poses to rabbinic subjectivity—the risk that they too might be subjugated, divorced, dismembered.[75] Yet even as Bavli Gittin uses women's violation as a central metaphor for conceptualizing catastrophe, it gives little expression to women's emotional lives. These tales do not spur the rabbis to recognize women's subjectivity, or to empathize with a woman's wounds. For all that sexual violation serves as a powerful narrative trope for expressing rabbinic pain and violation, Bavli Gittin's tales of sexual violence routinely displace women's suffering. They gesture instead in a different direction, toward the pathos of the nation, the agony of the rabbis, the suffering of God.

---

75. A. Cohen, "Beginning Gittin," 93.

2

Sex in the Shadow of Rome

SEXUAL VIOLENCE AND THEOLOGICAL LAMENT
IN BAVLI GITTIN'S DISASTER TALES

IN BAVLI GITTIN'S account of the Roman destruction of Jerusalem, sexual violence evokes rabbinic horror over the desecration of the temple. Its stories portray Roman conquest as a sexual assault, a destruction enacted in part through the bodies of women. When the Roman general Titus finally breaches the walls of Jerusalem and raids the temple, the Talmud recounts how he seizes a woman, enters the holiest space of the sanctuary, unfurls a Torah scroll, rapes her on the altar, and then pierces the veil that surrounds the Holy of Holies. In this tale, a woman's violated body symbolizes and accentuates the desecration of the temple by the Roman conquerors. A similar collision between brutality and sacrality appears in the tale of Tsafnat bat Penuel, daughter of the high priest, who was assaulted all night by her captor and then sold to another man in the market. By portraying the exposure and brutality borne by a woman of the most illustrious priestly lineage, Bavli Gittin uses Tsfanat's corporeal experience of exposure and brutality to recall the defilement of the temple and the desecration of the priestly altar. These narratives make use of pervasive Roman symbolism of imperial dominance as a form of "sexual conquest"—a visual and narrative ideology that imagines the subject population as a feminine body, sexually dominated by the virile might of the conqueror.[1] But while rabbinic tales participate in a familiar Roman

---

1. My thinking on the sexual and gender implications of Roman colonial power is indebted to the work of Daniel Boyarin, Davina Lopez, and Joseph Marchal. My interest in the gendered body as a locus for the expression of ideology and the negotiation of power has been shaped by the work of Virginia Burrus, Elizabeth Castelli, and Dale Martin. See D. Boyarin, *Unheroic Conduct*; D. Boyarin, *Dying for God*; J. Boyarin and D. Boyarin, *Powers of Diaspora*; Davina C. Lopez, *Apostle to the Conquered*; Joseph Marchal, *The Politics of Heaven: Women, Gender, and Empire in the Study of Paul* (Minneapolis: Fortress Press, 2008); Virginia Burrus, *The Sex*

discourse, they use the symbolism of sexual conquest to express rabbinic lament and violation at the hands of Rome. Charged tales of sexual violence allow the rabbis to voice both lament and revulsion, coding Roman conquest as a desecration of the altar and an affront to God.

Within Bavli Gittin, stories of rape and violation forge a critical connection between imperial domination and sexual violence, a connection that has often gone unseen.[2] Scholars working on rabbinic responses to sexual violence have largely focused on the rabbis as legal jurists, probing how rabbinic law conceptualizes and responds to rape or other forms of sexual violence.[3] This is critical work, particularly as it illuminates the ramifications of rabbinic law for women, captives, slaves, and others who face sexual violence. Yet this focus on the rabbis as legal jurists can obscure the reality of rabbinic powerlessness in the face of Roman violence.[4] In this chapter, I draw attention to the colonial context of many rabbinic tales of sexual violence, highlighting rabbinic fears about the dangers faced by Jewish women and the ways in which conquered men were also subject to sexual risk. Assessing the Roman imperial context, David Mattingly

---

Lives of Saints: An Erotics of Ancient Hagiography (Philadelphia: University of Pennsylvania Press, 2007); Elizabeth Castelli, *Martyrdom and Memory: Early Christian Culture Making* (New York: Columbia University Press, 2004); and Dale B. Martin, *The Corinthian Body* (New Haven: Yale University Press, 2006).

2. David Mattingly discusses the connection between imperialism and sexuality in the context of the Roman Empire and more recent colonial contexts, arguing that Roman imperialism had a profound effect on the development of Roman sexual mores and practices. Examining sexual violence and Native American genocide, Andrea Smith argues for a strong connection between sexual violence and colonial power, emphasizing that rape functions not only as means of reinforcing male dominance over women but also as an expression and enactment of colonialism. Both Mattingly and Smith emphasize the degree to which scholarly accounts of these periods have tended to separate discussions of sexuality from assessments of imperial power or colonial violence. Mattingly, *Imperialism, Power, and Identity*, 94–121; Andrea Smith, *Conquest: Sexual Violence and American Indian Genocide* (Cambridge MA: South End Press, 2005).

3. Important discussions of rabbinic responses to sexual violence appear in Biale, *Women and Jewish Law*; Hauptman, *Rereading the Rabbis*; Judith Romney Wegner, *Chattel or Person? The Status of Women in the Mishnah* (New York: Oxford University Press, 1988); and Irshai, "Rape in Jewish Law."

4. Catherine Hezser's treatment of social structure in rabbinic Palestine emphasizes that the rabbis could only rarely draw upon institutional authority to legitimate their social power and that they largely lacked the ability to impose their religious program. Instead, their authority (such as it was) was primarily personal in nature, based on their reputation and the status afforded the rabbinic role by various members of the community. Catherine Hezser, *The Social Structure of the Rabbinic Movement in Roman Palestine* (Tübingen: Mohr Siebeck, 1997). Seth Schwartz stresses the profound effect of imperial domination on the development of Jewish culture—suggesting the importance of reconceptualizing rabbinic prowess in light of their subject status vis-à-vis Greco-Roman power. Schwartz, *Imperialism and Jewish Society*.

observes, "the psychological taint of sexual humiliation and degradation has been a powerful tool for sustaining social difference between rulers and ruled in many colonial societies."[5] Whether or not the rabbinic tellers of these tales were themselves directly subject to Roman sexual violence, they were, I suggest, shaped by a context in which imperial sexual threat was a recognizable reality.

Focusing attention on the vulnerability of the rabbinic body allows us an alternative vantage point to consider the imprint of Roman colonialism on the construction of rabbinic masculinity, sexuality, and social power. Reading Bavli Gittin's rape narratives as a form of resistance literature allows us to better understand the cultural and theological import of their sex and gender politics. As I have argued in the previous chapter, Bavli Gittin's account of the destruction treats sexual violence in a strikingly different way. It does not link conquest with women's sexual transgression, nor does it portray sexual sin as repaid through violence enacted upon a woman's body. In Bavli Gittin, corporeal and sexual assault receives no divine sanction. Rape is marked out as violence, an act of violation that reveals the brutality of the conqueror. These stories express elements of rabbinic resistance to imperial domination, emphasizing Jewish resilience even in the midst of intense suffering. Yet even as rabbinic narratives portray in vivid detail the brutality of Roman domination, I argue that the rhetorical use of rape as a symbol risks making instrumental use of those who experience violation, turning attention away from the physical and psychic experience of sexual assault. Bavli Gittin uses rape and sexual assault as a way of conceptualizing *divine* woundedness and *rabbinic* lament, thereby privileging the theological significance of Roman violation over the brutal body costs of imperial conquest.

Rape and/as Roman Domination in Rabbinic Literature

Despite a considerable gulf of geography that separates the Babylonian rabbinic academies from the heartlands of Rome, the cultural grammar of Roman conquest would surely have been recognizable and familiar to Babylonian rabbis. Recent scholarship has emphasized that Babylonian rabbinic worlds operated within a complex cultural landscape. As Yaakov Elman and Shai Secunda have shown, Babylonian rabbinic literature emerges within an Iranian cultural context. Analyzing the Bavli alongside Indo-Iranian literatures reveals potent parallels between the legal traditions, ritual practices, and cultural norms of Sassanian, Zoroastrian, and Babylonian rabbinic

---

5. Mattingly, *Imperialism, Power, and Identity*, 95.

communities.[6] Yet scholars of late antiquity are also increasingly recognizing the importance of cultural interactions *between* the Sassanian east and the Roman west. Richard Kalmin and Daniel Boyarin both situate rabbinic Babylonia within a shared cultural world that draws upon the intellectual currents of Roman Hellenism, Syriac Christianity, and a Sassanian culture increasingly attuned to engagement with Rome.[7] During the centuries of the Bavli's composition and redaction, the Sassanian and Roman empires were locked in fierce cultural and military rivalry. Art historian Matthew Canepa argues that, beginning in the third century, these two empires increasingly developed a mutually understandable language of symbolic gesture, artistry, and ritual performance that allowed them to make recognizable assertions of imperial power and majesty across cultural lines.[8] After a series of victories along the border, the Sassanian king Shapur I (r. 239/240–272) made a series of conquests in the eastern Roman Empire in which he captured and deported large numbers of people and resettled them within western Persian border provinces. A mainstay of Sassanian military practice, wartime population transfer brought an influx of Roman culture and learning into the Sassanian Empire, likely playing a significant role in the development of Syriac Christianity and the Christian school at Nisibis.[9] Richard Kalmin theorizes that Babylonian Jewish culture was likewise affected by the influx of Roman culture into the eastern parts of the Sassanian Empire, arguing for a significant "Palestinianization" of Babylonian rabbinic thought during the fourth century and beyond.[10]

---

6. Shai Secunda, *Iranian Talmud*. Yaakov Elman has pioneered critical research on the relationship between early Iranian legal texts and rabbinic tradition. For a helpful introduction, see Elman, "Middle Persian Culture and Babylonian Sages," 165–197.

7. D. Boyarin, "Hellenism in Jewish Babylonia," D. Boyarin, *Socrates and the Fat Rabbis*; and Richard Kalmin, *Jewish Babylonia*.

8. Canepa has documented an extensive degree of artistic and cultural interaction between Sassanian and Roman empires. He argues that Shapur I and later Sassanian kings frequently captured Roman artisans and used them to commemorate Persian battlefield triumphs, commandeering not only their persons but also their technical skill and artistic repertoire as a display of Sasanian prowess and might. Canepa, *Two Eyes of the Earth*, 67, 78, 188.

9. Kettenhofen, "Deportations," http://www.iranicaonline.org/articles/deportations; Frye, *History of Ancient Iran*, 296–303; Canepa, *Two Eyes of the Earth*, 27–29; and Wiesehöfer, *Ancient Persia from 550 BC to 650 AD*, 201. On the School of Nisibis, see Becker, *Fear of God and the Beginning of Wisdom*.

10. Palestinian traditions had long circulated in Babylonia; Kalmin emphasizes that this was not a new phenomenon, but an increase and intensification of the amount of Palestinian influence. Kalmin, *Jewish Babylonia*, 3–8, 174.

While the precise lines of transmission that conveyed Palestinian rabbinic traditions and Hellenistic cultural motifs to the Babylonian rabbinic academies were surely complex and varied, my work assumes that Roman ideologies of imperial conquest would have been recognizable and comprehensible to the Babylonian rabbis. Despite the Bavli's greater geographical distance from the historical fact of the Roman conquest of Judea in 70 CE, the Babylonian rabbinic communities were not insulated from Roman military power or imperial assertions. In commemorating and memorializing the Roman destruction of Jerusalem, Babylonian rabbinic texts display a complex engagement with potent motifs of Roman imperial conquest. When the rabbis use rape to lament Rome's violation of the temple, they make use of prominent Roman symbolism that linked military victory with sexual violence. Roman art and iconography consistently used women's bodies to represent conquered nations, figuring imperial triumph through the submissive and sexually violated bodies of conquered female nations.[11] The imagery of these portrayals is stark: Roman statuary commemorating triumph in battle commonly portrays Roman victory in explicitly sexual terms.[12] A well-known frieze at Aphrodisias in Asia Minor, for example, commemorates the Roman conquest of Britannia by showing Emperor Claudius seizing and raping a woman who personifies the subjugated province.[13] These Roman representations of victory were meant to inscribe the virile glory of imperial might. They use sexual violation to mark the humiliation and domination of a conquered land and people. In Roman imperial ideology, conquest feminizes vanquished men and nation alike.

Rabbinic destruction narratives make use of this potent cultural trope. But these rabbinic stories do not simply reinscribe the motif of the conquered nation as sexually violable. The rabbinic telling uses rape differently: to mark not the shame of the conquered but rather the moral degradation of the conqueror. Through mimicry that both makes use of and resists Roman ideologies of dominance as sexual violation, the narratives reveal fissures and cracks in Roman

---

11. Lopez, *Apostle to the Conquered*, 29. On the significance of these cultural motifs within rabbinic narrative, see David Stern, "Captive Woman."

12. This was also a significant motif in ancient Greece: See Edith Hall, "Asia Unmanned: Images of Victory in Classical Athens," in *War and Society in the Greek World*, ed. John Rich and Graham Shipley (London: Routledge, 1993), 108–133. Martin Kilmer discusses the use of male-male rape "to express complete dominance of another nation" in Greek pottery. Martin Kilmer, "'Rape' in Early Red-Figure Pottery," in *Rape in Antiquity: Sexual Violence in the Greek and Roman Worlds*, ed. Susan Deacy and Karen F. Pierce (Swansea: Classical Press of Wales, 2002), 137–138. On Greek colonization metaphors and their relation to marriage, sexuality, and rape, see Carol Dougherty, *The Poetics of Colonization: From City to Text in Archaic Greece* (New York: Oxford University Press, 1993).

13. Lopez, *Apostle to the Conquered*, 26–55.

conquest. In each of the three tales I examine, a gesture of unexpected agency highlights a moment of resistance to Roman domination. While recounting in brutal strokes the overt might and power of Rome, these narratives nevertheless suggest that the imperial project fails in subtle, but powerful ways to fully subdue the conquered Jewish subject. As we examine these tales, I draw attention to two different implications of the Bavli's representation of sexual violence. I highlight the protest impulse in these tales, uncovering how these stories express rabbinic resistance to Roman power. I also probe the ethical consequences of rabbinic representations of disaster, particularly the way rabbinic narrative portrayals of sexual violence eclipse attention toward the actual body costs borne by women, captives, and enslaved persons who were marginalized within the rabbinic world. The rabbinic refashioning of Roman rape symbolism represents an act of cultural and theological resistance to imperial domination. But these narratives also make instrumental use of women's pain to perform the cultural work of lamentation. These tales code Roman conquest as a desecration of the altar and an affront to God. By using rape as charged symbolic discourse to give voice to divine vulnerability and rabbinic loss, the rabbinic narratives shift the frame into theological lament, a choice that expresses rabbinic pathos and pain while silencing the significance of sexual violence against women and enslaved people.

In other contexts, Babylonian rabbinic sources often recognize rape as violence against women. As Judith Hauptman has emphasized, the Babylonian Talmud provides a number of important innovations that strengthen early Jewish legal responses to rape, seduction, and sexual violence.[14] In Bavli Ketubot 39a, for example, the Bavli rejects an argument that a woman who is raped receives compensation for pain only if she is thrust to the ground. In that passage, Rabbi Zeira argues that a woman feels pain even if she is raped on silk sheets.[15] Hauptman argues that later rabbis increasingly recognize women's suffering during rape—acknowledging not only physical but also psychological pain—and condemn rape as a crime, even if a woman experiences no physical wound.[16] By contrast, while the narrative portrayals of rape in Bavli Gittin highlight the brutality of Roman conquest and dramatize the Roman violation of the temple, these stories express little interest in women's suffering as such. In narratives in which rape is intertwined with Roman domination, rabbinic attention shifts away from the problem of women's pain to focus instead the suffering of the nation and the suffering of God.

---

14. Hauptman, *Rereading the Rabbis*, 77–101, esp. 96–97. On the mishnaic conceptualization of rape as primarily a crime against the father, see Wegner, *Chattel or Person*.

15. Biale, *Women and Jewish Law*, 244; and Hauptman, *Rereading the Rabbis*, 85.

16. In Bavli Ketubot 51b, Rava condemns forced sex, even if it ultimately results in a woman's pleasure or eventual consent. Hauptman, *Rereading the Rabbis*, 85–87.

Rape and the Altar: Sexual Violence in Titus's Conquest of the Jerusalem Temple

Bavli Gittin's account of the destruction uses sexual assault as a central symbol for conceptualizing the physical and spiritual desecration of the Jerusalem Temple.[17] The narrative likens Titus's invasion of the temple to an act of rape, using a woman's body to embody the reality of destruction. Bavli Gittin 56b reads:

> Titus said:
>> *Where is their God, the Rock in whom they take shelter?*
>> (Deuteronomy. 32:37)
>
> This is Titus the wicked one, who reviled and blasphemed against Heaven.
> What did he do?
> He seized a whore (*zonah*),
>> entered the holy temple,
>> spread out a Torah scroll,
>> and performed a sin upon it.
>
> He drew a sword[18] and cut into the curtain that veiled the Holy of Holies,
>> but a miracle occurred and blood bubbled forth.
>
> He went out, believing he had killed God,[19]
>> as it is written:
>>> *Your enemies roar within your holy place;*
>>> *they regard their signs as true signs.* (Psalms 74:4).
>
> Abba Ḥinan says:
>> *Who is strong like you, YHVH?* (Psalms 89:9)
>
> Who is as strong and as hard as You?
> For You hear the insults and blasphemies of that wicked one and remain silent.

---

17. A version of this story also appears in Leviticus Rabbah, which has been analyzed by Galit Hasan-Rokem and Joshua Levinson. See Galit Hasan-Rokem, "Within Limits and Beyond: History and the Body in Midrashic Texts," *International Folklore Review* 9–10 (1993–1995): 5–12; Galit Hasan-Rokem, "Narratives in Dialogue: A Folk-Literary Perspective on Interreligious Contacts in the Holy Land in Rabbinic Literature of Late Antiquity," in *Sharing the Sacred: Religious Contacts and Conflicts in the Holy Land*, ed. Arieh Kofsky and Guy G. Stroumsa (Jerusalem: Yad Izhak Ben Zvi, 1998), 109–129; and Joshua Levinson, "'Tragedies Naturally Performed': Fatal Charades, Parodia Sacra, and the Death of Titus," in *Jewish Culture and Society under the Christian Roman Empire*, ed. Richard Kalmin and Seth Schwartz (Leuven: Peeters, 2003), 349–382.

18. This phrase is missing in the Munich 95 manuscript, but appears in the Vatican 130 and Vatican 140 manuscripts, as well as in the Soncino printing of 1488 and the Vilna printed edition. The St. Petersburg RNL Evr. I 187 is fragmentary at this point and does not include this section of text.

19. The manuscripts literally read "believing he had killed *himself*," but this is a pious euphemism.

In this tale, Titus seizes a woman, brings her into the sacred space of the temple, spreads out a Torah scroll, and violates her on the parchment that contains the divine word. Then Titus draws his sword and cuts into the veil that surrounds the Holy of Holies, symbolically penetrating the sanctuary. Titus's triumphant phallus is figured as victorious, both through the symbol of the bloodied sword and the rape itself. The blurred boundaries between woman and veil intertwine the violence done to the woman and to the sanctuary.[20] As Daniel Boyarin has shown, rabbinic literature commonly figures the Torah as a desired and desirable woman, the ultimate object of rabbinic eros.[21] Titus's sexual assault collapses the violated woman and the physical form of the Torah into a single female body, vulnerable to the conqueror.

The Titus narrative also depicts a stark inversion of the sanctity of the altar and the Holy of Holies. According to rabbinic tradition, the high priest alone could enter the Holy of Holies at only one moment each year, the afternoon of Yom Kippur. In preparation for the ritual, the high priest was required to maintain strict ritual purity, even avoiding physical proximity to his wife.[22] When Titus enters the temple, he transgresses on every score: he lacks the genealogical lineage of the priesthood and his sexual violence inverts the priest's ascetic discipline. By having Titus bring a whore into the temple, the Bavli also activates a longstanding polemic against temple sexuality, bringing to mind the biblical and rabbinic caricatures of "temple harlots" and illicit, idolatrous sexuality.[23] By

---

20. The version of this tale that appears in Leviticus Rabbah 22:3 accentuates even more brutally the blurred boundaries between the woman, the Torah, and the temple. The desecration of the temple begins with Titus brandishing his sword, slashing the curtain, and raping two women on a spread-out Torah scroll, and then withdrawing his bloody sword. By positioning the rape in the midst of the penetration of the Holy of Holies, Leviticus Rabbah deliberately mingles the physical sanctity of the temple and the body of the women. As Levinson notes, "the narrator has skillfully displaced the concluding action. The sword should have appeared after the first threesome, since presumably it is bloodied by penetrating the curtains and not the women. This is a classical type of 'ungrammaticality' which . . . equates both of Titus's penetrative acts; his bloodied *gladius* has violated and conquered both bodies—both incorporeal and corporeal space." Levinson, "Tragedies Naturally Performed," 369.

21. D. Boyarin, *Carnal Israel*, 134–166.

22. Günter Stemberger, "Yom Kippur in Mishnah Yoma," in *The Day of Atonement: Its Interpretations in Early Jewish and Christian Traditions*, ed. Thomas Hieke and Tobias Nicklas (Leiden: Brill, 2011), 121–138.

23. On the Bavli's association between prostitutes and idolatry, see Simcha Fishbane, *Deviancy in Early Rabbinic Literature: A Collection of Socio-Anthropological Essays* (Leiden: Brill, 2007), 91–92. Michael Satlow argues that rabbinic literature commonly draws a link between Jewish-gentile intercourse and idolatry in *Tasting the Dish: Rabbinic Rhetorics of Sexuality* (Atlanta: Scholar's Press, 1995), 90–91, 104–105. Most of the cases that Satlow cites focus on the power of gentile women to draw Jewish men into idolatry.

associating Titus with idolatrous sexuality, the Bavli figures his conquest as the ultimate violation of God. Titus is anti-priest and arch-idolater, the one who profanes what the high priest holds sacred. But Titus does not simply desecrate the sacred place. The Bavli's story emphasizes the violence that Roman assault does to the rabbinic experience of sacred communion. As Joshua Levinson has shown, rabbinic texts often figure the Holy of Holies in term of sacred eros, a site of intimate divine and human congress. Titus's violence turns the site of sacred encounter into a place of rape.[24]

The Bavli uses the rape of a woman to imagine the rape of God, deploying the symbolic force of sexual violence to articulate the inexpressible injury that Roman conquest does to the divine. In the narrative, the veil stands in for the ephemeral divine body. It is the veil, not the body of the woman, that bleeds after Titus's assault. The physical rape is portrayed as bloodless, while the pierced cloth spurts actual blood. The Bavli presents this as a miracle, but it is surely a strange form of miraculous intervention, a miracle that underscores the depth of divine loss. Right after the penetration of the veil, the Bavli emphasizes that the God of Israel is not *actually* slain. In the rabbinic account, Titus misunderstands the sign and believes himself to be God's killer. After the passage quoted above, the talmudic narrative goes on to highlight God's victory over the arrogant Roman general, a story I will discuss in detail in a later chapter. An overconfident Titus taunts the God of Israel to make war upon him—only to die in agony as a mosquito bores for seven years into his brain.[25] The full narrative emphasizes divine power and agency, manifest through the tiny mosquito that brings down the mighty general. While the rape scene portrays Titus as the victorious conqueror, demonstrating his conquest of Jerusalem through his defilement of the temple and violation of a woman on the altar, the larger story depicts *his* destruction at the hands of Israel's God.

The scene in the temple concludes differently, however, with a haunting acknowledgment of God's silence in the face of assault. Glossing Psalms 89:9 that asks, "Who is strong like you, YHVH?," Abba Ḥinan describes God as one who "hears the insults and blasphemies of the wicked one and you remain silent." Abba Ḥinan reads this silence as strength in the face of insult and violation. Through intertwined images of the woman raped and the veil pierced by the conqueror's sword, the Bavli laments the war wounds of a feminized God.[26] This is a striking,

---

24. Levinson, "'Tragedies Naturally Performed,'" 369–370.

25. Bavli Gittin 56b.

26. Levinson describes this as the "effeminization" of God. Levinson, "'Tragedies Naturally Performed,'" 369.

daring theological move—a motif that allows the Bavli to set the stage for a portrayal of God as suffering under Roman occupation. Yet by using rape to voice
divine vulnerability and rabbinic loss, by centering attention on the symbolic
significance of rape, the narrative obscures the embodied physicality of sexual
violence. By presenting Titus's actions as a crime against God, the Bavli directs
attention away from the woman's pain.

Temple Rape and the Zonah: Fashioning the Rabbinic Whore

Following the counsel of feminist critic Trinh T. Minh-Ha, to "pause and look
more closely than is required, to look at what one is not supposed to look at,"[27]
I want to turn our attention more closely to the woman in this tale. The text
describes her as a *zonah*, a word which rabbinic texts commonly use to describe
a woman who engages in lewd or illicit sexual acts (*zenut*). In rabbinic culture,
both men and women are stigmatized for engaging in *zenut*, but the word *zonah*
is specifically applied to women; the Bavli has no equivalent terminology that
characterizes a man as a fornicator. Accordingly, I translate *zonah* as "whore"—a
translation that reflects the moral charge of the word and captures its gendered
nature. The more neutral "prostitute" fails to capture the stigma associated with
the term *zonah* and conveys a professional status that may be inaccurate. In rabbinic Jewish contexts, we cannot assume that a woman categorized as a *zonah*
worked in the sex trade. As Christine Hayes has demonstrated, rabbinic texts use
zenut to describe any kind of sexual intercourse that does not result in a valid
marriage. The Bavli's terminology of *zenut* is also unconcerned with issues of
women's consent; it does not matter, from a halakhic standpoint, whether illicit
sex is forced or consensual.[28] Rabbinic legal thought categorizes a Jewish woman
as a *zonah* after sexual intercourse with a person she is not permitted to marry.[29]

While the Bavli's audience is expected to regard the woman as essentially
identified with and stigmatized by and illicit sex, the text offers no insight into

---

27. Trinh T. Minh-Ha, *When the Moon Waxes Red: Representation, Gender, and Cultural
Politics* (New York: Routledge, 1991), 114.

28. In the Bavli's customary halakhic usage, the term *zonah* appears most commonly in discussions of priestly marriage and expresses concern about priests' genealogical purity. It designates
a woman who is "a prohibited outsider with whom marriage is not legally possible." Hayes,
Gentile Impurities, 172.

29. J. Simcha Cohen, *Intermarriage and Conversion: A Halakhic Solution* (Hoboken, NJ: Ktav,
1987), 123.

her prior sexual history. The term *zonah* elides two possibilities. If the woman had previously worked as a prostitute, she may have been particularly vulnerable to sexual violence and unprotected by cultural norms that might more successfully shield an elite rabbinic woman. The other possibility is that the woman's status as *zonah* was forged through rape. A woman without a prior history of sex work could become a *zonah* on account of Titus's seizure. If so, an uncritical translation of *zonah* as prostitute effaces this act of brutality and identifies the woman solely in terms of her (forced) involvement in sexual sin. By characterizing her as a *zonah*, Bavli Gittin draws narrative attention away from her suffering, deemphasizing her status as Titus's victim and highlighting her active involvement in the temple's desecration.[30] While the rabbinic tale uses rape to express the rabbis' own symbolic violation at the hands of Rome and to lament the violation of God through the penetration of the sanctuary, rabbinic discourse forges no empathy with the violated woman. Her body figures in this tale as a marker of the nation's vulnerability, an instrument of the temple's ruin.

Captivity and Sexual Conquest: Sexual Violence, Enslavement, and Empire

The Titus narrative draws attention to a critical lacuna in rabbinic legal discussions of interethnic unions. Most halakhic texts focus their attention on the permissibility (or lack thereof) of gentile women as sexual partners for Jewish men. While the rabbis clearly prohibit sexual relations between Jewish women and gentile men, they address sexual relations between Jewish women and gentile men in far less detail. David Novak suggests that the rabbinic focus on sexual relationships between Jewish men and gentile women reflects social and gender dynamics that made men more able to seek out sexual liaisons than women.[31] Yet the realities of war, captivity, and enslavement clearly created situations in which Jewish women experienced sexual contact with non-Jewish men. The tale of Titus in the temple suggests that rabbinic responses to these unions generated moral revulsion and outrage—not simply because they regarded intercourse

---

30. The Bavli's lack of empathy for the *zonah* in this tradition seems to me in keeping with Judith Baskin's assessment that biblical and rabbinic traditions "often display a romanticized view of prostitutes—as long as they are not Jews." Baskin, "Prostitution: Not a Job for a Nice Jewish Girl," in *The Passionate Torah: Sex and Judaism*, ed. Danya Ruttenberg (New York: New York University Press, 2009), 24.

31. David Novak, "Jewish Marriage: Nature, Covenant, and Contract," in *Marriage, Sex, and Family in Judaism*, ed. Michael J. Broyde and Michael Ausubel (Lanham, MD: Rowman & Littlefield, 2005), 72.

between Jewish women and Roman men as a sexual transgression, but because these encounters made manifest the bitter realities of conquest and domination.

Through narratives of sexual subjugation and rape, Bavli Gittin gives poignant voice to the central role of sexual violence in forging Roman conquest and domination, as well as the intimate connection between war, sexual violence, and enslavement.[32] Ancient and late-antique Jewish sources attest to a widespread fear that defeat in battle will lead to the rape of Jewish women as well as the captivity and enslavement of men, women, and children. The Testament of Judah, for example, details the feared consequences of national defeat: a man's exile from his native land, the rape or murder of his family, and his own captivity, castration, and enslavement.[33] In the book of Judith, the threatened community likewise pleads with God, "not to allow their infants to be carried off and their wives to be taken as booty, and the towns they had inherited to be destroyed, and the sanctuary to be profaned and desecrated to the malicious joy of the Gentiles."[34] Especially in cultures that frame masculinity in terms of the ability to protect and provide for women, wartime rape inscribes the impotence of defeated men through the violated bodies of "their" women. Beyond the incalculable violence done to its explicit victims, rape also does psychic violence to bystanders who are unable to intervene. Family and community experience viscerally their inability to protect victims, to shield them from the conqueror.[35]

---

32. Because of the nature of my sources, I focus on representations of rape in rabbinic literature. I do not assume we can reconstruct from rabbinic texts the actual experiences of women, captives, or enslaved persons who faced sexual violence. I bring historical evidence of the connection between imperial conquest, enslavement, and sexual vulnerability not to assert that rabbinic texts are accurate portrayals of a particular historical situation, but to situate these narratives within a broad historical and social context in which imperial conquest was bound up with sexual risk. While these texts are not historiographical portrayals of particular acts of sexual assault, they are also not simply narratives of rabbinic fantasy.

33. Testament of Judah 23:3–5.

34. Judith 4:12.

35. Describing an account of a child forced to watch while soldiers brutalized and murdered his parents and sisters while a lieutenant kept his eyes open so that "he would see and remember this for a long time," Franz Fanon underscores how torture and sexual assault are meant to convey conquest not only to the primary victims of violence but also to reveal the powerlessness of those who cannot prevent it. Frantz Fanon, *A Dying Colonialism*, trans. Haakon Chevalier (New York: Grove Press, 1967), 26. My thinking about Fanon's response to sexual violence has been influenced by the scholarship of T. Denean Sharpley-Whiting, particularly her critique of the way in which white feminists have often characterized Fanon as a misogynist, without fully engaging the racial and postcolonial dimensions of his work. T. Denean Sharpley-Whiting, *Frantz Fanon: Conflicts and Feminisms* (Lanham, MD: Rowman & Littlefield, 1998), 16–17.

While war might generate sexual assault in the immediate aftermath of battle, imperial expansion also led to widespread taking of captives, many of whom were likely subject to sexual violence as a condition of their enslavement.[36] The previous chapter discussed the trope of marriage in captivity, in which captive women and men were sexually conscripted to produce the next generation of enslaved labor.[37] But beyond the master's desire to breed children who would grow up in slavery, enslaved persons were also vulnerable to their master's desires.[38] Slavery provided high-class Romans with a ready supply of sexually available subordinates. As Bettina Eva Stumpp suggests, high-class Romans had no need for brothels, because they had access to slaves.[39] Rabbinic law regulating the marital status of women who are ransomed or rescued from captivity takes for granted that women would experience sexual contact during their captivity.[40] But enslaved men also faced sexual risk. Roman sources attest to widespread use of male slaves

---

36. Hezser argues that Jewish enslavement by Rome was particularly widespread during the first and second Jewish revolts, noting the repeated mentions of this practice in Josephus's accounts of Titus and Vespasian's campaigns (*Jewish Slavery*, 221–229). Jerome attests to the sale of innumerable captured men, women, and children at a slave market near Hebron, while the seventh-century history *Chronicon Paschale* suggests that an abundance of Jewish slaves in Roman slave markets after the Bar Kokhba revolt made their price extremely low (Jerome, *Commentary to Jeremiah* 31:15.6; *Chronicon Paschale*, vol. 1, p. 474, ed. L. Dindorf [Bonn: E. Weber, 1832]). See also William Harris, "Towards a Study of the Roman Slave Trade," *Memoirs of the American Academy in Rome* 36 (1980): 118–125, and "Demography, Geography, and the Sources of Roman Slaves," *Journal of Roman Studies* (1999): 62–72. On slavery in warfare in the Sassanian Empire, see Jan Willem Drijvers, "Rome and the Sasanid Empire: Confrontation and Coexistence," in *A Companion to Late Antiquity*, ed. Philip Rousseau (Oxford: John Wiley and Sons, 2012), 441–454.

37. Walter Scheidel suggests that "natural reproduction" accounted for more than three quarters of the slave population in the early Roman Empire. "Quantifying the Sources of Slaves in the Early Roman Empire," *Journal of Roman Studies* 87 (1997): 156–169. For a discussion of the role of slave reproduction in Jewish law, see Kriger, *Sex Rewarded, Sex Punished*.

38. My thinking about the intersection of sexual violence and slavery is indebted to the work of Bernadette Brooten, who emphasizes the profound role that slavery plays in shaping Jewish, Christian, and Muslim conceptions of gender, body, and personhood—as well as to Adrienne Davis, who calls for attention to what she terms "the sexual economy of slavery." See Brooten, *Beyond Slavery*; and Adrienne Davis, "Don't Let Nobody Bother Yo' Principle: The Sexual Economy of American Slavery," in *Sister Circle: Black Women and Work*, ed. S. Harley (New Brunswick, NJ: Rutgers University Press, 2002), 103–127.

39. Bettina Eva Stumpp, *Prostitution in der römischen Antike* (Berlin: Akademie-Verlag, 2001), 27.

40. In both halakhic and aggadic texts, the rabbis address the situation of women taken captive—whether as a direct consequence of war or more opportunistic kidnappings for ransom. In legal terms, the rabbis' concern with women's captivity centers upon marriage law, which rests upon the rabbinic assumption that captive women have been sexually active during their period of captivity. Unmarried women taken captive after the age of three are presumed

by Roman masters.[41] In her work on slavery in late antiquity, Jennifer Glancy argues that anxiety over the prospect of becoming a slave formed a significant backdrop to late antique conceptions of manhood. The threat of losing control over one's bodily self-determination, of becoming physically at risk, hangs like a shadow over Roman and Christian conceptions of slavery.[42]

The Depths of the Sea: Gender, Enslavement, and Sexual Violation

Bavli Gittin's narratives attest to the profound connection between enslavement and sexual violation in the aftermath of the conquest of Judea. The following tale recounts the fate of four hundred young male and female captives who threw themselves into the sea instead of allowing themselves to be enslaved and used for prostitution. Bavli Gittin 57b recounts:

> Rav Yehudah said Shmuel said:
>   (and some say, Rabbi Ami said;
>   and some say it was taught in a *baraita*)
> An account:
> Four hundred young men and young women were captured[43]
>   and sensed what they were wanted for.
> They said to themselves,
>   "If we drown ourselves in the sea,
>   we will enter the life of the world to come."
> The eldest among them interpreted the verse:
>   *The Lord said, "I will retrieve from Bashan,*
>   *I will retrieve from the depths of the sea."* (Psalms 68:23)

---

not to be virgins, a status that means they are unable to marry priests and are entitled to a smaller ketubah. According to rabbinic law, married men are required to ransom their wives if they are taken captive—and nonpriestly men are obligated to take them back as wives. Since priests are not allowed under rabbinic law to cohabitate with a woman who has had sexual experience with another man, a priest whose wife is captured is required to ransom her and return her to her family home. On ransom obligations within Jewish law, see Louis Epstein, *The Jewish Marriage Contract: A Study in the Status of the Woman in Jewish Law* (New York: Jewish Theological Seminary, 1927), 164–168.

41. Williams, *Roman Homosexuality*.

42. Glancy, *Slavery in Early Christianity*, 25, 98.

43. The St. Petersburg RNL Evr. I 187 adds "among the nations," but this phrase does not appear in the Munich 95, Vatican 130, or Vatican 140 manuscripts, nor in the Soncino or Vilna printings. There are no other significant variations in the text of these manuscripts.

I will retrieve from Bashan [means]:
    From between the teeth (*bein shinei*) of lions
I will retrieve from the depths of the sea:
    Those who drown in the sea.

As soon as the young women heard that,
    they all jumped and threw themselves into the sea.
The young men reasoned amongst themselves
    according to a *qal veḥomer* (a fortiori argument):
        "If women, for whom this is the accustomed manner [of sex],
            respond in such a way,
        Then we, for whom this is not the accustomed manner,
            should do so as well."
So they also jumped into the sea
    and regarding them Scripture says:
        It is for Your sake that we are slain all day long,
        that we are regarded as sheep to be slaughtered. (Psalms 44:23)

The story begins by signaling the captives' self-awareness, making clear their recognition that they will be subject to sexual slavery. Bavli Gittin uses a phrase that offers a rare glimpse into the captives' interiority: they sensed within themselves (*hirgishu be'atzman*) what they were wanted for. Despite their large numbers, the four hundred young men and women feel this truth as a single body. Their first words give collective expression to their lament and desperation. Once the captives articulate their communal desire to drown themselves for the sake of eternal life, the narrative singles out a particular voice: the voice of the eldest, who affirms that God will lift up those who find themselves in dire straits, "between the lions' teeth." There is no miraculous rescue here, at least not for the physical body. The narrative also gives little overt sign of divine power: God's people are captive on a slave ship and the choices they face are stark. Nonetheless, the narrative promises spiritual rescue, positing suicide as defiance of Roman domination. En route to their enslavement, the young captives assert their resistance by choosing death on their own terms.

Jewish law and literature has long engaged the question of whether death is preferable to enslavement, idolatry, or sexual violation. Examining ancient and late antique discourse of death before enslavement, Catherine Hezser argues that in Josephus, the embrace of suicide instead of the humiliation of slavery appears as a heroic virtue, a practice that reveals a Jew's ultimate fidelity to God and unwillingness to serve a Roman master. Hezser emphasizes that Josephus's treatment of the subject has a significant gender dimension. Josephus's male speakers make impassioned calls for accepting death rather than enslavement, while his women prove more willing to submit to slavery in order to preserve their own lives and the lives of their families.[44] Bavli Gittin's narrative inverts this motif, using the women to dramatize and inspire suicide rather than sexual slavery. After the eldest captive speaks, the collective body fragments into two gendered groups. The young women jump immediately, while the young men deliberate. They decide to jump only after considering the women's example, basing their decision upon the established rabbinic principle of *qal vehomer*. A rabbinic *qal vehomer* reasons that if a less serious matter warrants a stringent response, then a more serious matter must also be treated with (at minimum) the same degree of strictness.[45] Based on an assumption that male-male intercourse is forbidden while male-female intercourse is permitted, the young men claim that their violation will be more serious than that of the women.

The gendered dimensions of this exchange are striking on two counts. First, the Bavli's use of the *qal vehomer* portrays the men as engaged in rational, legal discourse. They engage in the culturally sanctioned practice of argumentation according to the law, while the women's suicide appears borne of passion and fear. Second, the appeal to a *qal vehomer* emphasizes a gendered difference in Bavli Gittin's assessment of sexual violation. The *qal vehomer* begins by asserting that "this" is the "accustomed manner" (*darkhan*) for women, but not a part of men's experience. The Bavli grounds its reasoning in the principle that male-male sex is transgressive, while male-female intercourse can be licit.[46] While Bavli Gittin does not, it seems to me, actively intend to sanction rape as a permissible act, the *qal vehomer's* "this" fails to distinguish between consensual male-female sex and sexual violence. The Bavli reifies the basic permissibility of male-female coupling in a way that fails to resist violence against women. Through the young men's reasoning, Bavli Gittin makes plain its profound fear of men's sexual violation. But the Bavli's terror at the prospect of male rape reinscribes women's sexual violation as an ordinary fact of captivity. It brackets the rape, failing to distinguish between the sexual slavery of Roman captivity and the ordinary course of women's lives. Through a laconic analogy that equates the present situation of forced prostitution with women's ordinary sexual experience, the *qal vehomer* refuses a

---

44. Hezser, *Jewish Slavery*, 224–227.

45. For a discussion of this form of argumentation, see Strack and Stemberger, *Introduction to the Talmud and Midrash*, 18.

46. As Satlow has demonstrated, rabbinic literature also uses the phrase *lo kedarkha* to describe anal intercourse between a man and a woman. He argues that while this phrase "is often translated as unnatural sex/intercourse, neither the phrase itself nor any other rabbinic rhetoric implies the attachment of an argument from nature to anal intercourse. Both anal and vaginal intercourse were seen as part of the same legal category, as intercourse." The same phrase also appears in rabbinic literature in a variety of (nonsexual) legal contexts to signal behavior that differs from prevailing custom. Satlow, *Tasting the Dish*, 238–241.

distinction between sexual violence and commonplace sexual encounter. By naturalizing women's experience of rape, Bavli Gittin's reasoning fashions a kinship between the rabbinic bedroom and the sexuality of the slave ship, while presenting violence against men as the ultimate violation.[47]

The Destroyer Has Come Upon Me: Tsafnat bat Penuel and the Power of Lament

The final story I examine in this chapter recounts the capture and violation of Tsafnat bat Penuel, who was the daughter of the high priest in Jerusalem. Bavli Gittin 58a reads:

> Reish Laqish said:
> An account of a certain woman whose name was Tsafnat bat Penuel—
>> Tsafnat because all gazed (*tsofin*) at her beauty,
>> and the daughter of Penuel because she was the daughter
>>> of a high priest who served at the Holy of Holies—
>>>> who was used sexually by her captor the entire night.
> Afterward, he dressed her in seven garments
>> and took her out to sell her in the market.[48]
> A certain man came who was extremely ugly.
> He said to him, "Let me see her beauty."
> He said to him,
>> "Empty one! If you wish to buy, then buy!
>> For her beauty is unmatched in the entire world."
> He said to him, "Even so, [let me see her.]"
> He stripped off six wraps—
>> and she tore the seventh and rolled in the dirt.
> She said before God,
>> "Lord of the World, even if You have no compassion on us,
>> have You no compassion for the sanctity of Your great name?"[49]

---

47. The Jerusalem Talmud makes this reasoning explicit in a passage that discusses the redemption of captives: "If a man and a woman (in prison) are threatened with exposure to prostitution, the redemption of the man has precedence." Yerushalmi Horayot 3, 48b.

48. This phrase is missing in Soncino printing of 1488 and the Vilna printed edition, but appears in Munich 95, Vatican 130, Vatican 140, and Saint Petersburg RNL Evr. I 187 manuscripts.

49. The manuscripts include a number of variations in Tsafnat's question. The Vilna and the Soncino printed edition put the final verb in the imperfect, while the manuscripts have it in

Regarding her, Jeremiah lamented:

Daughter of my people—put on sackcloth and strew dust on yourselves!
Mourn, as for an only child;
wail bitterly, for suddenly the destroyer is coming upon us. (Jeremiah 6:26)
It does not say "upon you," but "upon us,"
for it is as if to say—
the Destroyer has come upon Me and upon you.

Expressing a motif that appears in many of Bavli Gittin's destruction narratives, the account of Tsafnat bat Penuel emphasizes a sharp contrast between beauty and brutality.[50] As I will discuss in the next chapter, Bavli Gittin uses the tales of beautiful bodies in extremis to express the incalculable loss that captivity and violation brings not just to individual victims but also to Jewish communal identity. Through the story of violated beauty, the Bavli articulates the devastating desacralization of Roman conquest. The tale begins by situating Tsafnat within an illustrious priestly family. Her father's name means "Face of God," a name that underscores the religious power of the priesthood and evokes the high priest's right to come before the Holy of Holies and to stand amidst God's presence.[51]

As the daughter of a high priest, Tsafnat's capture and rape symbolizes not simply a personal or family tragedy, but a disaster for the entire nation. By turning the daughters of priests into the sexual objects of depraved Roman masters, the Bavli makes plain the violence of the world that exists beyond rabbinic boundaries. Bavli Gittin's narrative accentuates the brutality of Tsafnat's transition from hiddenness to exposure. The destruction exposes her body to Roman desire. The tale begins by situating her within the high priest's household, "concealed" by

---

the perfect tense. The Munich 95 and Saint Petersburg RNL Evr. I 187 manuscripts describe the divine name as "great" (*gadol*), while the Vilna and Soncino have it as "mighty" (*gibor*), and the Vatican 130 and Vatican 140 include no adjective.

50. Stern argues that the Tsafnat tale is one of many rabbinic narratives that reflect elements of the Greco-Roman romance genre, which often feature protagonists who have sterling moral qualities and exquisite physical beauty; their beauty commonly catapults them into erotic tests or undesired sexual situations, thereby generating the plot of the romance. Stern, "Captive Woman," 91–127.

51. Regarding the name Penuel, Tal Ilan writes, "this person, designated 'face of God' sees God face to face" (206). The same name also appears in Luke 2:36, as the daughter of Hannah. Ilan notes that people identified with the title of "high priest" in rabbinic literature do not always accord with more historically reliable sources on the high priesthood and persons who occupied that office. (34) Tal Ilan, *Lexicon of Jewish Names in Late Antiquity*, vol. 1. (Tübingen: Mohr Siebeck, 2004).

the stringent cultural rules governing priestly daughters. Even her captor conceals her beauty, albeit for a devastatingly different end. When her captor decides to sell her in the market, he covers her with seven garments, veiling her beauty from the sight of the buyer. He lures the man who comes to buy with tales of the captive women's hidden beauty. Yet the rumor of beauty is not enough for the buyer. Where a rabbinic man would see his bride's body only after he affirmed the sanctity of their marriage, Roman captivity and enslavement allows Tsafnat to be stripped even before she is sold. The first six of the veils are taken from her, but she takes the seventh in her own hands. This action marks a significant if subtle shift in agency. Tsafnat strips away the final veil, rips her garment, and rolls in the dirt—gestures that evoke rituals of mourning and lamentation.[52]

Tsafnat's words give potent expression to rabbinic lament, a mode of religiosity that Tod Linafelt argues has been too often devalued among modern readers.[53] The Bavli couples her lament with religious protest, using a women's voice to articulate a haunting, dangerous question. Tsafnat cries out to God, "Lord of the World, even if You have no compassion on *us*, have You no compassion for the sanctity of Your great name?" Tsafnat's first phrase calls God to account for apparent failure to respond to violence, but her final question laments the wound to God's own dignity—the injury that the violation of her human body has done to God. While she gives voice to the possibility that God lacks compassion for the suffering people as such, she also asserts that God undoubtedly remains concerned with the sanctity of the divine name. That sanctity, she argues, has been degraded by the violence of Roman conquest. Tsafnat's lament raises the theological stakes of her own pain, positioning her violation as suffering that wounds God's own self.

As in the Titus tale, a woman's rape once again gives immediate rise to concern for God. But where rabbinic exegesis in the Titus story emphasizes God's strong silence and ultimate victory over the Roman conqueror, the Tsafnat tale offers an alternate portrayal of God's experience of disaster. Through rabbinic interpretation of Jeremiah 6:26, Bavli Gittin suggests that "the Destroyer" assails not only the Jews but also the Jewish God. The narrative emphasizes divine vulnerability, portraying God as one who experiences profound injury. Strikingly, the Bavli's narrative grants God no voice in response to Tsafnat's question. The passivity of the wounded God in the Bavli's account contrasts with other

---

52. Tearing the clothes and putting dirt or dust on the head appear frequently in the Hebrew Bible as signs of mourning. Xuan Huong Thi Pham, *Mourning in the Ancient Near East and the Hebrew Bible* (Sheffield, UK: Sheffield Academic Press, 1999), 25–27.

53. Linafelt, *Surviving Lamentations*, 2–4.

well-known rabbinic narratives in Lamentations Rabbah that emphasize how God weeps in response to the destruction and in which God becomes a speaking subject who responds to the sufferer's cry.[54] In Bavli Gittin's account, the divine subject has been rendered mute. The Bavli's anonymous rabbinic narrator acknowledges the destruction that has come upon the daughter and the Divine alike, articulating a lament that claims a woman's pain as injury to God.

Through narratives of sexual subjugation and rape, Bavli Gittin's account of the destruction of Jerusalem gives poignant voice to rabbinic grief and violation at the hands of Rome. Through subversive mimicry that highlights the brutality of imperial conquest through sexual domination, these rabbinic narratives stigmatize Roman savagery and galvanize moral outrage at the brutality of the conqueror. While these stories narrate unflinchingly the catastrophe of Roman destruction, elements within each of these tales accentuate Jewish resistance and resilience beneath the conqueror's shadow. Yet the narrative use of rape as a symbol to express divine and rabbinic lament has dangerous implications for women, enslaved people, and others who are vulnerable to the embodied experience of sexual violence. Even as these narratives give voice to rabbinic protest against Roman brutality, they serve to silence the suffering of the most direct victims of Roman violence. These tales make instrumental use of women's suffering to articulate rabbinic or divine loss. In the Titus narrative, concern for God and temple obscures rabbinic concern for the woman on the altar. In the tale of the captured four hundred, the fear of male sexual risk eclipses rabbinic attentiveness to women's pain. By drawing the eye toward the grief of God and the rabbinic sages, the Bavli's focus on theological lament overwrites attention to the violence borne by human bodies. Only in the final narrative does an alternate voice emerge, as Bavli Gittin imagines the lament of a priestly daughter in a way that allows God's suffering to echo through a woman's cry of pain.

Bavli Gittin uses sexual violence as a powerful metaphor for the violation of the Jewish nation and the Jewish God, generating revulsion toward the brutality and sexual immorality of the conqueror and giving voice to rabbinic and divine lament. But symbolic use of rape to express theological and national grief does not necessarily translate into empathy for victims of violence. In this chapter, I have argued that Bavli Gittin's narrative use of rape symbolism primarily serves to express the suffering of the nation and the suffering of God—not the suffering of women. In the next chapter, however, I show that in one important respect, Bavli Gittin's stories of sexual violence and captivity *do* lead the rabbis to

---

54. For discussion of Lamentations Rabbah narratives, see Stern, *Parables in Midrash*; Kraemer, *Responses to Suffering*, 140–146; and Linafelt, *Surviving Lamentations*, chap. 5.

articulate a more egalitarian response to bodily risk. When it comes to imagining the beautiful Jewish body in captivity, Bavli Gittin turns away from a familiar rabbinic trope that holds women culpable for the consequences of their beauty. Conventional rabbinic narratives frequently castigate women for the way that female body beauty leads men into sin. But Bavli Gittin's stories, I argue, recognize the beautiful Jew as the victim, not the instigator of violence. These narratives portray both Jewish women and men as objects of covetous Roman desire. As with Bavli Gittin's representations of sexual violence, the beauty tales also use subversive mimicry to reveal the brutality of the conqueror and to critique the Romans for their lack of sexual restraint and self-control. But where Bavli Gittin's metaphor of sexual violence privileges male theological lament over women's embodied suffering, its beauty tales reveal a striking equivalence between male and female bodies in distress. The Bavli's outrage at Roman brutality overwrites the commonplace misogyny that frequently pervades conventional rabbinic accounts of women's beauty. Before the avarice of the conqueror, Bavli Gittin recognizes both women and men as victims of unrestrained Roman desire.

3

Conquered Bodies in the Roman Bedroom

THE GENDER POLITICS OF BEAUTY IN BAVLI GITTIN'S DESTRUCTION TALES

BAVLI GITTIN'S ACCOUNT of the Roman conquest of Judea lingers on the bitter fate of Jewish men and women taken captive by Rome. While many of these stories also appear in Lamentations Rabbah and other rabbinic compilations, this chapter analyzes a distinctive aspect of Bavli Gittin's tales: their emphasis on the exquisite beauty of the conquered Jewish subject. In these stories, I argue, the beauty of the conquered body performs potent cultural work, making visceral and apparent the intense vulnerability of Jewish flesh. Beauty draws the captive Jew into spaces of acute moral and physical danger, exposing the conquered subject to Roman sexual violence and degradation. The splendid Jewish body, violated by the conqueror, becomes a locus for expressing rabbinic loss and lament. Alongside the cultural work of lamentation, however, the rhetoric of Jewish beauty also serves a potent anti-imperial purpose. In Bavli Gittin's narratives, I assert, beauty gives expression to rabbinic resilience, encoding the rabbis' refusal to inscribe the Jewish body with the marks of domination. Bavli Gittin deploys the beautiful body to articulate the moral virtue of the Jew in captivity and to narrate the survivability of conquest. As in the last chapter, where I demonstrated that Bavli Gittin's stories of sexual violence critique Roman brutality and deny moral victory to the conqueror, this chapter asserts that Jewish beauty tales likewise issue a striking critique of Roman domination. In the hands of Bavli Gittin's storytellers, Jewish beauty becomes a potent force for excoriating the depravity of Roman desire, for making visible the twin vices of lust and luxury that power Roman greed.

Perhaps the most surprising dimension of these tales lies in the way they refuse the usual gender politics of beauty. In conventional rabbinic discourse, the beautiful body is sharply gendered. While men's physical splendor is imagined as a mark of spiritual virtue, women's beauty is most commonly associated with danger. Rabbinic narratives frequently regard beautiful women as a threat to male piety, portraying women's beauty as a potent force that threatens to destabilize the social order and erode rabbinic men's virtue. Conventional rabbinic thought guards against what I call "beauty-risk" by constraining women's voice, visibility, and mobility. Rather than exhorting rabbinic men to greater control over their sexual impulses, rabbinic narrative frequently places the onus of protecting male virtue on women—imposing limits on how women speak, how women are seen, and where women can go. Such limits are particularly acute in the Babylonian Talmud, which, as Ishay Rosen-Zvi has shown, regards the male subject as profoundly vulnerable to sexual desire.[1] But Bavli Gittin's narratives of Roman conquest reveal a striking departure from the Bavli's usual rhetoric of beauty risk. Rather than castigate the victims of violence for their own violation, these tales place the blame squarely on the sexual aggressor: they imagine both Jewish women and men as the objects of depraved Roman desire.

Luxury and Lust in the Roman Bedroom: Jewish Beauty and Imperial Critique

In a striking cluster of tales about the fate of beautiful captives, Bavli Gittin uses the violation of the beautiful Jewish body to mourn the incalculable devastation that Roman conquest brings. The stories begin in Bavli Gittin 58a, with a narrative that likens the captive Jewish body to a precious jewel, more splendid than gold:

> *Zion's precious people, worth more than fine gold* (Lamentations 4:2)
> What does "worth more than fine gold" mean?
>   You might say it means they were covered in gold.
> But it was said in the house of Rabbi Shila:
>   Two coin-weights of gold descended into the world—
>   one is in Rome and the other is spread among the rest of the world
>   [so Zion's people could not have been covered in gold.]
> Rather, it means that their beauty put gold to shame.

> The nobles of Rome used to grasp their signet rings during sex
> but from this point onward,
>   they brought Jews and bound them to the feet of their beds during sex.
> One of the Jews said to the other: "Where is this written?"

1. Rosen-Zvi, *Demonic Desires.*

He said to him:
"All the other diseases and plagues
that are not mentioned in this book of Torah,
[the Lord will bring them upon you, until you are destroyed.]"
        (Deuteronomy 28:61)
He said to him: "How far am I from that place?"
He said to him, "Another scroll-sheet and a half."[2]
He said to him, "Had I reached it, I would not have needed you."[3]

The passage begins with a curious exegesis of Lamentations 4:2, in which an anonymous speaker suggests that the ancient people of Zion were literally covered in gold. What shall we make of this incongruous image of gold-plated Israelite flesh? Through this tradition, flesh becomes likened to an edifice, a monument: the physical bodies of Jerusalem's people are corporeal embodiments of Jerusalem's golden splendor. The Bavli ultimately rejects this idea in favor of a more straightforward reading: the people are not gold themselves, they are more beautiful than gold. They outshine the precious metal. The luster of their physical bodies puts even gold to shame.

Yet consider the Bavli's reasoning more closely. The rabbis do not reject the image of the gold-plated Jew because it seems a strange or forced reading of the verse. They reject the notion of golden Israelite flesh because gold is in short supply! Bavli Gittin cites a tradition attributed to the house of Rabbi Shila that claims only a minute amount of gold descended into the world.[4] Rome possesses half the store, while the rest of the gold has been spread out among the remaining nations. Jerusalem's people could not have been covered with precious metal, Bavli Gittin concludes, for there was not enough gold to go around. The resource

2. Vatican 130, JTS Rab. 1718.93–100 and JTS Rab. 1729.64–67 read only "a scroll-sheet and a half." The Vilna and the Soncino printed edition read, "It extends another scroll-sheet and a half."

3. JTS Rab. 1718.93–100 adds, after this, "Another sign: Where is this written? In that place. Say to him: If I had reached there, I would not have asked you."

4. A full version of the "ten measures" tradition appears in Bavli Kiddushin 49b and in Esther Rabbah 1:17 to Esther 1:3, associating a large number of ethnic, regional, or identity groups with possession of nine out of ten measures of certain identifying characteristics. As Rivka Ulmer argues, these traits reveal stereotypical rabbinic evaluations of the relative virtues and vices of other cultures. Carol Bakhos notes that the ethnic terms are used here as "types," quite distinct from narrated encounters with particular individuals. Rivka Ulmer, *Egyptian Cultural Icons in Midrash* (Berlin: Walter de Gruyter, 2009), 196–198; Carol Bakhos, *Ishmael on the Border: Rabbinic Portrayals of the First Arab* (Albany: State University of New York Press, 2006), 71–73.

shortage is not an entirely neutral claim: the lack of gold in the world is partly a function of outright rarity, but more a reflection of Roman avarice. The rabbinic claim that Rome possesses the lion's share of the world's wealth echoes a negative assessment of Roman luxury and opulence that is widespread in rabbinic sources; here, I suggest, it foreshadows Bavli Gittin's critique of Roman conquest as an expression of greed. Such avarice comes into sharp focus in the next scene. Bavli Gittin recounts how Roman elites used to grasp their signet rings during sex, a narrative motif that imagines the Roman noble as deriving sexual pleasure from caressing the material marker of his own power and status. In the wake of the Roman conquest of Jerusalem, the Jews have become a replacement for those jewels. Captive Jews now adorn the bedposts of the Roman conquerors.

To understand the significance of the metaphor of the Jew as jewel, we must return to the biblical verse that launches this narrative. The opening verses of Lamentations 4 use metaphors of gold and jewels to fashion the physical beauty of Jerusalem's residents into a corporeal sign, a manifest expression of the sanctity of the city before its fall. The opening pericope imagines Jerusalem as a city whose splendor resides not only in glittering gemstones, but in the shining faces of her people, a people once valued above the finest gold. Lamentations 4:1–2 reads:

> 4:1 Alas, the gold is dulled,
>   the purest gold has lost its luster.
> The holy gems are strewn
>   at every street corner.
>
> 4:2 Zion's precious people,
>   worth more than fine gold;
> alas, they were valued as earthen pottery,
>   the work of a potter's hands.[5]

In Lamentations 4:1, the evocation of gold and gems calls forth the splendor of Jerusalem, imagining the city as a site of inestimable value. Yet the purity of the gold has degraded; it no longer glitters with its original light.[6] Jerusalem's holy gems lie scattered like refuse in the street, their beauty exposed when it should be protected. Cast into the intensely public space of the street corner, the jewels are unguarded, uncovered, free for the taking. The transformation of these

---

5. The translation draws from the Jewish Publication Society translation and that of Adele Berlin, *Lamentations: A Commentary* (Louisville: Westminster John Knox Press, 2002).

6. As Berlin observes, "This gold is dulled from dirt, not from tarnish. It is not that the gold itself has gone bad, but that the treatment it has received has ruined it." Berlin, *Lamentations*, 104.

two material treasures gives potent expression to the changes that have befallen the people of Jerusalem. The dulled gold reveals the diminishment of their physical beauty, while the scattered gemstones evoke the vulnerability of the beautiful body.

Bavli Gittin's tale literalizes the metaphor. Its Jews are bound to Roman beds, glittering like diamonds. In Lamentations 4:2, the biblical writer uses the motif of the holy gems to mourn the violation of the sacred places, the travesty of holy vessels strewn through the street. In the Bavli's exegesis, however, these glittering stones have taken on corporeal form. By imagining the Jewish captive as a holy jewel, Bavli Gittin imbues Jewish flesh with the sanctity of the sacred precincts. It lodges in the captive Jewish body the splendor of Jerusalem, the luminous loveliness of the city before its fall. But like the gems in Lamentations, these Jewish bodies have become beauty out of place, beauty that is coveted and claimed by the conqueror. The dynamics of space, place, and exposure that surround the jewels underscore the danger that Roman desire for luster and luxury poses to the beautiful Jewish body. Bavli Gittin's exegesis shifts the physical place in which the scattered jewels are found. In Lamentations 4:1, the poet laments, "The holy gems are strewn at every street corner." In the biblical scene, the intensely public site of the street corner reveals the holy jewels to plebian eyes, replacing the highly mediated private access of the priests with a newfound accessibility to the traffic of the open street. Bavli Gittin, by contrast, imagines a more intimate exposure. Within the narrated aftermath of the Roman destruction, the Bavli situates the captive Jews within the private space of the Roman bedchamber. Where the priests who cultivated the holy spaces of the temple were subject to heightened strictures of sexual abstention and expected to live according to the dictates of intensified personal and sexual virtue, the Roman bedroom plunges the "jewels" into a place of sexual exhibition. The exegetical move forges a contrast between the idealized temple priest and the decadent Roman master, who forces the Jewish captive to decorate lurid Roman rites. Bound within the confines of the Roman bedroom, the captive Jews are degraded by their setting, forced to adorn and endure the sexual exploits of their Roman masters.[7]

While Roman nobles used to caress their signet rings while engaging in sexual relations, they now bind beautiful Jewish men to their bedposts

---

7. Mattingly argues that Roman sexual permissiveness is profoundly intertwined with Roman imperialism, that it operates within a cultural milieu that expects an elite man to practice sexual decorum within the context of his marriage, but permits and perhaps even encourages sexual opportunism with people of lower social status, particularly those marked as the objects of imperial conquest. Mattingly, *Imperialism, Power, and Identity*, 96–98.

instead. The motif of the signet ring, which recurs three times in the larger *sugya*, appears to symbolize a potent combination of elite decadence, temporal power, and moral degradation. By providing a new setting for Jerusalem's "holy jewels," the Roman signet ring serves to concretize the realities of Roman conquest and imperial dominance over the beautiful bodies of Zion's captured people. The final lines of the narrative underscore the bodily risk that male beauty brings in the conquest of captivity. Though the passage never recounts an explicit act of sexual penetration, the story gives oblique voice to the prospect of male rape.[8] The tale ends with an expression of cynicism and despair, as one captive questions whether the Torah foresees such degradation. His companion responds by affirming that even this violation—so shameful, perhaps, that it could not be mentioned by name—is encompassed within the bitter expanse of God's curse.

Yet this tale, I argue, is not only a register of Jewish degradation. Bavli Gittin's portrayal of the beautiful Jewish body also levels a powerful critique against Roman avarice and sexual immorality. In the Bavli's telling, Roman conquest reveals not only imperial ambition or desire for political power, but a desire to capture and possess Jewish beauty. By imagining the Jewish body as a spoil of war—as a precious material object desired and claimed by the conqueror—Bavli Gittin calls upon a potent discourse within Roman moral thought that criticizes sexual, sensual, and material self-indulgence (*luxuria*). Ancient Roman moralists asserted a powerful connection between *luxuria* and licentiousness. "For Romans," Catharine Edwards writes, "luxury and lust were cognate vices; those susceptible to sexual temptation, it was felt, were also prone to indulge to excess their appetites for food, drink, and material possessions."[9] Through vibrant imagery that likens the captive Jewish body to the splendor of finest gold and precious stone, Bavli Gittin portrays Roman conquest as an insatiable desire for opulent luxury and wealth that is also inextricably linked with sexual depravity. By linking rich extravagance and sexual immorality, the Bavli activates a critique of Roman decadence made also by ancient Roman writers who inveighed against

---

8. On the uses of same-sex desire and the threat of male rape in captivity to critique the moral virtue of the conqueror, see Mark D. Jordan, *The Invention of Sodomy in Christian Theology* (Chicago: University of Chicago Press, 1997), 10–28.

9. Edwards argues that because modern moral thinkers rarely assert a fundamental connection between luxury and sexual immorality, scholars approaching Roman morality have tended to treat these issues as two distinct fields of study and overlooked the important conceptual connections between them within Roman thought. Catharine Edwards, *The Politics of Immorality in Ancient Rome* (New York: Cambridge University Press, 1993), 5. Mark Jordan also discusses the critical view of *luxuria* in late antique and medieval Christian thought, particularly the association that develops between *luxuria* and sexual sin. Jordan, *Invention of Sodomy*, 29–44.

the "softening" of the state, the decline of proper masculine self-control.[10] As it narrates the fate of Jewish beauty in captivity, Bavli Gittin aims to expose the moral decay at the heart of Roman conquest, challenging both the virility and virtue of the conqueror.[11]

Sexual Risk in Captivity: Beauty and Danger in the Context of Colonialism

Shortly after the tale of the bound Jewish captives, Bavli Gittin 58a tells three more beauty tales: the story of the young Ishmael ben Elisha in a Roman prison, rescued by Rabbi Yehoshua ben Ḥanania; the tale of Ishmael ben Elisha's son and daughter, who were forced by their captors to marry each other; and the tale of the priestly daughter Tsafnat bat Penuel, a captive woman whose beauty is unmatched throughout the world. While versions of the first two tales appear in separate places in Lamentations Rabbah, Bavli Gittin has drawn these stories into a narrative cluster that highlights the particular risks and vulnerabilities of Jewish beauty in captivity.[12] In Bavli Gittin, tales of beautiful Jewish bodies reveal the intertwined corporeal and spiritual risks borne by Jews in and after Roman conquest. For the rabbis, beauty serves as a powerful locus for grappling with the tragedy and terror of Roman conquest, expressing vivid rabbinic fears of sexual exploitation and assault upon Jewish bodily integrity. The loveliness of the Jewish body becomes a liability, as beauty thrusts the captive Jew into the throes of brutality. Bavli Gittin 58a continues:

The rabbis taught:
An account of Rabbi Yehoshua ben Hanania
   who was walking through a great city in Rome.

---

10. Edwards emphasizes the connection between manliness and morality in Roman thought. She argues that most Roman moralists' accusations of immorality are directed not at foreigners, women, or slaves, but against elites and emperors, at those who claim themselves to be honorable and upstanding Roman men. Edwards, *Politics of Immorality*, 20–25.

11. Jennifer Knust examines the uses of sexual slander as a means of demonizing opponents and critiquing political leaders in the late ancient world. Noting the strong political implications of sexual immorality, she argues that Christians also used sexual polemic against the Romans. "By arguing that non-Christians are depraved, ruled by the passions, and guilty of incest and adultery," Knust maintains, "Christian authors from the New Testament period onward called the authority of their rulers into question." Jennifer Knust, *Abandoned to Lust: Sexual Slander and Ancient Christianity* (New York: Columbia University Press, 2005), 11.

12. The tale of Rabbi Yehoshua ben Hanania appears in Lamentations Rabbah 4:3, while the story of the two children of the high priest appears in Lamentations Rabbah 1:47.

They said to him,

> "There is a young man in prison
> with lovely eyes and a beautiful face,
> with his curly hair arranged in locks."

He went and stood at the entrance of the prison and said:

> *"Who was it who gave Jacob over to despoilment*
> *and Israel to plunderers. . . ?"* (Isaiah 42:24)

The young man answered [with the continuation of the verse]:

> *". . . Surely, the Lord against whom they sinned,*
> *in whose ways they would not walk*
> *and those teaching they would not obey."*

Rabbi Yehoshua ben Hanania said,

> "I am certain that this one is a teacher in Israel.
> By God, I will not budge from here until I ransom him,
> no matter the amount they have set for him."

He did not budge until he had ransomed him for a very high amount,

> and it was not many days until the young man
> was a teacher of traditions in Israel.

Who was he?

Rabbi Ishmael ben Elisha.

In this narrative, Rabbi Yehoshua ben Hanania is traveling through Rome when he hears of a beautiful young man imprisoned in a Roman jail. The rumors the rabbi hears emphasize the beautiful features of the boy's body: lovely eyes, a beautiful face, curly hair all in locks. By narrating the striking beauty of the captive's physical form, the narrative accentuates the danger posed by his imprisonment.[13] While the tale itself gives no intimation of sexual or physical assault, other rabbinic traditions attest to the great risk borne by Jewish youths in Roman prisons. As a Palestinian aphorism notes, "A Jewish boy in prison is doomed to prostitution."[14] But if beauty propels the captive into danger, it also becomes the source of his rescue. Corporeal beauty serves, in this tale, as the first intimation of Jewish identity. Rabbi Yehoshua originally comes to suspect that the captive is a Jew not because of his words or because of his piety, but because of his splendid physical

---

13. On the prison as a site of danger, see Sofía Torallas Tovar, "Violence in the Process of Arrest and Imprisonment in Late Antique Egypt," in *Violence in Late Antiquity: Perceptions and Practices*, ed. Harold Allen Drake (Burlington, VT: Ashgate Publishing, 2006), 101–110.

14. Yerushalmi Horayot 3, 48b.

form. It is the report of extraordinary beauty that initially draws the rabbi to the prison gates, that leads him to listen for the captive voice.

Though beauty provides the impetus for the encounter between rabbi and captive, the confirmation of the imprisoned boy's Jewish identity emerges through a call-and-response recitation of Isaiah 42:24, a verse that explains Israel's degradation and despoilment as a consequence of sin and a refusal to obey divine command. Through his appeal to this verse, Rabbi Yehoshua calls upon the captive to affirm that the divine hand has orchestrated his present circumstances. When Ishmael answers, his words not only recognize God's role in orchestrating disaster, but acknowledge Israel's culpability for catastrophe. His capacity to complete the verse not only confirms his identity as a Jew, but affirms the depth of his devotion. I have argued in a previous chapter that Bavli Gittin's sugya shows a striking tendency to avoid linking Roman conquest with Jewish sin or portraying catastrophe as a form of divine chastisement. Here, however, through its appeal to Isaiah 42:24, the Bavli makes an explicit evocation of the sin-punishment paradigm and appears to endorse this framework as a cornerstone of Jewish piety. Young Ishmael's evocation of the verse serves to confirm his fidelity to the God of Israel despite his dire situation. With the prison as his proving ground—a place made particularly dangerous in the Roman captivity by the beauty and youth of his captive body—Ishmael uses the verse to express a martyr's acceptance of his fate. That a martyriological stance is suggested here is made likely not only through the inherent risks of the prison scene, but through the identification of the sage. Rabbinic traditions frequently number Rabbi Ishmael ben Elisha among the celebrated sages who accepted martyrdom during the Hadrianic persecutions.[15] Our tale treats young Ishmael through a classic martyriological lens. As Raʿanan Boustan has argued, rabbinic martyr narratives frequently emphasize the extraordinary piety of individual martyrs, "whose excellence is realized through their heroic conduct under conditions of extreme duress."[16] But while

---

15. The historical identification of the martyred Rabbi Ishmael is difficult; the earliest sources that explicitly identify him as Rabbi Ishmael ben Elisha are relatively late sources, Avot de-Rabbi Natan A 38 and Avot de-Rabbi Natan B 41. The tradition of the martyrdom of Rabbi Ishmael also appears in Mekhilta de-Rabbi Ishmael, Neziqin 18 on Exod 22:22 (Lauterbach ed. 3:142–143) and in the Story of the Ten Martyrs. On the reception and development of this tradition in rabbinic midrash, see Menahem Kister, *Studies in Avot de-Rabbi Nathan: Text, Redaction, and Interpretation* (Jerusalem: Hebrew University, 1998), 188–191. On the significance of the Rabbi Ishmael traditions for the development of the Story of the Ten Martyrs, see Raʿanan S. Boustan, *From Martyr to Mystic: Rabbinic Martyrology and the Making of Merkavah Mysticism* (Tübingen: Mohr Siebeck, 2005), 71–77.

16. Boustan, *From Martyr to Mystic*, 99. Boustan argues that rabbinic theologies of martyrdom are strikingly conservative in their approach to theodicy. Despite the Bavli's willingness to

the recitation of the verse allows our hero to proclaim his fidelity to God even in a place of tremendous bodily risk, the narrative ultimately follows a strikingly different path. The story of Rabbi Ishmael ben Elisha is Bavli Gittin's only tale of successful redemption, the only account Bavli Gittin offers of a Jew rescued after capture. In this tale, the splendid rabbinic body remains intact even amidst the perils of Roman captivity, undiminished by its ordeal. Beauty is ransomed from the Roman prison and the sage is restored to his rightful place as teacher in Israel.

In Bavli Gittin, the story of Rabbi Ishmael's rescue from Roman captivity is immediately followed by a narrative that recounts the fate of Ishmael's beautiful children when they were taken captive. The sister and brother, both extraordinarily beautiful, are separated during captivity but brought together in a forced marriage by their masters. Bavli Gittin 58a continues:

> Rabbi Yehudah said Rav said:
> An account of the son and the daughter of Rabbi Ishmael ben Elisha,
>   who were captured by two masters.
> Later, the two masters happened to be in the same place.
> One said, "I have an enslaved man
>   whose beauty is unlike that of any other in the world."
> The other said, "I have an enslaved woman
>   whose beauty is unlike that of any other in the world."
> They said, "Come, let us marry them to each other
>   and divide their children."
> They brought them into the chamber
>   and one sat in one corner
>   and the other in the opposite corner.
> He said, "I am the priest from the line of high priests,
>   and I shall marry a slave girl?"
> And she said, "I am a priestly daughter from the line of high priests,
>   and I shall marry a slave boy?"

---

engage alternative responses to suffering and theodicy in other genres, Boustan maintains that Babylonian martyr narratives continue to explain a martyr's suffering through the notion of sin and punishment. "The Babylonian Talmud," he writes, "does not betray any marked tendency to modify the explanatory framework upon which earlier examples of rabbinic martyrology had traditionally depended." Boustan, *From Martyr to Mystic*, 69. On the innovative stance of certain currents within the Babylonian Talmud to matters of suffering, see Kraemer, *Responses to Suffering*, 184–210; Yaakov Elman, "Righteousness as its Own Reward: An Inquiry into the Theologies of the Stam," *Proceedings of the American Academy for Jewish Research* 72 (1990–1991): 35–67; Yaakov Elman, "The Suffering of the Righteous in Palestinian and Babylonian Sources," *Jewish Quarterly Review* n.s. 80 (1990): 315–339.

They wept the entire night.
Once dawn broke,
> they recognized each other and fell upon each other,
> moaning and weeping until their souls departed.

Regarding them, Jeremiah lamented:
> *For these I weep, my eyes flow with tears.* (Lamentations 1:16)

While the previous tale recounted the successful rescue of Rabbi Ishmael ben Elisha, this story relates the tragic end of Ishmael's son and daughter, whose self-willed deaths in captivity offer them their only escape from the sexual degradation of captivity. Bavli Gittin emphasizes their exquisite beauty—a detail that does not appear in the Lamentations Rabbah version.[17] In the Bavli's account, each master assesses the value of his captive, pronouncing them "unlike that of any other in the world." It is the very singularity of their beauty that prompts the captors to bring the man and woman together, as they force them into a marriage that will produce enslaved children for their masters. While captivity could have befallen them regardless of their physical features, beauty becomes the spark that propels them into an even deeper tragedy: the incestuous inversion of the sexual-spiritual purity of the priesthood. Both identify themselves in terms of their priestly lineage, using their priestly status to underscore the particular degradations they face in captivity. The association between priests and beauty is a powerful trope, a narrative convention reinforced by biblical and rabbinic legal traditions that stress the importance of physical perfection among priests who serve at the altar.[18] But the notion of priestly beauty extends far beyond the legal framework that obligates priests at the altar to be without blemish. In these tales, corporeal beauty becomes a material expression of Jewish virtue, as physical beauty evokes the sacrality of Jerusalem and the temple. Because beauty serves as a potent sign of Jewish sanctity, its violation makes tangible and corporeal the

---

17. Galit Hasan-Rokem has offered a detailed comparison of the Lamentations Rabbah and Bavli versions of this tale. She notes that the discussion of the children's beauty appears only in the Babylonian Talmud and is not mentioned in any of the Lamentations Rabbah manuscripts. Hasan-Rokem, *Web of Life*, 208, n. 29.

18. On the significance of the unblemished priestly body in biblical and rabbinic texts, see Belser, "Reading Talmudic Bodies"; Saul Olyan, *Disability in the Hebrew Bible: Interpreting Mental and Physical Differences* (New York: Cambridge University Press, 2008); Ishay Rosen-Zvi, "The Body and the Book: The List of Blemishes in Mishnah Tractate Bekhorot and the Place of the Temple and Its Worship in the Tannaitic Beit Ha-Midrash" [Hebrew], *Madaʿei Hayahadut* 43 (2005/6). Jeremy Schipper and Jeffrey Stackert, "Blemishes, Camouflage, and Sanctuary Service: The Priestly Deity and His Attendants," *Hebrew Bible and Ancient Israel* 2, no. 4 (December 2013): 458–478.

devastating desacralization of Roman conquest. The priestly body becomes a locus of threatened sanctity, expressing through its own flesh the violated ruins of Jerusalem. The body of the priest remains an unsheltered edifice in a brutal world, exposed to the conqueror and vulnerable to desecration.

As the tale unfolds, the rabbinic storyteller draws upon motifs of corporeal beauty, sexual risk, and mis/recognition to underscore the perils of the captives' situation. When the two are first brought together, captivity renders them unable to recognize each other. Initially, they weep not for the incestuous relationship that their captors demand, but for their own bitter loss of status. While they each identify themselves with the long lineage of the priesthood, they see only a slave as their fated partner in marriage. As Galit Hasan-Rokem has shown, the tragic irony of the tale is intensified by the dramatic delay in recognition, as the two captives slowly come to understand what the reader has known from the start: that "the true source of catastrophe" lies not in the vast difference between them, but in the fact that they are too much alike.[19] It is not until dawn breaks that the siblings come to realize the true horror of their circumstances, to recognize that acceding to their masters' demand will force an even greater violation—a transgression of the incest taboo. Yet the bitter knowledge that recognition brings finally affords them a certain degree of agency, as it propels them to grief deep enough to induce their souls to rebel against the demands of enslavement. Through death, Bavli Gittin allows Rabbi Ishmael's children to find release. The verse from Lamentations mirrors the captives' own tears, as the prophet Jeremiah weeps over beauty degraded and forced from this world.

Reconfiguring Rabbinic Beauty Risk: Gender and Beauty that Draws the Gaze

Bavli Gittin's emphasis on the beauty and vulnerability of the priestly body also finds potent expression in the final narrative in this sequence, the account of Tsafnat bat Penuel, the beautiful daughter of a high priest who is seized by the Romans, sexually violated by her captors, and then stripped and sold in the marketplace to an extremely ugly man. In the previous chapter, I discussed the use of sexual violence in this story, arguing that Bavli Gittin uses this narrative to voice a

---

19. As Hasan-Rokem emphasizes, Lamentations Rabbah accentuates even more elaborately the dramatic tension of the siblings' eventual recognition, a tendency that aligns with its greater emphasis on the trope of the transformed and unrecognizable body, a motif I will discuss in the next chapter. Hasan-Roken, *Web of Life*, 28.

protest against Roman brutality. In this chapter, I return to the story of Tsafnat to analyze the way beauty discourse furthers the Bavli's critique of Roman violence. For ease of reference, I repeat the full narrative here:

> Reish Laqish said:
> An account of a certain woman whose name was Tsafnat bat Penuel—
>> Tsafnat because all gazed (*tsofin*) at her beauty,
>> and the daughter of Penuel because she was the daughter
>>> of a high priest who served at the Holy of Holies—
>>>> who was used sexually by her captor the entire night.
> Afterward, he dressed her in seven garments
> and took her out to sell her in the market.[20]
> A certain man came who was extremely ugly.
> He said to him, "Let me see her beauty."
> He said to him,
>> "Empty one! If you wish to buy, then buy!
>> For her beauty is unmatched in the entire world."
> He said to him, "Even so, [let me see her.]"
> He stripped off six wraps—
> and she tore the seventh and rolled in the dirt.
> She said before God,
>> "Lord of the World, even if You have no compassion on us,
>> have You no compassion for the sanctity of Your great name?"[21]
> Regarding her, Jeremiah lamented:
>> *Daughter of my people—put on sackcloth and strew dust on yourselves!*
>> *Mourn, as for an only child;*
>> *wail bitterly, for suddenly the destroyer is coming upon us.* (Jeremiah 6:26)
> It does not say "upon you," but "upon us,"
>> for it is as if to say—
>> the Destroyer has come upon Me and upon you.

---

20. This phrase is missing in Soncino printing of 1488 and the Vilna printed edition, but appears in Munich 95, Vatican 130, Vatican 140, and Saint Petersburg RNL Evr. I 187 manuscripts.

21. The manuscripts include a number of variations in Tsafnat's question. The Vilna edition and the Soncino printing put the final verb in the imperfect, while the manuscripts have it in the perfect tense. The Munich 95 and Saint Petersburg RNL Evr. I 187 manuscripts describe the divine name as "great" (*gadol*), while the Vilna and Soncino have it as "mighty" (*gibor*), and the Vatican 130 and Vatican 140 include no adjective.

Following a familiar pattern, Bavli Gittin's narrative begins by emphasizing the exquisite bodily beauty of the captive Jew. Like the previous tale of the two captive children of Rabbi Ishmael ben Elisha, this story frames Tsafnat's beauty through the valuation of the Roman who seizes her. In the eyes of her captor, she is "unmatched" in the entire world. The story juxtaposes Tsafnat's beauty with the repulsiveness of the man who comes to buy her. The narrative sets up a diametric opposition between these two figures, highlighting the paradigmatic aspects of each character. Tsafnat is not simply lovely; she is a woman whose exquisite beauty has no equal. Her purchaser is "extremely ugly," a man whose face is meant to mirror his depravity.[22] In order to express moral outrage at the mistreatment of the priestly daughter, Bavli Gittin emphasizes the aesthetic violation of this coupling. Jewish beauty has been bought and claimed by ugly Rome. Tsafnat's rape is not only the violation of her person, but a transgression of the strict sexual rules that govern the purity of the priestly line. The motif of priestly beauty uses the physical form of the body to express the sanctity and spiritual integrity of Jerusalem. In the symbolic economy of the Bavli's beauty discourse, Tsafnat's violation is not only a defilement of Jewish flesh, but the desecration of sancta.

But while beauty drives the degradation plot and is meant to heighten the reader's sense of violation at Roman hands, beauty also surfaces earlier in the tale as a sight that captivates the rabbinic gaze. Through a symbolic etymology of Tsafnat's name, Bavli Gittin links the priestly daughter with the Hebrew word *tsofin* (to gaze).[23] As it describes Tsafnat through the phrase "all gazed at her beauty," the tale activates a potent rabbinic discourse that treats women's beauty as a source of spiritual danger and sexual temptation. Rabbinic literature commonly portrays beauty in sharply gendered terms. As Ra'anan Boustan has shown, rabbinic sources commonly associate male beauty with spiritual virtue.[24] Women's beauty, by contrast, is frequently linked with risk. In many rabbinic narratives, the sight or sound of a beautiful woman lures men into danger.[25] Female

---

22. David Stern notes that the contrast between his extreme ugliness and her intense piety and beauty is a typical convention of the Greco-Roman romance genre. Stern, "Captive Woman," 95.

23. Ilan, *Lexicon of Jewish Names*, 425.

24. Ra'anan Boustan shows how rabbinic narrative frequently uses male beauty to emphasize the power, holiness, and sanctity of a particularly idealized rabbinic man. Boustan, *From Martyr to Mystic*, 119–124.

25. Judith Baskin discusses the common rabbinic motif of women as temptresses, emphasizing the way in which rabbinic gender legislation is often "motivated by a desire to circumscribe, defuse, and control" women on account of the sexual temptation they pose for men. Judith Baskin, *Midrashic Women: Formations of the Feminine in Rabbinic Literature* (Hanover: Brandeis University Press, 2002), 30. See further discussion in Satlow, *Tasting*

beauty works on men regardless of female intent. While beauty is rarely figured as an active evil in rabbinic sources, it remains a powerful force: drawing the male gaze and kindling male lust, endangering marriage bonds, and posing moral danger to male piety.[26] Women's beauty is figured as a risk—to rabbinic men's virtue. When the rabbis constrain how women are seen, where they may go, and how their voices are heard, they do so in order to protect men from sexual arousal, defusing sexual danger by limiting men's exposure to female beauty.[27]

Tales of Jewish beauty set within a colonial context shift these gender dynamics in important ways. In conventional rabbinic accounts, when the Bavli assumes the primacy of rabbinic authority and social control, beauty-risk is almost always gendered as a characteristic of female beauty. Beauty-risk represents the subversion of masculine control, revealing the dangerous and destabilizing capacity of a beautiful woman to erode masculine virtue. It is especially potent when it causes an otherwise righteous rabbinic man to lose control of his desire. As Tal Ilan has observed, the Babylonian Talmud tends to emphasize a woman's culpability for causing men to sin, an orientation exemplified by the case of a pious young woman who prays to God that "no man sin because of me" or the story of the beautiful daughter of Yosi of Yodkarat, whose father discovers a man making a chink in the wall to gaze at her—and who calls upon her to "return to her dust, lest men stumble on your account."[28] Though Tsafnat's extraordinary beauty affords the rabbinic narrator ample opportunity to critique Tsafnat for drawing the male gaze, Bavli Gittin's telling steadfastly refuses to consider her responsible for the terror that befalls her or to inveigh against her beauty. Instead, Bavli Gittin places lovely women alongside beautiful men as corporeal witnesses to Israel's spiritual splendor—and turns its moral critique against the brutality of the conqueror.

---

the Dish, 155–167. Judith Hauptman argues that the rabbinic discourse of gender separation emerges out of a rabbinic idea that men were "easily aroused in the presence of women and therefore did not trust themselves to be alone with them." Hauptman, *Rereading the Rabbis*, 30.

26. Ishay Rosen-Zvi emphasizes that while the rabbinic literature presents both women and men as having a *yetzer*, the Bavli is primarily interested in men's engagement with and against their *yetzer*. By focusing on men's conquest over the *yetzer*, it seems to me that these texts situate both the *yetzer* and the female body-beauty that stimulates it as a source of danger over which men must strive to become victorious. Rosen-Zvi, *Demonic Desires*, 120–126.

27. On rabbinic anxieties about women in markets and other public spaces, their efforts to articulate domestic space as women's space, and the disconnect between such cultural ideals and actual women's practice, see Cynthia Baker, *Rebuilding the House of Israel: Architectures of Gender in Jewish Antiquity* (Stanford, CA: Stanford University Press, 2002).

28. Bavli Sotah 22a; Bavli Ta'anit 23b-24a. See Tal Ilan, *Massekhet Ta'anit: Text, Translation, and Commentary*. (Tübingen: Mohr Siebeck, 2008), 231–236.

By highlighting the physical dangers and sexual vulnerabilities of the beautiful male body, Bavli Gittin's account of the destruction articulates a new politics of bodily risk. As Bavli Gittin narrates Jewish experience under the dominance of foreign powers, beauty is no longer an outside force that threatens a rabbinic man's virtue. It has become a property of his own body, one that makes him subject to the threat of violation and corporeal danger. The Romans desire Jewish men because of the splendor of their bodies, because of the loveliness of their form. In these contexts, beautiful Jewish men become the victims of colonialist aggression. Beauty-risk renders them vulnerable. They too become subject to the avarice and lust of Rome. In this colonialist setting, Bavli Gittin places the culpability clearly on the conqueror, exposing and critiquing the greed and unrestraint of those who see and desire and despoil Jewish beauty. By recognizing the beautiful male body as the victim of Roman desire, Bavli Gittin reformulates conventional notions of beauty-risk. While ordinary rabbinic discourse focuses on constraining women's presence in order to contain the risk their beauty poses to Jewish men's piety, these tales rebuke the sexual aggressor. Where conventional notions of beauty-risk stigmatize or circumscribe women's behavior lest their beauty "provoke" rabbinic desire, these tales critique Roman men for their failure to exercise proper masculine self-control. When Bavli Gittin imagines Jewish men as the victims of Roman conquest, it recognizes the culpability of the one who acts on unrestrained desire—and affirms the moral innocence of the individual who is subjected to another's lust. When it narrates tales of Jews in captivity, Bavli Gittin extends this empathy to women as well. In colonized contexts, stories of women's beauty also reveal the moral limits of the conqueror and evoke outrage on behalf of women wronged. In the shadow of Roman dominance, beauty becomes a shared risk, a body burden borne by both women and men.

In this chapter, I have argued that Bavli Gittin narrates beauty's bitter cost, as Jewish bodies come face to flesh with the brutal underside of Roman imperium. The beautiful Jewish body captivates the Roman gaze. It endures Roman lust. It is dragged through the streets and trussed up in the conqueror's bedchambers. Despite these dangers, Bavli Gittin portrays beauty as an indelible fact of the Jewish body, a material reality that endures the desecrations and predations of imperial conquest. As the Bavli recounts tales of beauty in danger, it overturns the usual gender dynamics of beauty and danger to recognize both men and women alike as vulnerable subjects of Roman lust. While conventional rabbinic discourse frequently castigates women for the consequences of their own beauty, Bavli Gittin's beauty discourse operates differently. As it situates beauty in the context of imperial power, Bavli Gittin recognizes the beautiful individual as victim of the conqueror's desire. Its valuation of beauty thus reveals an unexpectedly egalitarian response to the fate of male and female bodies in distress.

Yet for all that Bavli Gittin's beauty tales empathize with the plight of the beautiful body in danger, my own ethical commitments lead me to a pose another set of questions: How does the fantasy of the enduring beautiful body disenfranchise bodies that are *not* beautiful? How is this notion of beauty constituted, and what bodies does it leave behind? Bavli Gittin's tales repeatedly fashion a sharp contrast between beauty and ugliness, using beauty to signal virtue and ugliness to demarcate both corporeal and moral deviance. As disability studies theorists have argued, the deployment of beauty as a marker of both aesthetic and moral judgment has long helped constitute the disabled body as abject and undesirable.[29] Amidst the symbolic equation of beautiful bodies and spiritual virtues, what becomes of the bodies reshaped by war and violence? Where are the ugly, the ordinary, the disfigured, the maimed? As Bavli Gittin recounts the idealized aesthetics of the heroic body, as it recalls the tragedies borne by its lovely and obdurate flesh, the fates and fortunes of these other bodies shift to the margins of memory. In the next chapter, I turn to Lamentations Rabbah to trace a different narrative trajectory, a trajectory of changed flesh—of bodies marked and marred by conquest and violence, of bodies disabled by the brutalities of war and famine.

---

29. In an influential work, David Mitchell and Sharon Snyder have analyzed the narrative representations of disability and the metaphoric freight that disabled bodies are frequently made to bear. Mitchell and Snyder, *Narrative Prosthesis*. More recently, Tobin Siebers has argued that—despite the widespread assumption that disabled bodies are not beautiful—disability represents a central element within modern art and aesthetics, that it is precisely the presence of disability that makes critics more likely to laud the aesthetic excellence of a piece. Tobin Siebers, *Disability Aesthetics* (Ann Arbor: University of Michigan Press, 2010). The idealization of particular bodily forms has far-reaching implications beyond disability studies. For a critical assessment of the racial implications of late antique aesthetic ideology, see Shawn Kelley, "Race, Aesthetics, and Gospel Scholarship: Embracing and Subverting the Aesthetic Ideology," in *Prejudice and Christian Beginnings*, ed. Laura Nasrallah and Elizabeth S. Fiorenza (Minneapolis: Fortress Press, 2009), 191–210.

4

Disability Studies and the Destruction of Jerusalem

RABBI TSADOK AND THE SUBVERSIVE POTENCY
OF DISSIDENT FLESH

ROMAN CONQUEST LEAVES its mark on Jewish flesh. Whether through the physicality of war itself, the privations of famine, or the brutalities of sexual violence and enslavement, imperial dominance has powerful effect on the corpus of the conquered. As the previous chapter has shown, early Jewish texts forge a potent connection between the Jewish body and the city of Jerusalem, likening the Jew to a "holy jewel" within the sacred city. Even after the destruction of Jerusalem, I argued, Bavli Gittin emphasizes the striking beauty of the captive Jewish body, using motifs of Jewish beauty to evoke the profound vulnerability of conquest and castigate the Romans for avarice and greed. In this chapter, I turn my attention to Lamentations Rabbah to uncover an alternate strand in the representation of the conquered body: the idea that catastrophe brings about an indelible change in Jewish flesh. I focus particularly on two tales of Rabbi Tsadok, a celebrated priest who was said to have fasted for forty years in a failed attempt to stave off the destruction of the temple. While Rabbi Tsadok makes only a brief appearance in Bavli Gittin's account of the destruction, he is the subject of a more substantial set of narrative traditions in Lamentations Rabbah. This chapter reads the Rabbi Tsadok traditions through the prism of disability studies theory to analyze the political significations of corporeal resistance to Roman regimes and to parse the cultural implications of the notion that Jewish flesh is physically transformed by catastrophe and colonial assault.

By staging an encounter between the fasting Rabbi Tsadok and the Roman general Vespasian, these tales probe the possibility that the body might serve as a locus for Jewish resistance. They also reveal the stark corporeal costs of Rabbi

Tsadok's activist intervention: his emaciated flesh, his blackened skin and his weakened body, altered by repeated fasts. In this chapter, I read the Rabbi Tsadok stories as narratives of acquired disability, narratives in which disability carries a potent, political charge. In these tales, I argue, physical disability performs two distinct, if intertwined pieces of cultural work: it laments the tangible loss wrought by Roman conquest and it protests Roman dominance. Even as the rabbis use disability to give visceral expression to the brutality of Roman conquest, they also use the disabled Rabbi Tsadok to resist and resignify the cultural logic of imperial victory, written in and through the flesh.

My reading of disability amidst these tales of empire echoes and extends the conclusions that Daniel Boyarin has drawn with regard to gender in rabbinic narrative. Boyarin argues that imperial conquest restructures social conceptions of gender, feminizing subject populations and reshaping colonized conceptions of manhood. Rabbinic stories, Boyarin maintains, valorize the "sissy-boy" cultures of the rabbinic academy above the brutal, warlike, "bully-boy" masculinity of imperial Rome. In such ways, rabbinic discourse claims this symbolic feminization as a valorized alternative to Roman dominance, turning a cultural script of domination into a subversive form of resistance.[1] Imperial expansion, I contend, also uses disability to imagine and refashion the colonized subject. In the cultural grammar of conquest, defeat disables the nation. War itself is indelibly intertwined with disability.[2] Warfare operates through the deliberate production of disability, as the bodies of combatants come to be killed, to bear wounds, to be maimed. Even beyond the ordinary facts of battle, the symbolic discourse of conquest is bound up with disablement. Victors often subjugate the bodies of the conquered through calculated acts of mutilation, through the intentional

---

1. On the gender implications of imperial power and colonial dominance in rabbinic contexts, see D. Boyarin, *Unheroic Conduct*; D. Boyarin, *Dying for God*; and J. Boyarin and D. Boyarin, *Powers of Diaspora*.

2. Nirmala Erevelles emphasizes the urgency of considering war in the context of feminist disability studies. Noting the surprising lack of attention to disabilities produced through war in the scholarly literature of both first- and third-world feminist scholarship, she argues that "the violence of imperialism is instrumental not only in the creation of disability but also in the absence of public recognition of the impact of disability in the third world" (118). Nirmala Erevelles, "The Color of Violence: Reflecting on Gender, Race, and Disability in Wartime," in *Feminist Disability Studies*, ed. Kim Q. Hall (Bloomington: Indiana University Press, 2011), 117–135. See also Maria Berghs, *War and Embodied Memory: Becoming Disabled in Sierra Leone* (Aldershot: Ashgate, 2012); Daniel R. Morrison and Monica J. Casper, "Intersections of Disability Studies and Critical Trauma Studies: A Provocation," *Disability Studies Quarterly* 32, no. 2 (2012); Maurice E. Stevens, "Trauma's Essential Bodies," in *Corpus: An Interdisciplinary Reader on Bodies and Knowledge*, ed. Monica J. Casper and Paisley Currah (New York: Palgrave Macmillan, 2011), 171–186.

production of impairment.[3] Wounded, marked, and disabled bodies make tangible the brutal incursions of imperial power. Imperial conquest *produces* disability, both as a material reality and as a discursive effect. But the victors do not have the final word. In rabbinic narrative, the subjugated body becomes a potent site of resistance, a site for grappling with trauma and violation—and a site through which rabbinic storytellers flip the script and resignify the meanings of disability to challenge Roman dominance over the Jewish body.[4]

Conceptualizing Disability: Beyond the Diagnosable Body

Lamentations and Lamentations Rabbah are rife with images of bodies changed by war and famine: emaciated bodies, bodies that thirst, bodies with shattered limbs, bodies scarred by violence. Despite the visceral corporeality of these depictions of bodily change, readers may well ask: Are these images of bodily transformation expressive of disability? At first glance, these texts do not evoke familiar categories of disablement. These passages make no mention of *mumim*, the category of body blemishes that biblical sources often use to describe impairment.[5] Nor do they feature the familiar triad of the blind, the deaf, and the lame, a commonly evoked constellation of disabled bodies in early Jewish sources.[6] Conventional discourse tends to associate disability with a set of specific, identifiable physical, mental, or sensory impairments. In highly medicalized cultures,

---

3. On the use of tattoos as a means of marking enslaved persons and prisoners of war, see C. P. Jones, "Stigma: Tattooing and Branding in Graeco-Roman Antiquity," *Journal of Roman Studies* 77 (1987): 139–155.

4. On the relationship between disabled bodies and Roman imperial conquest in early Christian narrative, see Carter, "The blind, lame and paralyzed" (John 5:3)," 129–150 and Betcher, *Spirit and the Politics of Disablement*, 128.

5. The term *mum* first appears in the Hebrew Bible to enumerate conditions that disqualify a priest from offering a sacrifice at the altar in Leviticus 21:17–23. The underlying criteria for classifying a condition as a blemish are difficult to discern. Some biblical *mumim* are visible to the eye, while others are not normally seen; some involve conditions that affect a person's senses, while others affect the physical structure of the body or the body's symmetry. See Olyan, *Disability in the Hebrew Bible*. For discussion of the category of *mum* in biblical and rabbinic texts in relation to contemporary disability studies theory, see Belser, "Brides and Blemishes." On conceptions of bodily blemishes and physical difference in biblical literature and the Ancient Near East, see Schipper, *Disability Studies and the Hebrew Bible*, 64–72.

6. On these categories in rabbinic literature, see Judith Z. Abrams, *Judaism and Disability: Portrayals in Ancient Texts from the Tanach through the Bavli* (Washington, DC: Gallaudet University Press, 1998).

disability is frequently imagined as a matter that demands diagnosis and repair.[7] It is a condition of the exceptional body, an anomaly that marks out cognitive or corporeal difference. Disability thus registers most saliently for readers when it is a discrete mark of sensory or physical impairment.

I argue, however, that holding fast to an essentialist conception of disability leads readers to overlook its cultural significance. First, fixed notions of disability obscure the way disability as a concept and category has shifted across cultures and over time. Biblical and rabbinic texts have no single term that aligns precisely with the modern Western category of disability.[8] Instead of treating disability as a stable, essential category that demarcates a clear set of somatic or mental impairments, disability studies scholars recognize disability as a fluid, flexible category. What constitutes a disability? A body or mind that deviates in certain stigmatized ways from what Rosemarie Garland-Thomson has called the "normate" body or mind.[9] Disability studies probes a culture's categories of disablement, examining how they are constituted and the social functions they serve. Notions of disability reveal a broader set of cultural practices: the registers through which a culture marks power, capacity, and weakness; the perceptions of beauty that idealize particular body forms; the way a culture grapples with deviance and difference, with trauma and loss, with the vulnerabilities of the body, with pain.[10] For cultural historians, disability serves as a potent category of analysis not simply for

7. Michel Foucault's influential study of the rise of medical institutions emphasizes how the modern position of the body within the field of medicine, subject to scrutiny and diagnosis by physicians, increasingly fashioned bodily difference into pathology and deviance. Michel Foucault, *The Birth of the Clinic: An Archeology of Medical Perception*, trans. A. M. Sheridan Smith (New York: Vintage Books, 1975). For a critical analysis of diagnosis and the medicalization of disability, see also David T. Mitchell and Sharon L. Snyder, "Re-engaging the Body: Disability Studies and the Resistance to Embodiment," *Public Culture* 13, no. 3 (2001): 367–389.

8. In its biblical context, the term *mum* includes certain physical characteristics (such as a broken arm) that most moderns do not consider a disability. Nor does it encompass deafness, which is marked as a stigmatized identity in biblical sources, but never considered a *mum*. Despite these differences, I find the modern scholarly conception of disability to be a useful frame for analyzing corporeal difference in rabbinic contexts. Rather than using the term disability to signal a stable, unified category of somatic or mental impairments, I use the terminology of disability to signal the way diverse bodily conditions operate within a given culture to generate a marked, stigmatized difference. See the introduction to this volume and Belser, "Judaism and Disability"; Belser and Lehmhaus, "Disability in Rabbinic Judaism."

9. Rosemarie Garland-Thomson has coined the term "normate" to politicize the notion of a normal body and to call attention to its inverse—"the figure outlined by the array of deviant others whose marked bodies shore up the normate's boundaries." Garland-Thomson, *Extraordinary Bodies*, 8.

10. On the significance of disability as a category for cultural analysis, see Mitchell and Snyder, *Narrative Prosthesis*; Garland-Thomson, "Integrating Disability, Transforming Feminist Theory"; Alison Kafer, *Feminist, Queer, Crip*.

its capacity to illuminate the facts of individual difference, but to trace the cultural and political significance of ability and debility discourse, that is, to parse the social significance of the disabled body.

In this chapter, I push the notion of disability beyond the diagnosable body, beyond the contours of the exceptional form. While I occasionally focus on figures whose bodily difference might mark them as disabled according to a conventional metric of individual impairment, I am more interested here in the way that disability can encompass entire communities affected by famine and siege, entire communities debilitated through imperial conquest and the brutality of war.[11] Lamentations portrays the corporate body of Israel as disabled by disaster. Catastrophe reshapes the corporeal form of the nation, reshaping the physicality of an entire population. A whole people have been changed—the flesh and form of their bodies altered by assault, their capacities diminished by famine and war. While conventional notions of disability frame impairment as the province of an individual body, I argue that stigmatized corporeal difference can be scripted onto entire populations. Bodily devastation is writ large through social and structural violence. Treating disability solely as an exceptional "accident" of fate veils the relationship between disability and violence, between disablement, domination, and colonialist power.[12] As Jasbir Puar has argued, disability is "*endemic to* disenfranchised communities."[13] Bodies bear the consequences of ethnic, gender, and class marginality. Among those who occupy the underside of imperial expansion, disability is rarely an exceptional condition. It is not an unusual case, but a pervasive experience of subjugated bodies. Disability is central to the corporeal architecture of domination.

Bodies Transformed: Catastrophe, Conquest, and Corporeal Change in Lamentations

The recognition that bodies are changed by conquest already appears in the Hebrew Bible. Lamentations is a biblical book haunted by the memory of a city, a city whose ruin is imagined through the devastation of the female body. Jerusalem is portrayed as a woman disfigured by grief, reshaped by famine, and shattered by the material

---

11. See Nirmalla Erevelles, *Disability and Difference in Global Contexts: Enabling a Transformative Body Politic* (New York: Palgrave Macmillan, 2011).

12. My thinking about the relationship between disability and colonial politics, particularly the contemporary intersections of disablement and race, has been shaped by the work of Mel Y. Chen, *Animacies: Biopolitics, Racial Mattering, and Queer Affect* (Durham: Duke University Press, 2012).

13. Jasbir Puar, "Coda: The Cost of Getting Better: Suicide, Sensation, Switchpoints," *GLQ: A Journal of Lesbian and Gay Studies* 18, no. 1 (2012): 154.

consequences of war and famine. Images of corporeal change give visceral narrative voice to the material impact of conquest, narrating disaster through the diminishment of the body. As Lamentations recounts the fall of the holy city, it paints a vivid contrast between the present and the past. In days of old, before disaster struck, the people of Jerusalem were splendid and dazzling. Their bodies, Lamentations claims, glimmered like jewels. These corporeal metaphors play a significant role in rabbinic narrative, as the last chapter has shown. Both Lamentations Rabbah and Bavli Gittin portray the Jewish body as a jewel, literalizing the metaphors of the biblical writer. But while Bavli Gittin portrays Jewish beauty as a bodily quality that endures despite conquest, Lamentations Rabbah imagines Jewish bodies as utterly transformed. Domination brings about somatic estrangement; it changes the very physicality of the Jewish people. In the wake of Roman conquest, the body has become unrecognizable. Jewish flesh is lastingly changed.

The fourth chapter of Lamentations recounts the bitter disasters that have befallen the people of Jerusalem, the cruelty to which they have been reduced because of famine. In several verses within this passage, Lamentations highlights the physical and moral toll that hunger brings:

> 4:3 Even jackals offer their teat,
> suckle their cubs.
> But my daughter-people have turned cruel,
> like ostriches in the wilderness.

> 4:4 The baby's tongue sticks
> to his palate from thirst.
> Little children beg for bread,
> and no one gives them a crumb.

> 4:5 Those who feasted on delicacies
> lie starving in the streets.
> Those reared in crimson
> have embraced refuse heaps . . .

> 4:10 With their own hands, caring women
> cooked their children.
> They became their sustenance,
> amidst the shattering of my daughter-people.[14]

---

14. This and all subsequent translations of Lamentations are drawn from the Jewish Publication Society translation and that of Adele Berlin, *Lamentations: A Commentary* (Louisville: Westminster John Knox Press, 2002).

In these verses, the biblical writer makes plain the transformation of Zion's people. Where Jerusalem's residents used to feast on delicacies, they now lie skeletal and famished in the streets. While they were once reared in the luxurious purples of imperial privilege, they now dig through dung heaps and seek sustenance from refuse. Note the physicality of the biblical language, the way it uses the body to convey both material and existential crisis. Lamentations 4:4 evokes the bodily experience of thirst, the dryness of the tongue within a parched mouth. In early Jewish thought, water is a rich symbol of divine abundance; its absence is a sign of spiritual crisis, as much as a material one. In besieged Jerusalem, the water of life can no longer be found.[15]

While this passage chronicles the physical change famine imposes on the bodies of famished Jerusalemites, it underscores the brutal moral transformation that starvation brings in its wake. Consider the scathing indictment of Lamentations 4:3. Though even wild jackals nurse their young, Jerusalem's starving people turn away from the need of their babes; little children beg for bread but go forth empty handed. The discourse of animality serves to rebuke the unnatural lack of maternal care and concern that Jerusalem's mothers show after the destruction.[16] Even the jackals, the biblical writer claims, possess a nurturing instinct that Jerusalem's mothers have lost.[17] Lamentations 4:10 closes this passage with a devastating inversion of maternal care. Once-compassionate women cook their children with their own hands, as desperate hunger severs family bonds and turns mothers into murderers.[18] Through images of cannibalism and brutality, the writer castigates the ethical reduction of Zion's people. Destruction does not simply level the city;

---

15. On the symbolic significance of drought in rabbinic discourse, see Belser, *Power, Ethics, and Ecology in Jewish Late Antiquity*.

16. Animal studies theorists have drawn attention to the use of animal discourse to draw a sharp moral line between the human and the bestial. Rhetorical appeal to animality has often served to accentuate faultlines *within* human communities, as associations of animality are used to naturalize and grant moral significance to differences of class, gender, disability, race/ethnicity, and sexuality in order to map marginalized others outside the realm of the human. For an introduction to animal studies, see Aaron Gross and Anne Vallely, eds., *Animals and the Human Imagination: A Companion to Animal Studies* (New York: Columbia University Press, 2012). For a discussion of the complex signification of the category "animal" and its rhetorical uses, see Aaron Gross, "The Question of the Creature: Animals, Theology, and Levinas' Dog," in *Creaturely Theology: On God, Humans, and Other Animals*, ed. Celia Deane-Drummond and David Clough (London: SCM Press, 2009), 121–137.

17. Berlin observes that jackals and ostriches are often associated together in biblical literature, appearing also in Isaiah 34:13, Micah 1:8, and Job 30:29. They "share the characteristics of inhabiting ruins and uttering eerie cries that sound like keening. Like jackals and ostriches, Zion's people preside over a ruin." Berlin, *Lamentations*, 106.

18. Hasan-Roken notes the way that Lamentations Rabbah uses images of a mother eating her son and a son unknowingly eating his father's corpse to express the "total inhumanity of

it devastates its moral capacity. In the poet's evocative phrase, the utter inhumanity of famine "shatters" the moral and physical integrity of those God calls "my daughter-people (*bat-ami*)."

The emphasis on the material transformation of the body in the aftermath of destruction is particularly prominent in Lamentations 4:7–8. In these two verses, the biblical writer contrasts the people's physical form before Jerusalem's fall with the stark bodily change that catastrophe brings:

> 4:7 Her nobles[19] had been brighter than snow,
>   whiter than milk.
>   Their bodies had been ruddier than coral,
>   their physique sapphire.
>
> 4:8 Now their faces are darker than black;
>   they are unrecognizable in the streets.
>   Their skin has shriveled on their bones;
>   it has become as dry as wood.

These two verses chronicle the material consequences of destruction, marking out the corporeal terrain of catastrophe. The change in Israel's circumstance has altered the physical form of the Israelite body. In keeping with the previous verses, Lamentations 4:7 uses vivid colors to characterize the physical stature of Jerusalem's people. Before destruction, the body is associated with opulence and wealth; the verses deploy a bright and vibrant palette: sapphire, pure white, crimson, and coral.[20] As catastrophe unfolds, the imagery changes; "the colors are erased from the picture and all that remains is dullness and blackness."[21] In

---

starvation." Hasan-Rokem, *Web of Life*, 143. On the discourse of cannibalism as a classic marker of famine and siege, see S. Cohen, "Destruction: From Scripture to Midrash," 22.

19. Berlin argues that the verse refers not to Nazirites, but to aristocrats—to those who wear a crown or wreath. Berlin, *Lamentations*, 101.

20. The meaning of *gizrah*, translated here as "sapphire," is difficult. Berlin argues that the meaning should be understood in terms of the radiance or shining nature of the Israelites' physique. In Exodus 24:10 and Ezekiel 1:26, sapphire is used to connote "brilliant, shiny, sparkling, of good color." Berlin, *Lamentations*, 108. On rabbinic midrashic motifs that link this word with *gezerah*, "decree," see Alexander, *Targum of Lamentations*, 167.

21. Berlin, *Lamentations*, 104. On the racialized valuation of brightness and the significance of brightness and dullness as a means of marking ethnic skin-color differences in late antiquity, see Shelley P. Haley, "Be Not Afraid of the Dark: Critical Race Theory and Classical Studies," in *Prejudice and Christian Beginnings: Investigating Race, Gender, and Ethnicity in Early Christian Studies*, ed. Laura Nasrallah and Elisabeth Schüssler Fiorenza (Minneapolis: Fortress Press, 2009), 27–50.

the discursive world of Lamentations, black is frequently imbued with negative connotations.[22] The rabbinic Targum to Lamentations intensifies this imagery, translating this verse as: "Darker than the blackness of the exile."[23] But while the Targum uses blackness to signal the metaphysical and spatial displacements of disaster, Lamentations stresses the physical change that destruction brings. Jerusalem's people have lost the fairness of their skin, the brightness of their countenance. Though their forms once gleamed like sapphires, their faces have grown dark. As Gay Byron has argued, the language of blackness conveys a powerful set of ethno-political significations in the ancient world, mobilizing notions of ethnic difference, geographical distance, foreignness, and marginality.[24] These verses invest Zion's people with a visible marker of ethnic difference. They mobilize notions of racial-ethnic otherness to express a sense of bodily estrangement. The people have become "foreign" in every sense of the word.

As Lamentations recounts the destruction of Jerusalem, it uses this repeated motif of bodily change to make tangible the visceral impact of conquest. Lamentations 4:8 chronicles national loss through the shifting terrain of face, skin, and bone. The verse describes the skin of the Jerusalemites as shriveled on their bones, likening their living flesh to dry wood. Where the people's limbs were once ruddy, their vigor has faded. Their skin has shriveled and desiccated. Destruction has changed the people beyond recognition. When they are seen in the streets, they are no longer known. Even as the people of Jerusalem move through the streets and squares of the ruined city, they pass without recognition through the city's public spaces. Disaster has remade their physicality, changed their bodies into unfamiliar forms. Destruction has rendered them unrecognizable.

---

22. Lamentations often uses words for night, darkness, and blackness in negative contexts. In addition to its use in Lamentations 4:8, the writer uses darkness imagery with a negative intention in 2:1, 2:19, 3:2, and 5:10. F. W. Dobbs-Allsopp, *Lamentations* (Louisville: Westminster John Knox Press, 2002), 53–54. On the racial implications of color prejudice in religious thought, see Robert Earl Hood, *Begrimed and Black: Christian Traditions on Blacks and Blackness* (Minneapolis: Fortress Press, 1994). On the importance of revaluing the symbolic implications of darkness, see Vincent Wimbush, "Reading Darkness, Reading Scriptures," in *African Americans and the Bible: Sacred Texts and Social Structures*, ed. Vincent Wimbush, 1–43. (New York: Continuum International, 2000).

23. Alexander, *Targum of Lamentations*, 167.

24. Gay L. Byron, *Symbolic Blackness and Ethnic Difference in Early Christian Literature* (New York: Routledge, 2003). On early Christian uses of ethnic reasoning for religio-political purpose in the context of the Roman Empire, see Denise Kimber Buell, *Why This New Race: Ethnic Reasoning in Early Christianity* (New York: Columbia University Press, 2005).

Fasting Instead of Famine: Rabbi Tsadok and Bodily Resistance to Imperial Regimes

The biblical book of Lamentations recounts the corporeal and psychic toll that conquest imposes on the bodies of the Jerusalemite people, revealing the way that famine reshapes their physical and moral capacities. These biblical verses chronicle the corrosive effects of extreme hunger, the desperation that befalls the Israelite people in the wake of starvation. Yet hunger is not always a negative condition. In striking contrast to the degradation that follows a famine, early Jewish sources recognize a potent spiritual agency that emerges out of *intentional* hunger—the deliberate renunciation of food associated with fasting. If famine is imposed upon a population, fasting is a ritual practice that accentuates the agency of the one who chooses to go without food. The intentionality of a fast is a critical dimension of its efficacy. Fasting gains its spiritual charge not from the physical absence of nourishment, but in the willing renunciation of food at a moment when it is still possible to eat. It is not the raw fact of hunger that drives fasting's potency, but the act of abstention. The dynamics of the rabbinic fast are particularly apparent in the practice of fasting to break a drought. As I have argued elsewhere, rabbinic rain fasts make deliberate use of a voluntarily weakened body to anticipate and avert a crisis to come.[25] Rain fasts make visible the threat of famine, revealing an awareness of human vulnerability and human culpability in the face of crisis. Rabbinic fasting practice deploys abstention in the potent actionable moment when hunger can still be framed as a choice, before it is forced upon a population. If drought persists, famine will be inevitable.

In rabbinic accounts of the destruction of Jerusalem, the power of the fasting body emerges most strikingly in the stories of Rabbi Tsadok, a celebrated priestly figure who fasts for many years to attempt to prevent the destruction of Jerusalem.[26] Bavli Gittin contrasts the extensive fasting of Rabbi Tsadok with the

---

25. I offer a lengthy discussion of rabbinic fasting practice in Belser, *Power, Ethics, and Ecology in Jewish Late Antiquity*. On fasting and dimensions of rabbinic asceticism, see Eliezer Diamond, *Holy Men and Hunger Artists: Fasting and Asceticism in Rabbinic Culture* (New York: Oxford University Press, 2004).

26. Sonia Pilz argues that Rabbi Tsadok's decision to turn away from food is connected to a story in Bavli Yoma 23a, which describes how two priests rush toward the place of sacrifice and are so eager to perform the sacred duties that one priest stabs the other in order to prevent him from performing the sacrifice. Rabbi Tsadok witnesses the murder, which he takes as condemnation of an entire community that has allowed the sacred rituals to become a site of jealousy, greed, and violence. Pilz suggests that this tale stands in the backdrop of the fast described in Lamentations Rabbah and Bavli Gittin. Rather than continuing to consume the tainted sacrifice of a murderous priesthood, Tsadok "turns his own body into an offering" through his fast. Pilz, *Food and Fear*, 98–118.

foolishness of Marta bat Boethus, a wealthy Jewish woman who starves on the streets of Jerusalem. While I discuss Marta's tale in more detail in the final chapter of this book, consider the depiction of Rabbi Tsadok in Bavli Gittin 56b:

> She ate from the shriveled figs of Rabbi Tsadok
>   and was overcome.
> For Rabbi Tsadok sat and fasted for forty years,
>   so that Jerusalem would not be destroyed.
> When he ate anything, it could be seen from the outside
>   [because he was so thin.]
> When he was regaining strength,
>   they brought him dried figs
>   and he sucked them and threw them away.

Bavli Gittin portrays Rabbi Tsadok's fast as an extensive, deliberate attempt to stave off catastrophe. For forty years, he has fasted to prevent the destruction of Jerusalem, an attempt to hold crisis at bay through the medium of his own body. Rabbi Tsadok's fasts script the looming catastrophe onto his flesh, rendering his body transparent. As the Bavli details, everything that goes inside him can be visible from the outside. Yet despite the rigors of his fast, Tsadok's body remains profoundly resilient. Like many pious rabbis and wonder-workers, Rabbi Tsadok proves able to survive on meager nourishment.[27] His story serves as a striking counterpoint to Marta's tale, in which a wealthy woman starves on the streets of Jerusalem. The two stories narrate strikingly different trajectories of agency. Marta grasps at very figs that nourished Tsadok, but rather than sustain her, the dried husks become her downfall. He deploys deliberate hunger in an attempt to avert crisis; she suffers famine, dying despite her desperate attempts to forage. His is a fasting body, hers a famished one.

---

27. A famous example is Rabbi Ḥanina ben Dosa, who is described as subsisting on a handful of carobs from week to week. In his study of poverty in Greco-Roman Palestine, Gildas Hamel notes that the fruits of the wild carob tree were considered a typical poor man's food and actually used primarily as fodder for animals. The human consumption of carobs was synonymous with living in poverty. Hamel reads the rabbinic narratives of Ḥanina ben Dosa as well as Shimon bar Yoḥai and his son, who lived for twelve years in a cave hiding from the Romans and eating carobs, to suggest that that "only extraordinary individuals could subsist on so meager a food." Gildas Hamel, *Poverty and Charity in Roman Palestine: First Three Centuries C.E.*, Near Eastern Studies, vol. 23 (Berkeley: University of California Press, 1989), 16–17. For further discussion of this motif of "wondrous provision," see Antoinette Clarke Wire, *Holy Lives, Holy Deaths: A Close Hearing of Early Jewish Storytellers* (Atlanta: Society of Biblical Literature, 2002).

Unlike the starving woman, whose death becomes emblematic of the terrible
disaster that befalls Jerusalem, Rabbi Tsadok's deliberate cultivation of a weakened body becomes a sign of rabbinic resilience amidst devastation. While his
body is weakened, Tsadok's ability to endure the rigors of a forty-year fast signals
a profound spiritual and physical discipline.[28] Rabbi Tsadok surfaces once more
in Bavli Gittin's account, as the Bavli narrates Rabbi Yoḥanan ben Zakkai's negotiation with the Roman general Vespasian. As Vespasian prepares to depart to
become emperor, he grants Rabbi Yoḥanan ben Zakkai a request:

> [Vespasian] said to him:
>   "I am going, and I will send someone else.
>   Ask me something, and I will give it to you."
> [Rabbi Yoḥanan ben Zakkai] said to him:
>   "Give me Yavneh and its sages,
>   and the line of Rabban Gamliel,
>   and physicians to heal Rabbi Tsadok."

This exchange between Vespasian and Rabbi Yoḥanan ben Zakkai is a potent
moment in Bavli Gittin's account of the destruction, the moment when the rabbinic leader has the opportunity to wrest from the conqueror some small measure of protection for the Jewish people. As Jeffrey Rubenstein has shown, Bavli
Gittin's version of this story portrays Rabbi Yoḥanan ben Zakkai in an ambivalent light, critiquing his meager requests and his willingness to be content with
merely "saving a little."[29] Yet Yoḥanan's requests lay the foundations for the rescue
of the rabbinic movement. From out of the ruins of Jerusalem, the tale offers an
origin story for the legendary rabbinic center at Yavneh. It recounts how Rabbi
Yoḥanan ben Zakkai preserved the line of Rabban Gamliel, protecting the family
that would occupy the office of the patriarch and provide religious and political
leadership for the Palestinian Jewish community for generations to come. Given
these significant political gestures, what shall we make of the third request? The
healing of Rabbi Tsadok operates as a potent symbol of the possibility of repair.
Even amidst the bitter realities of conquest, our tale promises, Roman physicians
will come to nourish and nurture the devoted Jew whose body was spent in opposition to the destruction. They will return him to strength, devoting their knowledge and craft to the restoration of his flesh. In Bavli Gittin, the healing of Rabbi

---

28. Eliezer Diamond, *Holy Men and Hunger Artists.*

29. Rubenstein, *Talmudic Stories,* 157–159, 169–173.

Tsadok becomes a rabbinic redemption tale, a story that uses the rehabilitation of the pious Jewish body to imagine the possibilities of life after destruction.

The Body Politics of Fasting: Rabbi Tsadok in Lamentations Rabbah

Lamentations Rabbah offers two different narratives of Rabbi Tsadok, both of which complicate the neat tale of repair and redemption that appears in Bavli Gittin. The midrash first introduces Rabbi Tsadok in a lengthy account that details how Rabbi Yoḥanan ben Zakkai negotiates with the Roman general Vespasian while he was besieging Jerusalem and eventually wins the right to bring his loved ones and relatives out of the city before it falls. While the full narrative is lengthy and not necessary to analyze here in its entirety, let us look more closely at the description of Rabbi Tsadok. Lamentations Rabbah 1:31 reads:

> They went and found him at the city gate.
> When Rabbi Tsadok came before him, Rabbi Yoḥanan rose up.
> Vespasian said,
>   "You rise up before this small, shriveled old man?"
> Rabbi Yoḥanan said to him,
>   "By your life, had there been one more like him
>   then even had you double the troops,
>   you would not have been able [to conquer Jerusalem]."
> Vespasian said to him,
>   "What is his strength?"
> Rabbi Yoḥanan said to him,
>   "He eats but a single fig,
>   and he can teach one hundred sessions."
> Vespasian said to him,
>   "Why is he so reduced (*ḥashik*)?"
> Rabbi Yoḥanan said to him,
>   "From his many fasts and self-afflictions."

Lamentations Rabbah 1:31 draws attention to the physical form of Rabbi Tsadok, which it uses to illuminate a striking difference in rabbinic and Roman perception. In the midrash, the Roman general is taken in by surface appearances. When Vespasian first sees Rabbi Tsadok, the one figure Yoḥanan has chosen to rescue, the general asks why the rabbi has made such efforts to honor and rescue such a "small, shriveled old man." Rabbi Yoḥanan's response maintains that Tsadok's visible weakness conceals an unexpected strength. Had there been another man of his stature in Jerusalem, Vespasian could never have conquered the city. But while we might be tempted to read this tale as a contrast between physical and spiritual power, the midrash emphasizes that Rabbi Tsadok's capacity arises from his emaciated body. When Vespasian asks about the source of "his strength," Rabbi Yoḥanan boasts that Rabbi Tsadok can teach a hundred sessions in the rabbinic academy with no more sustenance than a single fig.[30] When Vespasian asks about the state of Rabbi Tsadok's body, Yoḥanan praises the intensity of Rabbi Tsadok's regimen of fasts and self-afflictions. The term ḥashik, which our midrash uses to characterize Rabbi Tsadok's body, portrays his body as meager and skinny; it can also connote darkness, reminiscent of Lamentations' depictions of the biblical bodies that are not only weakened, but blackened by famine and distress.

The striking transformation of Rabbi Tsadok's physical form is a testament to the intense corporeality of fasting as a religious practice. Fasting calls forth divine attention through the language of the flesh.[31] In contrast to the residents of Jerusalem who starve once disaster has come, Rabbi Tsadok's hunger predates the siege of Jerusalem. His fasts anticipate and aim to prevent the bitter famine that strikes the city once the Roman conquest is at hand. Recall that, at least according to the Bavli's tradition, Rabbi Tsadok has fasted for a period of forty years. Given the intentionality of his fasting practice, I read his refashioned body as a deliberate change of the flesh, a willful practice of corporeal transformation. Through his fast, Rabbi Tsadok shapes the arc of his own body's destiny. But though his practice works by transforming the landscape of his own flesh, Rabbi Tsadok aspires to broader social transformation. His shriveled body is a site of corporeal resistance whose strength is affirmed by rabbi and Roman alike.

Curing Tsadok: Roman Rehabilitation and the Taming of the Dissident Body

While the central section of Lamentations Rabbah 1:31 celebrates the efficacy of Rabbi Tsadok's fast, the midrash goes on to recount Rabbi Tsadok's bodily restoration. Our midrash relates how Vespasian himself summons doctors to tend to the frail rabbi, who painstakingly feed him to gradually expand his stomach

---

30. The fig is a staple of the ancient Mediterranean diet, popular and widely available; dried figs were an important source of nourishment, especially during hard winters. John Cooper, *Eat and Be Satisfied: A Social History of Jewish Food* (Northvale, NJ: Jason Aronson, 1993), 12.

31. On the body as a locus for expression in rabbinic fasting practice, see Belser, *Power, Ethics, and Ecology in Jewish Late Antiquity*, 121–124.

and return his body to health. Vespasian's physicians rehabilitate Rabbi Tsadok's body, erasing the corporeal signs that fasting inscribed in his flesh. Lamentations Rabbah 1:31 continues:

> Vespasian sent for doctors
>   and they fed him little by little
>   and gave him drink little by little
>   until his body was restored.
> Eleazar, his son, said to him:
>   "Father, give them their reward in this world,
>   so they will not have merit with you in the world to come."
> He gave them [the skill of] calculation with fingers
>   and the Roman balance scale.[32]

As it concludes the Rabbi Tsadok tale, Lamentations Rabbah 1:31 narrates the restoration of the fasting body through the expert intervention of imperial physicians. Though the midrash ties Rabbi Tsadok's strength to his deliberately weakened body and celebrates the potent religious capacity of the fasting sage, it ultimately undoes the physical transformation his fasting has wrought.

How shall we understand Vespasian's intervention? I find it quite curious that the Roman general makes such efforts to cure Rabbi Tsadok. Our midrash is set during the time of the Roman siege. At this very moment, the Roman army has surrounded the city. Vespasian is actively starving the people of Jerusalem, even as he feeds and restores the body of Rabbi Tsadok. That he should "send for doctors" to painstakingly hydrate and nourish a frail fasting rabbi is striking and strange. We could, of course, read Vespasian's medical intervention as a benevolent act, an expression of the general's commitment to keep his promise to Rabbi Yoḥanan. Sonia Pilz suggests that this tale's emphasis on cure turns the story "into a vehicle for healing national trauma," that the figure of Rabbi Tsadok allows the rabbis to craft the destruction of Jerusalem into "a holistic saga of survival."[33]

She reads the Roman medical intervention as a maternal act, reminiscent of the way one might nurture and feed a small child. "Roman food nourishes Jewish survival," she argues, "and Roman strength protects the bearers of Jewish knowledge and tradition." In Pilz's view, the rabbinic tales impart a visceral lesson about

---

32. The term *qartstion*, which Jastrow translates as "the Roman balance," is often called the charistion, associated with Charistion, a Greek scholar of geometry from the second century BCE. Marcus Jastrow, *Dictionary of the Targumim, Talmud, and Midrashic Literature* (London: Luzac & Co., 1903), 667.

33. Pilz, *Food and Fear*, 131.

the urgency of accommodation to Roman authority. Jewish survival hinges on the good will of the powers. Like Tsadok, Pilz asserts, "Judaism also survives due to Roman mercy." [34]

While our story may imagine the healing of Rabbi Tsadok as an expression of Roman benevolence, I suggest a different possibility: that cure is not a kindness. Cure functions in this tale as a barbed articulation of Roman dominance, a medical intervention that presses imperial power onto Jewish flesh. In our story, Vespasian has come to recognize the subversive power of the disabled body, deployed against the state. He deploys his physicians in an attempt to defuse the body's force, to defang its capacity. Rabbi Yoḥanan claims that Rabbi Tsadok's shriveled body, weakened through fasting and prayer, is the Jews' most powerful weapon against Roman assault. When Vespasian feeds Rabbi Tsadok, he is attempting to neutralize the power of the rabbi's chosen fast. Like authorities who force-feed protesters who have committed to a hunger strike, the Roman general countermands the rabbi's capacity to fast. Vespasian denies Rabbi Tsadok sovereignty over his own body, claiming for Rome the power to rehabilitate Jewish flesh. The portrait of healing as a power play surfaces again in the final lines of our tale, once the cure is complete. Even though Rabbi Tsadok's body is restored to health, his son offers no gratitude to Vespasian or his lackeys. Instead, he urges his father to give them their reward immediately—to discharge his debt to them as expeditiously as possible, lest they have a claim upon him in the world to come. Eleazar treats the imperial physicians as interlopers, not saviors. He wants his father free of them.

The Body that Will Not Heal: Rabbi Tsadok and the Persistence of Changed Flesh

Lamentations Rabbah later recounts a second story of Rabbi Tsadok—a tale that counters these motifs of Roman healing and bodily restoration. In Lamentations Rabbah 4:11, the midrash claims that Rabbi Tsadok's body has been permanently changed. In this tale, the effects of destruction have a profound, lasting effect on the Jewish body. Lamentations Rabbah 4:11 reads:

They are unrecognizable in the streets... (Lamentations 4:8)
Rabbi Eliezer, son of Rabbi Tsadok said:
May I see the consolation—
    for though my father lived on all those years after the destruction,

---

34. Pilz, *Food and Fear*, 137–138.

his body never returned to the way that it was,
    to fulfill that which was written:
. . . *their skin has shriveled on their bones;*
    it has become as dry as wood. (Lamentations 4:8)

This midrash uses Rabbi Tsadok to exemplify the physical transformation
described in Lamentations 4:8, a biblical verse that declares that the people of
Jerusalem will no longer be recognized in the streets. In this tale, Rabbi Eliezer
recalls the bodily transformation brought on by his father's extensive ascetic
efforts to prevent the destruction. His physical body is permanently shrunken
by his own fasting, diminished through the intensity of his abstentions. In
Lamentations Rabbah 4:11, Rabbi Tsadok's son reports that his father's body does
not return to its pre-destruction condition. Though his father lives on for years,
his body is never restored to its original state.

What shall we make of the midrashic assertion that Rabbi Tsadok's flesh
will not heal, that the sage retains a disabled body through the remaining years
of his existence? As the midrash draws our attention on the incurable body of
Rabbi Tsadok, it uses the marked body to convey the permanence of destruction.
Within the symbolic grammar of the midrash, Rabbi Tsadok's unhealed body
remains a sign of the enduring physical effect of exile and conquest. Rabbi Eliezer
is forced to grapple with the changed body of his father, to admit the enduring
transformation of familiar flesh. His father occupies the liminal space between
the known and the unknown, pressed between the memory of what was and
the impossibility of return. We hear his son's lament, the grief that cannot be
assuaged. In this tale, the disabled body gives tangible expression to the uncon-
soled state of the nation, to the unresolved wound of exile.

But Rabbi Tsadok's body is not, I suggest, solely a symbol of enduring distress.
Reading the Tsadok tales through the prism of disability studies theory, we can
recognize the utility of the disabled body as a site of cultural protest.[35] Recall my
argument that Vespasian's healing of Rabbi Tsadok should not be understood as a
straightforward act of benevolence, that the healing of Rabbi Tsadok functions

---

35. Garland-Thomson argues that disabled body is culturally provocative, a sight that "disrupts
the expectations of the complacently normal." Disability activists and performance artists, she
asserts, often deliberately deploy disability to overturn entrenched assumptions about beauty
and otherness, forcing viewers to confront the limits of accepted cultural narratives about
disability. Rosemarie Garland-Thomson, "Staring Back: Self-Representations of Disabled
Performance Artists," *American Quarterly* 52, no. 2 (2000): 335. On the political dimensions
of the embrace of embodied difference among disability artists, see Snyder and Mitchell, "Re-
engaging the Body," 381–386. For a discussion of the performative dimensions of disabled bodies in rabbinic literature, see Belser, "Reading Talmudic Bodies."

as an expression of Roman power and dominance. Against the backdrop of Vespasian's medical imperialism, Tsadok's unhealed body becomes a potent marker of corporeal resistance. The uncured body stands as a defiant register of destruction, a scar that will not be erased. The body that does not heal becomes a visceral expression of rabbinic memory. Like Augustine's Christian martyrs who bear the scars of their holy wounds even in the afterlife, Rabbi Tsadok carries a story of destruction and resistance pressed into his skin.[36] The story of his flesh articulates the potent witness of the body that does not heal, the body whose physical change demands we reckon with the impossibility of repair. It also gestures, I suggest, toward the possibility that the disabled body is itself an expression of resistance, a provocation in its own right. The practice of "rehabilitating" a body involves rendering that body capable again, according to the normative dictates of dominant culture.[37] Rabbi Tsadok's unhealed body attests to the cultural potency of unrehabilitated flesh. Rabbi Tsadok refuses to perform for the powers. His is a body that will not work for empire, that will not be an "able" body beneath imperial regimes.

A Stranger at the Gate: Gender Indeterminacy and the Unrecognizable Body

In Lamentations Rabbah 4:11, Rabbi Tsadok's defiantly disabled body serves as a striking alternative to Bavli Gittin's notion of the heroic body, unbowed by the cruelties of captivity and conquest. As my last chapter has argued, Bavli Gittin's narratives place a strong emphasis on the enduring beauty of the captive Jew, celebrating the body that remains unchanged despite Roman domination. Lamentations Rabbah, by contrast, proves willing to linger with a different

---

36. On the bodies of martyrs in Augustine's eschatology, see Kristi Upson-Saia, "Resurrecting Deformity: Augustine on the Scarred, Marked, and Deformed Bodies of the Heavenly Realm," in *Disability in Judaism, Christianity and Islam: Sacred Texts, Historical Traditions and Social Analysis*, ed. Darla Schumm and Michael Stoltzfus (New York: Palgrave Macmillan, 2011), 107. For a broader consideration of the disability implications of bodily transformation in the afterlife in early Christian thought, see Moss, "Heavenly Healing."

37. While medical approaches to disability assume the urgency of rehabilitating the disabled body, disability studies theorists stress that the cultural power afforded to cure and rehabilitation can further stigmatize disability. Medical intervention can, without a doubt, be desirable and beneficial for individual bodies. Yet rehabilitation also treats the disabled body as a site of pathology, as a deviant body in need of repair. It functions as a means of regulating bodily difference. For a critique of dominant cultural efforts to regulate disability through the production of more normalized bodies, see Davis, *Enforcing Normalcy* and Lennard Davis, *Bending Over Backwards: Essays on Disability and the Body* (New York: New York University Press, 2002).

truth: that the body is changed by conquest, that flesh is remade in the shadow of Roman power. Through this second tale of Rabbi Tsadok, Lamentations Rabbah imagines the possibility that the disabled body might also harbor possibilities for rabbinic resistance. In these tales of Rabbi Tsadok's changed flesh, Lamentations Rabbah lays claim to an alternate mode of corporeal heroism: a heroism that lies not in the classical ideal of untouched beauty, but in the concrete, material endurance of a body harrowed by war or famine.

Yet even this gesture toward an alternative body politics, as I have sketched it here through the figure of Rabbi Tsadok, remains bound up with rabbinic notions of manhood. Just as Bavli Gittin's account of Rabbi Tsadok places the sage in striking contrast to Marta bat Boethus, a once-wealthy woman who starves on the streets of Jerusalem, Lamentations Rabbah 4:11 also juxtaposes Rabbi Tsadok against the figure of an unnamed woman, whose transformed body is afforded no capacity for resistance. Immediately after it relates Rabbi Eleazar's account of his father's unhealed body, Lamentations Rabbah 4:11 continues:

> Another version:
> *They are unrecognizable in the streets . . .* (Lamentations 4:8)
> Rabbi Eliezer bar Tsadok said:
>> There was a poor person
>> who came and stood at the door of my father's house.
> My father said to me:
>> "Go and see! Perhaps he is one of the people of Jerusalem."
> I went and I found that she was a woman.
> Her hair had fallen out
>> and there was no person who knew whether she was woman or man
>> and she asked for nothing but a single dried fig
>>> to fulfill that which was written:
> *. . . their skin has shriveled on their bones;*
> *it has become as dry as wood.* (Lamentations 4:8)

Glossing the same verse that launched the tale of Rabbi Tsadok, the midrashist recounts a story that highlights the unknowability of the post-destruction body. In this story, Rabbi Eliezer meets a stranger at the gate—a figure his father believes is a man, who he perceives as a woman. The ambiguity of the stranger's form is accentuated by lack of hair, a detail the midrashist uses to veil the stranger's gender and render it indeterminate. The midrash treats the gender-ambiguous body as evidence of destruction, a form of social unmaking that has unbound the cultural markings of gender from the flesh. As gender theorists have argued, gender functions as a cultural script, as a means of asserting and shaping the social and cultural meanings of body and self.[38] Within the symbolic discourse of the midrash, the unrecognizability of the figure's gender condenses the intense cultural devastation of conquest. As the hair is shorn away, as the body is changed by the privations of poverty and famine, as the moorings of culture give way before the brutality of conquest, gender itself appears to unravel and come undone.

Yet despite this striking image of gender ambiguity, the feminine remains a critical signifier within the narrative. Amidst the depravities of destruction, the midrash claims that "no person" can discern whether the body of the stranger is male or female. While the stranger's gender remains inscrutable to people who pass on the street, the midrashist positions Rabbi Eliezer as capable of seeing beneath the surface.[39] He recognizes her womanhood. By claiming the gender-indeterminate body as a woman, Rabbi Eliezer's recognition allows the midrash to position her as the antithesis to the idealized feminine body of Jerusalem. Eliezer's confirmation of her true gender drives home the corporeal devastation borne by the city as woman. Jerusalem has become an anonymous body, stripped not only of her splendor but also of her sex.[40] According to the cultural logic of the midrash, the unrecognizability of her body testifies to the profound somatic undoing that conquest has wrought. Jerusalem has become a woman shorn of hair, with flesh that destruction has utterly changed. She is the daughter who cannot be recognized, the daughter whose body has lost the cultural scripts that allow it to signify. Her body has become inscrutable. Without the beauty and bodily integrity that made her a woman, she might well be taken for a man.

By pairing these two tales of bodily change, Lamentations Rabbah underscores the difference gender makes in navigating devastated Jerusalem. The midrash

---

38. Judith Butler, *Gender Trouble: Feminism and the Subversion of Identity* (New York: Routledge, 1990).

39. In analyzing halakhic responses to gender ambiguity in rabbinic literature, Charlotte Fonrobert emphasizes that rabbinic discourse aims to "enforce and normativize congruence between sexed bodies and gendered identities." Charlotte Fonrobert, "The Semiotics of the Sexed Body in Early Halakhic Discourse," in *How Should Rabbinic Literature Be Read in the Modern World*, ed. Matthew Kraus, 79–104 (Piscataway: Gorgias Press, 2006), 82. Sarra Lev argues that while the rabbis make strict halakhic gender distinctions on the basis of genitalia, they recognize the ambivalence and fluidity of gender in practice. Sarra Lev, "They Treat Him as a Man and See Him as a Woman: The Tannaitic Understanding of the Congenital Eunich," *Jewish Studies Quarterly* 17, no. 3 (2010): 213–243.

40. Ancient sources associate the forcible cutting off of a woman's hair with punishment and frequently portray shorn hair as a humiliation or source of bodily shame. Dio Chrysostom notes that a woman guilty of adultery would have her hair cut off. Dio Chrysostom, *Discourses*, trans. H. Lamar Crosby, Loeb Classical Library (Cambridge: Harvard University Press, 1951) 64.3. See discussion in Bruce W. Winter, *Roman Wives, Roman Widows: The Appearance of New Women and the Pauline Communities* (Grand Rapids: William B. Eerdmans, 2003), 82–83.

situates Rabbi Tsadok as a heroic figure, a paragon of rabbinic masculinity whose masterful control over his body represents the act of a spiritual adept. As Daniel Boyarin has shown, rabbinic culture often celebrates the "feminized" manhood of the sage.[41] In contrast to the brute strength of the Roman warrior, exemplified in these traditions by the general Vespasian, Rabbi Tsadok's body is weakened and shriveled. His strength lies elsewhere. On the sustenance of but a single dried fig, Lamentations Rabbah 1:31 claims that Rabbi Tsadok has the stamina to teach one hundred sessions in the rabbinic academy. It is precisely through the cultivation of physical weakness that Rabbi Tsadok is able to command cultural power. He marshals spiritual capacity through the deliberate disablement of his body. His physical debility stands as a revelation of spiritual potency, a marker of his ability to deploy the body for entirely different purpose. But "feminized" manhood is figured quite differently than femininity. Consider the contrast between Rabbi Tsadok and the unrecognized woman, who appears in our midrash as a symbol of degradation. She asks for but a single fig. While Rabbi Tsadok's fig affords him the capacity for herculean feats of pedagogy, for her, the fruit is nothing more than a beggar's meal. Like Marta bat Boethus, who dies while attempting to draw nourishment from Tsadok's cast-off husks, the woman at the gate is left with nothing but remnants. All of these figures bear upon their flesh the signs of Jerusalem's fall. But where Rabbi Tsadok's body carries the marks of his own efforts to stave off disaster, the woman's body tells no tale of agency. Though we might read her shorn head as a sign of grief, the language of the midrash refuses her even this small act of lament.[42] She has not torn her own hair; it has fallen, seemingly of its own accord. She gives no name, nor asks for anything beyond the most meager sustenance. She ghosts through the ruined city, unrecognized and unrecognizable.

In this chapter, I have argued that Lamentations Rabbah uses images of profound bodily change to evoke the dislocations and devastation of Roman conquest. In striking contrast to Bavli Gittin's beauty tales, which celebrate the idealized aesthetics of the heroic body, Lamentations Rabbah portrays the fall of Jerusalem as a diminishment of Jewish flesh. Where Jerusalem of old was once home to radiant beauties, the post-conquest body is a different specimen. Catastrophe has rendered the people unrecognizable. But such change is not only occasion for lament. As it recounts the two tales of Rabbi Tsadok, I maintain,

41. D. Boyarin, *Unheroic Conduct.*

42. The practice of cutting off hair in mourning appears in Isaiah 22:12, Jeremiah 16:6, Ezekiel 7:18, Amos 8:10, and Job 1:20, though certain practices of ritual hair-cutting are prohibited in Leviticus 21:5 and Deuteronomy 14:1–2.

Lamentations Rabbah affords the disabled body a potent capacity for corporeal resistance. Its stories illuminate the subversive potential of dissident flesh. But what of Bavli Gittin? In the next chapter, I push beyond the Bavli's fantasy of enduring beauty and trace the trail of blood and other fleshy residues of the body that run through Bavli Gittin's narratives, showing how they serve as a counter-discourse to the idealized notion of enduring Jewish beauty. Through provocative collisions between flesh and stone, Bavli Gittin charts another tale of lament and loss through the porous materiality of blood, earth, and bone. The land itself holds the last remains of these disposable bodies, this flesh that otherwise fails to meet the conditions for exemplary remembrance.

5

Materiality and Memory

BODY, BLOOD, AND LAND IN RABBINIC TALES
OF DEATH AND DISMEMBERMENT

RABBINIC ACCOUNTS OF destruction imagine the Jewish body as a potent site for representing catastrophe. In the last chapter, I argued that rabbinic narratives often use tropes of bodily diminishment and corporeal loss to make visceral the violence of conquest. Destruction, these sources suggest, transforms Jewish flesh so profoundly that it becomes unrecognizable. But it is not only the human body that is changed by catastrophe. In this chapter, I show how these narratives imagine a profound relationship between land and flesh, so that the land comes to mirror the estrangement and unrecognizability of the conquered body. In many ancient Jewish sources, the land itself is reshaped by disaster. Consider the writings of the first-century Jewish historian Josephus, as he describes the desolation of Jerusalem:

> The Romans . . . stripped the whole area in a circle round the town to a distance of ten miles. The countryside, like the city, was a pitiful sight; for where once there had been a lovely vista of woods and parks, there was now nothing but desert and the stumps of trees. No one—not even a foreigner—who had seen the old Judea and the glorious suburbs of the city, and now set eyes on her present desolation, could have helped sighing and groaning at so terrible a change; for every trace of beauty had been blotted out by war, and nobody who had known it in the past and came upon it suddenly would have recognized the place: he would have gone on looking for the city when he was already in it.[1]

---

1. Flavius Josephus, *Jewish War* 6.1.1 (Chapter and section numbers align with Whiston

Josephus's description of Jerusalem emphasizes the tremendous change that has come upon city and countryside alike. War has blotted out Jerusalem's beauty, recasting her sightlines and altering her vistas. Memory plays a critical role in Josephus's narration of sight. When Josephus describes the affective experience of beholding ruined Jerusalem, he focuses on those who have *seen* and *known* Judea of old. Memory is both a requirement for grief and a goad to heartbreak. The stumps of felled trees stand as a visible scar, a tangible reminder of past glory now laid waste. But memory has become an uncertain guide, an unstable map. Josephus narrates destruction through images of unrecognizability and estrangement. To stand in the midst of the ruins is to experience a geographic dislocation, to find oneself in a place that cannot be recognized. Anyone who knew Jerusalem of old "would have gone on looking for the city," even though they were already there.

In Bavli Gittin's narratives of the destruction of Judea, disorientation and memory also serve as powerful literary loci for grappling with the tangible consequences that Roman conquest has for the land.[2] Consider the Bavli's account of the devastation of King's Mountain, a site rabbinic tradition associates with the failed Bar Kokhba revolt in 135 CE.[3] Traditions about the majesty of King's Mountain appear in Palestinian and Babylonian rabbinic sources, both of which underscore its vast population and many cities. Bavli Gittin 57a recounts:

> King Yannai had sixty myriad cities on King's Mountain—
>   and each had a population that equaled
>   those who went out from Egypt [during the Exodus],
>   save for three cities that had double as many
>   as those who went out from Egypt.

By recounting the great multitudes on the mountain, such traditions emphasize the magnitude of the destruction and underscore the tremendous casualties it

---

edition). Translation follows *The Jewish War: Revised Edition*, trans. G. A. Williamson (New York: Penguin Books, 1981), 337.

2. I begin with Josephus because his account of seeing the ruined city gives potent expression to the way that conquest alters the land, provoking an experience of estrangement and disorientation. While similar notions surface also in certain rabbinic sources, I do not intend to suggest that rabbinic sources are consciously adopting or reworking Josephus. On the relationship between rabbinic sources and Josephus's accounts of destruction, see Zellentin, "Jerusalem Fell after Betar."

3. The identity of the mountain is uncertain. On the various identifications in ancient sources, see Judah Nadich, *Legends of the Rabbis: Jewish Legends of the Second Commonwealth* (Northvale, NJ: Jason Aronson, 1994), 387.

caused. Through a comparison that links the cities' population with the people of the Exodus, the tradition situates the disaster as an inversion of God's redemptive power, turning back the thrust of Israel's liberation. As the Bavli's passage unfolds, the erstwhile glory of King's Mountain becomes a source of contention, as the Palestinian sage ʿUlla contests the elaborate description of its pre-destruction splendor:

> ʿUlla said: I myself saw that place
>> and it could not hold even sixty myriad reeds!
> A certain Sadducee said to Rabbi Ḥanina: You tell lies!
> [Rabbi Ḥanina] said to him:
>> There it is written, "A glorious land" (*erets tsvi*).
>> Just as the skin of a deer (*tsvi*) cannot contain its flesh
>>> [for the hide shrinks, once the animal has been killed],
>>> so too the Land of Israel.
>> When it is inhabited, it expands.
>> But when it has no inhabitants, it shrinks.

The argument between ʿUlla and the sages highlights the conflict between what the rabbis remember and what they can see. Drawing upon his own "eyewitness" testimony, ʿUlla protests that King's Mountain could hardly hold such vast numbers. ʿUlla's skepticism is echoed by a Sadducee, who disputes with Rabbi Ḥanina and accuses him of telling lies. In response, Rabbi Ḥanina counters by explaining that the land itself has shrunk. Drawing on the dual meaning of the word *tsvi*, Rabbi Ḥanina likens the land of Israel to a deer. Elsewhere in rabbinic literature, this midrashic comparison has positive and beneficent implications. In Bavli Ketubot 112a, for example, rabbinic evocation of Israel as the "land of the deer" (*erets tsvi*) underscores the miraculous bounty of the land; just as the skin of a deer cannot contain its flesh, so the land of Israel cannot contain its produce. In the Gittin tradition, by contrast, the association of the land with the skin of a deer takes on a more sinister connotation: just as the hide of a deer contracts after it has been skinned, so too the land shrinks when it has few inhabitants. Rabbinic recollection attempts to preserve a now-obliterated reality, while ʿUlla's counter-testimony reveals that the mountain's former glory is scarcely imaginable to the post-destruction gaze.

The shrinking of King's Mountain underscores a profound responsivity between people and place: depopulation brings about a contraction in physical geography. In Rabbi Ḥanina's telling, destruction has permanently altered not just the face of the land, but its very features. The physical capacity of the land has been transformed; it is shrunken and diminished. Where Josephus' account of the denuded countryside with its stumps of felled trees laments the visible marks that war and conquest leave upon the face of the land, rabbinic traditions about the shrinking of King's Mountain suggest that the land has undergone an even deeper change, a transformation in the very materiality of the mountain. With the loss of its people, the place has become small and insignificant. Such narrations of transformed terrain and altered place serve as an important registrar for marking the meaning of catastrophe. They make concrete the enduring nature of disaster, lodging loss in the very land itself. The claim that the land itself has been materially diminished inscribes the permanence of destruction on the physical geography of Judea.

While Bavli Gittin's account of King's Mountain gives striking expression to the notion that the land of Israel was indelibly changed by conquest, the rest of Bavli Gittin's account of the destruction places relatively little emphasis on the land's desolation. In Lamentations Rabbah, several midrashim evoke the pathos of destruction through a tremendous outpouring of grief: Jerusalem weeps and God cries with her, the angels and the people of Israel alike shed tears.[4] When Jerusalem mourns, the midrash asserts, "heaven and earth weep with her, the sun and the moon, the stars in their constellations, the mountains and the hills."[5] Lamentations Rabbah and Yerushalmi Ta'anit both describe destruction and exile as an experience that affects not only the Jews, but also the more-than-human world: the birds of the air have fled, the animals are gone from the land. Even the fish have gone into exile, traveling through the great deep (*tehom*) to accompany Israel to Babylonia.[6] By contrast, Bavli Gittin's narratives give less attention to the lamentation of the land or its nonhuman creatures. Unlike the Palestinian texts, Bavli Gittin's account of destruction rarely personifies the land. It does not tell how the hills and mountains weep. Instead, it lingers on the pathos

---

4. On the significance of lamentation and its connection with the material body, particularly a female or feminized male body, see Galit Hasan-Rokem, "Bodies Performing in Ruins: The Lamenting Mother in Ancient Jewish Texts," in *Lament in Jewish Thought: Philosophical, Theological and Literary Perspectives*, ed. Ilit Ferber and Paula Schwebel (Berlin: Walter De Gruyter, 2014), 33–63.

5. Lamentations Rabbah, Buber edition 1:1 (30b); Soncino edition 1:23. The text that appears in the Buber edition is more expansive, making mention of the weeping of the sun and the moon, as well as the weeping of the constellations. Both versions preserve the "earthy" laments of the mountains and the hills.

6. Yerushalmi Ta'anit 4:5, 25a–b; Lamentations Rabbah Petiḥta 34. In the Yerushalmi, this passage underscores not only the diminishment of the land of Israel after conquest, but also God's intention to bring the best of the land to Babylonia in order to prepare it for the exiles. A similar tradition appears in Bavli Shabbat 145b, though the Bavli's passage serves instead to emphasize the preeminence of Babylonia over Palestine.

of human flesh, using the land to underscore the visible signs of *human* grief. The land becomes a site that calls attention to the blood and tears of women and men whose bodies bear the visceral imprint of conquest.

But Bavli Gittin's account of destruction, I argue, is not indifferent to the land. The Bavli's portrayal of destruction is rife with what feminist materialist theorist Stacy Alaimo calls "transcorporeality," literary images that emphasize "the interconnections, interchanges, and transits between human bodies and nonhuman natures."[7] In Bavli Gittin's accounts of catastrophe, brutalized bodies bleed over into the soil, run into the rivers, and seep into the sea. Flesh leaves its trace upon the rocks. The remains of the slain become a material part of the landscape. As a contemporary environmental theorist, Alaimo's attention to transcorporeality aims to disrupt a particularly modern notion that posits the human as separate from and sovereign over a dull and disembodied nature. Attending to the transcorporeal dimensions of rabbinic narrative, I suggest, can illuminate important dimensions of rabbinic discourse—not because the rabbis participate in the modern fantasy that human bodies can be neatly cordoned off from their environments, but precisely because rabbinic narrations frequently blur the boundaries between human bodies and the rest of the material world. Bavli Gittin's transcorporeal imagery creates a memory of place haunted by the corporeal. The rocks and rivers of Judea bear the blood and viscera of murdered thousands, retaining some physical trace of the nameless dead. Destruction is a human crisis, but it is a crisis that bleeds and seeps into the land itself.

In this chapter, I argue that Bavli Gittin's images of intermingled body and soil are marked with anxious instability: subject to erasure by the land itself, even as the text aims to anchor memory in place. Though Bavli Gittin strives to mark and memorialize Jewish blood sinking into the dirt and the sea, the tangible remains of Jewish death are all too easily washed away, rendered ephemeral. In the narratives that follow, I parse Bavli Gittin's portrayal of death in the land, paying particular attention to the way the flesh and fluids of the human body mingle with the rocks and the rivers, the soil and the sea. I argue that these portrayals of seeping and bleeding in the land are intimately intertwined with broader questions of defeat and survival: how a death is remembered and how it is erased, what passage the body leaves and where memory is lodged. Examining Bavli Gittin's account of the defeat of Betar, this chapter shows how Bavli Gittin uses the material imprint of blood to endow the land with moral agency, to invest the land with presence that survives death. But I caution against the tendency

---

7. Alaimo, *Bodily Natures*, 2.

to frame these tales in terms of resistance and resilience.[8] I linger deliberately with stories that speak of slaughter, that tell of body parts and blood seeping into Judea's soil and stones. These passages, I argue, constitute an important counter-discourse to Bavli Gittin's celebration of the heroic body, which I discussed in an earlier chapter. Alongside those tales of spectacular Jewish survivals and heroic acts of resistance, Bavli Gittin chronicles the fate of the defeated body, the body overrun by Roman conquest. Through transcorporeal imagery that emphasizes the blurred boundaries between blood, flesh, river, and soil, Bavli Gittin fashions body and land alike as victimized by Roman incursion, marked and maimed by Roman dominance. The land harbors the material remains of the dead, as the fluids of the human body mingle with the physicality of place. Unlike the tales of beautiful captives I examined in chapter 3, which celebrate the singular identity of the heroic subject, Bavli Gittin's account of the fall of Betar preserves few details of the self. The land becomes a graveyard for the nameless, for those remembered only as part of a multitude, for those whose bodies have come entirely undone.

Blood and Bone in the Land: Probing the Material Traces of Conquest in Bavli Gittin

Natural symbolism plays a powerful role in Bavli Gittin's account of the fall of Betar, the third and final catastrophe that concludes its chronicle of the devastation of Judea. A fortress associated with the failed Bar Kokhba revolt, Betar is remembered through vivid naturalistic imagery. Trees, rocks, rivers, stone, and soil play a significant part in Bavli Gittin's account of catastrophe. Similar elements appear also in Palestinian narratives of destruction; in this, the Bavli's tales are not unique. By recounting disaster in ways that underscore the close relation between human flesh and material place, these rabbinic texts lodge disaster in the physicality of the land itself. Consider the beginning of this section of text, Bavli Gittin 57a:

> Betar was destroyed on account of the shaft of a litter.
> It was the custom when a boy was born to plant a cedar

---

8. Ilana Szobel has critiqued the tendency for Israeli and American interpreters to frame narratives of trauma or woundedness primarily in terms of recovery, and I am indebted to her for an early conversation about this work that helped me articulate the importance of focusing on victimhood and counter-redemptive narrative. See Szobel, *Poetics of Trauma*. Seth Schwartz, in his retrospective response to critics of *Imperialism and Jewish Society*, has also discussed scholarly resistance to the claim that the Jews who survived successive Roman assaults "simply exhausted their capacity to resist," an argument that he believes has faced challenges in part due to its "apparent antiromanticism." Schwartz, "Was There a 'Common Judaism,'" 16.

and when a girl was born to plant an acacia tree,
    and when they were wed,
    they cut off branches and made a bridal canopy from them.
One day, the daughter of Caesar was passing through.
The shaft of her litter broke,
    so [the Romans] cut from a cedar and brought [the branches] to her.
[The Jews] fell upon them and beat them.
[The Romans] went and told Caesar: "The Jews are rebelling against you!"
    and he came against them.

This passage portrays the Jewish revolt as an impassioned, spontaneous response to Roman soldiers' desecration of a Jewish wedding custom, which the soldiers mistook for evidence of a widespread rebellion. I will take up the political dimension of these stories in the next chapter. At present, I focus on the natural symbolism embedded within the Bavli's account, which uses the "cut branches" to signal the disruptions of Roman presence. In this passage, the Romans inadvertently incite Jewish violence when they cut branches from a certain cedar tree, which had been designated for use in the marriage ritual of a local Jewish youth. That the Romans are ignorant of this custom is hardly surprising; the intentional use of specific tree branches to create a marriage canopy is nowhere else attested as a Jewish wedding tradition.[9] Yet the symbolic significance of the custom is easy to parse: the trees, planted at the time of the children's birth, are intended to mirror the intertwined lives of the couple as they come together in marriage to create a new home. The ritual invests the human pair with the fortunes of their trees, using the branches to symbolize their now-intermingled lives. The cut branches— taken from the tree by the wrong hands, for the wrong purpose—reveal the bitter imprint of Roman conquest.[10] The symbolism evokes the potent gender politics of colonial presence: the Romans strip the branches from the man's tree in order to bolster the fortunes of an elite Roman woman, thereby denying them to his Jewish wife. Roman presence in the land shatters the symbolic harmony

9. Though the practice Bavli Gittin describes does not correspond to any known Jewish marriage customs, the use of tree imagery to connote blessing is common in rabbinic texts. Tree imagery also makes frequent positive appearance in Zoroastrian religious sources, and tree branches have a prominent role in Zoroastrian liturgy and ritual. The *barsom*, a bundle of sacred twigs frequently cut from the pomegranate tree, is used both in daily liturgical prayer and in other religious rituals. M. F. Kanga, "Barsom," *Encyclopædia Iranica*, vol. 3, no. 8 (1988), 825–827, http://www.iranicaonline.org/articles/barsom-av.

10. On the negative symbolism of tree cutting in early Jewish sources, see Marianne Luijken Gevirtz, "Abram's Dream in the Genesis Apocryphon [1Qap Gen]: Its Motifs and Their Function," *Maarav 8* (1993): 229–243.

of the marriage canopy. Caesar's daughter displaces the Jewish wife; her passage through the land unsettles the creation of the Jewish family and unmakes the Jewish future.

In the passages that follow, Bavli Gittin uses images of Jewish blood mingling with the soil and waterways of Judea to make Roman power visceral and manifest. Bavli Gittin 57a continues:

> *In blazing anger, He has cut down all the horns* (qeren) *of Israel.*
>   (Lamentations 2:3)
> Rabbi Zeira said that Rabbi Abahu said that Rabbi Yoḥanan said:[11]
> These are the eighty [thousand][12] horns of war (*qarnei milḥamah*)
>   that entered the fortress of Betar at the time it was conquered,
>   and they killed men, women, and children there
>   until blood streamed into the great sea.
> Perhaps you will say that the sea was near? It was farther than a mile!

> It was taught:
> Rabbi Eliezer the Great said,
>   "There are two rivers in the valley of Yadaim.
>   One flows this way and the other flows that way,
>   and the sages measured
>   that there were two parts water to one part blood."
> It was taught in a baraita:
>   For seven years, idolaters cut their grapes from the blood of Israel,
>   without needing manure.

In these passages, the physical geography of the land becomes an anchor for the Bavli's recollection of slaughter. The sages describe how the rivers run red and blood streams into the sea, how the land itself is fertilized as it absorbs the life-blood of the fallen. The motif of "waters running red" is a common literary trope,

---

11. There is some variation in the attribution of this teaching. The translation follows the version that appears in Munich 95 and the Vilna edition. Vatican 140, JTS Rab. 1718.93–100, and JTS Rab. 1729.64–67 attribute the teaching to Rabbi Ḥiyya bar Abba. The Vatican 130 and the Soncino printing attribute the tradition to Rabbi Zeira, Rabbi Abba, and Rabbi Yoḥanan.

12. The Vilna edition has been amended in order to add the word thousand, in order to align this passage with a parallel Palestinian tradition. Yerushalmi Taʿanit 4:8, 68d reads: "Rabbi Yoḥanan said: Eighty thousand pairs of horn blowers (*toqei-qarnot*) besieged Betar, and each and every one was in command of many soldiers." As part of its exegesis of Genesis 27:22, Lamentations Rabbah 2:4 asserts that Hadrian killed eighty thousand myriads in Betar and that eighty thousand horn blowers besieged Betar. The word "thousand" does not appear in any Bavli Gittin manuscripts.

a poet's flourish, a phrase whose very familiarity leaches its power. Yet rabbinic discourse refuses to let these motifs collapse into the well-worn lexicon of lament. Bavli Gittin's passage does not simply paint with the broad brushstrokes of memory; it insists on measuring the distance, quantifying the ratio of blood to water. Measurement works to overcome the hyperbole of metaphor, to insist on the quantifiable physicality of catastrophe. The apparatus of measurement preserves the enormity of the loss, seeking to confirm the sages' accounts of disaster in the face of incredulity or disbelief. Through dint of the rabbinic evidentiary gaze, Bavli Gittin records the composition of the waterways, the span of distance from fortress to sea, the number of years the Romans harvested the fruit of slaughter. Against the doubts of their imagined interlocutors, the rabbis measure and mark the trail that blood leaves, as it runs through the contours of place.

The rabbinic lament for blood in the land unfolds within an interpretive frame that once again underscores Bavli Gittin's tendency to avoid the theological trope of divine anger and Jewish sin. Our passage begins with a striking interpretation of Lamentations 2:3, one that displays Bavli Gittin's characteristic tendency to minimize God's direct responsibility for the destruction of Judea. In its original biblical context, Lamentations 2:3 describes how God "cuts down" a wayward people, hewing the "horns" of Israel. In the Hebrew Bible, the horns serve as a vivid symbol of the glory and strength of Israel.[13] The biblical motif of the "hewn horns" has a clear message: God has "cut off" Israel's glory.[14] The Bavli's tradition, by contrast, moves in a different direction. Reversing the thrust of the biblical verse, Bavli Gittin's exegesis shields God, shifting the plain sense of the verse so that God is no longer the one who brings about Israel's execution. The horns no longer represent the people of Israel, slain by God in response to divine anger. Instead, they serve as signs of Roman military strength, a testament to the

---

13. The notion that Jews have horns has a long and notorious history within anti-Jewish discourse, beginning with what Ziva Amishai-Maisels argues is Jerome's "purposeful mistranslation" of Exodus 34:29; this trope has often served to associate Moses and the Jews with the demonic. Yet the biblical conception of the horn as a sign of glory also has a robust afterlife. Lamentations Rabbah 2:6 portrays horns as a symbol of Israel's radiance; the Patriarchs, Moses, the priests, the Levites, and the entire people of Israel are variously imagined as being endowed with horns. In early Byzantine art, a horn often signals the anointing of a prophet; here too the wicked have physical horns that are "cut off" to signal the loss of their power. Ziva Amishai-Maisels, "Demonization of the 'Other' in the Visual Arts," in *Demonizing the Other: Antisemitism, Racism, and Xenophobia*, ed. Robert S. Wistrich (New York: Routledge, 1999), 44–72. See also Ruth Mellinkoff, *The Horned Moses in Medieval Art and Thought* (Berkeley: University of California Press, 1970).

14. This reading is intensified in the Palestinian midrash tradition. Lamentations Rabbah 2:6 uses the biblical verse to assert that God, in great anger, has stripped splendor and dignity from Israel and given these "horns" of power and majesty to the nations.

vast number of soldiers who assault the fortress of Betar. In a blatant act of rein-
terpretation, Bavli Gittin rereads the verse so that Rome—not God—becomes
the agent of Israel's slaughter. With their myriad horns of war, the Roman legions
breach the fortress and conquer it, slaying the men, women, and children of
Betar. The Bavli's account gives no theological explanation for the disaster; it
avoids any hint of Jewish culpability for catastrophe. Divine violence has no part
in the Bavli's interpretation. In Bavli Gittin's telling, God has been almost entirely
eclipsed from the scene.

What shall we make of this silence? It is difficult, of course, to claim conclu-
sive significance for the gaps and absences within rabbinic narrative. The rabbis
who told and retold these traditions may have expected their listeners to embed
these stories within a familiar theological frame. They may have recounted these
tales in a milieu where God's role in disaster was so obvious as to go unspoken. Yet
I wish to sketch a different possibility, for I find in Bavli Gittin's narrative choices
a striking and recurring aversion to read destruction through the lens of divine
anger and collective wrongdoing. Particularly when read in comparison with parallel Palestinian traditions, Bavli Gittin repeatedly avoids the claim that catastrophe is a consequence of Jewish sin. By muting these familiar tropes, Bavli Gittin
opens up narrative space to imagine differently the theological consequences of
crisis, to reconfigure God's role in national loss and catastrophe. Though God's
capacity for violence is central to the biblical verse, the Bavli's God does not bring
about Jewish military defeat. It is Roman anger that blazes at Betar, at the cost of
Jewish blood.

That blood lingers in the land, leaving visceral traces of Jewish bodies in the
rivers and fields of Judea. In Bavli Gittin's telling, the mingling of water, soil, and
flesh becomes a form of memory-making, an assertion that loss leaves its own
tracks in the land. But the land, it seems, remains an uneasy partner in this act of
remembrance. Bavli Gittin's tradition maintains that Jewish blood lends a perverse fertility to the fields of Judea. For seven years, it asserts, the Romans needed
no other medium to fertilize their crops. That the Bavli builds this image around
the grape harvest only accentuates its symbolic force. Central both to Jewish
religiosity and to foreign ritual, grapes occupy a fraught borderland between the
permissible and the idolatrous.[15] Jewish defeat opens a space for the Romans to
harvest the grapes and subvert the richness of Judea's fields for nefarious purpose.
The vivid transcorporeal imagery of Bavli Gittin's account heightens the stakes of

---

15. On the tensions surrounding grapes and wine in rabbinic thought and the importance
that refraining from gentile wine has for the construction of rabbinic identity, see Jordan
Rosenblum, *Food and Identity in Early Rabbinic Judaism* (New York: Cambridge University
Press, 2010), 81–83.

this subversion, revealing the cannibalism of the colonial project. Jewish blood nourishes the fields and flows into the fruit. The bodies of those slaughtered at Betar become nothing more than dung, making fertile the lands now claimed by the conqueror. The Roman harvest is more than a plunder of produce. It is a seizure of Jewish flesh, an act of devouring.

The renewed fertility of the land thus stands as an inverse reflection of the material impact of conquest, a reminder of the impartiality of earth. Where Josephus's ruined Jerusalem mirrors Jewish defeat, Bavli Gittin's productive fields become an inverted sign of catastrophe. The fruitfulness of the land simultaneously reveals and belies Jewish loss. A similar ambiguity persists in the images of rivers that run with Jewish blood. At first glance, the rivers appear as an unequivocal sign of catastrophe. But here too, the natural world proves to be an unreliable marker, an ambivalent means of monumentalizing loss. Will the blood register for more than a moment, before its physical presence is carried into the sea? How long will the rivers preserve the trace of massacre? Water cannot retain a stable afterimage of death. That Rabbi Eliezer the Great must *recall* the blood measured by the sages, that he cannot see for himself the memory of the dead made visible in the valley of Yadaim, acknowledges the transience of the transcorporeal. The material marks of death run through the rivers and into the sea, but their visible presence dissolves in the blink of an eye. Memory is both manifest and ephemeral, coming undone even as it is being made.

Encountering the Unquiet Dead: Zechariah and the Bubbling Blood

This tension between the rabbis' insistence on the land as a site of remembrance and their recognition of the land as an ephemeral site of erasure becomes manifest in Bavli Gittin's account of Zechariah and the bubbling blood, a tale that counters the notion that Jewish blood is absorbed by the land without a trace. This story circulated widely in late antiquity and the Middle Ages, with diverse versions attested in rabbinic, Syriac, Arabic, and Ethiopic literature.[16] In Bavli Gittin's version of the Zechariah tale, the Babylonian general Nebuzaradan enters the temple precinct during the first

16. For a discussion of the textual history of the various versions of this narrative in late antiquity, see Richard Kalmin, *Migrating Tales: The Talmud's Narratives and Their Historical Context* (Berkeley: University of California Press, 2014), 130. See also Richard Kalmin, "Zechariah and the Bubbling Blood: An Ancient Tradition in Jewish, Christian, and Muslim Literature," in *Jews, Christians and Zoroastrians: Religious Dynamics in a Sasanian Context*, ed. Geoffrey Herman (Piscataway: Gorgias Press, 2014), 203–251.

conquest of Jerusalem and sees blood bubbling up. Troubled and disturbed by the sight, he eventually secures a confession from the Israelites that this is the unquiet blood of a Jewish prophet, slain by the Jews because he prophesied against them.[17] Nebuzaradan seeks to appease the prophet and quiet the blood by killing more Jews upon the site of the original murder. While the Babylonian general eventually succeeds in stilling the blood, his quest leads him to fear the price that will be exacted for his own murderous deeds, and he ultimately repents and converts to Judaism. In this chapter, I focus particularly on the way that the Zechariah legend operates within the larger narrative context of Bavli Gittin. I argue that the central motif of the bubbling blood amplifies—and attempts to ameliorate—tensions over materiality and memory within Bavli Gittin's account of death and disaster.

Immediately after Rabbi Eliezer's teaching about the measure of blood in the river of Yadaim, Bavli Gittin 57b recounts the tale of Zechariah:

> Rabbi Ḥiyya bar Avin said in the name of Rabbi Yehoshua ben Qorḥa:
> A certain elder[18] told me:
> In this valley, Nebuzaradan, chief of the guards,
>   killed two hundred and eleven myriads,
> and in Jerusalem, he killed ninety-four myriads upon a single stone—
>   and their blood went forth until it touched the blood of Zechariah
>   to fulfill that which is written: *Blood touches blood* (Hosea 4:2)
> He saw the blood of Zechariah, that it was boiling and rising.
> He said, "What is this?"
> The Israelites said to him,

---

17. The identification of Zechariah is difficult. Many interpreters have suggested that the narrative refers to Zechariah ben Yehoiada (2 Chronicles 24:17–22), but as Betsy Halpern Amaru observes, that figure is never clearly identified as a prophet. In the New Testament, Matthew 23:35 has Jesus accuse the people of killing "Zechariah son of Berechiah, whom you slew between the shrine and the altar," in a passage that imagines judgment coming forth from the righteous blood of all those who were slain. See discussion in Betsy Halpern Amaru, "The Killing of the Prophets: Unraveling a Midrash," *Hebrew Union College Annual* 53 (1983): 153–180 and Sheldon Blank, "The Death of Zechariah in Rabbinic Literature," *Hebrew Union College Annual* 12–13 (1937–1938): 327–346. Richard Kalmin suggests that the quest for a specific historical figure may in fact be a mistake; "perhaps the significance of the name Zechariah—"God Remembers" or "Remember God"—provides a key to the significance of the name in these diverse contexts." Kalmin, *Migrating Tales*, 136.

18. The Vilna edition and the Soncino printing read, "a certain elder among the people of Jerusalem."

"This is the blood of sacrifices whose blood was poured out."[19]
He brought blood, but it was not the same.[20]
Nebuzaradan said to them,
  "If you tell me, well and good.
  If not, I will comb your flesh with iron combs."
They said to him,
  "What can we say to you?
  There was a prophet among us who used to rebuke us,[21]
    and we rose against him and killed him
    and for many years, his blood has not come to rest."
He said, "I will appease him."
He brought the Great Sanhedrin and the Lesser Sanhedrin
  and he killed them over [the blood],
  but it did not rest.
He brought young men and young women and he killed them over it,
  but it did not rest.[22]
He brought children from the schoolhouse and he killed them over it,
  but it did not rest.
He said to him, "Zechariah, Zechariah!
  I have destroyed the good ones among your people.
  Will it satisfy you if I destroy them all?"
When he said this to him, it rested.
At that very moment, he felt remorse.
He said,
  "If this is so for a single soul,[23]

19. JTS Rab. 1718.93–100 and JTS Rab. 1729.64–67 state, "This is the blood of the offerings that we offered before the Holy One, blessed be He." The phrasing parallels the version found in Bavli Sanhedrin 96b.

20. This line is absent in Munich 95. Bavli Sanhedrin 96b states, "He brought the blood of bulls and deer. He compared it, but it was not the same. He brought all kinds of blood. He compared it, but it was not the same."

21. The Vilna edition and the Soncino printing add, "with the words of heaven." JTS Rab. 1718.93–100 and JTS Rab. 1729.64–67 state, "who used to prophesy against us regarding all that we did, and we killed him on Yom Kippur, which fell upon Shabbat."

22. The killing of the young men and young women is absent in Munich 95 and Vatican 140. JTS Rab. 1718.93–100 and JTS Rab. 1729.64–67 include this phrase and also add that Nebuzaradan brings eighty thousand young priests and kills them over the blood, but it does not rest. The killing of the priests appears also in Bavli Sanhedrin 96b, as well as in the Palestinian sources.

23. I have translated this phrase according to the Vatican 130, St. Petersburg RNL Erv. I 187, JTS Rab. 1718.93–100, JTS Rab. 1729.64–67, and the Vilna, which read: "If this is so for a

then what of this man, who has slain so many souls?

How much the more so!"

He fled, caused a rift in his house, and converted.

The Rabbis taught: Naʿaman was a resident foreigner,

Nebuzaradan was a righteous convert,[24]

the grandsons of Haman learned Torah in B'nei Baraq,

descendants of the grandsons of Sisera learned Torah in Jerusalem,[25]

and descendants of the grandsons of Sennaḥrib learned Torah in Rome.

Who were they? Shemaya and Avtalion.

In keeping with a recurring motif that shapes Bavli Gittin's account of the destruction of Betar, the Zechariah narrative is shaped by imagery that blurs the line between flesh, blood, and land. As in the previous tales we have examined, slaughter and death mark a material collapse of the boundaries between people and place. When the Babylonian general Nebuzaradan enters Jerusalem, he slaughters ninety-four myriads "on a single stone"—and their blood drains into the porous rock until, in an evocative alchemical gesture, it "touches the blood of Zechariah" and causes it to rise up, boiling. Through this narrative, Bavli Gittin counters the ephemeral nature of the earth's capacity to

---

single soul," (*U'mah ʿal nefesh 'aḥat*). The Munich 95 and the Soncino printing read: "If this is so for those [who kill] a single soul," (*U'mah hem ʿal nefesh 'aḥat*). Vatican 140 states, "If it is thus for those who have not killed but a single soul," (*Halalu shelo hargu 'ela nefesh 'aḥat*). The parallel narrative in Bavli Sanhedrin 96b also has significant variations in the text. The Vilna edition reads, "If this is so for those who destroy a single soul, what will become of this man?" Kalmin offers the following translation from the Yad Harav Herzog I manuscript: "If Israel, who violated the law by killing one person [was punished severely,] I, who destroyed so many Jews, how much the more so [will I be punished severely?] Kalmin, *Migrating Tales*, 148–149.

24. St. Petersburg RNL Erv. I 187, JTS Rab. 1718.93–100, and JTS Rab. 1729.64–67 stop the list of converts with Nebuzaradan, concluding instead with an exegesis of Ezekiel 24:8, a verse that Babylonian and Palestinian sources alike use to anchor the blood-sin associated with Zechariah's murder. They assert that the blood of the slain prophet was left uncovered on a bare rock. According to Leviticus 17:13, any Israelite or resident foreigner who hunts and kills a kosher animal must "pour out its blood and cover it with earth." Zechariah's blood, by contrast, was not poured upon the ground, nor covered with earth. The rabbis marshal Ezekiel 24:7–8 to assert that the blood of the slain prophet was left uncovered on a bare rock, which provides an etiological explanation for the ravages of destruction; the people's impious treatment of the prophet's blood arouses God's fury and causes God to take vengeance on the people. Palestinian versions of the Zechariah narrative incorporate this exegesis more prominently, as an introduction to the account of the bubbling blood. Bavli Gittin's version references it more obliquely, in a coda to the narrative in which the rabbis exegete several verses associated with the destruction.

25. The Vatican 140 manuscript identifies the descendant of Sisera's grandson as Rabbi Ishmael ben Elisha.

remember with a tale of spilled blood that endures unquiet for generations. This tale challenges the central tension of the previous tales: the recognition that the land, sea, and soil do not retain the memory of the dead. The earth all too easily swallows slaughter; the signs of human catastrophe refuse to endure.

The Zechariah tale counters the transience of these tangible marks of catastrophe by fashioning the unquiet blood of the prophet into a presence that lingers in the land. Against the image of land that absorbs and neutralizes blood, Bavli Gittin's Zechariah tale posits a land that remembers, that feels for one particular death, one beloved man. In the story, the bubbling blood becomes a visible sign of murder—a material residue of the Israelites' slaughter of their prophet. The tale begins with a strikingly ironic gesture: the Babylonian general Nebuzaradan, who has just slaughtered thousands of Israelites during his seizure of Jerusalem is, we learn, distressed by the sight of uncanny blood. While death and slaughter cause him no apparent moral concern, blood that refuses to rest demands investigation and remedy. In response to Nebuzaradan's questions, the Israelites endeavor to hide their culpability for the unquiet blood. They try to convince the general that the bubbling blood is properly sacrificial, using the sanctified blood of the animal as a shield for human depravity. But the general sees through the ruse. In a gesture that recalls a variation of rabbinic "blood science," Nebuzaradan performs a comparative analysis of sacrificial and bubbling blood to assay that the substance is not the same.[26] Threatened with torture—facing the flaying of their own flesh, the exposure of their own blood—the Israelites confess to Zechariah's murder. In response, the Babylonian general appoints himself to the task of appeasing the slain prophet. The exchange, I suggest, is meant to shock. This is a man who has murdered myriads, who extracted the truth of Zechariah's demise only by threatening the integrity of Jewish flesh. How shall he propitiate the prophet, save by more death?

Nebuzaradan's efforts lead to a mounting death toll: members of the Sanhedrin, young men and young women, even children. But while Nebuzaradan's actions surely underscore the brutality of conquest, the incongruous image of the Babylonian general slaying thousands to appease a Jewish prophet and still the signs of Jewish sin also casts a critical light on a conventional principle of prophetic theology: that Israel's God will use the nations as a means of chastising

---

26. On the attention the rabbis pay to the diagnosis of blood and its connection to the construction of rabbinic authority, see Charlotte E. Fonrobert, *Menstrual Purity: Rabbinic and Christian Reconstructions of Biblical Gender* (Stanford: Stanford University Press, 2000) and Shai Secunda, "Talmudic Text and Iranian Context: On the Development of Two Talmudic Narratives," *AJS Review* 33, no. 1 (2009): 45–69.

Israel for its sins.[27] In this narrative, Nebuzaradan becomes a veritable embodiment of this theological claim, attempting to exact sufficient death and devastation to satisfy the wronged prophet who stands in for a wronged and vengeful
God. His final question to Zechariah—"I have destroyed the good ones among
your people. Will it satisfy you if I destroy them all?"—exposes the brutality
espoused by such a theology. Nebuzaradan's question reveals the apparent limit-
lessness of the prophet's desire for vengeance, his demand for atonement through
human sacrifice. The dialogue seems to invite the reader to imagine a similar
question posed before God, to grapple with the question of whether God's own
appeasement might similarly demand Jewish blood.

Nebuzaradan's critique is effective; it stills the bubbling blood. Though the
Babylonian general's poignant question allows the prophet ease, it stirs disquiet
in Nebuzaradan's own heart. The encounter with Zechariah's strange, enduring
blood forces the conqueror to grapple with the consequences of the deaths he
himself has caused. At the close of the tale, Nebuzaradan acknowledges the terrible consequences exacted from the Israelites for their slaughter of a single soul
and becomes aware of the recompense that surely awaits him. This moment of
internal dialogue is rich with theological assumptions. The general portrays the
first destruction of Jerusalem—his own handiwork—as the consequence of the
Jews' murder of Zechariah. But rather than treat the slaughter as a sign that
God no longer feels concern for the wayward people, Nebuzaradan assumes
that his own slaughter of the Jews will also have far-reaching consequences. He
too will be called to account for the deaths that he has caused. Just as the blood
of God's slain prophet lingers in the land and must be appeased, Nebuzaradan
assumes that the blood of God's other children will *also* cry out for justice. In
response, Nebuzaradan flees and becomes a righteous covert. The Bavli's telling
concludes by nestling the Babylonian general among an illustrious line of erstwhile enemies who have become part of Israel, whose descendants now learn
and teach Torah.

The motif of Nebuzaradan's conversion appears only in the Bavli; it does not
appear in the Palestinian versions of this tale. The conversion, I argue, underscores the theological and ethical claims of the Bavli: that even the notorious
Nebuzaradan comes to recognize the significance of each individual life and
fears the consequences of his brutal murder of myriad Jews. The import of
Nebuzaradan's conversion is particularly apparent when Bavli Gittin's telling

---

27. For an analysis of a critical engagement with "chastisement" theology in another rabbinic narrative, see my discussion of Bavli Ta'anit 23a's portrayal of Ḥoni the Circle Maker in
relation to the biblical prophet Habakkuk. Belser, *Power, Ethics, and Ecology in Jewish Late
Antiquity*, 160.

of the Zechariah tale is compared to the parallel Palestinian traditions. The Palestinian versions of this tale also conclude with a dramatic "conversion"—but not of Nebuzaradan! Instead, the Palestinian telling dramatizes the stirring conversion of God, from a posture of strict justice toward an embrace of mercy and compassion. [28] Consider the final portion of the story, as it appears in Yerushalmi Ta῾anit 4:7, 69a–b:

> At that moment, Nebuzaradan rebuked Zechariah.
> He said to him,
>   "Do you want me to destroy your entire nation on your account?"
> At that moment, the Holy Blessed One was filled with compassion.
> He said, "If this one, who is flesh and blood and cruel,
>   is filled with compassion for my children,
>   what of Me, about whom it is written:
>   *For the Lord your God is a compassionate God;*
>   *He will not fail you nor will He destroy you.*
>   *He will not forget the covenant with your fathers.* (Deuteronomy 4:31)
>   How much the more so should I have compassion?"
> At that moment, God motioned to the blood
>   and it was swallowed in its place.

In this dramatic concluding scene, the Yerushalmi imagines God "learning" the virtue of compassion from the cruel conqueror. When Nebuzaradan protests Zechariah's unquenchable demand for blood, his stance causes God to recall the covenant and be filled with compassion for the people.[29] If even the brutal conqueror quails before the slaughter of an entire people, God reasons, surely the Holy One must also have mercy?

The Yerushalmi's emphasis on God's embrace of mercy over strict judgment accords with the larger thrust of the Palestinian versions of this tale, which emphasize the problem of Jewish sin. Earlier in the narrative, in a section not quoted here, the Yerushalmi recounts "the seven sins" Israel committed when they murdered Zechariah. Not only are they culpable for innocent bloodshed, for the killing of a priest who was a prophet and a judge, they also defiled the

---

28. In a recent analysis of the development of the Zechariah legend, Richard Kalmin argues that the Zechariah story likely originated as a Christian tale, meant to dramatize God's rejection of the Israelites after they murdered the prophet in the Jerusalem Temple. As Kalmin has demonstrated, the Palestinian rabbinic versions of the tale underscore God's enduring compassion for Israel. Kalmin, *Migrating Tales*, 130.

29. Kalmin, *Migrating Tales*, 138.

courtyard of the temple and committed the crime on the Day of Atonement, which itself fell upon the sabbath. By piling transgression upon transgression, the Yerushalmi heightens the Israelites' moral fault.[30] Against such a backdrop, the Yerushalmi concludes with a dramatic evocation of divine mercy. God recalls the covenant and the promise not to destroy the people. When the Yerushalmi's God quiets Zechariah's blood, it functions as a visible sign that God will no longer hold the people's transgressions against them—that God will not continue to demand Jewish blood.

Much has been made of the absence of God from the Bavli's account— perhaps too much, as Richard Kalmin has suggested.[31] Like Kalmin, I agree that the Bavli's version imagines God as an operative presence behind the scenes of the narrative. The difference between these tales, I maintain, lies not in the presence or absence of God, but in the way that God is portrayed. In the Palestinian narratives, God appears first as an arbiter of justice, then as a source of compassion. The Palestinian tale is primarily invested in chronicling the transformation of the divine heart, in narrating this profound shift from judgment to mercy. Bavli Gittin's tale, by contrast, gives us no stirring tale of divine conversion. While it inarguably regards the slaying of Zechariah as a serious transgression, it does not dwell upon Israelite sin. It places no special emphasis on the link between culpability and catastrophe. Bavli Gittin's telling neither highlights the ravages of divine justice, nor dramatizes the return of divine compassion. Instead of showcasing the transformation of God's character, Bavli Gittin's narrative emphasizes the moral conversion of the Babylonian general, who is moved to repentance through his encounter with Zechariah's unquiet blood.

What is it about the blood that provokes such profound moral change? While Nebuzaradan's curiosity is first compelled by the uncanny sight of roiling, bubbling blood, his remorse emerges as he confronts the implacable brutality required to bring it to rest. When Nebuzaradan calls out to Zechariah after he kills the elders, the youths, and the children, when he confronts the prophet and asks him whether he desires still more death, might we not hear an intimation that the hardened Babylonian general has himself become sick of slaughter? When Nebuzaradan reasons that "this" is the price exacted for the murder of even a single soul, Bavli Gittin surely means us to imagine the

---

30. Blank suggests that rabbinic tellers were troubled by the fact that their punishment does not seem to have been commensurate with the crime; thus the addition of the "seven sins" motif, which serves to amplify the nature of the Israelites' transgressions. Blank, "Death of Zechariah," 341.

31. Kalmin, "Zechariah and the Bubbling Blood," 230.

warlord tallying the consequences of his own deeds and quailing at the cost. Yet to see the Babylonian general's conversion as motivated solely by fear misses, I suggest, an important dimension of his character. Nebuzaradan's repentance is spurred by the sight of Zechariah's unquiet blood, by his efforts to still the haunting that lingers after murder has been done. It is the sight of the blood—its tangible persistence, its material presence—that grounds Nebuzaradan's newfound conviction that God will not forget the death of even a single soul. The blood that lingers in the land marks, for Nebuzaradan, the import of a single death.

While the persistence of the bubbling blood stands as a provocative sign that brings about Nebuzaradan's conversion, it carries, perhaps, a different resonance within the larger context of Bavli Gittin's account of catastrophe. Amidst the murdered bodies that seem to pass from this earth without a trace, the myriad deaths that have been swallowed by the ground and sea without apparent protest, the bubbling blood marks the conservation of Zechariah's memory. Zechariah's unquiet blood stands as an uncanny insistence that murder cannot be easily erased, that the land itself remembers and retains the life-blood of each individual soul. In this textual moment, the land becomes a symbolic registrar of the sacred, a material matrix of remembrance. But the reader is left wondering whether the promise of remembrance is, in fact, as democratic as Nebuzaradan assumes. Is Zechariah not an exceptional figure, a man whose potent blood marks him as different from the unnamed thousands, the dead that litter the fields of Judea, whose blood has been swallowed without a trace?

In Bavli Gittin's telling, Zechariah's bubbling blood initiates a transcorporeal fantasy of remembrance. In this encounter between porous earth and human viscera, the earth itself resists the easy absorption of Zechariah's life-force. The blood-sign emerges in the unquiet relations between hallowed land and human flesh. Might we read the bubbling blood as a mark of the land's own resistance, its refusal to swallow and neutralize blood that is unsanctified, blood that has been improperly spilled? The blood itself is a potent force, a catalyst. Zechariah's unquiet blood has the power to capture Nebuzaradan's attention, to stay the brutality of conquest. The blood forces the conqueror to confront the consequences of death, spurring the general to protest its futility, its waste. The blood leads him to remorse and repentance, bringing about an ethical transformation that culminates in ethno-religious conversion. As a living prophet, Zechariah had no power over the Israelites. In life, he failed to bring about the moral conversion of his own people. But where the living man falters, the blood proves capable. Even in death—especially in death—the prophet Zechariah has the power to call injustice to account.

Reading for Resistance: Slaughter and Martyrdom in Lamentations Rabbah

While Bavli Gittin's Zechariah tale underscores the striking potency of the murdered prophet through the uncanny presence of his bubbling blood, the notion that spilled blood can serve as a catalyst for the moral transformation of the conqueror rests uneasily amidst the Bavli's chronicle of dead and dismembered bodies. If Zechariah's tale affords the slain prophet some manner of posthumous victory, it is—as Nebuzaradan himself suggests—a victory that comes at brutal, bitter cost. Having parsed the Zechariah tale as an expression of the transcorporeal relations that blur the boundaries between blood and land, I wish to turn now to the question of how we read the dissolution of body and earth, how we linger with loss, how we tarry with ruin. Thus far, I have offered a reading of Zechariah's story that has highlighted the agency and potency of the corpus, a reading that has aimed to redeem the violated body of the prophet at the center of the tale. Rather than leave this reading as my final word on the Zechariah legend, let me also critique my own interpretive inclination. Even as I highlight the moments of resistance that emerge in Bavli Gittin's narratives, I note how such a hermeneutical frame aligns with my own interests as a reader. Amidst the hauntings of history and memory, amidst graveyards ancient and modern, I want to both acknowledge and resist the urgency of this desire to wrest some form of survival from the textual remains of brutalized bodies, to craft an account of catastrophe that showcases the resilience of spirit and flesh.

While certain aspects of Bavli Gittin's narrative affirm the resilience of the captive body and the conquered land, reading Bavli Gittin's stories solely in these terms risks eclipsing an important dimension of the text: its exhaustion, its acknowledgment of defeat, its recognition of the futility of protest. To articulate this point, I turn to a well-known martyrological tale, the story of the mother of seven sons, which appears in strikingly different form in both Lamentations Rabbah and Bavli Gittin.[32] Lamentations Rabbah 1:16 recounts the suffering of Miriam bat Tanḥum, whose seven sons were killed at the command of the Roman emperor for refusing to bow before an idol. Lamentations Rabbah 1:16 begins as follows:

---

32. The well-known tale of the mother and her seven sons, first attested in Jewish sources in 2 Maccabees 7, makes frequent appearance in rabbinic literature: Bavli Gittin 57b, Lamentations Rabbah 1:16 ed. Buber, Lamentations Rabbah 1:50 ed. Soncino, and Pesikta Rabbati 43:4. My treatment of the Lamentations Rabbah tradition follows the Buber edition. See Robert Doran, "The Martyr: A Synoptic View of the Mother and Her Seven Sons," in *Ideal Figures in Ancient Judaism: Profiles and Paradigms*, ed. John J. Collins and George W. E. Nickelsburg (Chico: Scholars Press, 1980), 189–221.

This is the story of Miriam bat Tanḥum,
    who was taken captive with her seven sons.
What did the ruler do to her?
He imprisoned each one alone.
He brought out the first and said to him,
    "Bow before the image, just as your brothers have bowed."
He said, "Heaven forbid!
    My brothers did not bow, and I also will not bow."
He said to him, "Why?"
"For it is written in the Torah, *'I am the Lord your God.'*" (Exodus 20:2)
He commanded that he be killed.

The midrash continues by enumerating the identical scenario for five more sons. It relates the deaths of Miriam's six sons using stylized, patterned language, varying only the verses that the children use to affirm their fidelity to Israel's God. But when it arrives at the seventh son, the midrash unfolds a more elaborate dialogue:

He brought the seventh, who was the youngest among them.
He said to him,
    "Bow before the image, just as your brothers have bowed."
He said, "Heaven forbid!
    My brothers did not bow, and I also will not bow."
He said to him, "Why?"
"Because we have already sworn to our God
    that we will not exchange Him out of fear,
        as it is written, *You have affirmed the Lord today* (Deuteronomy 26:17)
And just as we have sworn to Him,
    so He has sworn to us
    that He will not exchange us for another nation,
    And God has affirmed today." (Deuteronomy 26:18)
He said to him,
    "If so, then I will throw this ring before the image.
    You bring it to me, so that they will see and say,
        'He has fulfilled the command of Caesar.'"
He said to him, "Woe to you, Caesar.
    Should I fear you, a king of flesh and blood,
    and not the king of kings, the Holy Blessed One,
        who is God of all the world?"

When the boy refuses to bow, Caesar offers to throw down his ring before the idol so that the boy can pick it up and thereby appear to accede to the ruler's command. The boy refuses. He reaffirms his loyalty to the Eternal, disdaining Caesar's power as transient and ephemeral. In contrast with the King of Kings, to whom our Jew offers allegiance, the Roman emperor is mere "flesh and blood." For all his temporal might, he too is a mortal man, subject to the vicissitudes of time and death. The scene culminates in an extensive theological debate between the Roman emperor and the Jewish boy, a dialogue rife with charged contestations over power, capacity, and disability:

[Caesar] said to him, "Is there a God in the world?"
He said to him,
    "Woe to you, Caesar. Do you see a world without an owner?"
He said to him, "But does your God have a mouth?"
He said to him,
    "Of your idolatry, it is written,
        They have mouths, but do not speak. (Psalms 115:5)
    But of our God, it is written,
        By the word of God, the heavens were made." (Psalms 33:6)

He said to him, "But does your God have eyes?"
He said to him,
    "Of your idolatry, it is written,
        They have eyes, but do not see. (Psalms 115:5)
    But of our God, it is written,
        The eyes of the Lord your God are always upon it." (Deuteronomy 11:12)

He said to him, "But does your God have ears?"
He said to him,
    "Of your idolatry, it is written,
        They have ears, but do not hear. (Psalms 115:6)
    But of our God, it is written,
        God listened and heard." (Malachai 3:16)

He said to him, "But does your God have a nose?"
He said to him,
    "Of your idolatry, it is written,
        They have a nose, but do not smell. (Psalms 115:6)
    But of our God it is written,
        God smelled the pleasing scent." (Genesis 8:21)

He said to him, "But does your God have hands?"
He said to him,
   "Of your idolatry, it is written,
      They have hands, but do not feel (Psalms 115:7)
   But of our God, it is written,
      My hand has founded the earth. " (Isaiah 48:13)

He said to him, "But does your God have feet?"
He said to him,
   "Of your idolatry, it is written,
      They have feet, but do not walk. (Psalms 115:7)
   But of our God, it is written,
      'He will stand with his feet, on that day' (Zechariah 14:4)
      and *'He will stand and tread upon the high places of the earth.'*"
         (Micah 1:3)

He said to him, "But does your God have a throat?"
He said to him,
   "Of your idolatry, it is written,
      They do not make sound with their throats. (Psalms 115:7)
   But of our God, it is written,
      His mouth is sweet; all of him is lovely. " (Song of Songs 5:16)

[Caesar] said,
   "If He has all of these qualities,
      why does he not save you from my hand
      as He saved Hananiah, Mishael, and Azariah?"
He said to him,
   "Hanaiah, Mishael, and Azariah were worthy
      and fell into the hands of a worthy king.
   But we are guilty (*ḥayyvim*),
      and we have fallen into the hand of a guilty and merciless king
      so that he may exact our blood.
   For the Holy Blessed One has many bears and many leopards
      with which to strike us,
   but the Holy Blessed One has given us into your hand
      only in order to exact our blood from your hand in the future."
Immediately, [Caesar] commanded that he be killed.

In this passage, the midrash stages a lengthy exchange between the two figures, in which Caesar names attributes of the human body and asks whether Israel's

God possesses them. While readers steeped in the expectations of medieval Maimonidean philosophy might expect a sharp denial of such anthropomorphic accounts of the divine presence, our midrash revels in recounting the corporeality of Israel's God. Reworking a familiar biblical polemic that the gods of the nations "have eyes, but cannot see,"[33] Lamentations Rabbah 1:16 emphasizes the corporeal capacity of Israel's God, in contrast to the disempowered deities of the nations. The distinction the midrash crafts between God and idolatry is not between form and formlessness, but between agency and incapacity. Disability serves as a rhetorical tool to illustrate the powerlessness of idols. Their inability to see, hear, walk, talk, and save stands in sharp contrast to the ultimate capacity of Israel's God, whose eyes survey the entire world, whose ears listen and hear, whose hands have laid the foundation of the earth, whose feet stand firm upon the Mount of Olives, and whose speech comes forth from His mouth.[34] The power and agency of Israel's God is rooted in a decidedly corporeal presence, in the physicality of flesh.

Yet having enumerated such an effusive recitation of God's potent capacity, the divine defense leaves itself open to the emperor's final question: "If your God has all these attributes, why does He not save you from my hand?" With this question, Caesar attempts to reaffirm the power of mortal human flesh, to reinscribe the visceral strength of the murderer over the apparently more intangible physicality of the divine body. The Jew's heroic speech summons forth a divine presence endowed with (super)human power. Caesar's words put this specter to the test: Can this God rescue its passionate defender from the imperial grip? Or will God's powerlessness be revealed, the slack divine hand broadcast through the death of this child? Our young Jew refuses the terms of Caesar's question. It is not God's power to save that is in question, he avers. Instead, it is his own righteousness that stands suspect. Lamentations Rabbah defuses the question of divine disability by having the captive boy affirm the justice of his own death. Caesar can kill the Jews only because they are condemned by divine decree. But the logic of the midrash does not rely solely on the trope of Jewish culpability. In defending the (in)action of his God, the boy argues that it is Caesar's own character that makes a critical difference. When God saved three Jews from Nebuchadnezzar's flaming furnace, it is not only the Jews

---

33. Psalms 135:15–17 and Psalms 115:4–7.

34. Such rhetoric is a significant dimension of biblical depictions of idolatry. See Rebecca Raphael, *Biblical Corpora: Representations of Disability in Hebrew Biblical Literature* (New York: T&T Clark, 2008), 40–49; Saul Olyan, "The Ascription of Physical Disability as a Stigmatizing Strategy in Biblical Iconic Polemics," *Journal of Hebrew Scriptures* 9, no. 14 (2009): 2–15.

who were worthy; the boy claims that God saved them from "a worthy king." Caesar's cruelty, by contrast, leads God to deliver the children to him only so that he can be repaid by God in turn. Unlike Nebuzaradan, whose encounter with Jewish blood ultimately provokes moral transformation, Caesar is locked within his own cruelty.

Theologically, Lamentations Rabbah 1:16 offers a complex, unresolved assessment of suffering and divine justice. By fashioning the seventh child into the figure of the willing sacrifice who accepts his own slaughter with trust and faith, the midrash releases its God from the doubter's noose. It rescues divine capability, at the cost of Jewish blood. Yet through the figure of Miriam bat Tanḥum, the grieving mother, the tale also underscores the pathos of the sons' deaths, the tragedy of their loss. Lamentations Rabbah 1:16 concludes:

His mother said, "By your life, Caesar!
    Give me my son, so that I may kiss him and embrace him."
They gave her her son,
    and she uncovered her breast and let him suckle milk
    in order to fulfill that which is written:
        Honey and milk are under your tongue. (Song of Songs 4:11)
His mother said to him, "By your life, Caesar!
    Give my neck and his neck to the sword at once!"
He said to her, "Heaven forbid! I will not do it,
    for it is written in your Torah,
        You shall not kill the baby bird and its mother on the same day.
        (Leviticus 22:28)
The young boy said to him,
    "Wicked one! Have you observed the entire Torah,
        except for this verse?"
Immediately, they took him from her to kill him.

His mother said to him,
    "My son, do not fear.
    You are going to be near your brothers,
        and you will be within the bosom of Abraham our father.
    Say to him, in my name:
        'You built one altar and did not sacrifice your son,
        but I built seven altars and I sacrificed my sons upon them.'
    And more:
        'For you it was a test, for me it was in earnest.'
Once he was killed, the sages estimated the age of the boy
    and found that he was six and a half years and two hours old.

At that very hour, all the nations of the world cried out and said:
"What is it with their God?
He does all this to them and they are slain for His sake at all times."
They said that after several days,
that woman climbed up to the roof and threw herself down and died.
They said of her:
A joyful mother of children. (Psalms 113:9)
And the Holy Spirit says:
For these things I weep. (Lamentations 1:16)

The final portion of the midrash sanctifies Miriam's sacrifice through the discourse of martyrdom. The midrash offers its readers a startling scene of bodily intimacy between mother and son, as Miriam not only kisses and hugs her child, but also offers him milk from her breast.[35] When Caesar reiterates his command to kill the child, Miriam comforts her son by imagining him exchanging her breast for Abraham's bosom; his martyrdom is portrayed as a seamless transition from the corporeal embrace of the mother to the shelter of the father's breast. But where Abraham's ordeal was a "mere test," Miriam lauds her own embodied sacrifice: she has built seven altars, one for each murdered child.

But if these dimensions of the midrash valorize the piety of the martyr, the narrative also excoriates the violence of empire and raises haunting questions about divine justice. Miriam begs Caesar to kill her together with the last child, but Caesar refuses, citing Leviticus 22:28, a verse that forbids a person from killing both mother and offspring on the same day. For rabbinic audiences, the verse has a barbed edge; it frequently serves as a means of critiquing divine justice.[36] In our midrash, Caesar uses the verse in an attempt to sanctify his actions, to present himself as a "moral man." Yet the seventh son makes mock of Caesar's attempt to veil his barbarism in the illusion of piety, refusing his attempt to sanctify brutality. The nations of the world cry out, questioning God's justice, even as they affirm

---

35. On the significance of nursing and suckling as a symbol for the transmission of Jewish identity, see Ellen Davina Haskell, *Suckling at My Mother's Breasts: The Image of a Nursing God in Jewish Mysticism* (Albany: State University of New York Press, 2012), 15–34. On the evocative parallels between this text and the well-known early Christian martyrdom of Perpetua, see Hasan-Roken, *Web of Life*, 123.

36. The use of the mother bird motif to pose the question of theodicy and divine justice appears prominently in the Palestinian Talmud's account of Elisha ben Abuya, which appears in Yerushalmi Ḥagigah 2:1, 77b–c. See Jeffrey Rubenstein, *Talmudic Stories*, 91; Alon Goshen-Gottstein, *The Sinner and the Amnesiac: The Rabbinic Invention of Elisha ben Abuya and Eleazar ben Arach* (Stanford: Stanford University Press, 2000).

the Jews' loyalty to their God. In the final scene, as Miriam throws herself from the roof and dies, the midrash closes with two verses that juxtapose the "joy" of the mother with the pathos of the Holy Spirit. Highlighting the ironic contradiction, Hasan-Rokem observes, "The mourning of the human mother is now the fate of the Holy Spirit, whereas the mother is now joyful to play the heroine in a plot of martyrdom."[37] Through this martyological discourse, the midrash simultaneously laments Jewish suffering and uses it as an occasion to celebrate the heroic fidelity of Jewish commitment to God. For all Caesar's capacity to marshal the murderous architecture of the Roman state, he cannot silence Jewish protest. While the narrative makes plain the brute force of imperial dominance, it draws the reader to recognize the frailty of that power, its inability to exhaust the martyr's resistance.

Dismembering Resistance: Remembrance, Resignation, and the Exhaustion of Protest

As Lamentations Rabbah 1:16 illustrates, the discourse of martyrdom interprets death as the ultimate act of resistance to an unjust regime. The martyrological frame invests the dead and dying body with paradoxical power. It affirms the capacity of a brutalized body to refuse the logic of its torturers, to claim power even as life is extinguished.[38] Fashioned in this heroic mode, the martyr holds the power to deny the oppressor the ultimate victory. Yet such narrative choices are not ethically neutral. As an interpretive frame, the martyrological narrative aims to recuperate death, to overcome trauma and wounding. The expectation that the dead must die well, that victims must not only endure but also surmount their own violation, exacts a heavy burden. Though such a frame grants the individual a striking agency in the midst of crisis, it also asserts that something salvific must rise from the field of catastrophe and defeat. Such a discourse risks memorializing only those victims whose lives and deaths can be pressed into a heroic narrative, whose memories can be cast in the service of resistance.

---

37. Hasan-Roken, *Web of Life*, 119.

38. While the literature on martyrdom is immense, I acknowledge two scholars whose works are particularly influential for my own thinking. Elizabeth Castelli argues that Christian narratives of martyrdom function ideologically by overturning the dynamics of domination that frame the arrest, captivity, trial, and execution of the martyrs—often by contesting and inverting Roman concepts of law, piety, sacrifice, decorum, and spectacle. Castelli, *Martyrdom and Memory*. Daniel Boyarin has emphasized the significance of martyrdom in rabbinic narrative as an important mode of resistance to imperial power. Boyarin, *Dying for God*.

While some of Bavli Gittin's narratives push toward transformation, redemption, and resistance, other narratives go nowhere but the grave. They bear witness to endings, to rupture, to ruin that is not rebuilt or reconstituted. Consider another martyr tale, to which the Bavli turns after recounting the Zechariah story. Glossing Psalm 44:23, "It is for Your sake that we are slain all day long, that we are regarded as sheep to be slaughtered," Bavli Gittin recounts the story of four hundred young men and women who are taken captive by Rome and drown themselves in the sea. In this narrative, discussed in detail an earlier chapter, the young captives affirm that God will retrieve them from the depths. But God's promised "retrieval" is entirely eschatological; the flesh itself finds no rescue from the waters. By choosing death, the captives escape sexual enslavement; they refuse the fate their captors have decreed. In both scholarly and popular discourse, such choices are frequently celebrated as acts of resistance, as heroic reclamations of agency amidst the stark circumstances of captivity. Yet the interpretive frame of the "martyr victorious" risks overwriting other dimensions of ancient accounts of death and dying. Even as I recognize this strand within the Bavli's own narrative discourse, I wish also to read these tales against the grain, to push back against the romantic image of the martyr as the one who claims death as a victory, snatched from the brute force of the conquerors' grasp.

Let us turn to Bavli Gittin's account of the mother and her seven sons, a version whose minimalist prose is striking in comparison with the more elaborate, expansive account that appears in Lamentations Rabbah. Beginning with the same verse that that concludes the tale of the four hundred captives, Bavli Gittin 57b recounts:

> *It is for Your sake that we are slain all day long,*
> *   that we are regarded as sheep to be slaughtered.* (Psalms 44:23)
> Rav Yehudah said: This refers to the woman and her seven sons,
>   who were brought before Caesar.
> They brought the first and said to him, "Worship idolatry."
>   He said to them, "It is written in the Torah:
>   *I am the Lord your God.*" (Exodus 20:2)
> They led him away and killed him.
> They brought the next and said to him, "Worship idolatry."
>   He said to them, "It is written in the Torah:
>   *You shall have no other Gods before Me.*" (Exodus 20:3)
> They led him away and killed him.
> They brought the next and said to him, "Worship idolatry."
>   He said to them, "It is written in the Torah:
>   *One who sacrifices to another God shall be destroyed.*" (Exodus 22:19)
> They led him away and killed him.

They brought the next and said to him, "Worship idolatry."

He said to them, "It is written in the Torah:

Do not bow down to another God." (Exodus 34:14)

They led him away and killed him.

They brought the next and said to him, "Worship idolatry."

He said to them, "It is written in the Torah:

Hear, Israel! The Lord is your God; the Lord is one."

(Deuteronomy 6:4)

They led him away and killed him.

They brought the next and said to him, "Worship idolatry."

He said to them, "It is written in the Torah:

Know this day and lay it upon your heart

that the Lord alone is God in heaven above and on the earth below.

There is no other." (Deuteronomy 4:39)

They led him away and killed him.

They brought the next and said to him, "Worship idolatry."

He said to them, "It is written in the Torah:

You have affirmed . . . and God has affirmed . . .(Deuteronomy
26:17–18)

We have already sworn to the Holy One blessed be He

that we will not pass Him over for another God;

He too has sworn that He will not pass us over for another nation."[39]

Caesar said to him, "I will throw down for you my signet ring.

Bend over and pick it up,

and they will say that you accepted the authority of the king."

He said to him, "Woe to you, Caesar. Woe to you, Caesar.

For if your own honor is so precious to you,

how much more so the honor of the Holy Blessed One!"

---

39. There is considerable variation in the manuscripts, in terms of the verses recited by the children. My translation follows the Vilna edition and the Soncino printing. Exodus 20:2, the verse
that the Vilna and the Soncino attribute to the first child, is frequently absent in the manuscripts.
In Vatican 130, Exodus 20:2 is absent; the first child recites Exodus 20:3, the Vilna's second verse.
This version switches the order of verses three and four and adds a fifth verse, Deuteronomy
4:35. In Munich 95, neither verse 1 nor verse 3 appear; only six children are accounted for. The
first child recites the second verse, the second recites the fourth verse, the third recites the fifth
verse, the fourth recites the sixth, the fifth recites the seventh verse, and the sixth child recites no
verse but exchanges words with Caesar regarding the signet ring. In Vatican 140, the first verse
is skipped and only six children appear; the final child, however, still recites the final verse and
exchanges words with Caesar. In JTS Rab 1718.93–100 and JTS Rab 1729.64–67, the teaching
is attributed to Rav Yehudah in the name of Rav. These manuscripts skip the first verse and add
Deut. 4:35 in the fifth spot. They also enumerate the sons, rather than repeating "and the next."

As they led him away to be killed, his mother said to them,
   "Give him to me and let me kiss him a little!"[40]
She said to him, "My son, go and say to Abraham, your father:
   'You have bound one son upon the altar;
   I have bound seven altars.'"
Then she went up to the roof, threw herself down, and died.
A heavenly voice went forth and said:
   A joyful mother of children . . . (Psalms 113:9)[41]

While both Bavli Gittin and Lamentations Rabbah share the same basic structure and pattern, the Bavli's telling lacks many of the narrative details that invest the midrash with martyrological drama. Lamentations Rabbah focuses narrative attention on the mother. The opening lines assert that this is *her* story, that the tale will turn on what the ruler does to *her*.[42] The midrash amplifies her heroism, highlighting the trials that she endures and the extreme situation in which she finds herself. In her dialogue with Caesar, Miriam bat Tanḥum appears as a strong-willed woman who challenges the Roman emperor and proclaims herself willing to die before her child. By contrast, Bavli Gittin's telling minimizes the mother's role, not even affording her a name. She appears only in the abbreviated final scene, where she calls out for permission to kiss her son before he dies, and sends him forth with the instruction to recount her sacrifice before Abraham. While the Bavli's version preserves the basic structure of the mother's martyrdom, it eschews the narrative elements that freight the midrashic tale with emotional significance.

If the power of Lamentations Rabbah's account turns in part on the pathos of the suffering figures, the force of its martyrological claim emerges primarily in the exchange between Caesar and the seventh son. Echoing a classic martyrological motif, the midrash asserts that though the temporal ruler exercises demonstrable power over the bodies of the captive Jews, he cannot force them to submit to his authority, nor can he force them to acknowledge the legitimacy of his rule.[43] The ring-ruse, which appears in both Bavli Gittin and Lamentations Rabbah, serves

---

40. The mother's words to the guards are absent in the St. Petersburg RNL Evr. I 187 manuscript.

41. The mother's death and the heavenly voice are absent in the Vatican 130 manuscript.

42. Hasan-Rokem, *Web of Life*, 114.

43. In parsing the nature of the ring-ruse, it is worth considering whether the narrative imagines Caesar's offer as a conciliatory gesture, or whether the character of Caesar is imagined as tempting the Jew to illicit action. Candida Moss argues that early Christian martyr narratives often reveal the conflicting understandings of piety (*eusebeia*) among Romans and Christians, noting that Christians emphasized the exclusivity of piety, so that acts of reverence for the

as a key site of Jewish martyrological triumph. The scene aligns the emperor and the Jewish captive in a performance piece, designed to convince nameless onlookers of the Jew's assent to Roman sovereignty. By offering to throw down his signet ring instead of demanding that the final son bow to the idol (or before him, in Bavli Gittin), Caesar forfeits the desire for actual acknowledgement: the semblance of honor will serve. Both versions of our tale use this scene to broadcast Caesar's desperation and articulate the Jew's fidelity to God. Through the Jew's steadfast unwillingness to bend before Caesar, even to save his own life, these stories fashion death as a form of victory over imperial power.[44] But the two tales narrate this death within a strikingly different frame. In Lamentations Rabbah, the ring-ruse initiates an extensive theological dialogue between Caesar and the Jew. Through this complex and elaborate exchange, the midrash both advances a theological claim that Israel's God is triumphant over the powerlessness of the deities of the nations—and that Caesar's capacity to harm the Jews stems not from his own might nor his own righteousness, but is merely a role that God allows him, a role that will ultimately rebound to his own detriment.

Bavli Gittin's narrative, by contrast, is not particularly interested in affirming the power of God, nor even in promising Caesar's comeuppance. As the next chapter will make plain, other stories in Bavli Gittin's sugya do dramatize the eventual downfall of corrupt imperial powers. While such theological claims may be assumed by the redactors of our text, they do not emerge as an explicit theme within this story. Bavli Gittin's account of the mother and seven sons draws its readers toward a different emotional reality. This is a narrative that insists upon laying slaughter upon slaughter, that draws its final moral thrust from the mother's seven-fold loss. We are meant to hear, over and over again, the intertwined refrains: "They brought the next," and then "they led him away and killed him." The narrative gives us no

---

emperor became impious and religiously transgressive. From a Roman perspective, by contrast, "the gestures of deference and articulations of power implied in the discourse of piety were not exclusively religious but encompassed all manner of social and identity-grounded responsibilities." While Moss frames this redefinition of *eusebeia* as exclusively Christian, similar dynamics may also be at play in rabbinic discourses of idolatry. Candida Moss, "Resisting Empire in Early Christian Martyrdom Literature," in *Reactions to Empire: Sacred Texts in their Socio-Political Contexts*, ed. John Anthony Dunne and Dan Batovici (Tübingen: Mohr Siebeck, 2014), 151.

44. In an analysis of Bavli Sanhedrin 74a–75b, Aryeh Cohen has argued that passivity—the act of doing nothing—is an important and often overlooked dimension of martyrological narrative within rabbinic sources. While his analysis rests on a connection between sexual pleasure and idolatry that does not appear in this story, his argument that Bavli Sanhedrin 74a–75b constructs *kiddush haShem* (the sanctification of God's name=martyrdom) as a passive act strikes me as suggestive for reading Bavli Gittin's restrained narration of the seventh's son's posture vis-a-vis Caesar. Aryeh Cohen, "Toward an Erotics of Martyrdom," *Journal of Jewish Thought and Philosophy* 7 (1998): 227–256.

pause, offers no quarter. Death follows death, with each son persisting in his fidelity
to God and Torah. In the repetitive, stylized language of the tale, death becomes
routine. None of the characters acquires a name. Even the seventh son, on whom
Lamentations Rabbah lavishes such detail, stands for but a bare moment before
Caesar's throne. The story reads as a confirmation of brutality, a skeletal coda, a
sketch of a tale so well-known that it barely needs to be told.

Refusing the Redemptive: Lingering with Ruin and Dissolution

In this chapter, I have argued that a recurring strand in Bavli Gittin's story cycle
reveals a discourse that runs counter to the motif of heroic resistance. These narratives call us to linger with catastrophe, to bear witness to endings, to ruptures,
to ruin that is may never be restored. While some of Bavli Gittin's tales celebrate
the resilience of the captive Jew and undercut imperial power and prowess, we
must not let such narratives overwrite other discourses of disaster, of catastrophe. There are stories here that refuse the lure of the redemptive. Bringing such
discourse into focus asks us to read against the heroic grain: to *not* recuperate
a narrative, to *not* overcome the wounded body, to tarry with trauma without
expecting its repair. By highlighting the material remainders war leaves in the
landscape of Judea, Bavli Gittin illuminates the way conquest collapses body into
land, the way imperial might mangles blood and flesh and stone. Such collisions
emerge strikingly in a rabbinic discussion that unfolds just a few lines after the
tale of the mother and seven sons, in Bavli Gittin 57b–58a:

> Rabbah bar bar Ḥanah said that Rabbi Yoḥanan said:
> > Forty *se'ah* of tefillin capsules were found
> > on the heads of those killed at Betar.
> Rabbi Yannai said, in the name of Rabbi Ishmael:
> > Three heaps of forty *se'ah*.
> In a baraita, they taught:
> > Forty heaps of three *se'ah*.
> There is no contradiction here:
> > That was of the head, and this was of the arm.
>
> Rabbi 'Asi said:
> > Four *qav* of children's[45] brains were found upon a single stone.

---

45. The specification "of children" appears in the Munich 95, St. Petersburg RNL Evr. I 187,
Vatican 130, Vatican140, JTS Rab. 1718.93–100 and JTS Rab. 1729.64–67 manuscripts. The
phrase is absent in the Vilna edition and the Soncino printing.

'Ulla said: Nine *qav.*
Rav Kahana said, and some say Shila bar Mari: Where is this written?
> *Daughter of Babylon, you predator—*
> *A blessing upon the one who will repay you in kind*
> *for what you have inflicted upon us.*
> *A blessing upon the one who will seize your babies*
> *and dash them against the rock.* (Psalms 137:8–9)

This passage offers another chilling account of bodies undone in the land, bodies unmade through war and conquest. In this tradition, Bavli Gittin narrates bodily catastrophe through a material artifact of Jewish presence: the tefillin heaped amidst the bones of the dead. Tefillin are personal prayer amulets that contain tiny parchment scrolls with scribed verses from Torah, worn strapped to the arm and upon the forehead. Bavli Gittin recalls the recovery of tefillin amidst the dead of Betar, fashioning the abandoned amulets as a physical, material remnant of Jewish life and loss. The scene our narrative evokes has a striking historical resonance. Archeologists have discovered tefillin at several sites in the Judean desert, including some alongside letters associated with the Bar Kokhba uprising.[46] Though flesh and bone have decayed, the leather capsules with their parchment remain.

In Bavli Gittin's narrative, the abandoned tefillin evoke not only the dismemberment of the human body, but also the violation of the bond between a Jew and God. In the rabbinic imagination, tefillin are a rich symbol of fidelity and obligation. Tefillin evoke a Jewish commitment to divine commandment; the practice serves a veritable enfleshment of Deuteronomy's command to "bind these words as a sign upon your hand." Many ancient Jews treated tefillin as a powerful protective amulet, one aimed not only at preserving the life of the individual, but also the survival of the family and the land itself.[47] Rabbinic texts treat tefillin as a striking symbol of Jewish covenantal loyalty, a material expression of the connection between God and Jew. Bavli Berakhot 6a asserts that God also wears tefillin, a gesture through which the divine body comes to mirror the human.[48]

---

46. Tefillin commonly dated to the Bar Kokhba revolt have been found in three sets of caves in the Judean desert. See J. T. Milik, "Textes littéraires," in *Discoveries in the Judaean Desert*, vol. 2, ed. P. Benoit, J. T. Milik, and R. De Vaux (Oxford: Oxford University Press, 1961), 80–86. Y. Aharoni, "The Expedition to the Judean Desert, 1960, Expedition B," *Israel Exploration Journal* 11 (1961): 22–23. M. Morgenstern and M. Segal, "XHev/SePhylactery," in *Miscellaneous Texts from the Judaean Desert*, edited by James Charlesworth et al. Discoveries in the Judaean Desert Series, vol. 38 (Oxford: Oxford University Press, 2000), 183–191.

47. See Yehudah B. Cohn, *Tangled Up in Text: Tefillin and the Ancient World* (Atlanta: Society for Biblical Literature, 2008).

48. On the tradition that God wears tefillin, see Kimberley Patton, *Religion of the Gods: Ritual, Paradox, and Reflexivity* (New York: Oxford University Press, 2009), 258–262; Arthur Green,

The materiality of tefillin matters. Rabbinic legal thought regards the physical object itself as sacred, including tefillin in the list of items to be saved from fire on Shabbat, even if their rescue violates other laws of sabbath observance.[49] Abandoned tefillin are likewise a source of considerable rabbinic legal concern. Mishnah Eruvin 10:1–2 mandates that a person who finds tefillin has a responsibility to bring them to safety, even on Shabbat. If they are many, bundled together in ways that would make their return a greater violation of Shabbat strictures, one must remain with them until nightfall and then bring them in once Shabbat has ended. In a dangerous place, when a person must balance the sanctity of the tefillin against the risk of their own life, one should cover them before departing.[50] Yet in Bavli Gittin's telling, the tefillin are neither rescued nor reclaimed. Heaped among the dead, they become a material mark of a double dismemberment, a sundering of body and covenant.

In the final lines of this passage, Bavli Gittin turns to an explicit image of human flesh ruined against the rock, as the sages recall the measure of the brain matter found on a single stone. Once again, our passage uses transcorporeal imagery to highlight the material remainder of Jewish presence, figuring slaughter as an act that leaves a physical trace in the land. Our passage ends with the final verses of Psalm 137, words that praise the one who will ultimately exact vengeance on the conquerors—"repaying" the sufferings of the Jewish community in kind, by smashing the infants of the enemy against the rock. The conclusion of this psalm has long troubled modern readers, who have recoiled against its ethical implications, its exultation of revenge, its portrayal of the one who takes vengeance against the children of the enemy as "blessed."[51] For many late antique interpreters, this psalm articulated a striking application of measure-for-measure justice, an affirmation that God would require the brutality of oppressors in

Keter: The Crown of God in Early Jewish Mysticism (Princeton: Princeton University Press, 1997), 53–55.

49. Mishnah Shabbat 16:1.

50. See Cohn, *Tangled Up in Text*, 138.

51. On the ethical challenges that these lines have posed for modern Jewish and Christian interpreters, see David W. Stowe, "History, Memory, and Forgetting in Psalm 137," in *The Bible in the Public Sphere: Its Enduring Influence in American Life*, ed. Mark A. Chancey, Carol Meyers, and Eric M. Meyers (Atlanta: Society of Biblical Literature, 2014), 149–156. Athalya Brenner has argued for a translation of 'ashrei as "praised" or "confirmed," rather than "happy" or "blessed." While such a translation hardly removes the ethical difficulty, it changes the emotional valence of the utterance and no longer depicts the avenger as enjoying the cruelty of revenge. Athalya Brenner, "'On the Rivers of Babylon,' (Psalm 137), or Between Victim and Perpetrator," in *Sanctified Aggression: Legacies of Biblical and Post Biblical Vocabularies of Violence*, ed. Yvonne Sherwood and Jonneke Bekkenkamp (New York: T&T Clark, 2003), 90–91.

kind.[52] While modern commentators have often attempted to soften these verses by contextualizing them in light of ancient Near Eastern warfare or in terms of the satisfaction of divine justice, Athalya Brenner argues that such readings fail to grapple appropriately with "the vehemence of the last stanza, the cruel call of the powerless for revenge against their more powerful neighbors in exile."[53] These verses, Brenner asserts, force readers to confront the brutality of retaliation, the way a desire for vengeance all-too-often shapes the victim into one who is also simultaneously a perpetrator, in fantasy if not in practice.[54] In the next chapter, I probe the way that Bavli Gittin articulates fantasies of revenge and recompense, the way discourses of vengeance intertwine with motifs of triumph and transformation in the rabbinic literary imagination.

Despite the significant voice Bavli Gittin's narrative arc gives to a theology of repayment in kind, Rav Kahana's tradition does not actually articulate a triumphant theology of vengeance. While Bavli Gittin's use of Psalm 137 inarguably evokes certain strains of measure-for-measure justice, reading Rav Kahana's tradition solely through this lens obscures the pathos of the Bavli's discourse. In this passage, Psalm 137 functions not as an exaltation of eventual recompense, but as an anchor for acknowledging the depth of Jewish loss. Consider how the rabbinic deployment of Psalm 137 shifts the temporal frame of these verses. In its biblical context, the final strophe looks forward, prophesying the disaster that will eventually befall now-victorious Babylon, praising the one who will bring down the conquerors and impress upon them a grief that mirrors the Israelites' own. The rabbinic narrative, by contrast, looks backward. Surveying the ruins of a bitterly

---

52. Tracing pre-modern interpretations of Psalm 137, Susan Gillingham argues that there are significant differences between Jewish and Christian readings, with Jews using it to grapple with the material concerns of exile and suffering, while Christian readers more frequently spiritualize the psalm to refer to the "captivity" of the Church. Susan Gillingham, "The Reception of Psalm 137 in Jewish and Christian Traditions," in *Jewish and Christian Approaches to the Psalms: Conflict and Convergence*, ed. Susan Gillingham (New York: Oxford University Press, 2013), 64–82. Jonathan Magonet observes the striking absence of pre-modern Jewish concern regarding the final lines of the psalm, noting that the punishment was seen as fitting "the expectations of a just, measure-for-measure requital at the hands of God." Jonathan Magonet, "Psalm 137: Unlikely Liturgy or Partisan Poem? A Response to Sue Gillingham," in *Jewish and Christian Approaches to the Psalms: Conflict and Convergence*, ed. Susan Gillingham (New York: Oxford University Press, 2013), 83.

53. For an assessment of responses by modern commentators, see Stowe, "History, Memory, and Forgetting," 150; Brenner, "On the Rivers of Babylon," 86.

54. Brenner, "On the Rivers of Babylon," 89. Though she emphasizes that the "dialogic condition of being perpetrator as well as victim is a distinct human condition," Brenner is careful to emphasize the difference between actual and rhetorical violence. She argues that such an assessment is particularly urgent for Christian communities, "whose canonical traditions of kindness and forgiveness stand in stark contrast to historical, religiously motivated praxis against Jews."

remembered past, recalling the brains smashed against the stones of Judea, Rav Kahana attempts to anchor the present tragedy within scripture. While the rabbinic narrative never disavows the Psalmist's evocation of vengeance, this call is not the focal point of its narrative. Instead, the verse serves Rav Kahana's purpose as a different sort of prophecy—a reminder that the Psalmist foresaw the brutality of Roman conquest. [55] Reading the Psalmist's claim that the death of the conqueror's children will repay the empire for what it has inflicted upon its victims, Rav Kahana draws forth an indication that scripture has anticipated even this disaster, that it can encompass even the weight of the children's ruined skulls.

But what becomes of the ruin, the material markers of loss? The image of bone and brain against the rock evokes the symbolism of the tefillin—the leather capsules ruptured, the parchment exposed?—like the skulls of those who once wrapped them around head and hand. Destruction discloses the most intimate material of the self, the inner parts whose exposure signals the utter dissolution of the human person. While Bavli Gittin's earlier images of blood seeping into land and sea grapple with the tension between remembrance and erasure, these later images posit the striking endurance of material markers of loss. The rock does not absorb these bodily residues. The tefillin found at Betar remain as artifacts of slaughter, just as the brain matter of the murdered Jewish children lies preserved for later generations. Like the blood of Zechariah, some remnant of the slain endures in the land. The stone refuses to swallow the bitter remains of this offering. But where the blood of Zechariah serves as a source of potent transformation, turning the murderous general Nebuzaradan away from violence and toward repentance, the last remains of the dismembered children do not ultimately arc toward redemption. They become a scar upon the face of the land, a witness to brutality that leads only to a longing for more slaughter, a thirst for the enemy's pain.

---

55. That Psalm 137 reflects prophetic sight is made even clearer in an earlier passage in Bavli Gittin 57b, which asserts that "God showed to David the destruction of the First Temple and the destruction of the Second," both of which are evoked within the first lines of the psalm. See Kugel, *In Potiphar's House*, 174–175 and Gillingham, "Reception of Psalm 137," 66.

6

Romans Before the Rabbis' God

RABBINIC FANTASIES OF RECOMPENSE, REVENGE,
AND THE TRANSFORMATION OF FLESH

RABBINIC ACCOUNTS OF the destruction of Jerusalem and Judea are a potent
site for articulating fantasies of revenge and recompense. Such fantasies imagine a
world in which the conqueror comes to taste the brutal lash of his own violence,
in which seemingly intractable disparities of power are finally overturned. This
chapter examines how Bavli Gittin narrates encounters between Roman generals
and the rabbis' God, arguing that these tales become sites for grappling with a key
rabbinic eschatological claim: that God will eventually overturn Israel's oppressors. The chapter centers on the lengthy rabbinic tale of Titus's downfall after his
destruction of the temple, in which Titus repeatedly denies divine power and
seems at first to flaunt divine justice, but ultimately dies in agony after God sends
a mosquito to bore for years into his brain. Israel Yuval has argued that this tale
voices a pointed rabbinic polemic against Christianity, a refutation of Christian
supersessionist claims.[1] His reading is surely strengthened by the final scene in
the Bavli's tale, in which Titus's nephew raises his uncle, the seer Balaam, and
Jesus of Nazareth by necromancy and learns their terrible post-mortem fate: to
be scalded by boiling hot semen or excrement in the afterlife.[2] This passage has
its own tragic afterlife. It provoked the ire of medieval churchmen and played
a central role in medieval disputations over the Talmud, in which Jews were
condemned for heresy against their own doctrines. Eventually deleted from the

---

1. Yuval, *Two Nations in Your Womb*, 38–56.

2. Schäfer, *Jesus in the Talmud*, 82–94.

printed version of the Talmud by Christian censors, the rabbinic tale of Jesus's punishment has ushered in a long history of Jewish pain.[3]

Scholars have often sought to use the Titus tale to shed light on Jewish-Christian relations in late antiquity. While certain elements of the tale surely give potent expression to anti-Christian sentiment in the Bavli, I argue that an overemphasis on the "polemical" interpretive frame has flattened a crucial dimension of the text: its emphasis on God's capacity to overturn imperial power. Read within its larger narrative context, the thrust of the Titus tale does not center upon refutation of Christian scripture or Christian conviction. It takes aim at Christian imperium. In this chapter, I argue that the Titus narrative works to undercut the triumphalist assertions of Roman imperial power. The Bavli's text takes on a striking eschatological cast, as it narrates divine victory not only in the streets of Rome but also in the afterlife, where Titus affirms that Israel is God's beloved nation.[4] These rabbinic fantasies are expressed in striking corporeal terms: through images of bodily rupture and physical pain, as well as the humiliation and the degradation of the flesh, the unmaking of the imperial body. The Bavli's Titus tale undercuts the power politics of Roman-Christian authority, asserting that God can and will overturn the seemingly intractable structures of social and political dominance. Through striking images of the body as a porous and permeable space, these narratives challenge the notion of Roman-Christian power as sealed and sovereign—imagining the imperial body as vulnerable to divine incursion, open to divine touch.

Imperial Ignorance: Colonial Power and the Devastation of Judea

To understand Bavli Gittin's portrayal of the relationship between Romans and the God of the Jews, we must return to the question of how Bavli Gittin frames

---

3. On the history of Jewish-Christian disputations in the Middle Ages and the censorship of the Talmud, see Robert Chazan, "The Trial and Condemnation of the Talmud," *Tikvah Center Working Paper* 1 (2011) http://www.law.nyu.edu/sites/default/files/TikvahWorkingPapersArchive/WP1Chazan.pdf; Robert Chazan, "Christian Condemnation, Censorship, and Exploitation of the Talmud," in *Printing the Talmud: From Bomberg to Schottenstein*, ed. Sharon Liberman Mintz and Gabriel M. Goldstein (New York: Yeshiva University Museum, 2005), 53–59; Jeremy Cohen, *Living Letters of the Law: Ideas of the Jew in Medieval Christianity* (Berkeley: University of California Press, 1999), 317–363; Robert Chazan, "The Condemnation of the Talmud Reconsidered, 1239–1249," *Proceedings of the American Academy for Jewish Research* 66 (1988): 11–30; Jeremy Cohen, *The Friars and the Jews: The Evolution of Medieval Anti-Judaism* (Ithaca: Cornell University Press, 1982), 51–76; Judah M. Rosenthal, "The Talmud on Trial: The Disputation of Paris in the Year 1240," *Jewish Quarterly Review* 47 (1956–57): 58–76, 145–169; Chen Merhavia, *Ha-Talmud be-Rei ha-Nazrut* (Jerusalem: Mossad Bialik, 1970).

4. On biblical and rabbinic eschatology, see Jon D. Levenson, *Resurrection and the Restoration of Israel: The Ultimate Victory of the God of Life* (New Haven: Yale University Press, 2006).

the cause of the destruction. In comparison with other rabbinic narratives, I have argued, Bavli Gittin gives voice to a striking account of the reasons for the devastation of Jerusalem and Judea. Where most rabbinic traditions afford substantial weight to the discourse of Jewish sin, Bavli Gittin's narratives give little credence to the idea that Jewish transgression is to blame for catastrophe. Rather than portraying the destruction as a divinely orchestrated response to Jewish communal wrongdoing, Bavli Gittin's account emphasizes the political dimensions of destruction—the way destruction is bound up with imperial power and arrogance, with the violence, hubris, and ignorance of colonial dominance. The narrative opens with a tradition attributed to Rabbi Yoḥanan, which asserts that the three calamities came about through improbable causes. Bavli Gittin 55b begins as follows:

> Rabbi Yoḥanan said: What is it that is written (Proverbs 28:14):
>> *Blessed is the man who is always afraid (mefaḥed),*
>> *but the one who hardens his heart (maqshe libo) falls into misfortune.*
> Jerusalem was destroyed over Qamtsa and Bar Qamtsa.
> Tur Malka was destroyed over a rooster and a hen.
> Betar was destroyed over the shaft of a litter.

The text that follows is divided into three parts, each of which begins by recounting a series of improbable happenings that lead to disaster. All three explanatory tales highlight a moment of Roman error, a moment when Romans inaccurately interpret the meaning of Jewish practice. These small but striking Roman misunderstandings culminate in a mistaken claim that the Jews are in revolt, a claim that leads the Roman emperor to bring military force against the Jews. Compare the initial lines that introduce the destructions of Tur Malka and Betar, both taken from Bavli Gittin 57a:

> Tur Malka was destroyed over a rooster and a hen.
> When they processed out with the bride and the groom,
>> it was the custom to lead a rooster and a hen before them,
>> so as to say: "Be fruitful and multiply as the birds."
> A troop of Roman soldiers passed through and took [the birds] from them,
>> so [the Jews] fell upon [the soldiers] and beat them.
> They went and told Caesar: "The Jews are rebelling against you!"
>> and he came against them...
>
> Betar was destroyed on account of the shaft of a litter.
> It was the custom when a boy was born to plant a cedar
> and when a girl was born to plant an acacia tree,
>> and when they were wed,

they cut off branches and made a bridal canopy from them.
One day, the daughter of Caesar was passing through.
The shaft of her litter broke,
    so [the Romans] cut from a cedar and brought [the branches] to her.
[The Jews] fell upon them and beat them.
[The Romans] went and told Caesar: "The Jews are rebelling against you!"
    and he came against them.

These two passages reveal substantial parallels in structure and language. In each case, the inciting incident occurs when Roman soldiers pass by and, unaware of the significance of a Jewish marriage custom, disrupt the proceedings and spark a violent reaction that precipitates the Roman Empire's brutal response. In each case, Bavli Gittin uses the same formula to introduce the destruction and to attribute it to a particular cause (*'atarnegol utarnegolta hariv Tur Malka/'ashaqa dĕdispaq hariv Betar*). The narratives each introduce a custom (*havei nehigei*) that, while otherwise unknown, is established by the narrator as a significant local marriage practice in that place. Both tales recount how "one day" (*yoma had*), Romans are "passing by" (*hlf*). The details of the Roman presence differ: in the case of Tur Malka, a troop of soldiers seize a rooster and a hen that are instrumental to a local Jewish wedding custom, while in the case of Betar, they cut the branches of a symbolic tree to repair the litter of the emperor's daughter. In each case, the Romans violate Jewish custom and turn a festive occasion into cause for grief. Both accounts conclude with the same tightly narrated chain of events: the Jews react with violence (*nafal 'aleihu mahuneihu*), the Romans report to Caesar that the Jews are rebelling (*'atu 'amru lĕQesar mardu bĕkha Yehudai*), and Caesar attacks (*'ata 'aleihu*).

In both of these tales, imperial conquest is grounded in error, in Roman failures to accurately assess the colonial situation. The crises each turn on a pivotal moment of Roman ignorance and misinterpretation. In the accounts of Tur Malka and Betar, the soldiers desecrate Jewish traditions not through malice, but through ignorance. Not insignificantly, Bavli Gittin narrates two practices whose Jewish origins are unattested outside of this account. Rather than figuring our hapless Roman soldiers as violating a widely recognized custom, an ignorance for which they might more legitimately be held culpable, Bavli Gittin has the troop disrupt a local celebration whose Jewish significance is not broadly known. The soldiers misinterpret both the cause and context of Jewish violence; they mistakenly report that the Jews are rebelling against imperial authority. By figuring Roman military action as a zealous response to an inaccurate report, Bavli Gittin's narratives underscore the perilous position of elite figures. Caesar's tremendous power—and his corresponding dependence on subordinates—leaves him strikingly vulnerable to misinformation.[5] The Roman emperor brings an army to Judea to subdue what he thinks is an insurrection, never realizing that the violence is a spontaneous response to the soldiers' desecration of a Jewish wedding custom.

Bavli Gittin's explanation for the destruction of Jerusalem, which I will discuss in detail in the final chapter, also evokes similar themes. Its account is more elaborate and considerably more complex: Bar Qamtsa, a scorned and shamed Jew who was ejected from a feast, turns traitor and manufactures a situation whereby the rabbis are faced with a pernicious choice: sacrifice a blemished animal and violate the law or refuse the sacrifice and risk imperial ire. When the rabbis refuse to sacrifice, the Roman emperor concludes that they are in revolt—exactly as Bar Qamtsa had planned. In this account, Bavli Gittin frames the Roman mistake as the product of a deliberate ruse, the handiwork of a Jewish traitor. While the import of Bar Qamtsa's maneuverings have rightly attracted considerable scholarly attention, focusing solely on Bar Qamtsa's actions and the rabbis' response obscures the repeated trope of Roman mistake that links these three tales. In this tale too, the Roman emperor destroys Jerusalem on the basis of misinformation, because of a subordinate's false report. Whether deliberately manipulated or simply misled, Roman emperors are three times goaded into an attack that has no cause. In Bavli Gittin's telling, catastrophe is a product of imperial ambition, occasioned by a disastrous combination of Roman power, ignorance, and arrogance.

From a materialist perspective, the misinterpretations that undergird the Roman assault make little difference on the ground. The communities of Jerusalem, Betar, and Tur Malka are just as shattered, their people just as brutalized through Roman mistake as they might have been through a campaign of deliberate conquest. Yet I argue that Bavli Gittin's choice to interpret destruction through the lens of imperial ignorance has significant social and theological implications. Through these tales, Bavli Gittin unbinds the customary correlation between communal sin and catastrophe. In an important analysis of this tale in comparison with other rabbinic explanations for the destruction, David Kramer highlights the way this narrative minimizes God's role in bringing about the

---

5. Reflecting on the relationship between empire and ignorance in nineteenth-century European imperialism, Ann Laura Stoler argues that while the imperial project rests in part on an ardent and encyclopedic quest for knowledge, "one might be equally struck by how much imperial management produced and displayed the opposite: a nervous reticence about what to know" and how much imperial regimes favored "a bracketed know-how, stupefied states of ensured ignorance." Ann Laura Stoler, "Reason Aside: Reflections on Enlightenment and Empire," in *The Oxford Handbook of Postcolonial Studies*, ed. Graham Huggan (New York: Oxford University Press, 2013), 48.

destruction. "There is no sin, as such," he writes, "and therefore no room for pun-ishment."[6] Rather than focusing on God's role in bringing about divine justice, Bavli Gittin's redactors underscore catastrophe's *human* cause. Kraemer makes much of divine absence in this narrative. For Kraemer, Bavli Gittin's account is striking for its emphasis on divine silence, for God's distance from the destruc-tion. Bavli Gittin, he claims, affords God only the slightest of parts. Even God's active role in the punishment of Titus, Kraemer argues, "serves only to empha-size God's withdrawal in the other parts of the narrative."[7] Where Lamentations Rabbah emphasizes God's pathos and punishment in response to Israel's sin, Bavli Gittin offers what Kraemer calls a "remarkably naturalistic explanation" for the destruction.[8]

While Kraemer is right to emphasize the striking difference between Bavli Gittin's account and the prevailing theological responses to catastrophe in Lamentations Rabbah and other rabbinic texts, his framework overlooks an important dimension of the narrative: its political, counter-imperial thrust. Contra Kraemer's claim, I argue that God's presence *is* significant in Bavli Gittin's account. To see God's importance in the narrative, however, we must shift the theological frame. In Bavli Gittin's telling, destruction is neither a calculated act of divine punishment nor a deliberate divine intention. Bavli Gittin's account does not highlight Jewish sin or emphasize God's role as the ultimate architect of Jewish punishment. Instead, Bavli Gittin portrays God as the eventual force that brings down the conqueror, exacting corporeal vengeance on the body of the Roman emperor and other enemies of the Jews. Taking up a classic eschatological trope from the Hebrew Bible, Bavli Gittin's account of the destruction articulates a vivid vision of the divine promise: that God will ultimately overturn the dynam-ics of earthly power and transform the brutalities and injustice of the present age, that God will finally bring Israel's oppressors to heel, and lift up in their place the beloved nation that has suffered so profoundly in the current order.

Hubris and the Horizon of Catastrophe: The Hardened Heart in Bavli Gittin

Bavli Gittin signals this orientation with the opening lines of its narrative, Rabbi Yoḥanan's deployment of Proverbs 28:14, a biblical verse that praises fear as a

---

6. Kraemer, *Responses to Suffering*, 181.

7. Kraemer, *Responses to Suffering*, 182.

8. Kraemer, *Responses to Suffering*, 181.

character virtue and inveighs against the stubbornness and arrogance of those who set themselves against God's will. Consider again the opening lines of Bavli Gittin's account of the destruction, on Bavli Gittin 55b:

> Rabbi Yoḥanan said: What is it that is written (Proverbs 28:14):
> *Blessed is the man who is always afraid* (mefaḥed),
> *but the one who hardens his heart* (maqshe libo) *falls into misfortune.*
> Jerusalem was destroyed over Qamtsa and Bar Qamtsa.
> Ṭur Malka was destroyed over a rooster and a hen.
> Betar was destroyed over the shaft of a litter.

Proverbs 28:14 critiques the moral flaw of "hardening the heart," a biblical idiom used to condemn leaders whose stubborn refusal to submit to God's will results in disaster. In biblical contexts, the motif of the hardened heart is commonly used to portray the downfall of leaders whose actions run counter to the divine will. In the Hebrew Bible, the motif of the hardened heart appears most famously in the Exodus story, in the context of Pharaoh's refusal to release the Israelites from enslavement in Egypt. Because God hardens his heart (*'aqsheh et lev*), Pharaoh rescinds his own promise to let the Israelites go and pursues them, a military action that results in the drowning of his army in the Red Sea.[9] Pharaoh's "hard heart" leads him to rebel against the divine decision to free the Israelites. Narrating the political events that led to the Babylonian conquest of Jerusalem in 586 BCE, 2 Chronicles 36:13 uses a similar phrase to indict King Zedekiah for stubborn refusal to accede to God's design.[10] Zedekiah "hardened his neck and strengthened his heart" (*vayeqesh et 'arepo vaye'ametz et levavvo*); he refused to humble himself before the prophet Jeremiah or to fulfill the oath that he had

---

9. Exodus 7:3. Exodus uses three primary expressions to refer to the heart in this context: stiffening (*vayeḥezaq lev Par'oh*), becoming heavy (*kaved lev Par'oh*), and hardening (*'aqsheh et lev*). The first two expressions are by far the most common; the verb that echoes our Proverbs text appears only twice in this list, and in only one case does Exodus use it to make explicit mention of "hardening the heart." As Nahum Sarna observes, the Exodus narrative includes twenty references to the hardening or stiffening of Pharaoh's heart. Half emphasize Pharaoh's own choice to harden his heart and situate the stiff heart as an essential attribute of Pharaoh's own character, while the remaining half emphasize divine causality: God hardened Pharaoh's heart. Nahum Sarna, *JPS Torah Commentary: Exodus* (Philadelphia: The Jewish Publication Society, 1991), 23.

10. In 597 BCE, Nebuchadnezzar placed Zedekiah on the throne of Judah, but Zedekiah made an alliance with the Egyptians and rebelled against the King of Babylon. Nebuchadnezzar besieged Jerusalem and crushed the rebellion, plundering the temple and initiating the Babylonian exile. J. Maxwell Miller and John H. Hayes, *A History of Ancient Israel and Judah* (Philadelphia: The Westminster Press, 1986), 408–415.

sworn to the Babylonian ruler Nebuchadnezzar, in God's name.[11] In these passages, the biblical narratives reveal a particular form of human hubris, manifest in a leader's stubborn unwillingness to recognize that God's hand shapes the fate of nations and fashions the downfall of kings. Such leaders refuse to accede to God's design, particularly when it results in personal and national misfortune. They set themselves against political reversals and resist what the biblical author marks as the divine (if sometimes deeply unfortunate) course of history.

But what does this phrase mean, in the context of Bavli Gittin's stories? Rabbi Yohanan's appeal to Proverbs 28:14 troubled me from the very outset of this project, and its significance eluded me for most of the time I spent writing this book. I couldn't square the apparent message of the verse—its condemnation of the hard heart—with the rest of the narrative's apparent disengagement from questions of blame and sin. I found it easy to comprehend the rabbinic claim that the destruction of the temple was part of God's design. Destruction, according to this reading, is not a cataclysmic break in the order of things, but rather an event that fulfills part of God's ultimate plan, no matter how inscrutable such plans might appear in the moment. Yet the moral force of the verse is not simply the assertion that catastrophe can be God's will, but a promise that "hardening the heart," rebelling against God's plan, will result in misfortune. That misfortune had come upon the Jews was plain and apparent. But sifting through Bavli Gittin's stories, assessing the complex narrative portrayals of the destruction, I found it difficult to account for the full force of the verse—its indictment of a deliberate refusal to bow before God's will.

In his influential reading of the first portion of Bavli Gittin's narrative, Rubenstein suggests that Proverbs 28:14 is meant to critique the rabbis' refusal to take strong and deliberate action in response to Bar Qamtsa's blemished sacrifice. He reads "hardening the heart" as a refusal to act, as a failure "to take the necessary steps that would save the community from its plight."[12] While I appreciate Rubenstein's broader assessment of Bavli Gittin's critique of the rabbis' failure to exercise bold leadership, in this instance, I find his reading of the verse strained. In its biblical idiom, "hardening the heart" focuses most precisely on rebellion against divine authority. It indicts a refusal to accede to God's will, not a refusal

11. Similar to Proverbs 28:14, Proverbs 19:1 depicts the person with a "hardened neck" as a person who refuses to accept correction, a phrase that is used to describe the Israelites in Deuteronomy 10:16 and Jeremiah 7:26. Yoder argues that in the Hebrew Bible, the concept of the hardened heart is used to reveal God's hand in the fate of nations and to underscore God's role in orchestrating the downfall of kings. 2 Kings 17:4. Christine Roy Yoder, *Proverbs*, Abingdon Old Testament Commentaries (Nashville: Abingdon Press, 2009), 272.

12. Rubenstein, *Talmudic Stories*, 151.

to take action per se.[13] In this account, the rabbis seem too spineless to be properly accused of hardening their hearts. They are not arrogant; they do not set themselves against God's design. They exercise caution at every turn, so much so that their unwillingness to act plunges the community into disaster. If there is arrogance and rebellion in this narrative, surely it cannot be laid at the feet of the hapless rabbis who do not dare abrogate God's law, even though it seems the only way to spare their community from the emperor's wrath.

Who rebels against divine authority? Who dares God to challenge him? None other than Titus, the arrogant conqueror who believes he can flout God with impunity. The thrust of this verse, I argue, is not explanatory. It does not aim to give an account of why catastrophe comes upon the Jews, nor to enumerate the ethical failures that have brought disaster upon the nation. The rabbis, I maintain, do not use Proverbs 28:14 to explain *why* tragedy happens. Instead, I contend, the rabbis deploy Proverbs 28:14 to make a prophetic claim, to articulate the promise of future punishment that God will bring upon Rome. This is no moment of rabbinic self-critique, of reflective self-assessment about ethical failings. The verse indicts Roman hubris. When Rabbi Yoḥanan uses Proverbs 28:14 to ground his account of the destruction, he uses it to make a promise: that Rome will suffer the fate of Pharoah's kingdom, that misfortune will strike the conqueror. The tyrant's victory is only temporary. Like Pharaoh, the Roman emperor Titus has "hardened his heart" against God's will, but he too will eventually come to know the taste of God's power.

Recognizing the Divine Design: The Supple Heart of the Roman Emperor Nero

Before we turn to the Titus story, let us consider another Roman emperor, one Bavli Gittin portrays as Titus's polar opposite: the Emperor Nero, who ruled Rome at the start of the Great Revolt. Bavli Gittin's portrayal of Nero is quite curious. In most Jewish and Christian sources, Nero is notorious for his wickedness. Imagined as the embodiment of evil, Nero is commonly portrayed as the arch-oppressor of God's people, an eschatological antagonist, even the antichrist.[14]

---

13. In an explanatory note, Rubenstein emphasizes that the expression connotes stubbornness and obstinacy; he maintains that Pharaoh "obstinately refuses to let Israel go despite the ominous plagues" and that Bavli Gittin's host "also hardened his heart by refusing to let Bar Qamtsa remain at the banquet." Rubenstein, *Talmudic Stories*, 351, n. 44.

14. For an assessment of Nero's portrayal in Jewish and Christian traditions, see Harry O. Maier, "Nero in Jewish and Christian Tradition from the First Century to the Reformation," in *A*

Such traditions build upon the widespread legends of *Nero redevivus*, the tradition voiced by a number of Roman historians that the Emperor Nero did not did actually die by suicide after escaping a palace coup, but fled to Parthia to reassemble an army, remains there in hiding, and will eventually return to punish his enemies. In Jewish and Christian imagination, the motif of Nero's return takes on an apocalyptic cast. Nero is the great persecutor, the one who "will return—often from the abyss—to wage war against the righteous."[15] According to the Sibylline Oracles, an apocalyptic Nero will return both to ravage the Jewish people and to destroy the Roman Empire. Though he will campaign against all the inhabitants of earth and attempt to destroy Jerusalem, God will raise up a messianic figure to oppose him and thereby bring about the final judgment.[16] In the Apocalypse of John, a revived Nero is imagined as the great beast, emerging from "the bottomless pit" to destroy Rome.[17] In the early-second-century Ascension of Isaiah, the apocalyptic Nero is portrayed as counterfeiting God's signs and wonders, thereby deceiving God's people and leading them to the false worship of Nero's own image.[18]

Bavli Gittin's tale reverses this portrayal on virtually every score, imagining Nero instead as a man so supremely sensitive to God's signs that he refuses to march upon Jerusalem and destroy the temple. Bavli Gittin 56a reads:

Companion to the Neronian Age, ed. Emma Buckley and Martin T. Dinter (Chichester: Wiley-Blackwell Publishing, 2013), 385–404.

15. Boustan, "Immolating Emperors," 215.

16. For apocalyptic portrayals of Nero, see particularly Sibylline Oracles 3.63–74 and 5.25–35, 93–110, 214–227, 361–385. More historically-minded portraits of Nero appear in Sibylline Oracle 4.119–124 and 137–139, where he is portrayed as a corrupt mother-killer, responsible for initiating the Jewish war. In this account, Nero is imagined as returning to destroy Rome as punishment for its persecution of the pious. In Sibylline Oracle 8.139–150, Nero will return to ravage "the nation of the Hebrews" and will thereafter destroy the Roman emperor. See Maier, "Nero in Jewish and Christian," 386–388.

17. Apocalypse of John, Revelation 13, and Revelation 17. See Steven H. Friesen, *Imperial Cults and the Apocalypse of John: Reading Revelation in the Ruins* (New York: Oxford University Press, 2001). On apocalyptic motifs in the Apocalypse of John, see David E. Aune, "The Apocalypse of John and Palestinian Jewish Apocalyptic," *Neotestanica* 40, no. 1 (2006): 1–33.

18. Ascension of Isaiah 3.13–14.22, especially 4.11. Maier identifies the Nero materials as a Christian fragment, interpolated into a pre-existing Jewish text. He emphasizes that the motif of false signs amplifies an existing discourse in the New Testament that warns against the coming of false Christs and prophets who will arise and show false signs, to lead the elect astray. See Mark 13:22 and 2 Thessalonians 2:3–12. Maier, "Nero in the Jewish and Christian Tradition," 389.

He went and sent Caesar Nero against them.
When he arrived, he shot an arrow to the east—
    it went and fell in Jerusalem.
To the west—
    it went and fell in Jerusalem.
To the four directions—
    it went and fell in Jerusalem.[19]
He said to a child, "Tell me your verse!"
He said to him:
    "*I will take vengeance upon Edom,*
        through the hand of my people Israel." (Ezekiel 25:14)[20]
Nero said, "The Holy Blessed One desires to destroy his House
    and he desires to wipe clean his hands with that man [=me]!"
He fled and converted
    and Rabbi Meir came forth from his line.

In Bavli Gittin's account, Nero is sent to destroy the temple, but instead flees the Roman Empire and becomes a righteous convert, from whose line will come the illustrious Rabbi Meir.[21] As Anat Yisrael-Taran has observed, the trope of the foreign ruler who intends to destroy the Jews but instead ends up worshiping Israel's God has deep roots in Babylonian Jewish literature, tracing back to the example of Nebuchadnezzar in the book of Daniel.[22] The scenario is quite implausible in historical terms, even if we discount the fanciful account of Nero's conversion.[23]

---

19. There are some variations in the description of the arrow sign in the manuscripts: Vatican 130 and 140 mention only that Nero shot an arrow to the east and to the west; no mention is made of the four directions. According to JTS Rab. 1718.93–100, he shoots one way, then the other, then in all four directions. In JTS Rab. 1729.65–67, he shoots one direction, then in all four directions.

20. Munich 95 adds a suggestive comment, that the child stuttered when he spoke and said "adam" (man) instead of "Edom" (Rome).

21. Naomi Cohen has suggested that Rabbi Meir is identified as the legendary descendant of Nero because of a rabbinic tradition that his family resided in the general area where Nero was said, according to folk tradition, to have gone into hiding at the end of his life. Naomi Cohen, "Rabbi Meir, A Descendant of Anatolian Proselytes: New Light on His Name and the Historical Kernel of the Nero Legend in Gittin 56a," *Journal of Jewish Studies* 23 (Spring 1972): 51–59.

22. Daniel 2:46–47 and 3:28–29. Yisraeli-Taran, *Aggadot ha-Ḥurban*, 24–28 and 106–108.

23. Bastomsky has attempted an explanation of how rabbinic sources came to describe Nero coming to Jerusalem, despite the fact that Roman sources portray him as never having visited Judea. He suggests that the legend arose from a misinterpretation of the fourth Sibylline

Roman sources make no mention of Nero's alleged trip to Jerusalem. Nero was the reigning emperor at the time of the Jewish revolt; he is the one who commanded the generals Vespasian and Titus to assault Jerusalem. As Rubenstein observes, Bavli Gittin's assertion that Caesar "sent" Nero against the Jews serves as an important literary connection with other key moments in the broader narrative. In the opening sugya, Caesar "sent" a fine calf with Bar Qamtsa and later "sent" Vespasian to take the city.[24] But within Bavli Gittin's tale, the idea of being "sent" also serves to emphasize Nero's subordinate status in the narrative. It allows the Bavli to establish narrative tension between two reigning powers: the power of God and that of the invisible imperial hand that sends Nero to ravage Jerusalem.[25]

When Nero comes to Jerusalem, he does not immediately march upon the city. Instead, he stops to consult the divine will through a form of divination with arrows: using the arrow's flight to discern an appropriate route of travel.[26] Though Nero shoots arrows in various directions, each falls in the city. The message thus appears to be unambiguous. All arrows point toward Jerusalem. Yet Nero stops to consult a second sign, this time turning to a distinctly rabbinic oracle: the practice of discerning divine meaning by asking a child to recite his daily study verse. While the first sign presages a successful assault, the rabbinic sign reveals that God plans to use the Roman general to chastise the Jews—but that God will turn on him once the destruction is complete. In one of the manuscripts, the narrator adds that the child stuttered when he spoke and instead of "Edom," said "adam," thus making is clear that God would take vengeance not just on the nation, but on Nero himself.[27] While Nero would successfully

---

Oracle, which he maintains was likely known to the rabbis. S. J. Bastomsky, "The Emperor Nero in Talmudic Legend," *Jewish Quarterly Review* 59, no. 4 (1969): 321–325.

24. Rubenstein, *Talmudic Stories*, 145.

25. That Bavli Gittin's prose veils the identity of the one who sends Nero is suggestive in its own right, allowing the reader to consider the potential strategic collusion between divine and imperial power.

26. Divining the proper route to travel by arrows appears in Ezekiel 21:21, which describes how the king of Babylon consults the arrows when he stands "at the head of the two ways." Jeffers argues that the Ezekiel passage likely involves divination by arrows performed by inscribing place names or other words on headless arrows, casting them into a bag before withdrawing one. As an alternative, some divinatory practices use the flight of arrows (or thrown arrows) to indicate the appropriate direction of travel. Ann Jeffers, *Magic and Divination in Ancient Palestine and Syria* (Leiden: Brill, 1996), 190–194.

27. Munich 95. The motif of the stuttering child-oracle who "personalizes" a verse also appears in Bavli Ḥagigah 15b, when Rabbi Meir takes the heretic Elisha ben Abuya to consult with school children. See Goshen-Gottstein, *The Sinner and the Amnesiac*, 76.

serve as an instrument of God's desire to destroy the temple, the second sign prophesies that the Roman victory will not last. God will take vengeance upon the conqueror in the end.

Nero thus exemplifies the pious caution praised by Proverbs 28:14. His successful interpretation of the dual sign and his profound attentiveness to the subtleties of the divine will are highly valorized by Bavli Gittin. The narrative portrays Nero as an astute and sensitive interpreter, one who interprets as a rabbi should. The practice of deriving a divine message from a child's verse represents one of the most familiar and favored means of oracular consultation in rabbinic literature. It is a quintessentially rabbinic form of divination. The rabbinic interpreter regards the verse as an indirect form of divine communication; the verse is understood to apply to his own specific situation.[28] That the Roman general Nero makes successful use of this form of divination seems to presage the shift in identity that comes about at the end of the tale. In this tale, the non-Jewish sign spurs him on, while the Jewish sign cautions him. Were Nero interpreting according to Roman norms alone, he would not have discerned the danger posed by military success. It is Nero's ability to read the rabbinic sign that saves him. His actual conversion is spurred by his interpretive capacity. Because he can already read like a rabbi would, he becomes a Jew and becomes the progenitor of the illustrious Rabbi Meir.

Imperial Hubris: Titus's Divine Challenge and the Hardened Heart

If Bavli Gittin's account of Nero offers a surprisingly sympathetic portrait of the Roman general, valorizing his supple responsiveness to God's signs and his recognition of God's power, its portrayal of the Roman general Titus offers a striking counterpoint. Accounts of Titus appear in several rabbinic sources. Titus first appears in the tannaitic midrash Sifre Deuteronomy, a spare tradition that describes Titus entering the temple, slashing the curtain, and challenging God—together with a promise that God will demand immediate recompense for desecration of the divine name.[29] More elaborate accounts of Titus's blasphemy and subsequent punishment emerge in later Palestinian midrashim, offering a more developed account of Titus's sacrilege and dramatizing the punishment

---

28. On rabbinic divination practices in the broader context of Greco-Roman culture, see Saul Lieberman, *Greek in Jewish Palestine/Hellenism in Jewish Palestine* (1962; 1965; repr., New York: Jewish Theological Seminary of America, 1994), 194–195.

29. Sifre Deuteronomy, Ha'azinu, par. 328. See also Midrash Tannaim, p. 202.

he endured for his sin.[30] Bavli Gittin's narrative shares many features with the Palestinian stories, though it accentuates even more deliberately the motif of divine vengeance and the corporeal punishment of Israel's oppressors. In this tale, Bavli Gittin constructs an anti-hero whose blasphemy and hubris become his undoing. Since the Titus narrative is lengthy, I will analyze it in several parts. The passage begins in Bavli Gittin 56b:

> Titus said:
> > *Where is their God, the Rock in whom they take shelter?*
> > > (Deuteronomy 32:37)
> This is Titus the wicked one, who reviled and blasphemed against Heaven.
> What did he do?
> He seized a whore (*zonah*),
> > entered the holy temple,
> > spread out a Torah scroll,
> > and performed a sin upon it.
> He drew a sword[31] and cut into the curtain that veiled the Holy of Holies,
> > but a miracle occurred and blood bubbled forth.
> He went out, believing he had killed God,[32]
> > as it is written:
> > > *Your enemies roar within Your holy place;*
> > > *they regard their signs as true signs.* (Psalms 74:4)

As Bavli Gittin recounts Titus's victorious assault on the temple, the narrative emphasizes Titus's blasphemy, highlighting the way he challenges God's power

---

30. Genesis Rabbah 10:7; Pesikta de Rav Kahana 26; Leviticus Rabbah 20:5; Deuteronomy Rabbah (ed. Lieberman, 21). On the development of the amoraic tradition, see Yisraeli-Taran, *Aggadot ha-Ḥurban*. A version of the Titus tale also appears in Avot de-Rabbi Natan, Version B, 7; Menahem Kister has argued that this is a very late version, dating perhaps to the Gaonic period. Kister, *Studies in Avot de-Rabbi Nathan*, 217–222. The tale of Titus and the mosquito also appears in Muslim hadith. Shari Lowin has argued that the Muslim texts adapt the midrashic narrative in order to deploy similar motifs of divine punishment against Nimrod, the enemy king who persecuted Abraham, who is also regarded as a powerful ruler who dared challenge God. Shari L. Lowin, "Narratives of Villainy: Titus, Nebuchadnezzar, and Nimrod in the *Hadith* and *Midrash Aggadah*," in *The Lineaments of Islam: Studies in Honor of Fred McGraw Donner*, ed. Paul Cobb (Leiden: Brill, 2012), 261–296.

31. This phrase is missing in the Munich 95 manuscript, but appears in the Vatican 130 and Vatican 140 manuscripts, as well as in the Soncino printing and the Vilna edition. The St. Petersburg RNL Evr. I 187 is fragmentary at this point and does not include this section of text.

32. The manuscripts literally read "believing he had killed *himself*," but this is a pious euphemism.

and authority. The initial introduction of Titus describes him as a man who "reviled and blasphemed against Heaven" (*ḥeref vĕgidef klapei ma'alah*), using a phrase that suggests a deliberate and willful assault on divine power.[33] As I have discussed in an earlier chapter, Titus's violent entry into the sanctuary reveals his willingness to subvert sacred boundaries, to flout the precepts that govern access to the holiest places. The rape on the altar couples blasphemy with brutality. Titus's body is itself a weapon, an assault upon the sacred.[34]

To examine the significance of the Bavli's portrayal of Titus as a blasphemer, let us first consider Israel Yuval's insightful analysis of this story. Yuval reads the rabbinic Titus story as an inversion of popular late antique and medieval Christian legends that proclaim the destruction of the temple to be an act of vengeance for the crucifixion of Christ. Yuval highlights the key similarities—and strategic differences—between the rabbinic account and the Christian tales, in which Titus (or occasionally Vespasian) prays to be sent by God "to wreak vengeance on your enemies . . . to destroy them and to avenge your death."[35] The Bavli's account of Titus, Yuval maintains, is carefully constructed to challenge Christian discourse that claims the destruction of the temple as an act of divine vengeance for the death of the savior. "Against the Christian *vindicta salvatoris*," Yuval asserts, "stands a Jewish *vindicta Dei*," a tale that imagines God as taking revenge upon the brutal conqueror who has denied divine power, penetrated the sanctuary, and defied divine authority. I find Yuval's discussion of the parallels between the Christian and rabbinic legends important and insightful, though I ultimately draw different conclusions about the cultural significance of the narrative. Yuval sees the interaction between these tales in exclusively religious terms, as an expression of interreligious polemic. In the fourth century, once Rome became Christian, he argues, "the political struggle with the empire gave way to a religious debate between Christianity and Judaism."[36] In my view, however, asserting a sharp dichotomy between the religious and the political blunts the cultural force of this narrative. It also obscures the degree to which the Titus tale

---

33. Interpreting the command regarding the defiant and deliberate sinner in Numbers 15:30 who blasphemes against God, Sifre Numbers 112 (ed. Horowitz 121) offers an evocative explanation of this phrase, describing the blasphemer through the metaphor of "scraping out the dish." Some forms of blasphemy "impair the thickness of the vessel," wounding or diminishing God, while others do not. Idolatry, it asserts, "scrapes empty the entire dish and leaves nothing in it."

34. On the significance of the body as an expressive symbol in the Leviticus Rabbah traditions, see Hasan-Rokem, "Within Limits and Beyond."

35. Yuval, *Two Nations in Your Womb*, 45.

36. Yuval, *Two Nations in Your Womb*, 32.

evokes and parodies the myths and rituals of Pagan Rome, as Joshua Levinson has shown.[37] In Bavli Gittin's Titus tale, I argue, religiosity is inseparable from the political. Through Titus, the rabbis portray the destruction of the temple as an imperial assault on God's sovereignty. By recounting the vengeance God brings upon the body of the emperor, they tell of God's ultimate victory over Roman-Christian imperium.

The consequences of Titus's violent act of penetration become tangible through the veil, which bubbles blood after Titus tears it with his sword. As Yuval has argued, the rabbinic story cannot be fully understood without understanding the significance of the torn veil in early Christian discourse.[38] Matthew 27:50–51 links the tearing of the veil with Jesus's crucifixion on the cross. "Then Jesus cried again with a loud voice and breathed his last," Matthew writes. "At that moment, the curtain of the temple was torn in two."[39] For many Christian writers, the tearing of the veil reveals the significance of Jesus's sacrifice on the cross, his capacity to usher in a new mode of salvation. Jesus's death on the cross transforms the traditional paradigm of atonement, replacing the high priest's sacrifice of an animal on the altar with the singular self-sacrifice of the savior's flesh.[40] The Letter to the Hebrews makes this equation between veil and flesh explicit. Hebrews 10:19–20 argues that Christians should have "confidence to enter the sanctuary by the blood of Jesus, by the new and living way that he opened for us through the curtain, that is, through his flesh."[41] In Yuval's assessment, the Bavli's Titus story is a parody of this Christian belief. Where Christians imagine the veil to be symbolic of Jesus's divine flesh, torn and tortured upon the cross, Titus too "mistakenly thinks, as in Hebrews, that the veil itself is God."[42] By underscoring the limits of Titus's understanding, Bavli Gittin's telling aims to mock and discredit Christian theological claims about the veil.

---

37. On the allusions to Roman mythology in this rabbinic narrative, see Levinson, " 'Tragedies Naturally Performed,' " 349–382.

38. Yuval, *Two Nations in Your Womb*, 46–49. On parody in rabbinic literature, see Holger Zellentin, *Rabbinic Parodies of Jewish and Christian Literature* (Tübingen: Mohr Siebeck, 2011).

39. Matthew 27:50–51. Translation follows the Jewish Annotated New Testament.

40. The tearing of the veil has occasioned a vast amount of scholarship, both within biblical studies and Christian theology. For a helpful discussion, see Raymond E. Brown, *The Death of the Messiah: From Gethsemane to the Grave, A Commentary on the Passion Narratives in the Four Gospels*, 2 vols. (Garden City: Doubleday, 1994), 2:1098–1118.

41. Hebrews 10:19–20. Translation follows the Jewish Annotated New Testament.

42. Yuval, *Two Nations in Your Womb*, 47.

While Bavli Gittin's tale does indeed engage and refute such Christian assertions, I maintain that reading the narrative *solely* in terms of Jewish-Christian religious polemic flattens the religio-political complexity of the tale. The portrayal of Titus here is not simply a mockery of Christian belief. As Galit Hasan-Rokem has argued, the tale makes "a serious attempt . . . to understand and to depict the inner world of the Roman conqueror."[43] It gives poignant voice to the fear and suspicion with which many elite Greeks and Romans regarded the "Invisible God" of the Jews, even as it dramatizes the political and theological conclusions a pious Pagan would likely have drawn in the wake of a successful assault on the temple of a foreign deity. Even as the polemic of the tale works, as Yuval has argued, by projecting later Christian imperium retrospectively onto the Pagan emperor Titus, it also captures the political charge of an earlier period. Here again, I stress that the cultural work of the narrative also encompasses expressly political claims, not simply religious argumentation narrowly understood. The Titus tale does not simply criticize Titus for a theological misunderstanding or for false belief; it pits imperial power and prowess against the power of the God of the Jews. The Roman emperor, imbued in Roman mythos with divinity in his own right, stands as a rival and challenger to Israel's unseen God—a God who appears to have been pierced by the tyrant's bloodied blade.

The tale thus dramatizes Titus's ignorance, his misreading of the temple sign. By highlighting Titus's interpretive error with the torn veil, Bavli Gittin echoes its earlier claim that the three great Jewish calamities are sparked by Roman misinterpretation. Like Betar and Tur Malka, the tearing of the veil stands as another moment of imperial ignorance intertwined with brutality. Where other moments of Roman error pass without apparent consequence for the conquerors, Bavli Gittin uses the Titus tale to dramatize the dangers of Roman misjudgment. Titus's error becomes his (eventual) undoing. Through signs that lead Titus even more thoroughly into error, Israel's God lures the tyrant into a trap—drawing forth the hubris of the triumphant conqueror, only to destroy him utterly. Consider the way Bavli Gittin describes the penetration of the veil: "a miracle occurred and blood bubbled forth." That Bavli Gittin describes the blood as a miracle is quite curious. Surely we might readily imagine more effective modes of miraculous intervention, miracles that might repulse the conqueror from the inner precincts of the sanctuary or rescue the assaulted woman from the altar. Instead, Bavli Gittin emphasizes the "miracle" of the spurting blood, which appears to give material and tangible expression to the wound that Titus has done to God. How shall we understand this? On the most straightforward level,

---

43. Hasan-Rokem, "Within Limits and Beyond," 7.

we might understand the blood as miraculous because it is counter to nature, because we do not ordinarily expect cloth to bleed. But more significantly, I suggest, the spurting blood is miraculous because it serves as a *false sign*, because it misleads Titus and allows him to think that he has destroyed Israel's God. The significance of the blood as a false sign is underscored by Bavli Gittin's appeal to Psalm 74:4. Describing the destruction of the sanctuary, the Psalmist laments how "enemies roar within Your holy place/they regard their signs as true signs." In contrast to Nero, whose careful discernment and pious caution allowed him to avoid being misled by the initial sign, Titus is entirely taken in. The miracle of the blood convinces Titus that he has, indeed, vanquished the God of the Jews. Even as the sign registers the desecration of the sanctuary and marks a terrible assault upon the divine presence, it also allows Titus to believe that his victory is total—that he has emerged triumphant over Israel's God.

While Bavli Gittin's narrative focuses primarily on the way that the Roman generals Titus and Nero read the signs surrounding Roman victory, the story leaves upon a more haunting question: How shall a Jew understand the Roman conquest? Is there a sign here, a meaning to be drawn from these terrible events? Joshua Levinson has argued that the rabbinic Titus tale is told against the backdrop of a Roman theology of victory, which regards successful conquest as "the project of supernatural gifts which legitimated sovereignty and divine status alike."[44] If indeed such an understanding of conquest was widespread in late antiquity, then it surely performed potent cultural work not only among Roman audiences but also within Jewish communities. The rabbinic narrative gives voice to a "sign" which seems—on its surface—to confirm the Roman theology of victory, to imagine Titus as victorious over a penetrated and bleeding God. Yet the rabbinic narrative refashions the meaning of the sign, challenging the meaning of Roman victory. In my earlier analysis of the role that divine signs play in rabbinic discourse, I have argued that the Bavli often "challenges the straightforward interpretation of natural signs, articulating instead a discourse of hidden meaning in which signs often express a divine intention that runs counter to the expected meaning."[45] Bavli Gittin's blood sign does not simply mislead Titus; it could easily be read as confirmation of Roman ascendance by Jews. Yet against these conventional associations, our rabbinic tale refashions the transparent meaning of the temple destruction and the torn, bleeding veil. It subverts the claim that Roman victory serves as a sign of legitimized sovereignty. As with Nero, a surface reading of the sign appears to promise imperial success but actually presages

---

44. Levinson, "Tragedies Naturally Performed," 375.

45. Belser, *Power, Ethics, and Ecology in Jewish Late Antiquity*, 81.

God's ultimate victory. But where Nero's caution saved him from error, Titus's arrogance—his hardened heart—lures him to his doom.

Divine Restraint and Retribution: Responsivity and Recompense in the Titus Tale

While the larger arc of the Bavli Gittin's text dramatizes divine retribution against Titus, the narrative thus far lingers on the *absence* of divine action. To bring this motif into sharp relief, let us turn for a moment to the earliest rabbinic account of Titus's destruction of the sanctuary. Sifre Deuteronomy Ha'azinu, paragraph 328, reads:

> He will say: *Where are their gods?* (Deuteronomy 32:37)
> R. Nehemiah says:
>> This refers to the wicked Titus, son of Vespasian's wife,
>>> who entered the Holy of Holies,
>>> slashed the two curtains with his sword,
>>> and said, "If He is God, let Him come and protest!"
>> He said, "Moses misled them by telling them,
>>> 'Build an altar and offer burnt sacrifices upon it
>>> and pour out libations,'
>>> as it is said, *You shall offer one lamb in the morning
>>> and the other at twilight.* (Numbers 28:4)—
>>> *Let Him rise up and help you, let Him be your protection.*
>>> (Deuteronomy 32:38)"
> The Holy One will forgive anything,
>> but for desecration of His name, He requites immediately.

The tannaitic tradition gives a spare but potent account of Titus's sacrilege in the sanctuary. At the center of this tradition is the challenge the Roman conqueror issues to Israel's God. Standing in the midst of the temple's holiest place, with his sword still in his hands, Titus issues a brazen dare: "If He is God, let Him come and protest!" Sifre Deuteronomy underscores Titus's blasphemy by having the victorious emperor mock the impotence or indifference of Israel's God via verses from the Torah. Describing the biblical command to offer sacrifices as Moses "misleading" the Jewish people, the rabbis have Titus use scripture to underscore God's absence. When the tyrant quotes Deuteronomy 32:38, "Let Him rise up and help you, let Him be your protection," the silence is meant to echo. Through the figure of Titus, the conqueror who challenges God to intervene, the rabbinic text confronts the lack of divine response to Titus's desecration of the temple—using the brash arrogance of the conqueror, perhaps, to give voice to the reader's own doubts or misgivings.[46]

Sifre Deuteronomy's tradition concludes with a confident reaffirmation of divine power, asserting that God will requite "immediately" for the desecration of the divine name. The Sifre does not dramatize God's revenge against Titus. To learn what befalls the Roman conqueror, one must look to later rabbinic Titus tales. The later Palestinian midrashim and the Bavli offer detailed accounts of Titus's downfall, fashioning the arrogant emperor into a gruesome spectacle of divine justice. Yet even as Bavli Gittin's narrative affirms the tannaitic principle that divine retribution will follow Titus's blasphemy, it reconfigures the timing of God's response. Where the Sifre asserts (but does not depict) God's swift response to insult, Bavli Gittin gives voice to the notion that God waits, prioritizing deferred justice over immediacy. Bavli Gittin 56b continues:

> Abba Ḥinan says:
> *Who is strong like you, YHVH?* (Psalms 89:9)
> Who is as strong and as hard as You?
> For You hear the insults and blasphemies of that wicked one
>   and remain silent.
>
> The school of Rabbi Ishmael teaches:
> *Who is like You among the gods (ʾelim)?* (Exodus 15:11)
>   Who is like You among the dumb (ʾilmim)?
> What did he do?
> Titus took the curtain that veiled the Holy of Holies
>   and he made it into a kind of net
>   and he brought all the holy things that were in the sanctuary
>   and he placed them in it
>   and he took them back by ship, to go and be praised in his city—
> as it is said: *And then I saw the wicked buried—*
>   *those who came and went from the holy place*
>   *and who were forgotten in the city where they did such.* (Ecclesiastes 8:10)
> Do not read "forgotten" (*yishtakehḥu*), but "praised" (*yishtaḥevu*).
> Do not read "buried" (*qevurim*), but "gathering" (*qevutsim*).[47]

---

46. Adiel Schremer, *Brothers Estranged: Heresy, Christianity, and Jewish Identity in Late Antiquity* (New York: Oxford University Press, 2010), 29.

47. The order of these two phrases is sometimes reversed in the manuscripts. In Munich 95, Vatican 130, JTS Rab. 1718.93–100, JTS Rab. 1729.64–67, and München Bayerische

There are those who say:
  It truly was "buried," for even the hidden things were revealed to them.

In response to Titus's assault upon the Holy of Holies, Abba Ḥinan glosses Psalms 89:9 to describe God as "strong" and "hard." Abba Ḥinan's emphasis on God's hardness affirms divine masculinity via the conventional gender associations of the ancient world, which lauded the warm, dry hardness of a man over the cool, moist softness of women.[48] The language serves as a striking contrast to the symbolism of the penetrated veil, reinscribing God's firmness through images of masculine temperament and strength. What is the quality that exemplifies divine strength? For Abba Ḥinan, it is the capacity to endure insult—to preserve solid, stoic silence even in the face of blasphemy and affront. Silence, particularly the silence of one who *could* speak but who chooses instead to hold his own peace, was lauded by Greek and Roman writers as an exemplary masculine virtue. Silence was valorized when it was self-imposed, deliberate, and chosen. Intentional silence thus becomes an expression of masculine self-control, revealing a man's capacity to discipline desire. It becomes a marker of a self-mastery, a testament to a man's capacity to curb impulse and emotion.[49] As Adiel Schremer has argued, describing an earlier version of this tradition in the Mekhilta, the cleverness of this midrashic reading lies in its use of "a major Roman value, that of 'self-restraint,' in order to subvert the supremacy of Rome itself."[50] By framing divine silence as a masculine virtue, Abba Ḥinan claims God's inaction in response to the destruction of the temple as a sign of strength. Divine silence is not, as the Sifre's Titus charges, a sign of God's inability to act, nor is it, as Bavli Gittin's Titus imagines, proof that God is vanquished and defeated, that God is raped and bleeding on the altar, left for dead. Instead, Abba Ḥinan's tradition reconfigures silence as a sign of fortitude, a deliberate choice to hold back, to endure, to wait.

Staatsbibliothek Cod. hebr. 153, the rereading of "forgotten" comes before "buried." In the Vatican 140, the Vilna, and the Soncino print, the rereading of buried comes before forgotten.

48. A well-known articulation of this principle emerges in the work of the physician Galen, who associates masculinity with a temperament and physicality that is hard, dry, and hot. Susan P. Mattern, *Galen and the Rhetoric of Healing* (Baltimore: Johns Hopkins University Press, 2008), 103.

49. On the gendered nature of self-control in Roman culture, see Williams, *Roman Homosexuality*, 125–159; Brittany E. Wilson, *Unmanly Men: Refigurations of Masculinity in Luke-Acts* (New York: Oxford University Press, 2015), 97–100.

50. Schremer, *Brothers Estranged*, 31.

The next tradition extends and complicates this motif, contrasting God's silence with Titus's inability to speak. The tradition, attributed to the school of Rabbi Ishmael, plays with the language of Exodus 15:11, transforming a verse that praises God into a condemnation of Titus's singular hubris. The rabbinic reading rests upon the linguistic similarity between the word for god (*'elim*) and the word for mute (*'ilem*), allowing the interpreter to contrast God's greatness with Titus's ignorance and incapacity. Where God's silence is portrayed in our text as a deliberate act of restraint, a proper masculine virtue, Titus's silence is figured as a disability, a mark of inability and incapacity. While God chooses silence as an expression of strength, the mute Titus cannot speak. In the rabbinic imagination, as in Greek and Roman late antiquity, muteness carries associations of mental incapacity.[51] Roman and rabbinic sources alike assume that speechlessness is a sign of cognitive impairment, an association reinforced by modes of education that depended upon oral learning and recitation.[52] Thus, the rabbinic tradition intends to portray Titus as "dumb"—unable to speak and unable to reason. In crafting this contrast between God and Titus, the text draws also upon a familiar biblical polemic against idolatry. While the God of Israel is endowed with full sensory capacity, the gods of the nations are blind, deaf, and mute. That these deities are false gods becomes evident through the discourse of sensory impairment. With a masterful stroke, the rabbinic text applies this critique to Titus, deriding Roman imperial aspirations to divinity. Where Roman ideology deified the emperor ascendant, Bavli Gittin's narrative mocks Titus's acts as the height of hubris.

As Bavli Gittin describes Titus's plunder of the sanctuary, the narrative repeats the opening question: "What did he do?" In response, the text recounts how Titus fashioned the temple curtain into a carrying net so that he could haul away the stolen sacred things, to sail home and be feted as a victorious hero in the streets of Rome. The scenario again paints a vivid picture of Titus's temerity. His theft of the sacred objects, coupled with his audacious repurposing of the veil, reveal his utter fearlessness in the precincts of Israel's God. Confronted with another apparent confirmation of God's inaction in the face of assault, the rabbinic narrative appeals to Ecclesiastes 8:10 to anchor Titus's acts in scripture.

51. Christian Laes, "Silent Witnesses: Deaf-Mutes in Graeco-Roman Antiquity," *Classical World: A Quarterly Journal on Antiquity* 104:4 (2011): 451–473. On deaf-muteness in rabbinic sources, see Bonnie Gracer, "What the Rabbis Heard: Deafness in the Mishnah," *Disability Studies Quarterly* 23 (2003): 192–205; Abrams, *Judaism and Disability*.

52. For an important exception, see Bavli Ḥagigah 3a, which reports that the mute sons of Rabbi Yoḥanan ben Gudgada took part in rabbinic education and were eventually revealed to have expert knowledge of law and scripture.

Through the substitution of key words for others with a similar sound, the biblical verse is made to proclaim that the wicked conqueror will gather up the spoils of conquest and be praised for his victory. Through this rereading, the rabbis affirm that Titus's raid is not a violation of God's plan. It is encompassed within scripture. It is an *expected* assault, one that has been foretold. The promise of restitution for God and the Jews alike is, I argue, preserved in the very verse itself. Though the rabbinic interpretation substitutes new words for the old, this practice of reading allows a verse to signify on two levels simultaneously. It attests to a reality in which the victorious Titus is embraced as a hero, but it alludes also to a moment yet to come: a time when the wicked one will lie dead and buried, when he will be forgotten in the city he despoiled. Thus reconfigured, the verse functions as a palimpsest, a reused page that retains the traces of an earlier composition. Rabbinic revision does not fully overwrite the original text. Instead, it layers new words atop the old, even as it allows the original meaning to peek through.

The Death of the Tyrant: Corporeal Incursion in the Titus Tale

Thus far, Titus's desecration of the temple and his blasphemy against Israel's God has gone without resistance. No challenger arises to defend the sanctuary, and no miracle halts the assault. A victorious conqueror, Titus emerges from his initial challenge entirely unscathed. But the next scene shifts the dynamic of divine response. While Titus sees God's original inaction as proof of divine weakness, the rabbinic tale frames God's eventual action as purposeful and deliberate: a confirmation of God's capacity to overturn the tyrant's power. Instead of portraying Jerusalem as the site of divine recompense, the rabbinic tale imagines God confronting Titus in Rome, the seat of imperial authority. By displacing the divine response, the rabbinic tale thus imagines God as waiting to challenge the emperor on his own turf. It raises the stakes of the conflict, pitting Israel's God against Roman authority to reveal God's capacity to bring down the conqueror within the heart of imperial power. Bavli Gittin 56b continues:

> A spirit of the sea (*naḥshol shebayam*)[53] rose against him to drown him. He said, "It seems to me that their God only has power over the water.

---

53. The Munich 95, Vatican 140, JTS Rab. 1729.64–67, and München-Bayerische Staatsbibliothek, Cod. hebr. 153 manuscripts, as well as the Vilna edition and the Soncino printing read *naḥshol shebayam*; Vatican 130 and JTS Rab. 1718.93–100 read *naḥshol shel yam*.

Pharaoh came and [his forces] drowned in water.
    Sisera came and [his forces] drowned in water.[54]
    So too He rises against me to drown me in water.
    If He is so mighty,[55] let him come up onto dry land
        and make war against me!"

A heavenly voice went forth and said to him:
    "Wicked one, son of a wicked one,
    son of the descendants of Esau the wicked one!
    I have an insignificant creature in my world called the mosquito,
    which has an entrance, but no exit.[56]
    Come onto dry land and make war against her!"[57]

He arose onto dry land.
The mosquito came and entered into his nose
    and bored into his brain for seven years.
One day, he was passing by the gate of a blacksmith's house.
It heard the sound of the hammer and fell silent.
He said, "There is a remedy!"
From then onward,
    they brought a blacksmith before him to hammer.[58]
To a non-Jew, they gave 4 *zuz* [as payment.]
To a Jew, they said to him:
    "It is enough for you to see the one you hate."
From then onward—
    until it became accustomed to the sound.[59]

---

54. Mention of Pharaoh and Sisera are absent in JTS Rab. 1729.64–67 and JTS Rab. 1718.93–100.

55. JTS Rab. 1729.64–67 and JTS Rab. 1718.93–100 read "strong and mighty."

56. Vatican 140, the Soncino printing, and the Vilna edition add a question, "Why is it called an insignificant creature?

57. This phrase appears in Munich 95, JTS Rab. 1729.64–67, JTS Rab. 1718.93–100, the Soncino printing, and the Vilna edition; it is absent in Vatican 130, Vatican 140, and München-Bayerische Staatsbibliothek, Cod. hebr. 153.

58. Vatican 140, the Soncino print, and the Vilna read, "Every day," instead of "From then onward."

59. The Vilna specifies, "For thirty days, they did this."

It was taught: Rav Pinḥas ben ʿAruva[60] said:
> "I was among the great ones of Rome
> and when he died, they split open his brain
> and found within it something like a sparrow (*tsipor dror*),
>   two *selʿain* in weight."

In a baraita it was taught:
> It was the size of a two-year old dove,
>   two *liṭrin* in weight.[61]

Abaye said: "We have a tradition
> that its beak was copper and its talons were iron."

When Titus was dying, he said:
> "Let this man be burned
> and let his ashes be scattered among the seven seas
>   so that the God of the Jews[62] cannot find him
>   and bring him to judgment."

From the temple in Jerusalem, Bavli Gittin's Titus tale moves next to the sea, a scene that allows the Bavli to dramatize another dimension of Titus's hubris and heresy. As Titus sails home victorious from his conquest in Jerusalem, a dangerous storm assails his ship and threatens to drown him. Titus reacts, as Hasan-Rokem has observed, "with a strange mixture of provocation and insight."[63] Interpreting the storm through the prism of his own Pagan worldview, Titus understands his own experience as confirmation that Israel's God has power only over the sea. Israel's God is, in Titus's eyes, none other than "the Hebrew counterpoint of the Roman Neptune."[64] Titus draws upon the mythic history of the Jews to underscore his claim. During the Exodus from Egypt, God performed miracles of water—splitting the waters of the Red Sea to allow the Israelites to cross

---

60. The name of this sage varies in the manuscripts: Vatican 140, the Soncino, and the Vilna have "ʿAruva," while Munich 95, JTS Rab. 1718.93–100, and JTS Rab. 1729.64–67 have "ʿArukha." In Vatican 130, the name appears as "Shtikha," while München-Bayerische Staatsbibliothek, Cod. hebr. 153 reads "Shtiva."

61. JTS Rab. 1718.93–100 and JTS Rab. 1729.64–67 conclude here.

62. This reading follows Munich 95, Vatican 130, the Soncino printing and the Vilna edition; Vatican 140 and the München-Bayerische Staatsbibliothek, Cod. hebr. 153 read, "so that the Jews cannot find him."

63. Hasan-Roken, "Narratives in Dialogue," 115.

64. In the midrash, Titus draws examples from the generation of Enosh and the flood, as well as the drowning of Pharaoh and his army. Hasan-Rokem, "Narratives in Dialogue," 115.

and then drowning Pharaoh's army when they sought to pursue. Likewise, Judges 5:21 recounts the drowning of the armies of the Canaanite chieftain Sisera, how "the torrent Kishon swept them away."[65] Titus himself experiences God's deadly power through the sea storm that threatens his ship. Yet rather than responding with contrition or acknowledging divine sovereignty, the Roman general interprets the storm as proof of the *limits* of divine power. Titus dares God to challenge him on his own turf, to "make war" against him on dry land.

The rest of the tale unfolds as an answer to Titus's brash words, dramatizing the consequences of his hubris. The message of the tale is striking and clear. Assessing a parallel version of this tale that appears in Leviticus Rabbah 22:3, Galit Hasan-Rokem writes, "The narrative describes in concise and visually extremely effective terms Titus's blasphemous entrance into the Temple and his subsequent punishment—a mosquito devours his brain until he dies."[66] To grasp the subtle dynamics of the conflict between divine and imperial power in the Bavli's Titus tale, let us turn back to the first words of the passage. Bavli Gittin describes the sea storm as "*naḥshol shebayam*," a phrase which might either be translated as an ocean gale or as a spirit of the sea. I have chosen the later, with an eye to underscoring the parallelism of the two creatures that arises to challenge Titus—the mighty spirit of the sea and the insignificant mosquito. On the face of it, the difference between the sea-spirit and the mosquito seems at first to reinforce Titus's claims about God's power. At sea, divine power is manifest through the might of the sea, the stormy gale thrown up by a dangerous challenger. On land, the creature God calls forth to tangle with Titus is a miniscule being. But where Titus appears to evade the storm-spirit on sea without any narrated difficulty, he is plagued unto death by the tiny mosquito. Rather than tangling with a mighty creature and earning a hero's accolade, Titus succumbs to a miniscule challenger and dies an ignoble death in torment and agony. That Titus is felled by such a little creature underscores the limits of the tyrant's power. To bring down the might of Rome, God needs no more than a gnat.

Titus's death dramatizes God's power over Roman flesh. Bavli Gittin's tale is full of striking images of bodily incursion and corporeal rupture, imagining the sovereign Roman body as open to divine assault. Consider the (apparently insignificant) narrative detail the Bavli's tale includes about the mosquito, that it "has an entrance, but no exit." On first read, the detail seems a typical talmudic

---

65. Judges 5:21. On the motif of divine battles as an important dimension of biblical myth, see Michael Fishbane, *Biblical Myth and Rabbinic Mythmaking* (New York: Oxford University Press, 2005), 84.

66. Hasan-Rokem, "Narratives in Dialogue," 112.

digression. But by the end of the story, it has become a prescient assessment of Titus's own corporeal situation. His body too has an entrance with no exit, an orifice through which the mosquito can find access. But while the mosquito can get in, Titus cannot expel it. That the mosquito enters through his nostril is, perhaps, also significant. The nose is often figured in rabbinic sources as a marker of personal identity, something akin to a signature in the flesh.[67] In this narrative, the nose becomes a gateway, a means of slipping inside the skin. The entrance is easy; the violence comes after. Once the mosquito has entered Titus's body, it begins to penetrate his interior. For seven years, Bavli Gittin tells us, the tiny creature attacks his brain. In the Hebrew, the verb *naqar* (to pierce, to bore) has clear connotations of violence. Bavli Sanhedrin 130a uses a similar phrase, *yaqru et moḥo* "they pierce his brain," to describe the punishment the Romans decreed upon Jews who donned tefillin (prayer amulets) on their heads, in violation of the Roman decree.[68] In the Titus story, the pierced brain becomes a punishment for Titus's breach of God's law, his punishment for violating the sacred precincts. Might we imagine it also as a measure-for-measure punishment for the rape Titus commits upon the altar, a corporeal vengeance, a violation of the integrity of his own body?

By narrating the corporeal vulnerability of the conqueror, by revealing the porous and permeable nature of flesh, the Bavli exposes the frailty of empire. As a man, as an emperor, Titus is profoundly compromised. His body, his brain are no longer his own. He becomes unwitting host to a creature that transforms within his body, from mosquito into something like a bird. That the sages themselves weigh and measure the bird, that they endow it with a beak of copper and claws of iron, testifies both to its solidity as a distinct material object and to its unusual form. It is no natural bird, but a made thing—a creature of artifice and engineering. It grows inside him, transforming within his skull. The conqueror becomes its chrysalis, a shell for that which swells inside him. That the Bavli imagines the creature boring for seven years into Titus's brain underscores the enduring nature of Titus's penetration. In Bavli Gittin's tale, he is helpless before his assailant. He cannot drive it out. He cannot still it or silence it, without turning to another man for aid. When he discovers that the sound of a blacksmith's hammer will bring him peace, they bring a smith before him every day—until Titus's

---

67. The Hebrew term for nose, *ḥotem*, is derived from *ḥatam*, "mark" or "seal." Mishnah Yevamot 16:3 rules that the nose must be present in order to confirm the identity of a deceased individual, a statement confirmed again in Bavli Yevamot 120a.

68. In Judges 16:20, *naqar* is also the verb used to describe Samson's blinding, when the Philistines put out his eyes.

tormentor grows accustomed to the sound and ceases to respond. The blacksmith occupies a complex position before the emperor. On one level, the blacksmith holds a remedy for Titus's pain, a means of quieting the creature that stabs his brain. He becomes a physician, if an unconventional one, a man whose skilled trade allows him to ease the emperor's pain.

Yet the blacksmith also stands as a material witness to imperial agony, a spectator who gazes upon the emperor's distress. Bavli Gittin's narrative signals the import of this observation through its comment that a non-Jewish blacksmith was paid for his labor, while a Jew received no payment. To the Jew, they say, "It is enough for you to see the one you hate" in such distress, to look upon the suffering of the emperor who caused you and yours to suffer. Bavli Gittin's comment is a visceral confirmation of the dynamics of revenge that drive the tale. Through this dialogue, the Bavli imagines the sight of the emperor's pain as a potent currency. To see the tyrant brought down, to glimpse with one's own eyes the suffering that God brings upon the conqueror, is more valuable than coin. But let us not read too quickly past the colonial dynamics of the moment, the way the Jewish blacksmith is called to counter God's purpose. In this way, the imperial summons—the demand to hammer for Titus's pleasure, without pay—becomes another means of reinforcing Roman capacity to conscript the Jewish body, to extract labor with no reward. Even as Bavli Gittin's discourse unravels the stability of the imperial body, it recognizes the enduring imprint of imperial authority. Even here, at the height of his humiliation, the penetrated conqueror possesses the power to compel or enslave.

Titus and the Enemies of Israel: Corporeal Punishment and the Politics of the Afterlife

Against the visceral reality of Roman imperial might, the rabbinic Titus tale aims to make visible God's power. Through vivid images of corporeal punishment, the narrative reveals the tangible impact of divine authority on body and bone. In Michel Foucault's influential assessment, visible corporeal punishment serves as a means of manifesting the sovereign's power, reinforcing political authority through spectacles of bodily suffering. Some systems of punishment, as Foucault has emphasized, also seek to effect a transformation on the inner life of the criminal and to internalize discipline. Foucault draws a historical distinction between medieval externalizing regimes, which sought to use the spectacle of public corporeal punishment to make manifest the power of the sovereign, and modern internalizing regimes, which conceal the apparatus of punishment and aim to bring about the inner transformation of the person, to fashion the individual into a self-regulating agent of the state's authority and power. [69] As Beth Berkowitz has observed, however, elements of these two modes of punishment are present within rabbinic rituals of punishment. "Rabbinic criminal execution," Berkowitz observes, "slides back and forth between a medieval-style public manifestation of rabbinic power and a modern-style internalizing and concealing of that power."[70]

Within the Bavli's Titus tale, rabbinic discourse aims to deploy punishment as an external marker of divine sovereignty—and strives, albeit unsuccessfully, to bring about an inner transformation of Titus, to "reform" the criminal and render him a proper (humble) subject before God. In Bavli Gittin's tale, as we have examined it thus far, the first objective has been well accomplished. The splitting of Titus's skull and the revelation of the bird within serves as a spectacle of judgment, a corporeal punishment that makes divine power manifest through the dismembered body of the emperor. The second, however, the interior conversion by which the punished one comes to accept the authority of the regime and accede to its claims, remains in doubt. To consider Titus's relation to divine authority, let us turn first to a Palestinian version of the Titus tale, Leviticus Rabbah 22:3. The midrash recounts how Titus returns home to Rome and is acclaimed by the Roman citizens as a conqueror of the barbarians. He goes into the bathhouse, a quintessentially Roman institution, and a mosquito—appointed by God—flies up his nose and gnaws at his brain. In the Leviticus Rabbah version, Titus says:

> "Call for the doctors to split open the head of that man
>   so I can know with what the God of that nation has punished him!"
> They summoned the doctors
>   and they split open his brain
>   and found in it the likeness of a young dove,
>   and its weight was two litras.

Titus's words here represent a strikingly different response than in the Bavli. In Leviticus Rabbah's version, Titus recognizes that the God of Israel is punishing him. He calls for the doctors to split open his own head, an act that Joshua Levinson has read as strikingly reminiscent of Lucian of Samosata's parody of the Olympian family, in which the God Zeus calls the divine blacksmith Hephaestus and orders him to split open his head—from which emerges the Goddess

---

69. Michel Foucault, *Discipline and Punish: The Birth of the Prison* (New York: Vintage Books, 1979).

70. Berkowitz, *Execution and Invention*, 9.

Athena.[71] Both versions of the rabbinic tale engage in intertextual dialogue with the Roman myth: Leviticus Rabbah echoes Zeus's call to have his own head split in two, while Bavli Gittin's version makes evocative use of the blacksmith as the source of the powerful man's healing. Yet there are significant differences between the two tales. In Leviticus Rabbah, Titus instructs the doctors to split his skull, an act of self-destruction that also becomes a means of bringing about revelation. As he dies, Titus wants to know *how* he has been punished. He acknowledges divine power, admits that he suffers at God's hand, and wants to see the instrument of God's revenge. In this tale, Titus recognizes his own sin; he accepts the punishment and acknowledges the sovereignty of the one who punishes him. This acceptance, as Hasan-Rokem has argued, drives home a crucial theological message. "The pagan emperor, the very destroyer of the Temple," she asserts, becomes "the most effective mouthpiece to proclaim the monotheistic doctrine on the basis of his personal experience."[72]

The Bavli's telling unfolds differently. In Bavli Gittin's version, the skull splitting is a post-mortem inquiry, a means for the "great ones" of Rome (and the rabbis among them) to behold Titus's bizarre fate. Titus goes to his death still scheming to avoid God's justice, leaving instructions that his body be burned and his ashes scattered, lest Israel's God find him and call him to account for his crimes. While the Bavli's Titus has come to admit and to fear God's power, he still imagines himself able to avoid divine judgment. At the time of his death, the Bavli's Titus is only partially cowed. Yet in Bavli Gittin's telling, the emperor's death is not the final word. The Bavli's closing scene recounts Titus's fate in the afterlife, a text that portrays Titus in an eternal, undying state—his body burned and his ashes scattered anew each day, a divine punishment that mirrors his own earthly crimes against Israel's God. Bavli Gittin 56b–57a reads:

> Onqelos the son of Qaloniqos, the son of the sister of Titus
>   wanted to convert to Judaism.
> He went and brought up Titus out of his grave by necromancy
>   and asked him: "Who is important in that world?"
> Titus answered: "Israel."
> Onqelos asked: "What about joining them?"
> "Their [religious] requirements are many,
>   and you will not be able to fulfill them.
> Go and attack them in that world [=on earth] and you will be on top,

---

71. Levinson, "Tragedies Naturally Performed," 376–378.

72. Hasan-Rokem, "Narratives in Dialogue," 115.

as it is written: *Her adversaries have become the head*
(Lamentations 1:5).
　　Whoever harasses Israel becomes the head."
Onqelos asked: "What is your punishment?"
"What I decreed upon myself:
　　Every day my ashes are collected
　　　　and they pass sentence over me,
　　　　and I am burned
　　　　and my ashes are scattered over the seven seas."

He went and brought up Balaam out of his grave by necromancy
　　and asked him: "Who is important in that world?"
Balaam answered: "Israel."
"What about joining them?"
"*You shall not seek their peace, nor their prosperity
all your days forever.*" (Deuteronomy 23:7)
"What is your punishment?"
"With boiling semen."

He went and brought up Jesus of Nazareth/the sinners of Israel[73]
　　out of the grave and asked: "Who is important in that world?"
"Israel."
"What about joining them?"
"Seek their welfare, seek not their harm.
　　Whoever touches them,
　　　　it is as though he touches the apple of God's eye."
"What is your punishment?"
"With boiling excrement,
　　for one who mocks the words of the sages
　　　　is punished with boiling excrement."
Come and see the difference between the sinners of Israel
　　and the prophets of the nations of the world.

Where the Leviticus Rabbah account concludes with Titus's death scene, Bavli Gittin's tale pushes the narrative beyond the grave. In this narrative, Bavli Gittin recounts how a certain Onqelos calls up three nefarious figures, using necromancy to speak with their shades in the otherworld. Peter Schäfer has recently

---

73. For a discussion of the censorship and complex history of this passage, see Schäfer, *Jesus in the Talmud*, 141–144.

analyzed this text in terms of its portrayal of Jesus, arguing that the Bavli's tale makes mock of Christian claims regarding Jesus's eternal life and salvific power.[74] In keeping with my own focus, I will analyze this text primarily in terms of its contribution to the Titus legend, the way it completes the Bavli's portrayal of Titus's punishment and showcases in visceral detail the corporeal suffering he and other enemies of Israel experience in the afterlife.

Onqelos's inquiry unfolds in a neat tripartite structure, with our necromancer calling up three figures and asking each three questions. To the first inquiry, the response is unanimous: Israel is important in the next world; the Jewish people have status there that they do not in this present world. By underscoring the contrast between the present world and the world to come, this text uses the three sinners' own eyewitness testimony to affirm a key theological claim: that God will lift up the nation in the next world, in spite of their lowly position in this one. When Onqelos turns to the next question, however, the answers begin to diverge. As the prospective convert enquires about the prospect of joining the Jewish people, Titus asserts that it will be impossible for him. Their obligations are many, he avers, and Onqelos will not be able to fulfill them. Instead, Titus counsels Onqelos to follow his own example and content himself solely with the spoils of this present world. Harass Israel, he instructs, and Onqelos will at least be exalted for a time.

Through this exchange, Bavli Gittin's tradition highlights Titus's recalcitrance, his refusal to change, even in the afterlife. Where the Palestinian Titus acknowledges God's authority before he dies, the Babylonian Titus counsels persecution of God's people even as his own body is subject to perpetual punishment at God's hand. Titus will not compromise. Even after death, subject to punishment by a powerful sovereign, Titus refuses to budge. In counseling Onqelos to become a persecutor, even as he himself becomes an object lesson for the bitter fate of those who trouble God's beloved people, Titus becomes a corporeal embodiment of the obdurate flesh: the stubborn persistence of empire, its unyielding opposition to divine authority and divine desire. Against this backdrop of the intransigence of the imperial body, Bavli Gittin's tale dramatizes God's physical power over the body of the emperor. The flesh matters, in this tale. Galit Hasan-Rokem has emphasized "the rabbis' belief that the body is a vehicle for existential and theological fulfillment."[75] In keeping with rabbinic notions of measure-for-measure punishment, the tale brings down Titus through punishment that fits the crime. As Bernie Hodkin has observed, Bavli Gittin's

74. Schäfer, *Jesus in the Talmud*, 82–94.

75. Galit Hasan-Rokem, "Within Limits and Beyond," 5.

Titus tale accomplishes a measure-for-measure recompense for *both* of Titus's sins: death by mosquito for his denial of God's power and the burning of his own body for his burning of the temple.[76] Through this post-mortem encounter with the emperor, Bavli Gittin consigns the conqueror to an eternity of pain. Like a perverse inversion of the mythical phoenix, Titus's body is set alight anew each day. His undying flesh endures, forever dismembered in the afterlife.

The next two encounters similarly reinforce God's power over the bodies of those who threatened Israel. Onqelos calls forth Balaam, the non-Israelite prophet who is hired by the Moabite king Balak to curse the Israelites. In Numbers 22–24, the Hebrew Bible recounts how Balaam sought to fulfill the king's request, but instead found himself reciting a blessing upon the Israelites at God's behest. Rabbinic tradition judges Balaam harshly. Despite the favorable outcome of his act, rabbinic sources hold him accountable for his intent and emphasize that he later sought to cause the Israelites to curse themselves. Numbers 31:16 portrays Balaam as inciting Israel toward idolatry, counseling the Midianite women to entice the Israelite men to sexual sin and the worship of the Midianite deity Baal-Peor.[77] When called forth by Onqelos for advice regarding the people of Israel, Balaam recites Deuteronomy 23:7, a verse that originally instructed the Israelites to turn away from the Ammonites and Moabites—applied now to Israel. Schäfer suggests that the verse serves as a second curse against Israel, a post-mortem articulation of Balaam's original desire.[78] It also evokes a retrospective assessment of Balaam's own transgression. He himself did not seek Israel's peace, nor their prosperity—and for that, he continues to be held accountable. His own punishment fits his crime. For inciting Israel to sexual transgression, Balaam is punished with eternal immersion in boiling semen.

Finally, Onqelos turns to a third figure, described in some versions of the text as "the sinners of Israel" and in other manuscripts as "Jesus of Nazareth." Schäfer has argued, convincingly in my view, that Jesus was the original reading. A later hand changed the identity of the third individual, perhaps also adding the comparative remark about the difference between the sinners of Israel and the prophets of the nations.[79] When Onqelos asks again about Israel, Jesus (or the sinners

---

76. Bernie Hodkin, "Theologies of Resistance: A Reexamination of Rabbinic Traditions about Rome," in *Reactions to Empire: Sacred Texts in their Socio-Political Contexts*, ed. John Anthony Dunne and Dan Batovici (Tübingen: Mohr Siebeck, 2014), 176.

77. The incident at Baal-Peor is narrated in Numbers 25:1–18, though mention of Balaam does not appear; Numbers 31:16 connects the Baal-Peor to Balaam's advice.

78. Schäfer, *Jesus in the Talmud*, 86–87.

79. Schäfer, *Jesus in the Talmud*, 89–90.

of Israel) offer a strikingly different position, an allusion to Zechariah 2:12 that
counsels Onqelos to "seek their welfare, not their harm" because the people are
particularly beloved of God. Of the three, Jesus is the only figure whose experience in the afterlife has resulted in a transformation of the heart. Yet this post-
mortem conversion of character does not appear to mitigate his punishment. He
sits in boiling excrement, a punishment Schäfer argues is meant to parody the
New Testament claim that Christians who partake of Jesus's flesh in the Eucharist
gain eternal life. Instead, the Bavli tradition portrays Jesus as enduring eternal
punishment, with his own flesh afflicted by the byproducts of eating—rendering
unholy the very process that his followers profess has the power to save.[80] The
striking similarity of the punishment motif between the last two figures gives
the Bavli's final claim an ironic twist. As Schäfer has observed, "it hardly makes
much difference whether one sits in the Netherworld in boiling semen or in boiling excrement."[81] Despite the anonymous speaker's call to observe the difference
between the sinners of Israel and the prophets of the nations, the real distinction
lies only in their attitude toward Israel. In raw corporeal terms, both Jesus and
Balaam experience pain that also degrades and defames their flesh.

By calling three enemies of Israel to testify to their experience beyond the
grave, Bavli Gittin constructs an alternative arena for the practice of divine power.
Through these personal accounts of post-mortem suffering, Bavli Gittin's narrative makes a striking claim about the place of Jews in this and the next world.
Those who persecute Israel in the present, our text asserts, will experience pain
in the hereafter. The narrative gives vivid expression to a classical eschatological
motif, portraying the great reversal of fortune that will come about in the afterlife: those raised up in this world will be cast down, while those who are lowly
will be upraised. All three informants claim that Israel holds the paramount place
of importance in the next world—that Israel is, to echo the final speaker, "the
apple of God's eye." In this way, the Bavli's narrative offers a narrative embodiment of what Jon Levenson has argued is the overarching redemptive promise of
the Hebrew Bible: that God will overturn entrenched social realities, reverse the
fortunes of the poor and persecuted, and triumph over injustice and tyranny.[82]
The final scene in the Titus tale aims to upstage empire, to dethrone the tyrant
by casting his temporal power as a mere shadow of divine authority. Titus indeed
rose to power through the persecution of God's people. But his brief moment
of temporal triumph pales against an eternity of pain. Trapped in perennial

80. Schäfer, *Jesus in the Talmud*, 90–94.

81. Schäfer, *Jesus in the Talmud*, 89.

82. Levenson, *Resurrection and the Restoration of Israel*, 183.

torment, Titus must endure each day the unmaking of his own flesh: his body burned, his ashes scattered, his sovereignty and substance coming undone within God's mighty seas.

Torturing Titus in Sassanian Babylonia: Politics and Punishment in Bavli Gittin

In my analysis of the Titus tale, I have aimed to shift the way we see the conflict between Titus and the God of Israel, to underscore that the conflict dramatized in this tale is not simply a matter of religious conviction, but of political power. At stake in the Titus tale is not whether Titus "believes in" Israel's God in a narrow confessional sense, but whether he acknowledges divine sovereignty, whether he accedes to divine authority, whether he recognizes God's capacity to shape and discipline his flesh. In contrast to Nero, Titus is never fully "converted." Even as Titus is assailed by Israel's God, he refuses to change his posture toward the Jews. In refusing to submit, Titus's body becomes the rock against which Israel's God can demonstrate the immensity of divine power. As it narrates God's triumph over the body of the tyrant, Bavli Gittin fashions Titus's flesh into a symbol that reveals the fissures and frailties of the imperial project. His body, inhabited and assailed, burned and scattered to the seas, becomes a visceral sign of God's eventual victory over empire. In this tale, divine power proves itself able to penetrate and permeate imperial flesh.

Bavli Gittin's Titus tale is not simply a rehearsal of a well-worn trope that imagines evildoers suffering in the afterlife. The Titus tale lodges an attack against a specific figure, relishing the corporeal comeuppance that strikes the person of the emperor. Earlier narratives, Ra'anan Boustan has argued, eschewed such fantasies of violent vengeance. Describing a reticence of third- and fourth-century sources to engage in specific polemics against Roman rulers, Boustan asserts, "While Jews and Christians had available to them a robust idiom for describing the post-mortem suffering of the wicked, kings and generals among them, and while they could produce elaborate narratives concerning the final defeat of the emperor as risen Antichrist, they did not yoke these elements together to produce historically specific and politically charged visions of the afterlife throughout the first four centuries of the Common Era."[83] In the fifth and sixth centuries, however, Jewish writers begin "to generate tableaux of graphic violence directed specifically at the figure of the Roman emperor," expressions of antagonism and a "vivid discourse of retributive justice."[84] Boustan reads such images against the

---

83. Boustan, "Immolating Emperors," 217.

84. Boustan, "Immolating Emperors," 206.

increasingly common Byzantine motif of Jews as violent troublemakers, arguing that Jews internalized this discourse and made it their own. But what, I ask, might such tales mean? If late rabbinic sources are comfortable with such fantasies of violent retribution, how might these tales play out politically?

To parse the significance of the Bavli's Titus tale, I argue, we must consider what it means to tell this tale in the Sassanian Empire. Babylonian rabbinic Jews are not Roman subjects; they need not bow before the cultural might of Rome. In such a context, the Titus story does not serve as a straightforward subversion of the imperial regime. Of course, one might frame the salience of this tale in terms of historical memory, reading it as a revenge fantasy in which Babylonian rabbinic Jews imagine the comeuppance of the longstanding persecutors of the Jewish people. While such a reading might capture one dimension of the tale's cultural meaning, it defangs the political significance of the tale in the rabbinic present. To better situate Bavli Gittin's Titus tale in its Sassanian context, I suggest we reconsider Rome's significance as a political entity in the Sassanian Empire. While earlier scholarship often imagined Babylonia as geographically and culturally quite removed from the Roman Empire, scholars now increasingly recognize the border between the Roman East and the Sassanian West as significantly more porous. The persistent presence of military conflict between the two great empires, I argue, provides an important context for reading anti-Roman traditions in the Babylonian Talmud. In Sassanian Persia, Rome is not the empire ascendant. Rome is a rival, an enemy, and a challenger to Sassanian power. When the Babylonian Talmud revivifies traditional rabbinic anti-Roman discourse, it deploys that rhetoric against the enemy of its own emperors. For Babylonian rabbinic Jews, opposing the "evil empire" may well be politically expedient. Rather than destabilizing or subverting the dominant power structure, rabbinic critique of Rome aligns Babylonian Jewish identity with imperial Sassanian interests. Even as the Bavli's Titus tale takes aim at empire, it remains lodged within imperial politics, caught within the interstices of imperial power.

Can the Caged Bird Fly? Vengeance and the Colonized Imagination

How, then, shall we read the Titus tale? We are meant, it seems, to understand the Titus narrative as a triumph, a tale in which divine might is revealed as sovereign over the body and mind of the conqueror, a tale that demonstrates God's capacity to overturn empires and to plunge the enemies of Israel into torment in this world and in the next. But if the tale is a triumph, it is a triumph that haunts me with hard questions. It is a triumph that reveals the bitter imprint conquest leaves within the imagination, the way a world so deeply shaped by violence constrains the very contours of our longing. For all that the Titus tale has much to say about God's power over the corporeal flesh of the emperor, it offers only the most meager glimpse of a world refashioned according to a different order. If it gestures in the direction of rabbinic eschatology, it offers but the barest nod toward the restoration of Israel, a restoration sketched only through the eyes of those tormented in the afterlife. The rabbinic Titus tale lingers with revenge, rather than redemption. It draws forth a future in which the temple and the tyrant now have both been set ablaze. But what profit is there in the flames? Has hope become so scarred by violence and vengeance that torture is the only salve for conquest's wound?

To consider these questions, let us return for a moment to a significant motif in the Titus tale, the motif of the bird. When Titus dies, Bavli Gittin recounts, they split open his skull and discover that the tiny mosquito that flew into his nose has turned into an iron bird—a material mark of divine recompense, hammering within the body of the Roman conqueror. Levinson has argued that the appearance of a bird at the moment of Titus's death evokes the Roman ceremony of apotheosis, the divination of Roman emperors, a rite symbolized through the release of an eagle that carried aloft the soul of the emperor as it flew toward heaven.[85] In the rabbinic legend, Levinson suggests, the bird parodies Titus's imperial aspirations to divinity, a proposal I find quite insightful. Yet alongside these counter-imperial possibilities, I suggest that bird may also operate on another level: as a symbol of Israel, an expression of Jewish captivity and yearning. Consider the passage again, from Bavli Gittin 56b:

> It was taught: Rav Pinḥas ben ʿAruva said:
> I was among the great ones of Rome
> and when he died, they split open his brain
> and found within it something like a sparrow (*tsipor dror*),
>   two *selʿain* in weight.

---

85. Levinson, "Tragedies Naturally Performed," 379–380. On the Roman ritual, see Simon Price, "From Noble Funerals to Divine Cult: The Consecration of Roman Emperors," in *Rituals of Royalty: Power and Ceremonial in Traditional Societies*, ed. David Cannadine and Simon Price (New York: Cambridge University Press, 1987), 94–97. Price emphasizes that the release of the eagle, which became a standard part of the ceremony only in the second century, allowed all present to become witnesses to the apotheosis. That the rabbinic legend evokes the Roman rite is further suggested by the emphasis our text places on the burning of the imperial body as punishment. Price emphasizes that the pyre and the cremation of the emperor had central significance within imperial funeral rituals, even as standard burial practices in Rome shifted more toward inhumation.

In a baraita it was taught:
> It was the size of a two-year old dove,
>> two *liṭrin* in weight.
> Abaye said: "We have a tradition
>> that its beak was copper and its talons were iron."

The Bavli describes the bird as a *tsipor dror*, literally a "free bird." While the Hebrew word *dror* is commonly used to connote "freedom" and "release," Psalm 84:4 uses it as a kind of bird, variously identified as a sparrow, a swallow, a pigeon, or a dove.[86] The biblical verse sets *tsipor* and *dror* in parallel: "Even the sparrow (*tsipor*) has found a home, and the swallow (*dror*) a nest for herself in which to set her young, near Your altar, O, Lord of hosts, my king and my God."[87] In the Psalmist's metaphor, the worshiper becomes the bird, the one who desires to draw near to the divine, to find sanctuary in the shelter of God's holy place.[88]

The evocative image of the *tsipor dror* has been taken up by rabbinic and medieval writers alike as a potent symbol of freedom and constraint, expressed in the yearning of the bird to fly free. Within rabbinic literature, Mishnah Negaʿim 14:1 uses the phrase *tsipor dror* to describe the bird offering brought by a person who suffered an outbreak of *tsaraʾat*, a skin affliction that results in exclusion from the camp. As a ritual gesture, the sacrifice of the bird evokes a similar desire to return, a longing to be restored to one's place, to find and fashion a home.[89] For medieval Jewish writers, the image of the *tsipor dror* evokes a longing for freedom, amidst the realities of constraint. The medieval poet Judah Halevi plays with the phrase in his poem "West Wind," a poem that reflects his own pilgrimage to the Holy Land. On ship, awaiting a favorable wind, the speaker calls, "Let the wings of the swallow (*dror*) spread and set me free (*ve-tiqra-li dror*)." The image of the free bird calls forth the poet's quest to draw near to God's place—and alludes perhaps to Halevi's own desire for mystical union.[90]

---

86. The identification of the bird varies in the ancient literature. *Tsipor* indicates a small bird, likely a songbird. Regarding the identity of the *dror*, which appears elsewhere in the biblical corpus only in Proverbs 26:2, the Septuagint has "pigeon," Jerome translates as "sparrow," and the Targum includes the possibility of "dove." John Goldingay, *Psalms: Volume 2, Psalms 42–89* (Grand Rapids: Baker Academic, 2007), 590.

87. I have followed the Jewish Publication Society translation.

88. Goldingay, *Psalms*, 590.

89. Ari Kahn, "Freebird," *Orthodox Union*, April 16, 2015. https://www.ou.org/torah/parsha/rabbi-ari-kahn-on-parsha/freebird/#_ftn3.

90. Halevi longs for wind, Saperstein writes, "not only to free the ship from its stasis on the sea, but to free the poet's soul from the confines of a civilization that he has found to be

Glossing the verse in Psalms, the medieval exegete Abraham ibn Ezra asserts that the *dror* is a singing bird, "called this because it is not its manner to sing except when it is free."[91]

Within the Bavli's Titus tale, the *tsipor dror* is likewise poised between liberation and captivity, a symbol of freedom and also a reminder of the narrow crevices inhabited by the colonized. There is a songbird within, and it is trapped inside the tyrant. The bird becomes God's means of bringing down the empire, a covert thorn in the lion's paw. It is a strange creature, made of metal not feather and blood. Can it fly? Our text never gives this bird wings. If the *tsipor dror* is meant as a symbol of Israel, it is a reminder of how little room the Jews find under Roman rule, how little space there is to spread wing within the confines of the colonizer's mind. But it is also a promise, perhaps, a reminder that transformation happens even in the tightest of places, that God's touch can alchemize even the most brutal spaces, turn them into sites of wild possibility. Consider another tale of a strange bird, recounted in Bavli Shabbat 130a:[92]

> Rabbi Yannai said: Tefillin require a pure body,
>   like that of Elisha, man of wings . . .
> Why did they call him Elisha, man of wings?
> Because once the wicked kingdom decreed against Israel
>   that anyone who wore tefillin on his head,
>   his head would be pierced (*yaqru et moḥo*).
> But Elisha wore tefillin and went out to the market.
> A magistrate saw him.
> He fled, and the magistrate ran after him.
> As he overtook him, Elisha unbound the tefillin
>   and grasped them in his hand.
> The magistrate said to him, "What is in your hand?"
> Elisha said to him, "The wings of a dove."
> He opened his hand—and there were a dove's wings.
> Thus they called him Elisha, man of wings.
> And why did he say a dove's wings, and not some other bird?

---

spiritually enslaving, thereby enabling him to sing his song." Marc Saperstein, "Halevi's West Wind," *Prooftexts* 1, no. 3 (September 1981): 306–311. See also Martin Jacobs, *Reorienting the East: Jewish Traders to the Medieval Muslim World* (Philadelphia: University of Pennsylvania Press, 2014), 61–62.

91. Saperstein, "Halevi's West Wind," 309.

92. The tale also appears in Bavli Shabbat 49a.

Because the community of Israel is like a dove,
     as it is said: *the wings of a dove are sheathed in silver,*
       her pinions in fine gold. (Psalms 68:14)
Just as a dove's wings protect her, so too Israel—
     the commandments protect her.

As in the Titus tale, this rabbinic story uses the bird as a symbol of resistance to colonial regimes. The two tales share a resonant lexicon. Even beyond the shared motif of the transforming bird, this phrase the Bavli uses for the punishment decreed against Israel evokes the action of the creature that pierces Titus's brain (*naqar bemoho*), an echo that brings these two narratives into conversation.[93] But where Titus's bird is directed toward vengeance, Elisha's bird is turned toward rescue, perhaps even redemption. Produced through a generative piety coupled with a trickster's slight of hand, the bird in Elisha's hand seems a sign that God shelters the bold, those who dare to flaunt the distinctive marks of their Jewishness in the market, to spit in the face of repressive Roman decrees. If the bird is a reminder of God's power to make mock of imperial administrators and emperors alike, it is also a reminder, perhaps even a promise, that Israel may yet one day fly free.

And what of other meanings we might draw from this tale? If we were to read Titus's tale as a standalone narrative, we might indeed come to a triumphal conclusion about the overarching message of Bavli Gittin's account of disaster. Through the Bavli's Titus tale, the rabbis trace the tangible imprint of divine power pressed into imperial flesh, a revelation that first unfolds within the body's interior space and which ultimately culminates in a public spectacle before the great ones of Rome. The Titus tale articulates a sharp critique of colonial arrogance, emphasizing God's power to overturn empire, to exact recompense from the flesh and bone of the conqueror. But Titus is not the only Roman in this narrative. Hubris, in Bavli Gittin's telling, is not a character flaw endemic to powerful Roman elites. To challenge such a claim, we need only to recall the Bavli's striking account of the Roman general Nero, a man so attuned to God's signs that he forfeits his status and surrenders his place within Roman society. Nor does Bavli Gittin present all its Jewish figures as paragons of humility and sensitivity to God's will. In the next chapter, we examine tales that turn a critical eye toward the way high-status Jewish elites hold themselves distant from both the

---

93. My thinking about the effect that the repetition of unusual motifs or phrases have on the reader's experience of the Bavli has been shaped by Zvi Septimus, "Trigger Words and Simultexts: The Experience of Reading the Bavli," in *Wisdom of Bat Sheva: In Memory of Beth Samuels*, ed. Barry Scott Wimpfheimer (Jersey City, NJ: Ktav, 2009), 163–184.

material dimensions of disaster *and* the moral critique it might inspire. For the Bavli, hubris is not only an ethical failing that drives the great ones of Rome to dream of conquest; it also lodges closer to home, among the great ones of their own people who might imagine that wealth or circumstance will insulate them from catastrophe, from the risk conquest poses to their own flesh.

7

Opulence and Oblivion

CLASS, STATUS, AND SELF-CRITIQUE IN BAVLI GITTIN'S TALES OF FEASTING AND FASTING

THE OPENING LINES of Bavli Gittin's account of the destruction of the Second Temple and the devastation of Judea frame the catastrophe through a biblical verse, "Blessed is the man who is always afraid (*mefaḥed*), but the one who hardens his heart (*maqshe libo*) falls into misfortune" (Proverbs 28:14). In the previous chapter, I argued that the verse inveighs against the hubris and arrogance of the Roman conqueror, the general Titus who desecrates the sacred precincts, rapes a woman on the altar, pierces the veil, and then believes himself to have killed God. Titus's hubris leads him to challenge God on God's own terms—and to bear the brutal consequences of such arrogance, in this world and in the afterlife. The body matters here. The manifest corporeal suffering that Titus endures testifies to God's triumph over the tyrant, inscribing divine power in and through the flesh. The Titus tale affords Bavli Gittin a critical opportunity to challenge the power politics of Roman imperium, to undercut the emperor's claim to ultimate authority. Yet Titus is not the only face of human hubris in Bavli Gittin's narrative, not the only one whose elite status and illustrious social position lead him into danger. In this chapter, I probe the recurring motif of food and feasting to examine the Bavli's portrayal of elite Jewish experience before and after disaster. Through these tales, I argue, Bavli Gittin underscores the ethical cost of elite status by highlighting the physical and moral dangers of social privilege.

Most existing scholarship on food in rabbinic literature has focused on the way eating expresses Jewish identity, examining how particular culinary traditions, food abstentions, and table practices fashion a certain kind of Jewish difference.[1] By contrast, Bavli Gittin's food narratives include almost no distinctive markers of Jewishness. Instead, these tales draw attention to the social and political dynamics that drive conspicuous consumption and luxurious desires, as well as the material realities of hunger and famine. Food makes visible the politicized abundance of conspicuous consumption, the bountiful largess of wealthy patrons, the ritual practice of public fasting, and the abject disaster of famine. Through the recurring motif of food and its absence, the Bavli navigates the social and material implications of disaster—expressing both rabbinic culpability and human vulnerability through the fantasies of a well-stocked larder and the fear of gnawing hunger. These tales expose what Michael Dietler has called "the micropolitics of daily life," illuminating complex social dimensions of disaster.[2] They also allow the Bavli to take a self-critical stance toward ethical failings among Jewish elites. Stories of luxurious eating emphasize how corrosive concerns about status and shame often lead elites to protect their private interests by sacrificing the well-being of the broader community. By dramatizing the social allure of the feast, Bavli Gittin sheds light on the way that elite culture promotes spectacles of consumption that draw all eyes toward the privileged table. Bavli Gittin's feasting narratives make visible the way that wealth, luxury, and social privilege distance elites from the awareness of suffering in their midst. Through these tales, I argue, Bavli Gittin articulates striking concerns about the collateral costs of opulent wealth, calling attention to the way that extravagant luxury isolates and insulates those who dine at the fanciest tables from the gritty realities of violence and danger.

---

1. Two important works for the development of rabbinic food studies are David Kraemer, *Jewish Eating and Identity Through the Ages* (New York: Routledge, 2007) and Rosenblum, *Food and Identity*. Kraemer examines the history of Jewish eating, focusing primarily on the development of Jewish eating systems and the phenomenon of "transgressive" Jewish eating that pushes or breaks religious or cultural boundaries. Rosenblum examines how tannaitic sources craft distinctive Jewish identity through dietary regulations, cooking practices, and table fellowship, emphasizing how foodways communicate social identity.

2. Archeologist Michael Dietler argues that feasts and feasting rituals represent a critical area in which people express social, economic, and political relationships, describing feasts as both "inherently political and . . . a fundamental instrument and theater of political relations." Michael Dietler, "Theorizing the Feast: Rituals of Consumption, Commensal Politics, and Power in African Contexts," in *Feasts: Archaeological and Ethnographic Perspectives on Food, Politics, and Power*, ed. Michael Dietler and Brian Hayden (Washington: Smithsonian Institution Press, 2001), 66.

Feasting Politics: Status, Shame, and the Late
Antique Banquet

In one of the most famous tales in the Babylonian Talmud, Bavli Gittin attributes the destruction of Jerusalem to a disastrous late antique dinner party, to the bizarre and brutal consequences of a banquet gone wrong. When an anonymous host instructs his servant to invite a friend named Qamtsa to his feast, the servant instead brings Bar Qamtsa, his enemy, a mistake that sparks a disastrous chain of events that culminates in the destruction of the Temple. When the master finds the wrong man dining at his banquet, he refuses to play host to his enemy and throws Bar Qamtsa out of the feast. Seething with the shame of this public indignity, Bar Qamtsa resolves to turn informer, reports to Rome that the Jews are rebelling against the emperor, and then frames the Jews for sedition to provoke Caesar into an assault on Jerusalem. Bar Qamtsa prompts Caesar to send the Jews a calf to sacrifice as a test of their loyalty, but deliberately maims the animal so that it cannot be sacrificed according to rabbinic halakhah. Torn between the conflicting demands of appeasing the ruling kingdom and acting according to their own interpretation of the law, the rabbis' inaction provokes Rome's ire. Bavli Gittin 55b–56a reads:

> Jerusalem was destroyed over Qamtsa and Bar Qamtsa.
> A man who was friends with Qamtsa but who hated Bar Qamtsa
>   held a feast.
> He said to his servant: "Go and bring me Qamtsa."
> [The servant] went and brought him Bar Qamtsa.
> [The host] went and found him sitting there.
> He said, "Since you are my enemy, why did you come here?
>   Get up and go!"
>
> [Bar Qamtsa] said to him, "Since I have come, leave me alone
>   and I will give you money for what I eat and drink."
> [The host] said to him, "No."
> He said to him, "I will give you the money for half your feast."
> He said to him, "No."
> He said to him, "I will give you the money for your entire feast."
> He said to him, "No."
> [The host] seized him and forced him to get up and go.
>
> [Bar Qamtsa] said,
>   "Since the rabbis were sitting there and did not protest,
>   I will go and inform against them at the king's palace."

He said to Caesar, "The Jews are rebelling against you."

He said to him: "Says who?"

He said to him, "Send them an offering and see if they sacrifice it for you."

He sent with him a three-year-old calf.

As [Bar Qamtsa] was traveling, he caused a blemish on the upper lip—
  and some say, a cataract in its eye,
    which for us is a blemish but for them is not a blemish.

The rabbis reasoned that they should sacrifice it
  for the sake of peace with the kingdom.

Rabbi Zekhariah ben ʾAvkulos said to them:
  "They will say that blemished creatures may be sacrificed on the altar!"

They reasoned that they should kill him, lest he go and tell him.

R. Zekhariah ben ʾAvkulos said to them:
  "They will say that one who brings a blemished sacrifice
    should be killed!"

Rabbi Yoḥanan said:
  "The meekness of R. Zekhariah ben ʾAvkulos
    destroyed our temple,
    set fire to our sanctuary,
    and exiled us from our land."

The Bavli's story dramatizes the far-reaching consequences of a mistaken banquet invitation. But while the feast is a critical element in the tale, the rabbinic
account provides little discussion of the meal itself: food matters socially, not as
sustenance.[3] The banquet serves as a space to contest the host's lavish generosity and portray the intense danger of public shame. In the coveted social circles
of late antiquity, banquets helped shape elites' awareness of their own cultured
nobility, singling out the illustrious few from the plebian masses. Situating the
narrative within elite Roman and Sassanian feasting practices illuminates the way
the Bar Qamtsa story uses the visible space of the feast to communicate complex

---

3. In this respect, the rabbinic story is manifestly at odds with many Roman writers who focus
extensively on the food served at banquets. John D'Arms discusses the role of elaborate food
and drink in crafting the atmosphere of spectacle at elite Roman banquets, noting Macrobius's
opinion that food and drink are commonly on exhibition and parade, "more for show than
for nutritional use." See Macrobius, *Saturnalia*, trans. Robert A. Kaster, Loeb Classical
Library (Cambridge: Harvard University Press, 2011), 7.5.32. John D'Arms, "Performing
Culture: Roman Spectacle and the Banquets of the Powerful," in *The Art of Ancient Spectacle*,
ed. Bettina Bergmann and Christine Kondoleon (New Haven: Yale University Press,
1999), 303.

dynamics of friendship, loyalty, and hatred.[4] In elite Roman and Sassanian circles, banquets afforded hosts a privileged opportunity to display their largess and
demonstrate their esteem for their invited guests. Hosting an elaborate banquet
was a central strategy for representing oneself as a generous, urbane man.[5] Public
generosity granted the host considerable power and generated social debt—at
least until guests had the opportunity to reciprocate.[6]

Analyzing the talmudic narrative in light of Roman and Sassanian banquet
culture highlights the social significance of public feasting and heightens the
significance of Bar Qamtsa's mistaken invitation. By inviting the wrong man to
his master's banquet, the servant inadvertently forges a social bond between the
host and his enemy. When the host sees Bar Qamtsa at the feast, he refuses to
tolerate his enemy's presence. The host's abrupt command, "Get up and go!" reas-
serts control over the social space of the feast. But Bar Qamtsa resists. Threatened
with public humiliation and facing the prospect of eviction from the coveted
social space of the banquet, Bar Qamtsa negotiates for a chance to stay at the
table. "Since I have come," he says, "let me stay." He offers to compensate the
host for his own food and drink, thus relieving the host of the need to cover the
cost of his own plate. When that offer is rejected, Bar Qamtsa offers to pay half
the host's expenses and then to pay for the entire feast. But the host rejects Bar

---

4. While the Bar Qamtsa story is set in Palestine and concerns the behavior of Palestinian
Jews, the Bavli's narrative is likely shaped by a feasting culture common among both Roman
and Sassanian elites. Matthew Canepa suggests that, beginning in the late third century, both
Roman and Sassanian rulers used increasingly similar rituals of public display at banquets, rituals, and other public events to communicate visually to their own subjects and to each other
the majesty of their kingship and the magnificence of their largess. Canepa, *Two Eyes of the
Earth*, 188.

5. D'Arms emphasizes the importance of hosting in elite Roman culture: "For a Roman nota-
ble, the ostentatious exhibition of wealth was part of self-representation; it reinforced the great
man's sense of his own power over those personally bound to him by the ties of *clientela*, and it
set him and his social and political equals, the lofty few, apart from the rest of Roman society,
the obscure many." D'Arms, "Performing Culture," 308–309.

6. My thinking about feasting is shaped by anthropological thought on the social and political implications of gift exchange. Dietler emphasizes that while feasts are commonly viewed
primarily as a means of expressing social solidarity and reinforcing a sense of community,
they also create relationships of social superiority and inferiority. In this regard, he argues
that hospitality has great potential "to be manipulated as a tool in defining social relations."
Michael Dietler, "Feasts and Commensal Politics in the Political Economy," in *Food and the
Status Quest: An Interdisciplinary Perspective*, ed. Polly Wiessner and Wulf Schiefenhövel
(Providence: Berghahn Books, 1996), 91–92. Marcel Mauss emphasizes that agonistic forms
of gift exchange foster competitive and aggressive responses, in which shame plays a significant
role. By contrast, nonagonistic forms of gift exchange tend to foster relationships through hos-
pitality. Marcel Mauss, *The Gift: The Form and Reason for Exchange in Archaic Societies*, trans.
W. D. Halls (New York: W. W. Norton, 1990).

Qamtsa's bid, refusing to allow Bar Qamtsa to play generous provider to the other man's guests. Through the escalating negotiations, the Bavli reveals Bar Qamtsa's increasing desperation—his willingness to pay any price to avoid the stigma of forcible expulsion from the feast.

Many studies of rabbinic society have focused on the profound fear of shame within the intense study-house culture of rabbinic Babylonia.[7] Yet in elite late antique culture, *banquets* also evoked powerful fears about public shame. The cultural power of a banquet had a double edge: while elites could gain prestige through public attendance at the feast of a powerful patron, they also suffered scrutiny and risked considerable potential for shame. Public feasts made plain the realities of social status: guests' relative status was visible and on display through complex seating and serving hierarchies.[8] Classicist John D'Arms notes the widespread presence of Roman banquet anxieties in Roman sources, especially the fear of ridicule by the host or a more powerful guest. "At some banquets," D'Arms writes, "feelings of inferior status left guests convinced that they had been placed under sinister surveillance [*convivarum censura*, in Seneca's phrase] by their hosts or by powerful members of their hosts' households; in effect, they felt themselves transformed from watchers to watched."[9] Roman and Sassanian royals even used banquets to administer public punishment. After the late sixth-century Sassanian ruler Kosrow II regained his throne from a usurper, he brought the defeated general to a royal banquet in chains, to display his mutilated body before the jeers and mockery of guests, and then publically executed him. Another ruler, Kavadh I, rebuked a general for his failures on the battlefield by stripping him of his sash and other marks of favor at a royal banquet. Banquets were a potent space for expressing power through the use of public shame.[10]

---

7. Many interpreters connect this shame with the common rabbinic motif that the Second Temple was destroyed on account of causeless hatred. Such traditions appear in Tosefta Menaḥot 13:22, Yerushalmi Yoma 1:1 38c, and Bavli Yoma 9b. See Kraemer, *Responses to Suffering*, 176–177. By contrast, Jonathan Crane demonstrates that other rabbinic sources emphasize the ability to feel shame as a sign of moral development. Accordingly, Bavli Shabbat 119b describes *shamelessness* as one of the causes of the destruction of the Temple. Jonathan K. Crane, "Shameful Ambivalences: Dimensions of Rabbinic Shame," *AJS Review* 35, no. 1 (April 2011): 80.

8. Simon Malmberg, "Visualizing Hierarchy at Imperial Banquets," in *Feast, Fast or Famine: Food and Drink in Byzantium*, ed. Wendy Mayer and Silke Trzcionka (Brisbane: Australian Association for Byzantine Studies, 2005), 12–13. Canepa, *Two Eyes of the Earth*, 182–185.

9. D'Arms, "Performing Culture," 313. The quotation from Seneca appears in *Epistles,* trans. Richard M. Gummere, Loeb Classical Library (Cambridge: Harvard University Press, 1917), 47.8.

10. Canepa, *Two Eyes of the Earth*, 186.

Sabotage and Sacrifice: The Perils
of Imperial Generosity

Upon his ejection from the banquet, Bar Qamtsa expresses immediate and vehe-
ment anger—not at the host, but at the rabbis who failed to intervene on his
behalf. As Jeffery Rubenstein notes, the talmudic narrative includes no mention
of rabbinic presence at the Bar Qamtsa banquet.[11] Ironically, Bar Qamtsa's words
evoke rabbinic authority in order to condemn the rabbis' inaction. His remark
serves to rabbinize the story, bringing the elite banquet into the orbit of rabbinic
culture and introducing a rabbinic presence into what originally appeared to be a
nonrabbinic feast.[12] Bar Qamtsa's anger highlights the heightened stakes of rabbinic authority. It reveals the dramatic consequences of the original moment of
rabbinic silence—and the rabbis' failure to respond decisively once Bar Qamtsa
presents them with the sacrificial calf. Through this vivid portrayal of the terrible
price of rabbinic inaction, the rabbis shoulder responsibility for the devastation
that follows. In the rabbis' own accounting, their piety, prestige, and communal
leadership obligate them to an exacting standard of behavior. Their flaws are mag-
nified; their failures bear bitter fruit.[13]

---

11. Rubenstein, *Talmudic Stories*, 148.

12. The term "rabbinization" has been used to discuss the Bavli's tendency to describe early
Jewish wonder-workers and other nonrabbinic figures in ways that make them resemble rabbis, thereby appropriating these figures as proto-rabbis and bringing them into the realm of
rabbinic culture. Bar Qamtsa's remark seems to serve a similar purpose, retroactively situating the feast within rabbinic space. On the phenomenon of rabbinization in rabbinic literature, see William Scott Green, "Palestinian Holy Men: Charismatic Leadership and Rabbinic
Traditions," *Aufstieg und Niedergang der römischen Welt* II 19, no. 2 (1979): 619–647; Baruch
Bokser, "Wonder-Working and the Rabbinic Tradition: The Case of Hanina ben Dosa,"
Journal for the Study of Judaism 16 (1985): 42–92; Richard Kalmin, "Christians and Heretics
in Rabbinic Literature of Late Antiquity," *Harvard Theological Review* 87, no. 2 (April 1994):
155–169; and Richard Kalmin, "Holy Men, Rabbis, and Demonic Sages in Late Antiquity," in
Jewish Culture and Society under the Christian Roman Empire, ed. Richard Kalmin and Seth
Schwartz (Leuven: Peeters Press, 2003), 213–249.

13. A similar dynamic appears in other talmudic stories in which famous rabbis are rebuked or
suffer intense grief on account of seemingly minor ethical lapses, suggesting that the rabbis held
themselves to higher standards of piety—and often suffered on account of this expectation.
Bavli Nedarim 62a recounts a tradition about Rabbi Tarfon, who reportedly grieved "all the
days of his life" for making use of his status as a Torah scholar to save himself from murder. For a
discussion of this narrative, see Valler, *Sorrow and Distress*, 18–24. Jonathan Schofer argues that
a motif of "trivial sins" appears frequently in rabbinic literature, in which God punishes harshly
apparently minor transgressions committed by sages. Schofer argues that this motif emphasizes the ethical significance of a sage's every action and intention, no matter how minor. See
Schofer, "Protest or Pedagogy?"; and Jonathan Wyn Schofer, *Confronting Vulnerability: The
Body and the Divine in Rabbinic Ethics* (Chicago: University of Chicago Press, 2003).

Because the rabbis did not protest his treatment, Bar Qamtsa resolves to inform upon them before the Roman emperor. Bavli Gittin uses an idiomatic expression to describe the act of turning informer, describing Bar Qamtsa as going to "eat destruction" at the house of the king.[14] Denied satisfaction at the Jewish banquet, he aims to dine, at least symbolically, at the emperor's table.[15] Bar Qamtsa's "eating" goes hand in hand with a striking social advancement. His speech with Caesar is that of a trusted advisor, almost an equal. Bar Qamtsa not only *partakes* of imperial largess, he also manipulates it. Once he shifts his allegiance to Rome, he persuades Caesar to send a barbed "gift" to his erstwhile compatriots, a calf for sacrifice that will serve as a test of Jewish loyalty to Rome. By convincing Caesar to send the Jews an animal for sacrifice, Bar Qamtsa accentuates long-standing tensions over Jewish loyalty that were expressed through the symbolic performance of sacrifice. Though many Roman subjects made sacrifices to the reigning Roman emperor, Jews were generally allowed to make a sacrifice to the God of Israel on the emperor's behalf—a complex negotiation of loyalties that aimed to allow Jews to express the exclusivity of their religious commitments, while still demonstrating political allegiance to Rome.[16] Because the rituals of sacrifice were sites of complex and contested political and theological meanings, sacrifice was often a flashpoint for controversy and revolt.[17] Bar Qamtsa forces the rabbis to accommodate Caesar's dangerous gift. Imperial generosity entangles the Jewish community in the fraught politics of sacrifice—and exposes them to the spurned emperor's deadly rage.

---

14. The literal meaning of the expression is difficult to parse. In this form, it appears only in the construction *'okhlei karts'a*: to inform against. Jastrow defines the word *karts'a* as "biting, cutting, or destruction." Marcus Jastrow, *Dictionary of the Targumim,* 1425. Sokoloff comments that "the literal meaning of the phrase is uncertain." Michael Sokoloff, *A Dictionary of Jewish Babylonian Aramaic* (Baltimore: Johns Hopkins University Press, 2002), 1003. In Bavli Berakhot 58a, the phrase is used in a story that likewise pits the rabbis against the emperor: Rav Shila lashed a man who had sexual relations with an Egyptian woman, and the man went and informed upon him before the emperor.

15. In Roman culture, attendance at imperial banquets was one way that elites signaled their loyalty to the emperor. Malmberg, "Visualizing Hierarchy," 11–24.

16. E. Mary Smallwood, *The Jews under Roman Rule: From Pompey to Dioclecian: A Study in Political Relations* (1976; repr. Leiden: Brill, 2001), 147–148. Page citations are to the 2001 reprint edition. While many scholars have stressed the character of this accommodation as unique to Judaism, Miriam Pucci Ben Zeev argues that Roman emperors devised and accepted diverse forms of cultic practice as demonstrations of loyalty. Miriam Pucci Ben Zeev, *Jewish Rights in the Roman World* (Tübingen: Mohr Siebeck, 1998), 471–478.

17. On the symbolic significance of ingesting sacrificial food and the refusal to partake of sacrificed meat as a signal of revolt, see Rosenblum, *Food and Identity,* 50–52.

Patronage and Conspicuous Provision: Food, Famine, and Generosity in Wartime

Vespasian's siege of Jerusalem initiates the second cluster of food narratives in Bavli Gittin's account, which dramatize the political significance of food in the context of war. In the Roman world, famine was a deliberate strategy of war, not simply an inadvertent side effect of conflict.[18] Ancient accounts of cities under siege provide vivid portrayals of famine, often using depictions of cannibalism to dramatize the horrors and inhumanity within the besieged city.[19] The Bavli's discussion of Vespasian's siege highlights the political causes of famine, heightening the drama of the disaster by emphasizing that starvation was not inevitable. Bavli Gittin 56a reads:

> [Caesar] sent Vespasian against them.
> He came and besieged them for three years.
> In the city were three rich men:
>   Nakdimon ben Gurion,
>   Ben Kalba Savu'a,
>   and Ben Tsitsit Hakeset.
> Nakdimon ben Gurion—
>   the sun cut through [*nakdah*] [the clouds] on his account.
> Ben Kalba Savu'a—
>   for anyone who entered his house starving like a dog [*kalba*]
>   left satisfied [*sav'a*].
> Ben Tsitsit Hakeset—
>   because the fringes [*tsitsit*] [of his garment]
>   dangled from fancy cushions [*kesatot*];

---

18. Michael Sage emphasizes that Roman siege warfare depended primarily on wearing down the garrison through famine, in contrast to Greek strategies that made extensive use of war machines in order to breach a city's walls and allow invaders to storm the city. Michael M. Sage, *The Republican Roman Army: A Sourcebook* (New York: Routledge, 2008), 276–283. Hunger made a city significantly more likely to capitulate to a siege—and late antique war manuals discuss strategies for destroying crops, trees, and food stores, as well as methods for poisoning wells or water reservoirs. See discussion in Dionysius Ch. Stathakopoulos, *Famine and Pestilence in the Late Roman and Early Byzantine Empire: A Systematic Survey of Subsistence Crises and Epidemics* (Burlington, VT: Ashgate Publishing House, 2004), 46–48.

19. Noting that "no siege was complete without [the depiction] of a mother eating her child," Shaye Cohen emphasizes that this motif was already common in literature by the sixth century BCE, appearing in Lamentations 2:20 and 4:10. Cohen, "The Destruction: From Scripture to Midrash," 22. Sage also notes the widespread appearance of this trope in Roman sources (*Republican Roman Army*, 282).

and there are those who say—
because his seat [*kesoto*] lay among the great ones of Rome.

One said to them, "I will provide you with wheat and barley."
One said to them, "And I, with wine and oil."
One said to them, "And I, with wood."
The rabbis praised the wood,
    for Rav Ḥisda entrusted all of his keys to a servant,
        save for the woodshed,
    for Rav Ḥisda said,
        "One storehouse of wheat requires sixty storehouses of wood."
They had provisions enough for twenty-one years.
But there were some rebels among them.
The rabbis said to them, "Let us go and make peace with [the Romans]."
[The rebels] did not permit it.
They said to [the rabbis], "Let us go and make war against them."
The rabbis said to them, "It will not work."
[The rebels] arose and burned all the stores of wheat and barley,
    and there was famine.

In this scene, Bavli Gittin recounts how three wealthy men give provisions abundant enough to sustain Jerusalem for twenty-one years. [20] Unlike the anonymous host who refuses Bar Qamtsa a place at his table and thereby initiates the destruction of Jerusalem, this scene highlights three wealthy men whose patronage (could have) sustained Jerusalem.

The symbolic names of the three men exemplify aspects of idealized patronage: abundant generosity, great wealth, powerful social connections, and an intimacy with God that can bring about miraculous rescue. Ben Kalba Savuʿa satisfies everyone who enters his home, even though they arrive as ravenous as starving dogs. Unlike the anonymous host, Ben Kalba Savuʿa guarantees that all his guests leave satisfied. Ben Tsitsit Hakeset has powerful connections with Rome—his "seat" (*keset*) can be found among the Roman elite and his *tsitsit* dangle from his seat-cushion, visible markers of Jewish identity. The alternative explanation,

---

20. The tale is surely hyperbolic on this point—twenty-one years is an unrealistic amount of time in the context of ancient siege warfare. Even large, fortified cities rarely held out for more than a year when under siege. Analyzing the relationship between famine and siege warfare in the Roman and Byzantine empires from the mid-fourth to the mid-eighth century, Stathakopoulos notes that the duration of sieges varied. A year was common for a larger, well-fortified city, with smaller ones often capitulating in half that time. Of the cases he has collected, "no siege surpassed a period of 14 months." Stathakopoulos, *Famine and Pestilence*, 47.

that Ben Tsitsit Hakeset has his seat among "the great ones of Rome," seems a prescient foreshadowing of Titus's death scene, where Rav Pinḥas ben ʿAruva too was among the great ones of Rome to see the splitting of the tyrant's skull.[21] In contrast to Bar Qamtsa, who breaks with the Jewish community in order to affiliate with Rome, Ben Tsitsit Hakeset maintains the ability to engage with Rome and remain loyal to Jerusalem. Nakdimon's name recalls a rain miracle which allows him to provide for festival pilgrims during a time of intense drought. While the Bavli Gittin narrative does not retell the full story of Nakdimon's name, the sugya references a talmudic legend that recounts Nakdimon's prowess as a bountiful provider and a man whose great intimacy with God allows him to call forth miracles.[22] Yet despite their exemplary gifts and powerful connections, Jerusalem's patrons prove unable to protect the city. Famine occurs because "rebellious thugs" burn these gifts in a disastrous attempt to compel the people of Jerusalem to rise up and fight the Roman army. Jerusalem starves because of rebels who refuse the rabbis' suggestion to negotiate peace, not because of the Roman siege and not because of God. The tragedy of famine becomes even more acute because of its political, profoundly human cause.

Marta bat Boethus: The Tragedy of Women in Famine

The next scene contrasts the significant but ultimately fruitless generosity of three patrons of Jerusalem with the frivolous selfishness of Marta bat Boethus, a wealthy woman who starves to death on the streets of Jerusalem. Marta was a well-known figure for rabbinic audiences; several rabbinic texts mention her by name, always in the context of sumptuous wealth. In the tannaitic corpus, Marta bat Boethus appears as a paradigmatic example of a rich widow,[23] as the wife of the high priest Joshua ben Gamla,[24] and as the mother of two priests who brought private sacrifices to the Temple in a particularly distinctive manner that showcased their wealth

---

21. Bavli Gittin 56b. See discussion in Chapter 5.

22. An explanation of Nakdimon's name appears in Bavli Taʿanit 19b–20a. For a discussion of this narrative, see Belser, *Power, Ethics, and Ecology*, 132–136.

23. Sifre Deuteronomy reads: *You shall not . . . take a widow's garment in pledge*: whether rich or poor, even if she were [as rich as] Marta bat Boethus. Sifre Deuteronomy, Ki tetse, par. 281, to Deuteronomy 24:17 (ed. Finkelstein, p. 298).

24. Mishnah Yevamot 6:4 rules that a high priest may not marry a widow, but that he may marry a widow whom he betrothed *before* he became high priest. The Mishnah uses Marta as an example of the latter case, writing "There was the case of Joshua ben Gamla who betrothed Marta bat Boethus and the king nominated him high priest and he took her to wife."

and status.[25] In later rabbinic texts, however, Marta appears primarily as a symbol of tragedy—exemplifying the dire straits that befall wealthy women in the midst of disaster. Bavli Gittin's Marta tale is one of many rabbinic stories that recount the poverty of once-illustrious daughters and use their desperate circumstances to exemplify the tragedy of destruction.[26] Marta is, in Sonja Pilz's recent analysis, "a mirror and a symbol of the city of Jerusalem," her body used to illustrate the city's fall. She flourished while the temple stood, but she could not survive its ruin.[27]

Bavli Gittin recounts the tragic story of the last days of Marta bat Boethus, fashioning her into a symbol of pathos that embodies the misery and suffering of ruined Jerusalem. Bavli Gittin 56a reads:

Marta, the daughter of Boethus,
>   was the wealthiest woman in Jerusalem.
She sent forth her agent and said to him,
>   "Go and bring me bread of the finest flour from the market."
While he was gone, it sold.
He came and told her there was no fine flour,
>   but white flour remained.
"Go and bring it to me."
While he was gone, it sold.
He came and told her there was no white flour,
>   but poor-grade flour remained.

---

25. Tosefta Kippurim 1:13–14 describes "the case of the sons of Marta bat Boethus." Tal Ilan regards this case as another situation that dramatizes the wealth and prominence of Marta and her sons. Tal Ilan, *Mine and Yours Are Hers: Retrieving Women's History from Rabbinic Literature* (Leiden: Brill, 1997), 89–90.

26. Similar stories of wealthy women in distress give the woman's name as Miriam bat Boethus in Lamentations Rabbah 1:47, to Lamentations 1:16 (ed. Buber, p. 86); Miriam bat Nakdimon ben Gurion in Lamentations Rabbah 1:48, to Lamentations 1:16 (ed. Buber, p. 86) and in Pesikta Rabbati 29–30 (ed. Friedman, p. 140a); Miriam bat Shimʿon in Yerushalmi Ketubot 5:13 (30c); the daughter of Nakdimon ben Gurion in Tosefta Ketubot 5:9, Sifre Deuteronomy, Nitsavim, par. 305, to Deuteronomy 31:21 (ed. Finkelstein, p. 325), Bavli Ketubot 66a and Avot de-Rabbi Natan A:17 (ed. Schechter, pg. 65); or an anonymous Jewish woman in the Mekhilta de-Rabbi Ishmael, Baḥodesh 1, to Exodus 19:1 (ed. Horovitz-Rabin, 203–204). While the names of these distressed women vary and some details of their stories shift, the existence of many parallel stories suggest that these tales of once-prosperous women were culturally significant for the rabbis. For a close analysis of the development of this aggadic motif, see Burton Visotzky, "Most Tender and Fairest of Women: A Study in the Transmission of Aggada," *Harvard Theological Review* 76, no. 4 (October 1983): 403–418.

27. Pilz argues that Marta's story is used to draw a sharp line separating rabbinic Judaism from the temple-centered Judaism of the past; Marta's death, humiliation, and bodily devastation become a sign of the old order that has passed away. Pilz, *Food and Fear*, 50–51.

"Go and bring it to me."
While he was gone, it sold.
He came and told her that there was no poor-grade flour,
    but barley flour remained.
"Go and bring it to me."
While he was gone, the barley flour sold.

She took off her shoes and said,
    "I will go out and I will see. Perhaps I will find something to eat."
She put her foot in excrement and died.
Rabbi Yoḥanan ben Zakkai applied to her the verse:
And she who is most tender and dainty among you
    [so tender and dainty
        that she would never set a foot on the ground,
shall begrudge the husband of her bosom and her son and her daughter
        the afterbirth that issues from between her legs
        and the babies she bears;
she shall eat them secretly, because of utter want]. (Deuteronomy 28:56)

And there are those who say:
She ate from the shriveled figs of Rabbi Tsadok
    and was overcome.
For Rabbi Tsadok sat and fasted for forty years,
    so that Jerusalem would not be destroyed.
When he ate anything, it could be seen from the outside
    [because he was so thin.]
When he was regaining strength,
    they brought him dried figs
    and he sucked them and threw them away.
While she was dying,
    she brought out all the gold and silver that she had
    and threw it in the market.
She said, "Aie—what has it brought me?"
Thus it is written:
They shall throw their silver into the streets
    and their gold shall be treated as something unclean.
[Their silver and gold shall not avail to save them
    in the day of the Lord's wrath—
    to satisfy their hunger or to fill their stomachs.
Because [their beautiful adornments]
    made them stumble into guilt. (Ezekiel 7:19)

Bavli Gittin characterizes Marta as a frivolous and selfish aristocrat, a woman who refuses to moderate her high-class tastes even in times of crisis.[28] Marta's request for "finest flour" stands out as a culturally significant claim of elite status, reflecting a common Mediterranean preference for white bread as a mark of high status.[29] Barley bread, by contrast, commonly appears in rabbinic sources as food fit only for animals and for the poorest of the poor.[30] Through intensely patterned language that dramatizes the exchange between Marta and her agent over the declining quality of bread, Bavli Gittin highlights Marta's unwillingness to relinquish her high-class status. She holds out for the richest food her agent can find and thereby forfeits her opportunity to purchase anything at all.

When Marta resolves to go out and search for herself, the narrative emphasizes her elite "delicate" sensibilities, portraying her as physically unable to endure the harsh reality of besieged Jerusalem. Marta takes off her shoes, thereby fulfilling the curse articulated in Deuteronomy 28:56, which describes the downfall of a woman so tender and dainty that she would never let her bare feet touch the ground.[31] Other rabbinic texts use a similar association between wealthy women

28. In this narrative, the Bavli seems to exhibit strong disapproval for the practice of sustaining the formerly wealthy poor according to their previous social status. For a discussion of other sugyot that demonstrate the Bavli's increasing ambivalence toward the expectation that wealthy people who fall on hard times have a right to lavish provisioning at communal expense, see Alyssa Gray, "The Formerly Wealthy Poor: From Empathy to Ambivalence in Rabbinic Literature of Late Antiquity," *AJS Review* 33, no. 1 (2009): 101–133.

29. On the association between white bread and high-class status, see Andrew Dalby, *Siren Feasts: A History of Food and Gastronomy in Greece* (New York: Routledge, 1996), 93. Malmberg notes that access to high-quality foods was an important marker of class hierarchy in Roman society, with elite status often demarcated through elaborate displays of food and special dishes. Malmberg, "Visualizing Hierarchy," 14.

30. Pilz also draws attention to significance of barley and its association with animals, as well as the close connection between barley and excrement in the Peskita Rabbati version of the Marta tale, where Miriam bat Nakdimon picks barley grains out of the excrement of animals. Pilz, *Food and Fear*, 61. On barley as a low-class food, see Hamel, *Poverty and Charity in Roman Palestine*. Based on mishnaic texts, Sperber concludes that in the second century, wheat cost twice as much as barley (2 kabs of wheat is regarded as equivalent to 4 kabs of barley). Similarly, in the Edict of Diocletian of 301 CE, wheat was almost double the price of barley (100/60 denarii). Daniel Sperber, *Roman Palestine 200–400: Money and Prices*, 2nd ed. (Ramat-Gan: Bar-Ilan University Press, 1991), 112. Though the barley crop was often maligned, it was likely a critical crop for subsistence. Barley took a shorter time to mature, was more resistant to disease, and was better able to grow in thin, limestone soil that is characteristic of Greece, the Judean hills, and elsewhere in the Mediterranean world. Thomas Braun, "Barley Cakes and Emmer Bread," in *Food in Antiquity*, ed. John Wilkins, David Harvey, and Mike Dobson (Exeter: University of Exeter Press, 1995), 25–37.

31. Pilz underscores the significance of the fact that Bavli Gittin attributes this comment to Rabbi Yoḥanan ben Zakkai, the rabbi who negotiates with Vespasian for the founding of the rabbinic academy at Yavneh. The judgment on Marta, Pilz argues, is similarly a judgment on

and protected feet to portray Marta as the ultimate aristocrat. Lamentations Rabbah describes Marta going to see her husband, the high priest, on the day of Yom Kippur.[32] Even on the Day of Atonement, when one might expect an embrace of asceticism, Marta walks along carpets that were laid from the door of her house to the temple, so that her feet never touch the ground. The carpets, Pilz suggests, not only serve as a sign of Marta's spectacular wealth and privilege, they also insulate her from contact with dirt in the streets of Jerusalem.[33] Bavli Gittin inverts this image of "pampered feet" to portray Marta's tragic end. Until the destruction of Jerusalem, Marta never exposes her bare, tender toes.

By taking off her shoes, Marta enters into a direct encounter with the misery of Jerusalem. According to one version of the story, she dies from the shock of stepping into excrement. Within rabbinic narrative, the association between once-wealthy daughters and dung dramatizes the bitter change in the circumstances of these aristocratic women. In Bavli Ketubot 66b–67a, for example, Rabbi Yoḥanan ben Zakkai laments seeing the daughter of Nakdimon ben Gurion scavenge barley from the dung in horses' hooves. When she sees him, she covers herself up with her hair and begs for food—a narrative the Bavli uses to teach the importance of charity and to rebuke Nakdimon ben Gurion for not giving away enough of his fortune.[34] But unlike the more common motif of women who search for grain in dung, Bavli Gittin's Marta does not scavenge. Instead, our tale uses the excrement to highlight her delicacy and helplessness, emphasizing her inability to forage for food. She expires before she can seek out the nourishment that might be hidden in the midst of offal. Her tender flesh cannot withstand an unmediated encounter with excrement on the streets of Jerusalem. In the second version of her death, Marta *does* forage—attempting to sustain

---

the temple culture that has passed away. Pilz, *Food and Fear*, 85. On the interpretation of the verse, see Naomi G. Cohen, "The Theological Stratum of the Martha b. Boethus Tradition: An Explication of the Text in Gittin 56a," *Harvard Theological Review* 69 (1976): 188–189.

32. Lamentations Rabbah 1:47, to Lamentations 1:16 (ed. Buber, p. 86). The Leningrad manuscript gives the woman the name of "Marta." Printed editions read "Miriam." The names and stories of these two women are often interchanged in the literature. See Visotzky, "Most Tender and Fairest of Women."

33. Pilz, *Food and Fear*, 55.

34. The motif of women picking grains from dung appears widely: Bavli Ketubot 67a; Tosefta Ketubot 5:9–10; Yerushalmi Ketubot 5:13 (30b–c); Lamentations Rabbah 1:48, to Lamentations 1: (ed. Buber, p. 86); Sifre Deuteronomy *Nitsavim, pis. 305,* to Deuteronomy 31:21 (ed. Finkelstein, p. 325); Mekhilta de-Rabbi Ishmael, *par. Baḥodesh* 1, to Exodus 19:1 (ed. Horovitz-Rabin, 203–204), and Pesikta Rabbati 29–30 (ed. Friedman, p. 140a). In many cases, the sage who sees her is Rabbi Eliezer ben Tsadok. See extensive discussion of the relationship between these narratives in Visotzky, "Most Tender and Fairest of Women."

herself on the cast-off figs that Rabbi Tsadok used to sustain himself during his lengthy fast, when he sought to prevent the destruction of Jerusalem. Marta and Tsadok experience profoundly different perceptions of crisis: Marta is the pinnacle of unknowing, the woman whose obliviousness to the siege propels her into an arrogant, ignominious death. Tsadok is the ultimate visionary, the one who fasted for forty years in anticipation of the crisis, long before others recognized the danger.[35] Their divergent responses to the figs reveal a stark contrast between a rabbi fasting and a wealthy woman starving. While Rabbi Tsadok is revivified by the juice of a few figs, Marta dies trying to draw sustenance from his husks.[36] By contrast, Bavli Gittin portrays Marta as highly sensitive, a vulnerable body that cannot bear contact with the grim reality of besieged Jerusalem. Marta's delicacy becomes her death sentence.

Frivolity and Danger: Women's Wealth in Bavli Gittin's Narrative of Destruction

Marta's story stands within a long history of representing crisis through womanhood, a tradition in which visual and textual images of women's bodies become icons of disaster.[37] Marta's glorious wealth provides a backdrop against which the Bavli can narrate her spectacular fall. Anthony Saldarini suggests that the Babylonian Talmud uses Marta as a paradigm for the suffering and death among all Jerusalem's residents, positioning her as an extreme case that highlights the horror of the destruction. In Saldarini's view, Marta's wealth dramatizes the profundity of the crisis, revealing how the destruction brings suffering to all people, regardless of wealth.[38] Marta's story clearly underscores a theological claim that wealth will not save a person from suffering. The narrative concludes with a

---

35. In Bavli Yoma 39a–b, the Bavli attributes significance to forty years before the destruction, associating it with signs and portents that prefigure the destruction.

36. Rubenstein, *Talmudic Stories*, 154. Pilz reads the empty husks as a critique of Marta's values, her tendency to focus on concern for the "empty shells" of superficialities and appearances. Pilz, *Food and Fear*, 86.

37. Drawing upon longstanding biblical metaphors that imagine Jerusalem as a woman, Marta embodies both the glory and tragedy of the city, nation, and people. The motif of a devastated Jerusalem as a ruined woman appears most prominently in the book of Lamentations. For an analysis of rabbinic use of gender and destruction in Lamentations Rabbah, see Hasan-Rokem, *Web of Life*, especially Chapter 6.

38. Anthony J. Saldarini, "Good from Evil: The Rabbinic Response," in *The First Jewish Revolt: Archeology, History, Ideology*, ed. Andrea M. Berlin and J. Andrew Overman (New York: Routledge, 2002), 231.

sharp denunciation of wealth via the evocation of Ezekiel 7:19, and Marta's final words explicitly proclaim the uselessness of her riches. But Bavli Gittin portrays Marta's wealth in a particularly negative light, contrasting Marta's frivolity with the generosity of Jerusalem's patrons and emphasizing the way in which her own destruction came about because she failed to use her wealth well.

While Marta's final days are narrated in the context of famine, Bavli Gittin emphasizes that the cause of her death lies in her foolish unwillingness to relinquish her high-class desires. Marta begins the story in a position of considerable power, issuing precise instructions to her agent, setting the terms of her own purchase, and deploying her agent to insulate herself from the risks of the market.[39] But as the tale unfolds, the tale strips her of agency, neutralizing the utility of her wealth. By emphasizing the foolishness of her instructions, Bavli Gittin positions Marta as the architect of her own doom. Had she used her wealth judiciously at the start of the crisis or instructed her agent to purchase whatever food he could find, Marta might have escaped disaster. While Marta began the tale as a woman who does not need to go out because she has a servant to shop on her behalf, she becomes a woman who *should not* go out because she cannot survive on her own. The discourse of women's risk binds women's possibilities. Marta's death on the streets of Jerusalem reinscribes images of female dependency and vulnerability, underscoring the harsh costs that upper-class women pay when they are exposed to danger.

Through Marta's tale, Bavli Gittin crafts a striking contrast between a wealthy woman's frivolity and the patronage of three aristocratic men who seek to sustain Jerusalem. While each of these figures use wealth in a way that ultimately proves ineffective, the three men make a credible effort to deploy their riches for the good of the community. They provide consumable gifts of grain, oil, wine, and wood—with the Bavli quick to point out that "the rabbis praised the wood" as necessary for feeding the people. Patronage is not out of the question for Marta; wealthy women did serve as patrons in late antiquity. Josephus portrays Queen Helene of Adiabene as a major patron of Jerusalem, recounting how she sent her servants out to secure grain from Alexandria and figs from Cyprus in order to relieve a bitter famine.[40] Bernadette Brooten has also demonstrated that women

---

39. Cynthia Baker critiques scholars' tendency to view the market as a place devoid of women. She discusses the involvement of Jewish women in the market in light of rabbinic texts and the material culture of the Galilee, as well as analyzing the significance of gender in the market in rabbinic culture. Baker, *Rebuilding the House of Israel*, 77–112. See also Rosenblum, *Food and Identity*, 22.

40. Josephus, *Jewish Antiquities*, trans. Louis H. Feldman, Loeb Classical Library (Cambridge: Harvard University Press, 1965), 20:2:5.

made significant financial contributions to Jewish synagogues, serving as patrons of Jewish religious life and community.[41] But Bavli Gittin situates Marta as the antithesis of patronage, contrasting her elite desire for securing her own luxurious bread with the generous giving of the men who sustained Jerusalem. Her wealth brings no benefit to the city or its populace. When she relinquishes her riches at the end of the tale, she throws her silver and gold in the street. Even this final act of renunciation has no charitable purpose. With the bread gone from the market, what profit will her coins bring?

The Dangers of Privilege: Wealth, Servitude, and Unknowing in Bavli Gittin

Through the narrative of Marta bat Boethus, Bavli Gittin crystallizes a discourse of wealth as a physical and moral danger. By closing the tale with reference to Ezekiel 7:19, the Bavli uses Marta as fulfillment of a verse that prophesies a situation in which people will throw their silver into the streets, recognizing that wealth will neither save them from God's wrath nor fill their hungry bellies. But Ezekiel 7:19 does not simply condemn the uselessness of wealth; it situates wealth as an active source of danger: the people's riches "caused them to stumble into guilt." By deploying this verse to conclude the Marta tale, Bavli Gittin emphasizes a link between wealth and moral danger. In purely sociological terms, the Bavli's connection between riches and risk is inaccurate. Access to wealth provides immense material protection from the threat of famine. Ancient sources testify to the disproportionate risks that disaster and famine pose for people living in poverty.[42] Despite this lacuna, however, the Bavli's representation of the relationship between the master or mistress and the lower-status men who serve them does reveal an striking awareness of the ways elites may be at risk because of their dependence on others, thereby shedding light on the corrosive power of systems of servitude and slavery.[43]

Low-status, subordinate men play a critical role in driving the plot of the entire narrative. The Bar Qamtsa tale begins by attributing the destruction of the temple to a servant's mistake, describing the disastrous chain of events that unfold when the host's servant (*shama'eh*) fetches his master's enemy instead of his friend.

---

41. Bernadette Brooten, *Women Leaders in the Ancient Synagogue: Inscriptional Evidence and Background Issues*, Brown Judaic Studies 36 (Chico, CA: Scholars Press, 1982), 141–144.

42. Saldarini, "Good from Evil," 231.

43. I thank Bernadette Brooten for drawing my attention to this point and for stimulating conversation on the representation of subordinates and slaves in late antique texts.

While the narrative never returns to the servant's error, the entire plot is set in motion by his failure to follow precisely the master's instructions. In the Marta narrative, Bavli Gittin inverts the servant's character flaw. As the tale recounts the obsessive back-and-forth from Marta's home to the market, the sugya places at least partial blame on the hyper-punctiliousness of her agent (*shaluḥah*). As Jeffrey Rubenstein notes, the confusion between Qamtsa and Bar Qamtsa stems from a servant's minute but disastrous deviation in his instructions—but Marta's death rests in part on her agent's unwillingness to compromise his charge.[44]

Marta's reliance on an agent also plays a critical role in fostering her own disastrous ignorance of besieged Jerusalem. Not only does extravagant wealth diminish Marta's physical capacity to grapple with the gritty realities of famine and war, her patrician status insulates her from an awareness of suffering in the streets of Jerusalem. While Bavli Gittin makes no explicit critique of Marta's reliance upon an agent, the narrative dynamics suggest that her use of the agent veils her own awareness of the urgency of famine. Marta's use of the agent keeps her in the dark, obscuring the realities of famine. It fosters the tragic obliviousness that leads to her downfall. By accentuating the perils of wealth and the dangers that high status poses to elites, the tale diverts attention from the risks borne by the underclass. In the talmudic narrative, Marta's agent goes for her into the gritty streets of Jerusalem—the streets that proved toxic to Marta's tender flesh. Her agent bears the risk of this encounter, a danger that goes entirely unspoken by the text. This silence likely stems from the rabbis' intensely gendered discourse about women and danger in the marketplace.[45] Yet it also underscores a common tendency to overlook the ways that slavery, servitude, and other economically stratified labor systems force subordinates to bear risk by exposing lower-class bodies to danger.[46]

Celebration and Oblivion: Feasting and Slaughter on the King's Mountain

When it recounts the destruction of Tur Malka, Bavli Gittin once again uses a feast narrative to draw critical attention to issues of opulence, danger, and oblivion

---

44. "If in the first scene the servant confuses his instructions and invites the wrong person, in this case the servant does nothing, leading to death. Nonaction can be worse than wrong action—the moral of the story presented in microcosm." Rubenstein, *Talmudic Stories*, 154.

45. Baker, *Rebuilding the House of Israel*, 77–112.

46. Jennifer Glancy argues that late antique slaves often served as "body doubles" for their owners, physically insulating their owners from risk or violence. Glancy, *Slavery in Early Christianity*, 15.

to catastrophe. The story begins by evoking Rabbi Yoḥanan's original teaching that blames the destruction of Tur Malka (King's Mountain) on a rooster and a hen, once again recounting how a set of seemingly minor misunderstandings lead to disaster. Bavli Gittin 57a reads:

Tur Malka was destroyed over a rooster and a hen.
When they processed out with the bride and the groom,
    it was the custom to lead a rooster and a hen before them,
    so as to say: "Be fruitful and multiply as the birds."
A troop of Roman soldiers passed through and took [the birds] from them,
    so [the Jews] fell upon [the soldiers] and beat them.
They went and told Caesar: "The Jews are rebelling against you!"
    and he came against them.

[The Jews] had with them a certain man, Bar Droma,
    who could jump a mile—and he killed them.
Caesar took his crown and placed it on the earth.
He said: "Lord of All the World, may it not please you
    to surrender me and my kingdom to the hand of a single man."
Bar Droma was brought down on account of his mouth,
    for he said: "But You have rejected us, God.
    You do not march with our armies." (Psalms 60:12)
But David also said this!
David only wondered whether it was so.
While [Bar Droma was] on the toilet,
    a snake came and tore out his intestines and he died.

[Caesar] said, "Since a miracle was done for me,
    I will leave them alone this time."
He left them alone and they rejoiced—
    they ate and they drank
    and they lit lamps so abundant that the seal of a signet ring
    could be seen for more than a mile.
[Caesar] said: "The Jews are rejoicing greatly over me!"
So he returned and came against them.

R. 'Asi said: Three hundred thousand swordsmen ascended Tur Malka
    and they slaughtered them there for three days and three nights,
    while on the other side of the mountain,
    they celebrated and made merry,
    and one side did not know about the other.

According to the Tur Malka story, Jewish custom calls for communities to parade a rooster and a hen before a bride and groom on their wedding day to bring the new couple fertility. In the midst of this celebration, a troop of Roman soldiers snatch up the birds. The Jewish wedding guests mob the soldiers, who report to Caesar that the Jews are rebelling against imperial authority. Like the Bar Qamtsa story, the Tur Malka narrative rests on a critical misunderstanding: the soldiers believe the Jews are rising up in revolt, but Jewish violence is actually a spontaneous response to the soldiers' desecration of a Jewish wedding custom. Bavli Gittin once again emphasizes that Roman elites see rebellion where none is intended. The Bar Qamtsa tale likewise begins with a feast where a Jewish man is shamed by another Jew, turns informer, and then crafts an elaborate hoax with a blemished sacrifice that leads Caesar to think the Jews are rebelling against him. Caesar is vulnerable to Bar Qamtsa's machinations because he does not know the intricacies of Jewish sacrificial law and because he is duped by a treacherous informer. Set up by Bar Qamtsa's sabotage, Caesar regards the rabbis' unwillingness to sacrifice as an act of defiance and launches an unnecessary military campaign against the Jews. In the Tur Malka story, the feast is the final straw—not the first. Inverting the motif of the Jewish informer, the Tur Malka assault is first set in motion by *Roman* informants who give poor counsel because they fail to recognize their own culpability for causing violence. The soldiers' ignorance of Jewish customs leads them to mistake a wedding mob for an actual Jewish revolt and prompts another needless military action that nearly results in Caesar's destruction. Once again, subordinate men lead elites into error.

The narrative telescopes the conflict between Rome and the Jews to an engagement between two men: Bar Droma, the Jewish hero whose physical prowess allows him to kill the Roman forces; and Caesar, who pleads with God to avoid being subjected to the hand of this one man. Bavli Gittin's account links Caesar's ultimate victory with his humble stance before God, while connecting Bar Droma's downfall with his blasphemous claim, via Psalm 60:12, that God has rejected the people of Israel and does not march with their armies. Bavli Gittin describes Bar Droma's brutal end, narrating how a snake comes upon him while he is in the privy and tears out his intestines. It is a death scene that evokes the corporeal agonies of the previous chapter, a death meant to remind the reader of God's manifest sovereignty over the bodies of Roman and Jew alike. Caesar interprets Bar Droma's death as a miracle performed on his behalf and decides to leave the Jews alone.[47] When Caesar withdraws, the Jews rejoice with a great

---

47. This remark echoes an important moment earlier in the sugya, when Rabbi Yoḥanan is rebuked for failing to ask Vespasian to withdraw from the city and spare Jerusalem. See Rubenstein, *Talmudic Stories*, 356, n. 72.

feast—and the opulence of their celebration prompts Caesar to return and anni-hilate them. Through this image of the provocative feast, the Tur Malka story again dramatizes the dangerous repercussions of a banquet, linking the elaborate display of wealth with destructive emotions of anger or shame.

The final lines of the Tur Malka tale give haunting voice to the revelers' ignorance of the disaster unfolding just beyond their borders. Caught up in the extravagant celebration, half the people of Tur Malka feast in the midst of disaster—unaware of the brutal violence Caesar deploys on the other side of the mountain. With its description of the lavish lights that mark this feast, Bavli Gittin once again empha-sizes that wealth obscures the realities of war, famine, and crisis. The Bavli pays par-ticular attention to the extravagance of the Jewish victory banquet, describing how "they ate and they drank and they lit lamps so abundant that the seal of a signet ring" could be seen at a great distance. Though the lights of the feast illuminate the seal by which an elite man might mark his identity, the same lamps veil the brutal-ities of suffering. Despite (or perhaps because of) those glorious torches with their exuberant light, nothing illuminates the murders beyond their sight lines. With their attention fixated on the luxuries of the feast, the partygoers never glimpse the violence on the other side of the mountain.

Through its tales of feasting and famine, Bavli Gittin calls attention to the ethical cost of elite status, highlighting the physical and moral dangers of social privilege. In the story of Bar Qamtsa, the Bavli casts a critical eye on the social politics of elite banquets, dramatizing how a host and guest's personal intrigues over status and shame endanger an entire community. By linking Bar Qamtsa's treachery with the public humiliation of his expulsion from the feast, Bavli Gittin reveals the great lengths to which elites might go to preserve their own status or avenge its loss. Seething with the indignity of his exclusion from the host's banquet, Bar Qamtsa aligns himself with Roman power and turns informer for a taste of the emperor's bread. In the story of Marta bat Boethus, Bavli Gittin portrays the tragic downfall of an aristocratic woman as a consequence of her foolish unwillingness to forgo her taste for luxury. By linking Marta's wealth with frivolous desire in the midst of crisis, the Bavli suggests that social privilege insu-lates her from the reality of suffering, leaving her unable to accurately perceive the gravity of the situation. While the Bavli uses the Marta tale to articulate a gen-dered critique of elite women's frivolity that contrasts sharply with the generous provision of wealthy male patrons and visionary fasting rabbis, the final feasting tale extends Bavli Gittin's concern more broadly to encompass the moral danger of extravagance. Through the tale of Tur Malka, the Bavli intertwines opulence with oblivion: the bright lights that illuminate the lavish feast black out the vio-lence on the other side of the mountain, leaving the revelers unable to see the cost of luxury.

Ethics In the Midst of Empire: Sin, Suffering, and Self-Critique

Over the course of this book, I have argued that Bavli Gittin's response to the destruction of the temple sounds a strikingly different note. As it grapples with the suffering that engulfed Judea in the wake of the Roman conquest, Bavli Gittin eschews the familiar rabbinic claim that communal crisis is linked to collective sin, that the destruction of the temple represents God's chastisement for communal failings. Where other rabbinic voices aim to preserve the validity and vitality of the covenant by drawing out the sins that might explain the profundity and depth of Jewish suffering, Bavli Gittin takes a more political approach to the destruction, highlighting Roman conquest and minimizing the discourse of Jewish culpability for catastrophe.[48] What, then, shall we make of the self-critical dimensions of Bavli Gittin's account, its critique of elite Jewish hubris in the face of disaster? A reader might take the argument of this chapter to be a restatement of that familiar rabbinic claim, articulated perhaps with greater subtlety and more nuanced attention to the dynamics of status and social power, but at root, still the same: when suffering comes, sin is to blame. That would be, I believe, a misreading of these tales.

Of the stories I have examined in this chapter, the destruction of Tur Malka comes the closest to expressing this theology. Bar Droma is a figure cast in Titus's mold, a leader laid low by arrogance and hubris, perhaps even by blasphemy. In Bavli Gittin's account of Bar Droma's death, we hear an echo of the terrible recompense that came upon the conqueror. While Bavli Gittin's account of Bar Droma's death lacks the triumphal arc that shaped the Titus tale, while it does not relish his comeuppance or revel in his death, it nonetheless imagines his fate as a punishment for personal sin. In the visceral brutality of his death, it reminds the reader that God is sovereign over all human flesh, that Bar Droma himself remains subject to divine authority. Yet the thrust of the Tur Malka tale does not seem to be aimed at articulating divine vengeance for Bar Droma's overstep. Nor does our tale aim to indict the Jews of Tur Malka for their celebration, when the community is spared Caesar's wrath. Bavli Gittin does not fashion those deaths on the mountain as a moment of divine reckoning, an expression of God's judgment or justice. For all that this tale echoes with the sharp and bitter grief of those who feasted all unknowing while their kin were slain, it is not, I think, a condemnation of the revelers. Tur Malka is an indictment of Roman violence, another reminder of the ruthlessness of empire.

---

48. See Introduction and Chapter 1.

The final lines of our tale nuance the Bavli's self-critique in an important way. The Tur Malka tale takes a sharply critical stance toward Bar Droma's hubris, imagining him as a Jewish hero brought down at the height of his powers because he dares suggest that God no longer keeps faith with the Jewish people, that the tangible fact of tragedy reveals divine rejection. Bar Droma stands here as a difficult reminder that the Romans have not cornered the market on hubris, that arrogance is not only a character flaw that befalls the conqueror. In striking contrast to Bar Droma's brash pronouncement, Bavli Gittin valorizes Caesar's capitulation to the God of Israel, his humble deference as he lays his crown upon the ground, the honest surrender in his prayer. Yet for all that Bavli Gittin celebrates this moment of imperial submission, it does not embrace Caesar as a moral exemplar. Unlike Nero's deep relinquishment of status and his self-exile from empire, Caesar's is a momentary conversion, a necessity borne of emergency on the battlefield. It does not last. While Caesar will efface himself before Israel's God, he does not offer the same to his subjects. The final lines of the Tur Malka tale lay plain the limits of imperial humility. The Roman emperor might bow piously before Israel's God—but any insult, any hint of mockery from the Jews, he will repay with brutal violence.

In narrating the destruction of Jerusalem and the devastation of Judea, Bavli Gittin trains its eye on empire. Its critical discourse aims to pierce the power politics of Roman conquest, to protest the brutality of imperial dominance, to make plain the scar that Roman violence leaves upon Jewish flesh. Its narratives foretell that God's power will one day overcome the empire ascendant. But the critical discourse of Bavli Gittin's narrative does not take aim at Rome alone. Through these tales of opulence and oblivion, through stories that illuminate how luxury can draw the eye away from the realities of suffering and crisis, Bavli Gittin complicates its ethics and its politics. Just as its portrayals of Roman generals offer a complex portrait of the enemy's moral capacities, its assessment of its own people is likewise nuanced. For all that Bavli Gittin avoids castigating the victims of imperial violence for their sins, neither does it fashion them as angels. Bavli Gittin's Jews are not immune to the perils of arrogance, hubris, or callous disregard for pain.

Postlude—Theology in the Flames

EMPATHY, CATACLYSM, AND GOD'S RESPONSIVITY
TO SUFFERING IN BAVLI GITTIN

OVER THE COURSE of this book, you have followed me far. You have followed me into places of brutality and pain: across the killing fields of memory, to places of imprisonment, to Roman bedrooms and imperial slave ships, where captured Jews laid claim as best they could to shards of choice and circumstance. You have lingered with the flesh of those who found themselves on the underside of imperium: in the ruins of the street corners or the shattered bones of the temple, amidst bodies remade by rape or by the gnaw of hunger. You have come before the rock where cracked tefillin cases lie like unquiet revenants. You have probed the contours of constraint, tarried with the thin places of remembrance, where the last unspeakable traces of blood and loss sink into the arms of earth.

Will you follow me once more, through one last tale of tears?

In Bavli Baba Metsia 58b–59b, in the midst of a lengthy discussion about business fraud, as the Bavli discusses the problem of verbal wronging, the rabbis recount the story of a spectacular rabbinic argument, in which Rabbi Eliezer insists on the halakhic purity of a certain kind of oven. The Oven of Akhnai is a familiar tale, quite like that of Qamtsa and Bar Qamtsa, a story many readers of rabbinic literature have heard and told so many times that we are already sure we know how it goes. Rather than take up the ordinary mode of rabbinic disputation, Rabbi Eliezer rebuts his colleagues' claims with a stunning series of miraculous proofs, culminating with a heavenly voice that proclaims that the law is on his side. The other rabbis refuse to cede to such unconventional argumentation. The law, Rabbi Yehoshua famously claims, "is not in heaven." It is, instead, in the rabbis' own hands.

Every year, as I teach this story to my students, they are arrested by the audacity of this claim, and by the Bavli's image of a God who responds to Rabbi Yehoshua's words with the complex emotion of a parent whose children have grown into maturity and cleverness, a God who smiles and laughs and says, "My sons, my sons, they have defeated me!" Every year, I must push them to read on, to ask how this moment of divine pride and satisfaction gives way to a shattering catastrophe. The victorious rabbis turn on Rabbi Eliezer. They surround him, defame him, and subject him to the ban, refusing him a place within the rabbinic community. When Rabbi Eliezer learns his fate, he sinks to the ground and weeps. His grief calls forth a cataclysmic response, one that imperils the very fabric of the earth. Bavli Baba Metsia 59b reads:

> Rabbi Eliezer's eyes streamed with tears
> > and he took off his shoes
> > and removed [his seat] and sat on the ground.
>
> The world was smitten in one third of the wheat,
> > one third of the olives,
> > and one half of the barley.
> And some said that even the dough in the hands of women swelled up.
> It was taught:
> The destruction was so great on that day
> > that every place where Rabbi Eliezer cast his eyes—
> > > immediately, it caught fire.

Rabbi Eliezer suffers the bitter lash of public shame, a humiliation that rabbinic sources understand as a kind of social death.[1] In the Bavli's estimation, to subject a person to public shame, to whiten the face of a colleague before a multitude, is akin to murder.

In this tale, Rabbi Eliezer's grief is not his alone. His pain ricochets out through the world, shattering the harvest, brutalizing the land. The wheat, the olives, and the barley crop are decimated. Rabbi Eliezer casts fire wherever he looks. As the rabbi weeps, the world goes up in flames.

How shall we read this tale? We might, of course, take this story as a cautionary tale about the devastating consequences of violent speech, a reminder that shame can shatter a life, destroy a world. But to read the tale only as a rebuke

---

1. On the connection between the Oven of Akhnai and the Bavli's concern with shame, see Rubenstein, *Talmudic Stories*, 34–63. As Rubenstein has argued, the problem of shame is central to late Babylonian sources. In Rubenstein's estimation, the rabbinic study-house was a site of considerable social risk, "a place of verbal violence and danger. The injuries suffered were not physical, but emotional: shame and humiliation." Rubenstein, *Culture of the Babylonian Talmud*, 78.

against the rabbis who humiliate another sage silences an important dimension
of the story: the way it portrays God as profoundly responsive to human pain.
Bavli Baba Metsia 59b concludes our story with the words of Imma Shalom: "All
the gates are locked, except for the gates of wronging." Though the divine gates
are often shut before prayers, the tears of the wronged have a unique capacity to
stir divine action. Eliezer's pain evokes a powerful response from God.

It is not a particularly compassionate response, nor a measured one. Shame
prompts divine violence. It causes social convulsion. God's response to Rabbi
Eliezer's shame brings tremendous destruction to the world, a destruction that far
outstrips the scope and scale of the inciting incident. Is this divine punishment?
Perhaps. But I would argue that the frame of punishment is too thin a prism to
capture the texture of God's feeling. Divine responsivity seems to better account
for the dynamics of destruction in this tale. Bavli Baba Metsia's God is a God who
cannot countenance Rabbi Eliezer's tears, who is overwhelmed by his grief, who
feels his suffering so intensely that the divine response engulfs the entire world.
This is a God whose empathy comes utterly unbound, a God whose feeling shatters the earth in the wake of one man's pain.

A God, perhaps, who might destroy the temple in response to one man's shame?

Turn back with me, if you will, to the familiar terrain of Bavli Gittin. Across
the entire corpus of Bavli Gittin's account of the destruction of the temple and the
devastation of Judea, the Bavli offers only two explicit comments on the cause of
catastrophe. Both are bound up with an acute moment of pain. Bavli Gittin claims
that God burns the divine house and seals Israel's doom in response to two events:
first, the humiliation of Bar Qamtsa, whose public shame at the banquet begins
the entire chain of circumstance that culminates in catastrophe, and finally, the
tale of a hapless carpenter, who divorces his wife on the advice of his conniving
apprentice and ends up weeping into their cups while he serves them at the table.

Over the course of this book, I have argued that Bavli Gittin's account of the
destruction largely eschews claims that the destruction is caused by Jewish transgression. How, then, should we read these two statements? Are these two stories
a form of counter-theology, moments in which Bavli Gittin's rabbinic storytellers
return to the familiar trope that explains Jewish suffering in terms of sin? Such a
reading is surely possible. Rabbinic theology is famously multivocal.[2] Given the
strikingly unsystematic character of rabbinic theological thought, given the fact
that Bavli Gittin's stories incorporate the traditions and teachings of a wide range
of rabbinic storytellers, surely it should not surprise us to find passages within
this lengthy, complex story-cycle that strike a different theological note. But even

---

2. Belser, *Power, Ethics, and Ecology*, 9–15.

as I acknowledge that these two statements might go against the grain of Bavli Gittin's general approach to the destruction, I want to lay out another possibility: that they deepen and reinforce my claim that Bavli Gittin's stories offer an alternate understanding of God's place amidst suffering and catastrophe.

Rather than read these tales through the prism of sin and punishment, I propose a bold alternative: that these stories reflect an expression of divine empathy for two men who have been victims of acute social oppression. On its face, this assertion is hard to square with the apparent claim that God is *responsible* for destruction, that disaster reflects at least in some way God's own desire. Indeed, both of these traditions underscore that God brings about the destruction, that God burns God's own house. While rabbinic theology has often explained this act through the language of divine chastisement, the absence of a broader rhetorical appeal to sin in Bavli Gittin clears the field for a different possibility. What if God destroys the temple not as a calculated act of punishment against a sinful community, but as an act of self-sacrificial responsiveness to two men who bear the brunt of social violence? For all that it seems an utterly incomprehensible calculus, I wonder: might Bavli Gittin imagine the destruction of the temple and the devastations that follow as sparked by God's intense concern for human suffering?

This may well seem a shocking proposition, especially for those of us who have been steeped in the familiar explanatory logic of catastrophe as a consequence of sin. But think with me, if you will, through the prism of Baba Metsia's story. Unlike the narratives that surround the destruction of the temple, fraught as they are by later generations' need to explain and account for such a devastating loss, Baba Metsia's tale culminates in a destruction that has no historical referent. In that space, unburdened by the weight of history, we can more easily glimpse the textures of divine empathy. We might imagine the possibility of God's profound, if cataclysmic responsivity to the problem of human pain.

In Bavli Baba Metsia's story, the consequences of shame extend beyond the human parties who caused offense.[3] The devastation wrought by the shaming of

---

3. The notion that specific individuals are targeted for punishment in response to shame is already somewhat complicated by the fact that Bavli Baba Metsia shifts the primary antagonists over the course of the sugya. Rabbi Yehoshua appears as the primary opponent of Rabbi Eliezer in the first part of the narrative, while the conclusion focuses on the near death and eventual demise of Rabban Gamliel. While Rubenstein has offered two convincing accounts for the reasons for this shift—either because Rabban Gamliel as Patriarch represents rabbinic authority and bears ultimate responsibility for the ban or because the motif of Rabban Gamliel on a ship was borrowed from earlier tannaitic sources—I am struck by the literary and theological implications of the Bavli's willingness to so leave this incongruity in place. That the rabbi who dies in response to Rabbi Eliezer's prayers was not even present when he was first wronged emphasizes the notion that *God's* response extends far beyond the initial incident. Rubenstein, *Talmudic Stories*, 44, 55.

Rabbi Eliezer imperils the entire world. Major agricultural crops fall to ecological catastrophe, a disaster that will surely result in widespread famine. The wheat, the olives, and the barley did not take part in Eliezer's wrong, nor did the majority of the people who rely on the harvest. The fruits of the earth and the fortunes of the agrarian community are bound up in a drama of which they had no making. Eliezer's incendiary gaze targets not just the rabbis who caused him shame, but anything on which he rests his eye. In Bavli Gittin, shame also prompts a vast, sweeping act of destruction. The devastation extends far beyond the parties directly responsible for causing shame. Gittin's destruction is not directed toward the nameless host who put Bar Qamtsa to shame at his dinner party, nor even the rabbis who remained silent as Bar Qamtsa was thrown out of the feast. Shame plunges the people into a catastrophe not of their making. It sweeps up the entire populace, wrecking land and lives alike. This is no act of targeted divine punishment; it is a convulsion of feeling, an expression of unbounded pain.

Read with me, if you will, the Bavli's final mention of Bar Qamtsa, a tradition that appears not at the conclusion of the banquet narrative itself, but at the very close of Bavli Gittin's account of the destruction of Jerusalem, immediately after it has narrated Titus's eternal punishment in the afterlife. Bavli Gittin 57a reads:

> Come and see how great is the power of shame,
>> for the Holy One Blessed be He supported Bar Qamtsa,
>> destroyed His house,
>> and burnt His sanctuary.

How great is the power of shame. In this passage, Bavli Gittin asserts that God destroys the Second Temple as an affirmation of Bar Qamtsa, as a response to his humiliation, to the wronging he endures. It is an astonishing claim, all the more so because Bar Qamtsa is such a complex character, a man who has been wronged but who is himself also culpable for significant wrongdoing. Bar Qamtsa is hardly a striking exemplar of rabbinic moral values. After Bar Qamtsa transgresses one of the cornerstone principles of early rabbinic political thought—never involve the government in intra-Jewish affairs—the rabbis nearly put him to death to avoid confrontation with Rome. While Bar Qamtsa stands condemned by the rabbis and by many modern readers as a traitor and a tool, Bavli Gittin imagines God as empathizing with Bar Qamtsa's suffering. God espouses the cause of a notorious imperial informer, prompting a cataclysm of destruction that brings down the divine house and engulfs the holy sanctuary. There is something profoundly self-sacrificial about the divine response. Bavli Gittin imagines divine empathy as a matter so all-encompassing that it leads God to set God's own refuge aflame. Without regard for Bar Qamtsa's character flaws or political transgressions, God responds to the injustice of Bar Qamtsa's public humiliation. About matters of shame, God has no sense of proportion.

While both Bavli Gittin and Bavli Baba Metsia offer vivid accounts of divine destruction in response to shame, one important element is missing from the Bar Qamtsa tale: tears. In Bavli Baba Metsia, God's empathy and responsivity is particularly linked to human tears. Consider this passage in Bavli Baba Metsia 59a:

> Rav said: A person should be careful regarding wronging his wife,
>   for where her tears exist, wronging is near.
> Rabbi Eleazar said:
>   From the day that the temple was destroyed,
>   the gates of prayer were locked, as it is said:
>   *Even though I cry and shout, my prayer is shut out.* (Lamentations 3:8)
>   But even though the gates of prayer are locked,
>   the gates of tears are not locked, as it is written:
>   *Hear my prayer Lord and give ear to my cry;*
>   *do not be silent to my tears.* (Psalms 39:13)

A person who cries tears of shame activates God's empathy. In the tradition that opens this passage, Rav claims that a man must be particularly scrupulous about not wronging his wife, for her tears serve as a sign that verbal wronging is close at hand. Highlighting the significance of gender in this passage, Charlotte Fonrobert argues that the sugya takes up and redeploys a gendered cliché of female emotionality that is prominent in Greco-Roman discourse. Yet, as Fonrobert notes, Bavli Baba Metsia's sugya primarily draws attention to the tears of rabbinic men; it presents these men weeping in a way that calls forth the response of heaven.[4] Tears do not merely signal the presence of wronging, they also speak powerfully to God. While prayer has limited communicative utility since the destruction of the temple, tears have profound expressive power. While the one who prays is shut out from the divine presence, the sugya imagines tears attracting divine attention. The gates of tears are not locked. To tears, God will surely respond.

To find tears in Bavli Gittin's account, we must turn to Gittin's final story, the second time it articulates an explicit cause for the destruction. The narrative, which I discussed in detail in the first chapter of this book, begins when a carpenter's apprentice lusts after his master's wife. One day the carpenter needs money,

---

4. Charlotte E. Fonrobert, "When the Rabbi Weeps: On Reading Gender in Talmudic Aggadah," *Nashim: A Journal of Jewish Women's Studies & Gender Issues* 4 (2001): 56–83. For an analysis of sorrow and weeping in rabbinic literature, see Valler, *Sorrow and Distress.*

and he approaches his apprentice for a loan. The scheming apprentice sees his chance to steal his master's wife, and contrives a convoluted plot. He tells the master to send his wife to pick up the money, and then informs him that she has been sexually assaulted on the road. When the duped husband asks the apprentice for advice, he suggests divorcing her—and then claims the woman for his own. To make matters worse, the master borrows money from his apprentice in order to pay for the divorce, making him doubly indebted to his apprentice. The scoundrel suggests that the master work off his debt by serving at his table. From the midst of this portrait of servitude and oppression, Bavli Gittin 58a concludes:

> The apprentice and his new wife used to sit and eat and drink,
>   while the master would stand and serve them drinks
>   and the tears would flow from his eyes and fall into their cups—
>   and at that very hour,
>   the decree of judgment was sealed [against Israel].

While I find this tale profoundly troubling for its silencing of the woman's own suffering, I am nonetheless struck by the way the narrative fashions the husband's tears into a potent symbol of pathos, an expression of pain so profound that it brings about God's passionate response. That Bavli Gittin describes God's action as a decree of judgment underscores the apprentice's culpability, a culpability that grows to engulf the entire nation. Emotional devastation brings about catastrophe; the husband's grief seals Israel's fate.

What might we draw from this, beyond the old canard of violence repaid? Over the course of writing this book, I have let myself linger with this question and I have come to see within Bavli Gittin's tales a God who champions the wronged, a God who sides with those who bear the bitter lash of social violence. Bar Qamtsa and the hapless husband are neither of them spectacular exemplars of moral courage, nor of character. And yet, the Bavli's God is passionately moved by their suffering, profoundly responsive to their cries. This is a God so powerfully affected by the anguish of two ordinary and not especially virtuous men that God will destroy the divine house and plunge the world into disaster for their sake. Bavli Gittin's God, it seems, is a God who champions the victims of violence, a God so moved by heartbreak that God will let the sanctuary be overrun, let the temple go up in flames, rather than turn away from tears. And when catastrophe befalls the people, God's beloved ones? Bavli Gittin aligns God's presence not with the conquering armies, but with those who suffer violence and injustice. It is a powerful reorientation, one that positions God on the underside of imperium, in solidarity with bodies overrun by empire.

It is a powerful reorientation, and yet, it is not enough.

I come to these pages as a queer disabled Jewish feminist, as a scholar committed to a careful and critical parsing of the rabbis' own cultural moment, as well as to my own. For all that I recognize the ethical and theological promise of their project, I am acutely aware of the gaps, the absences in the Bavli's capacity for compassion. In crafting this book, I have sought to surface the figures who are pressed to the edges of the Bavli's memory, to uncover those whose presence leaves only the barest trace. I have tried to look and look again, to probe the textures of silence and loss, to trace those absences that barely register. This is a history of unshed tears, of unheard cries: the wronged wife, the raped whore, the slave boys bound to Roman beds, the daughters drowning in the sea—all the silenced voices that linger like a haunting in the margins of these tales. For me, they are a goad, a reminder, a call: to keep faith with the vanquished, with the wounded, with the wronged, with those whose bodies bear catastrophe's scar.

Bibliography

Abrams, Judith Z. *Judaism and Disability: Portrayals in Ancient Texts from the Tanach through the Bavli*. Washington, DC: Gallaudet University Press, 1998.

Aharoni, Y. "The Expedition to the Judean Desert, 1960, Expedition B." *Israel Exploration Journal* 11 (1961): 11–24.

Alaimo, Stacy. *Bodily Natures: Science, Environment, and the Material Self*. Bloomington: Indiana University Press, 2010.

Alexander, Philip S. *The Targum of Lamentations*. Collegeville: Liturgical Press, 2007.

Alon, Gedalia. "Rabban Joḥanan B. Zakkai's Removal to Jabneh." In *Jews, Judaism, and the Classical World*, translated by Israel Abrahams, 269–313. Jerusalem: Magnes Press, 1977.

Amaru, Betsy Halpern. "The Killing of the Prophets: Unraveling a Midrash." *Hebrew Union College Annual* 53 (1983): 153–180.

Amishai-Maisels, Ziva. "Demonization of the 'Other' in the Visual Arts." In *Demonizing the Other: Antisemitism, Racism, and Xenophobia*, edited by Robert S. Wistrich, 44–72. New York: Routledge, 1999.

Andersen, Francis I., and David Noel Freedman. *Micah: A New Translation with Introduction and Commentary*. Anchor Yale Bible Commentaries, vol. 24. New York: Doubleday, 2000.

Aune, David E. "The Apocalypse of John and Palestinian Jewish Apocalyptic." *Neotestanica* 40, no. 1 (2006): 1–33.

Bader, Mary Anna. *Tracing the Evidence: Dinah in Post-Hebrew Bible Literature*. New York: Peter Lang Publishing, 2008.

Baker, Cynthia. *Rebuilding the House of Israel: Architectures of Gender in Jewish Antiquity*. Stanford, CA: Stanford University Press, 2002.

Bakhos, Carol. *Ishmael on the Border: Rabbinic Portrayals of the First Arab*. Albany: State University of New York Press, 2006.

Baskin, Judith. *Midrashic Women: Formations of the Feminine in Rabbinic Literature*. Hanover: Brandeis University Press, 2002.

————. "Prostitution: Not a Job for a Nice Jewish Girl." In *The Passionate Torah: Sex and Judaism*, edited by Danya Ruttenberg, 24–35. New York: New York University Press, 2009.

Bastomsky, S. J. "The Emperor Nero in Talmudic Legend." *Jewish Quarterly Review* 59, no. 4 (1969): 321–325.

Becker, Adam. *Fear of God and the Beginning of Wisdom: The School of Nisibis and Christian Scholastic Culture in Late Antique Mesopotamia*. Philadelphia: University of Pennsylvania Press, 2006.

Belayche, Nicole. *Iudaea-Palaestina: The Pagan Cults in Roman Palestine (Second to Fourth Century)*. Tübingen: Mohr Siebeck, 2001.

Belser, Julia Watts. "Reading Talmudic Bodies: Disability, Narrative, and the Gaze in Rabbinic Judaism." In *Disability in Judaism, Christianity and Islam: Sacred Texts, Historical Traditions and Social Analysis*, edited by Darla Schumm and Michael Stolzfus, 5–27. New York: Palgrave Macmillan, 2011.

————. "Brides and Blemishes: Queering Women's Disability in Rabbinic Marriage Law." *Journal of the American Academy of Religion* 84, no. 2 (2016): 401–429.

————. "Disability, Animality, and Enslavement in Rabbinic Narratives of Bodily Restoration and Resurrection." *Journal of Late Antiquity* 8, no. 2 (2015): 288–305.

————. "Disability and the Social Politics of 'Natural' Disaster: Toward A Jewish Feminist Ethics of Disaster Tales." *Worldviews: Global Religions, Culture, and Ecology* 19, no. 1 (2015): 51–68.

————. *Power, Ethics, and Ecology in Jewish Late Antiquity: Rabbinic Responses to Drought and Disaster*. New York: Cambridge University Press, 2015.

————. "Judaism and Disability." In *World Religions and Disability*, edited by Darla Schumm and Michael Stoltzfus, 93–113. Waco: Baylor University Press, 2016.

Belser, Julia Watts, and Lennart Lehmhaus. "Disability in Rabbinic Judaism." In *Disability in Antiquity*, edited by Christian Laes, 434–452. New York: Routledge University Press, 2016.

Berghs, Maria. *War and Embodied Memory: Becoming Disabled in Sierra Leone*. Aldershot: Ashgate, 2012.

Berkowitz, Beth. *Execution and Invention: Death Penalty Discourse in Early Rabbinic and Christian Cultures*. New York: Oxford University Press, 2006.

Berlin, Adele. *Lamentations: A Commentary*. Louisville: Westminster John Knox Press, 2002.

Betcher, Sharon V. *Spirit and the Politics of Disablement*. Minneapolis: Fortress Press, 2007.

Biale, Rachel. *Women and Jewish Law: An Exploration of Women's Issues in Halakhic Sources*. New York: Schocken Books, 1984.

Bhabha, Homi K. *The Location of Culture*. New York: Routledge, 1994.

Blank, Sheldon. "The Death of Zechariah in Rabbinic Literature." *Hebrew Union College Annual* 12–13 (1937–1938): 327–346.

Bokser, Baruch. "Rabbinic Responses to Catastrophe: From Continuity to Discontinuity." *Proceedings of the American Academy for Jewish Research* 50 (1983): 37–61.

———. "Wonder-Working and the Rabbinic Tradition: The Case of Hanina ben Dosa." *Journal for the Study of Judaism* 16 (1985): 42–92.

Boustan, Raʿanan S. *From Martyr to Mystic: Rabbinic Martyrology and the Making of Merkavah Mysticism*. Tübingen: Mohr Siebeck, 2005.

———. "Immolating Emperors: Spectacles of Imperial Suffering and the Making of a Jewish Minority Culture in Late Antiquity." *Biblical Interpretation* 17 (2009): 207–238.

Boustan, Raʿanan S., Klaus Herrmann, Reimund Leicht, Annette Y. Reed, and Giuseppe Veltri, eds. *Envisioning Judaism: Studies in Honor of Peter Schäfer on the Occasion of his Seventieth Birthday*. In collaboration with Alex Ramos. 2 vols. Tübingen: Mohr Siebeck, 2003.

Boyarin, Daniel. *Carnal Israel: Reading Sex in Talmudic Culture*. Berkeley: University of California Press, 1993.

———. *Unheroic Conduct: The Rise of Heterosexuality and the Invention of the Jewish Man*. Berkeley: University of California Press, 1997.

———. *Dying for God: Martyrdom and the Making of Christianity and Judaism*. Stanford: Stanford University Press, 1999.

———. "Hellenism in Jewish Babylonia." In *Cambridge Companion to The Talmud and Rabbinic Literature*, edited by Charlotte E. Fonrobert and Martin S. Jaffee, 336–363. Cambridge: Cambridge University Press, 2007.

———. *Socrates and the Fat Rabbis*. Chicago: University of Chicago Press, 2009.

———. "Friends Without Benefits: Or, Academic Love." In *Sex in Antiquity: Exploring Gender and Sexuality in the Ancient World*, edited by Mark Masterson, Nancy Sorkin Rabinwitz, and James Robson, 517–535. New York: Routledge, 2015.

Boyarin, Jonathan, and Daniel Boyarin. *Powers of Diaspora: Two Essays on the Relevance of Jewish Culture*. Minneapolis: University of Minnesota Press, 2002.

Brady, Christian M. M. *The Rabbinic Targum of Lamentations: Vindicating God*. Leiden: Brill, 2003.

Braun, Thomas. "Barley Cakes and Emmer Bread." In *Food in Antiquity*, edited by John Wilkins, David Harvey, and Mike Dobson, 25–37. Exeter: University of Exeter Press, 1995.

Brenner, Athalya. "'On the Rivers of Babylon,' (Psalm 137), or Between Victim and Perpetrator." In *Sanctified Aggression: Legacies of Biblical and Post Biblical Vocabularies of Violence*, edited by Yvonne Sherwood and Jonneke Bekkenkamp, 76–91. New York: T&T Clark, 2003.

Brooten, Bernadette. *Women Leaders in the Ancient Synagogue: Inscriptional Evidence and Background Issues*. Brown Judaic Studies 36. Chico, CA: Scholars Press, 1982.

———, ed. *Beyond Slavery: Overcoming Its Religious and Sexual Legacies*. New York: Palgrave Macmillan, 2010.

———. "Sexual Surrogacy Enables Holy Celibacy: Euklia, Iphidama, and Maximilla in the Passion of Andrew." Harvard Women's Studies in Religion Program Colloquium, Cambridge, MA, March 28, 2012.

Brown, Raymond E. *The Death of the Messiah: From Gethsemane to the Grave: A Commentary on the Passion Narratives in the Four Gospels*, 2 vols. Garden City: Doubleday, 1994.

Bruggeman, Walter. *Isaiah: 1–39*. Philadelphia: Westminster John Knox Press, 1998.

Buell, Denise Kimber. *Why This New Race: Ethnic Reasoning in Early Christianity*. New York: Columbia University Press, 2005.

Burrus, Virginia. *The Sex Lives of Saints: An Erotics of Ancient Hagiography*. Philadelphia: University of Pennsylvania Press, 2007.

Butler, Judith. *Gender Trouble: Feminism and the Subversion of Identity*. New York: Routledge, 1990.

Byron, Gay L. *Symbolic Blackness and Ethnic Difference in Early Christian Literature*. New York: Routledge, 2003.

Camp, Claudia V. *Ben Sira and the Men Who Handle Books: Gender and the Rise of Canon-Consciousness*. Sheffield: Sheffield Phoenix Press, 2013.

Canepa, Matthew P. *The Two Eyes of the Earth: Art and Ritual of Kinship Between Rome and Sasanian Iran*. Berkeley: University of California Press, 2009.

Carter, Warren. "'The blind, lame and paralyzed' (John 5:3): John's Gospel, Disability Studies, and Postcolonial Perspectives." In *Disability Studies and Biblical Literature*, edited by Candida R. Moss and Jeremy Schipper, 129–150. New York: Palgrave Macmillan, 2011.

Castelli, Elizabeth. *Martyrdom and Memory: Early Christian Culture Making*. New York: Columbia University Press, 2004.

Chazan, Robert. "The Condemnation of the Talmud Reconsidered, 1239–1249." *Proceedings of the American Academy for Jewish Research* 66 (1988): 11–30.

———. "Christian Condemnation, Censorship, and Exploitation of the Talmud." In *Printing the Talmud: From Bomberg to Schottenstein*, edited by Sharon Liberman Mintz and Gabriel M. Goldstein, 53–59. New York: Yeshiva University Museum, 2005.

———. "The Trial and Condemnation of the Talmud." *Tikvah Center Working Paper* 1 (2011); http://www.law.nyu.edu/sites/default/files/TikvahWorking PapersArchive/WP1Chazan.pdf.

Chen, Mel Y. *Animacies: Biopolitics, Racial Mattering, and Queer Affect*. Durham: Duke University Press, 2012.

Childs, Brevard S. *Isaiah*. Louisville: Westminster John Knox Press, 2001.

Cohen, Aryeh. "Toward an Erotics of Martyrdom." *Journal of Jewish Thought and Philosophy* 7 (1998): 227–256.

————. "Beginning Gittin/Mapping Exile." In *Beginning/Again: Toward a Hermeneutics of Jewish Texts*, edited by Aryeh Cohen and Shaul Magid, 69–112. New York: Seven Bridges Press, 2002.

Cohen, J. Simcha. *Intermarriage and Conversion: A Halakhic Solution*. Hoboken, NJ: Ktav, 1987.

Cohen, Jeremy. *The Friars and the Jews: The Evolution of Medieval Anti-Judaism*. Ithaca: Cornell University Press, 1982.

————. *Living Letters of the Law: Ideas of the Jew in Medieval Christianity*. Berkeley: University of California Press, 1999.

Cohen, Naomi G. "Rabbi Meir, A Descendant of Anatolian Proselytes: New Light on His Name and the Historical Kernel of the Nero Legend in Gittin 56a." *Journal of Jewish Studies* 23 (Spring 1972): 51–59.

————. "The Theological Stratum of the Martha b. Boethus Tradition: An Explication of the Text in Gittin 56a." *Harvard Theological Review* 69 (1976): 187–195.

Cohen, Norman J. "'Shekhinta ba-Galuta': A Midrashic Response to Destruction and Persecution." *Journal for the Study of Judaism* 13 (1982): 147–159.

Cohen, Shaye J. D. "The Destruction: From Scripture to Midrash." *Prooftexts* 2, no. 1 (1982): 18–39.

Cohn, Yehudah B. *Tangled Up in Text: Tefillin and the Ancient World*. Atlanta: Society for Biblical Literature, 2008.

Cooper, John. *Eat and Be Satisfied: A Social History of Jewish Food*. Northvale, NJ: Jason Aronson, 1993.

Crane, Jonathan K. "Shameful Ambivalences: Dimensions of Rabbinic Shame." *AJS Review* 35, no. 1 (April 2011): 61–84.

D'Arms, John. "Performing Culture: Roman Spectacle and the Banquets of the Powerful." In *The Art of Ancient Spectacle*, edited by Bettina Bergmann and Christine Kondoleon, 301–319. New Haven, CT: Yale University Press, 1999.

Dalby, Andrew. *Siren Feasts: A History of Food and Gastronomy in Greece*. New York: Routledge, 1996.

Davis, Adrienne. "Don't Let Nobody Bother Yo' Principle: The Sexual Economy of American Slavery." In *Sister Circle: Black Women and Work*, edited by S. Harley, 103–127. New Brunswick, NJ: Rutgers University Press, 2002.

Davis, Lennard. *Enforcing Normalcy: Disability, Deafness, and the Body*. New York: Verso, 1995.

————. *Bending Over Backwards: Essays on Disability and the Body*. New York: New York University Press, 2002.

de Wet, Chris. *Preaching Bondage: John Chrysostom and the Discourse of Slavery in Early Christianity*. Berkeley: University of California Press, 2015.

Diamond, Eliezer. *Holy Men and Hunger Artists: Fasting and Asceticism in Rabbinic Culture*. New York: Oxford University Press, 2004.

Dietler, Michael. "Feasts and Commensal Politics in the Political Economy." In *Food and the Status Quest: An Interdisciplinary Perspective*, edited by Polly Wiessner and Wulf Schiefenhövel, 87–125. Providence: Berghahn Books, 1996.

———. "Theorizing the Feast: Rituals of Consumption, Commensal Politics, and Power in African Contexts." In *Feasts: Archaeological and Ethnographic Perspectives on Food, Politics, and Power*, edited by Michael Dietler and Brian Hayden, 65–114. Washington: Smithsonian Institution Press, 2001.

Dobbs-Allsopp, F. W. *Lamentations*. Louisville: Westminster John Knox Press, 2002.

Doran, Robert. "The Martyr: A Synoptic View of the Mother and Her Seven Sons." In *Ideal Figures in Ancient Judaism: Profiles and Paradigms*, edited by John J. Collins and George W. E. Nickelsburg, 189–221. Chico, CA: Scholars Press, 1980.

Dougherty, Carol. *The Poetics of Colonization: From City to Text in Archaic Greece*. New York: Oxford University Press, 1993.

Drijvers, Jan Willem. "Rome and the Sasanid Empire: Confrontation and Coexistence." In *A Companion to Late Antiquity*, edited by Philip Rousseau, 441–454. Oxford: John Wiley and Sons, 2012.

Eck, Werner. "The Bar Kokhba Revolt: The Roman Point of View." *Journal of Roman Studies* 89 (1999): 76–89.

Edwards, Catharine. *The Politics of Immorality in Ancient Rome*. New York: Cambridge University Press, 1993.

Elman, Yaakov. "The Suffering of the Righteous in Palestinian and Babylonian Sources." *Jewish Quarterly Review* n.s. 80 (1990): 315–339.

———. "Righteousness as its Own Reward: An Inquiry into the Theologies of the Stam." *Proceedings of the American Academy for Jewish Research* 72 (1990–91): 35–67.

———. "'Up to the Ears' in Horses' Necks (B.M. 108a): On Sasanian Agricultural Policy and Private 'Eminent Domain.'" *Jewish Studies, an Internet Journal* 3 (2004): 95–149.

———. "Middle Persian Culture and Babylonian Sages: Accommodation and Resistance in the Shaping of Rabbinic Legal Tradition." In *Cambridge Companion to Rabbinic Literature*, edited by Charlotte Elisheva Fonrobert and Martin S. Jaffe, 165–197. New York: Cambridge University Press, 2007.

Epstein, Louis. *The Jewish Marriage Contract: A Study in the Status of the Woman in Jewish Law*. New York: Jewish Theological Seminary, 1927.

Erevelles, Nirmala. "The Color of Violence: Reflecting on Gender, Race, and Disability in Wartime." In *Feminist Disability Studies*, edited by Kim Q. Hall, 117–135. Bloomington: Indiana University Press, 2011.

———. *Disability and Difference in Global Contexts: Enabling a Transformative Body Politic*. New York: Palgrave Macmillan, 2011.

Fanon, Franz. *A Dying Colonialism*. Translated by Haakon Chevalier. New York: Grove Press, 1967.

Fishbane, Michael. *Biblical Myth and Rabbinic Mythmaking.* New York: Oxford University Press, 2005.

Fishbane, Simcha. *Deviancy in Early Rabbinic Literature: A Collection of Socio-Anthropological Essays.* Leiden: Brill, 2007.

Fonrobert, Charlotte E. *Menstrual Purity: Rabbinic and Christian Reconstructions of Biblical Gender.* Stanford: Stanford University Press, 2000.

———. "When the Rabbi Weeps: On Reading Gender in Talmudic Aggadah." *Nashim: A Journal of Jewish Women's Studies & Gender Issues* 4 (2001): 56–83.

———. "The Semiotics of the Sexed Body in Early Halakhic Discourse." In *How Should Rabbinic Literature Be Read in the Modern World,* edited by Matthew Kraus, 79–104. Piscataway: Gorgias Press, 2006.

Fontaine, Carole R. "Hosea" and "A Response to Hosea." In *Feminist Companion to the Later Prophets,* edited by Athalya Brenner, 40–59 and 60–69. Philadelphia: Sheffield Academic Press, 1995.

Foucault, Michel. *The Birth of the Clinic: An Archeology of Medical Perception.* Translated by Alan Sheridan. New York: Vintage Books, 1975.

———. *Discipline and Punish: The Birth of the Prison.* Translated by Alan Sheridan. New York: Vintage Books, 1979.

Friesen, Steven H. *Imperial Cults and the Apocalypse of John: Reading Revelation in the Ruins.* New York: Oxford University Press, 2001.

Frye, Richard. *History of Ancient Iran.* Munich: Beck, 1984.

Garland-Thomson, Rosemarie. *Extraordinary Bodies: Figuring Physical Disability in American Culture and Literature.* New York: Columbia University Press, 1997.

———. "Staring Back: Self-Representations of Disabled Performance Artists." *American Quarterly* 52, no. 2 (2000): 334–338.

———. "Integrating Disability, Transforming Feminist Theory." *National Women's Studies Association Journal* 14, no. 3 (2002): 1–32.

———. "The Case for Conserving Disability." *Journal of Bioethical Inquiry* 9, no. 3 (September 2012): 339–355.

Gevirtz, Marianne Luijken. "Abram's Dream in the Genesis Apocryphon [1Qap Gen]: Its Motifs and Their Function." *Maarav 8* (1993): 229–243.

Gillingham, Susan. "The Reception of Psalm 137 in Jewish and Christian Traditions." In *Jewish and Christian Approaches to the Psalms: Conflict and Convergence,* edited by Susan Gillingham, 64–82. New York: Oxford University Press, 2013.

Glancy, Jennifer. *Slavery in Early Christianity.* Minneapolis: Fortress Press, 2006.

Goldenberg, Robert. "Early Rabbinic Explanations of the Destruction of Jerusalem." *Journal of Jewish Studies* 33 (1982): 517–525.

———. "The Destruction of the Jerusalem Temple: Its Meaning and Consequences." In *The Cambridge History of Judaism, Volume 4,* edited by Steven T. Katz. New York: Cambridge University Press, 2006.

Goldingay, John. *Psalms: Volume 2, Psalms 42–89.* Grand Rapids: Baker Academic, 2007.

Goshen-Gottstein, Alon. *The Sinner and the Amnesiac: The Rabbinic Invention of Elisha ben Abuya and Eleazar ben Arach*. Stanford: Stanford University Press, 2000.

Gracer, Bonnie. "What the Rabbis Heard: Deafness in the Mishnah." *Disability Studies Quarterly* 23 (2003): 192–205.

Gray, Alyssa. "The Formerly Wealthy Poor: From Empathy to Ambivalence in Rabbinic Literature of Late Antiquity." *AJS Review* 33, no. 1 (2009): 101–133.

Green, Arthur. *Keter: The Crown of God in Early Jewish Mysticism*. Princeton: Princeton University Press, 1997.

Green, William Scott. "Palestinian Holy Men: Charismatic Leadership and Rabbinic Traditions." *Aufstieg und Niedergang der römischen Welt* II 19, no. 2 (1979): 619–647.

Greengus, Samuel. *Laws in the Bible and in Early Rabbinic Collections: The Legal Legacy of the Ancient Near East*. Eugene: Wipf and Stock Publishers, 2011.

Gross, Aaron. "The Question of the Creature: Animals, Theology, and Levinas' Dog." In *Creaturely Theology: On God, Humans, and Other Animals*, edited by Celia Deane-Drummond and David Clough, 121–137. London: SCM Press, 2009.

Gross, Aaron, and Anne Vallely, eds. *Animals and the Human Imagination: A Companion to Animal Studies*. New York: Columbia University Press, 2012.

Gruen, Erich. *Heritage and Hellenism: The Reinvention of Jewish Tradition*. Berkeley: University of California Press, 1998.

Haberman, Bonna Devora. "Divorcing Ba'al: The Sex of Ownership in Jewish Marriage." In *The Passionate Torah: Sex and Judaism*, edited by Danya Ruttenberg, 36–57. New York: New York University Press, 2009.

Halberstam, Chaya T. *Law and Truth in Biblical and Rabbinic Literature*. Bloomington: Indiana University Press, 2010.

Haley, Shelley P. "Be Not Afraid of the Dark: Critical Race Theory and Classical Studies." In *Prejudice and Christian Beginnings: Investigating Race, Gender, and Ethnicity in Early Christian Studies*, edited by Laura Nasrallah and Elisabeth Schüssler Fiorenza, 27–50. Minneapolis: Fortress Press, 2009.

Hall, Edith. "Asia Unmanned: Images of Victory in Classical Athens." In *War and Society in the Greek World*, edited by John Rich and Graham Shipley, 108–133. London: Routledge, 1993.

Hamel, Gildas. *Poverty and Charity in Roman Palestine: First Three Centuries C.E.* Near Eastern Studies 23. Berkeley: University of California Press, 1989.

Harper, Kyle. *Slavery in the Late Roman World, AD 275–425*. Cambridge: Cambridge University Press, 2011.

Harris, William. "Towards a Study of the Roman Slave Trade." *Memoirs of the American Academy in Rome* 36 (1980): 117–140.

———. "Demography, Geography, and the Sources of Roman Slaves." *Journal of Roman Studies* 89 (1999): 62–75.

Hasan-Rokem, Galit. "Within Limits and Beyond: History and Body in Midrashic Texts." *International Folklore Review: Folklore Studies from Overseas* 9–10 (1993–1995): 5–12.

———. "Narratives in Dialogue: A Folk-Literary Perspective on Interreligious Contacts in the Holy Land in Rabbinic Literature of Late Antiquity." In *Sharing the Sacred: Religious Contacts and Conflicts in the Holy Land*, edited by Arieh Kofsky and Guy G. Stroumsa, 109–129. Jerusalem: Yad Izhak Ben Zvi, 1998.

———. *Web of Life: Folklore and Midrash in Rabbinic Literature*. Stanford: Stanford University Press, 2000.

———. "Rabbi Meir, the Illuminated and the Illuminating." In *Two Trends in the Study of Midrash*, edited by Carol Bakhtos, 227–244. Leiden: Brill, 2006.

———. "Bodies Performing in Ruins: The Lamenting Mother in Ancient Jewish Texts." In *Lament in Jewish Thought: Philosophical, Theological and Literary Perspectives*, edited by Ilit Ferber and Paula Schwebel, 33–63. Berlin: Walter De Gruyter, 2014.

Haskell, Ellen Davina. *Suckling at My Mother's Breasts: The Image of a Nursing God in Jewish Mysticism*. Albany: State University of New York Press, 2012.

Hauptman, Judith. *Rereading the Rabbis: A Woman's Voice*. Boulder: Westview Press, 1998.

———. *Rereading the Mishnah: A New Approach to Ancient Jewish Texts*. Tübingen: Mohr Siebeck, 2005.

Hayes, Christine. *Gentile Impurities and Jewish Identities: Intermarriage and Conversion from the Bible to the Talmud*. New York: Oxford University Press, 2002.

Hezser, Catherine. *The Social Structure of the Rabbinic Movement in Roman Palestine*. Tübingen: Mohr Siebeck, 1997.

———. *Jewish Slavery in Antiquity*. New York: Oxford University Press, 2006.

Hodkin, Bernie. "Repression and Romanization: Postcolonial Studies in Ancient Judaism." *Ancient Jew Review*, November 26, 2014. http://www.ancientjewreview. com/articles/2014/11/26/bbusbbpr9km137buti5qsso9e8gzx4.

———. "Theologies of Resistance: A Reexamination of Rabbinic Traditions about Rome." In *Reactions to Empire: Sacred Texts in Their Socio-Political Contexts*, edited by John Anthony Dunne and Dan Batovici, 163–177. Tübingen: Mohr Siebeck, 2014.

Hood, Robert Earl. *Begrimed and Black: Christian Traditions on Blacks and Blackness*. Minneapolis: Fortress Press, 1994.

Horsley, Richard, ed. *Hidden Transcripts and the Arts of Resistance: Applying the Work of James C. Scott to Jesus and Paul*. Atlanta: Society of Biblical Literature, 2004.

Ilan, Tal. *Massekhet Ta'anit: Text, Translation, and Commentary*. Tübingen: Mohr Siebeck, 2008.

Mine and Yours Are Hers: Retrieving Women's History from Rabbinic Literature. Leiden: Brill, 1997.

———. *Lexicon of Jewish Names in Late Antiquity*. Vol. 1. Tübingen: Mohr Siebeck, 2004.

Irshai, Ronit. "Rape in Jewish Law." Paper presented at the Society for Jewish Ethics Annual Meeting, Washington, DC, January 7, 2012.

Jacobs, Martin. *Reorienting the East: Jewish Traders to the Medieval Muslim World*. Philadelphia: University of Pennsylvania Press, 2014.

Jastrow, Marcus. *Dictionary of the Targumim, Talmud, and Midrashic Literature*. London: Luzac & Co., 1903.

Jeffers, Ann. *Magic and Divination in Ancient Palestine and Syria*. Leiden: Brill, 1996.

Jones, C. P. "Stigma: Tattooing and Branding in Graeco-Roman Antiquity." *Journal of Roman Studies* 77 (1987): 139–155.

Jones, Kenneth R. *Jewish Reactions to the Destruction of Jerusalem in A.D. 70: Apocalypses and Related Pseudepigrapha*. Leiden: Brill, 2011.

Jordan, Mark D. *The Invention of Sodomy in Christian Theology*. Chicago: University of Chicago Press, 1997.

Kafer, Alison. *Feminist, Crip, Queer*. Bloomington: Indiana University Press, 2013.

Kahn, Ari. "Freebird." *Orthodox Union*. April 16, 2015. https://www.ou.org/torah/parsha/rabbi-ari-kahn-on-parsha/freebird/#_ftn3.

Kaiser, Otto. *Isaiah 1–12: A Commentary*. Philadelphia: Westminster John Knox Press, 1981.

Kalmin, Richard. "Christians and Heretics in Rabbinic Literature of Late Antiquity." *Harvard Theological Review* 87, no. 2 (April 1994): 155–169.

———. "Holy Men, Rabbis, and Demonic Sages in Late Antiquity." In *Jewish Culture and Society under the Christian Roman Empire*, edited by Richard Kalmin and Seth Schwartz, 213–249. Leuven: Peeters Press, 2003.

———. *Jewish Babylonia Between Persia and Roman Palestine*. New York: Oxford University Press, 2006.

———. "Zechariah and the Bubbling Blood: An Ancient Tradition in Jewish, Christian, and Muslim Literature." In *Jews, Christians and Zoroastrians: Religious Dynamics in a Sasanian Context*, edited by Geoffrey Herman, 203–251. Piscataway: Gorgias Press, 2014.

———. *Migrating Tales: The Talmud's Narratives and Their Historical Context*. Berkeley: University of California Press, 2014.

Kamiankowski, Tamar. *Gender Reversal and Cosmic Chaos: A Study in the Book of Ezekiel*. New York: Sheffield Academic Press, 2003.

Kanga, M. F. "Barsom." *Encyclopædia Iranica*, Vol. 3, no. 8 (1988), 825–827. http://www.iranicaonline.org/articles/barsom-av.

Kelley, Shawn. "Race, Aesthetics, and Gospel Scholarship: Embracing and Subverting the Aesthetic Ideology." In *Prejudice and Christian Beginnings*, edited by Laura Nasrallah and Elizabeth S. Fiorenza, 191–210. Minneapolis: Fortress Press, 2009.

Kettenhofen, Erich. "Deportations." *Encyclopædia Iranica* 7, no. 3 (2014): 297–312.

Kilmer, Martin. "'Rape' in Early Red-Figure Pottery." In *Rape in Antiquity: Sexual Violence in the Greek and Roman Worlds*, edited by Susan Deacy and Karen F. Pierce, 123–142. Swansea: Classical Press of Wales, 2002.

Kirschner, Robert. "Apocalyptic and Rabbinic Responses to the Destruction of 70." *Harvard Theological Review* 78, no. 1–2 (1985): 27–46.

Kister, Menahem. *Studies in Avot de-Rabbi Nathan: Text, Redaction, and Interpretation* [Hebrew]. Jerusalem: Hebrew University, 1998.

Klawans, Jonathan. "Josephus, the Rabbis, and Responses to Catastrophes Ancient and Modern." *Jewish Quarterly Review* 100, no. 2 (Spring 2010): 278–309.

———. *Josephus and the Theologies of Ancient Judaism*. New York: Oxford University Press, 2012.

Knust, Jennifer. *Abandoned to Lust: Sexual Slander and Ancient Christianity*. New York: Columbia University Press, 2005.

Koltun-Fromm, Naomi. *Hermeneutics of Holiness: Ancient Jewish and Christian Notions of Sexuality and Religious Community*. New York: Oxford University Press, 2010.

Kraemer, David. *Responses to Suffering in Classical Rabbinic Literature*. New York: Oxford University Press, 1995.

———. *Jewish Eating and Identity Through the Ages*. New York: Routledge, 2007.

Kriger, Diane. *Sex Rewarded, Sex Punished: A Study of the Status of "Female Slave" in Early Jewish Law*. Boston: Academic Studies Press, 2011.

Krupp, Michael. "Manuscripts of the Babylonian Talmud," in *The Literature of the Sages. Vol. 1: Oral Tora, Halakha, Mishna, Tosefta, Talmud, External Tractates*, edited by Shmuel Safrai, 346–366. Philadelphia: Fortress Press, 1987.

Kugel, James L. *In Potifar's House: The Interpretive Life of Biblical Texts*. Cambridge, MA: Harvard University Press, 1994.

Labovitz, Gail. "Heruta's Ruse: What We Mean When We Talk About Desire." In *The Passionate Torah: Sex and Judaism*, edited by Danya Ruttenberg, 229–244. New York: New York University Press, 2009.

———. *Marriage and Metaphor: Constructions of Gender in Rabbinic Literature*. Lanham, MD: Lexington Books, 2009.

———. "The Purchase of His Money: Slavery and the Ethics of Jewish Marriage." In *Beyond Slavery: Overcoming Its Religious and Sexual Legacies*, edited by Bernadette Brooten, 91–106. New York: Palgrave Macmillan, 2010.

———. "More Slave Women, More Lewdness: Freedom and Honor in Rabbinic Constructions of Female Sexuality." *Journal of Feminist Studies in Religion* 28 (2012): 69–87.

Laes, Christian. "Silent Witnesses: Deaf-Mutes in Graeco-Roman Antiquity." *Classical World: A Quarterly Journal on Antiquity* 104, no. 4 (2011): 451–473.

Lapin, Hayim. *Rabbis as Romans: The Rabbinic Movement in Palestine, 100–400 CE*. New York: Oxford University Press, 2012.

Lefkowitz, Lori Hope. *In Scripture: The First Stories of Jewish Sexual Identities*. Lanham, MD: Rowman & Littlefield, 2010.

Lesses, Rebecca. "Exc(o)rcising Power: Women as Sorceresses, Exorcists, and Demonesses in Babylonian Jewish Society in Late Antiquity." *Journal of the American Academy of Religion* 69 (2003): 343–375.

Lev, Sarra. "They Treat Him as a Man and See Him as a Woman: The Tannaitic Understanding of the Congenital Eunich." *Jewish Studies Quarterly* 17, no. 3 (2010): 213–243.

Levenson, Jon D. *Resurrection and the Restoration of Israel: The Ultimate Victory of the God of Life*. New Haven, CT: Yale University Press, 2006.

Levinson, Joshua. "'Tragedies Naturally Performed': Fatal Charades, Parodia Sacra, and the Death of Titus." In *Jewish Culture and Society under the Christian Roman Empire*, edited by Richard Kalmin and Seth Schwartz, 349–382. Leuven: Peeters, 2003.

Lieberman, Saul. *Greek in Jewish Palestine/Hellenism in Jewish Palestine*. 1962 and 1965. Reprint, New York: Jewish Theological Seminary of America, 1994.

Linafelt, Tod. *Surviving Lamentations: Catastrophe, Lament, and Protest in the Afterlife of a Biblical Book*. Chicago: University of Chicago Press, 2000.

Lopez, Davina C. "Before Your Very Eyes: Roman Imperial Ideology, Gender Constructs and Paul's Inter-Nationalism." In *Mapping Gender in Ancient Religious Discourses*, edited by Todd Penner and Caroline Vander Stichele, 115–162. Leiden: Brill, 2007.

———. *Apostle to the Conquered: Reimagining Paul's Mission*. Minneapolis: Fortress Press, 2008.

Lowin, Shari L. "Narratives of Villainy: Titus, Nebuchadnezzar, and Nimrod in the *Hadith* and *Midrash Aggadah*." In *The Lineaments of Islam: Studies in Honor of Fred McGraw Donner*, edited by Paul Cobb, 261–296. Leiden: Brill, 2012.

Magonet, Jonathan. "Psalm 137: Unlikely Liturgy or Partisan Poem? A Response to Sue Gillingham." In *Jewish and Christian Approaches to the Psalms: Conflict and Convergence*, edited by Susan Gillingham, 81–88. New York: Oxford University Press, 2013.

Maier, Christl M. *Daughter Zion, Mother Zion: Gender, Space, and the Sacred in Ancient Israel*. Minneapolis: Fortress Press, 2008.

Maier, Harry O. "Nero in Jewish and Christian Tradition from the First Century to the Reformation." In *A Companion to the Neronian Age*, edited by Emma Buckley and Martin T. Dinter, 385–404. Chichester: Wiley-Blackwell Publishing, 2013.

Malmberg, Simon. "Visualizing Hierarchy at Imperial Banquets." In *Feast, Fast or Famine: Food and Drink in Byzantium*, edited by Wendy Mayer and Silke Trzcionka, 11–24. Brisbane: Australian Association for Byzantine Studies, 2005.

Mandel, Paul. "The Story in Midrash Eichah: Text and Style" [Hebrew]. M.A. thesis, Hebrew University, 1983.

———. "Midrash Lamentations Rabbati: Prolegomenon, and a Critical Edition to the Third Parasha" [Hebrew]. Ph.D. diss., Hebrew University, 1997.

———. "Between Byzantium and Islam: The Transmission of a Jewish Book in the Byzantine and Early Islamic Periods." In *Transmitting Jewish Traditions: Orality, Textuality, and Cultural Diffusion*, edited by Yaakov Elman and Israel Gershoni, 74–106. New Haven, CT: Yale University Press, 2000.

Marchal, Joseph. *The Politics of Heaven: Women, Gender, and Empire in the Study of Paul*. Minneapolis: Fortress Press, 2008.

Martin, Dale B. "Slavery and the Ancient Jewish Family." In *The Jewish Family in Antiquity*, edited by Shaye Cohen, 113–129. Atlanta: Scholars Press, 1993.

———. *The Corinthian Body*. New Haven, CT: Yale University Press, 2006.

Mattern, Susan P. *Galen and the Rhetoric of Healing*. Baltimore: Johns Hopkins University Press, 2008.

Mattingly, David J. *Imperialism, Power, and Identity: Experiencing the Roman Empire*. Princeton: Princeton University Press, 2011.

Mauss, Marcel. *The Gift: The Form and Reason for Exchange in Archaic Societies*. Translated by W. D. Halls. New York: W.W. Norton, 1990. Originally published as *Essai sur le Don*. Paris: Presses Universitaires de France, 1950.

Mays, James Luther. *Micah: A Commentary*. Philadelphia: Westminster John Knox Press, 1976.

McKane, William. *The Book of Micah: Introduction and Commentary*. Edinburgh: T&T Clark, 1998.

McRuer, Robert. *Crip Theory: Cultural Signs of Queerness and Disability*. New York: New York University Press, 2006.

Meir, Ofra. "The Subject of the Wedding in the Kin Parables in the Tales of the Sages" [Hebrew]. In *Studies in Marriage Customs*, edited by Issachar Ben-Ami and Dov Noy, 9–51. Jerusalem: Magnes Press, 1974.

Mellinkoff, Ruth. *The Horned Moses in Medieval Art and Thought*. Berkeley: University of California Press, 1970.

Merhavia, Chen. *Ha-Talmud be-Rei ha-Nazrut*. Jerusalem: Mossad Bialik, 1970.

Milik, J. T. "Textes littéraires." In *Discoveries in the Judaean Desert*, vol. 2, edited by P. Benoit, J. T. Milik, and R. De Vaux, 80–86. Oxford: Oxford University Press, 1961.

Millar, Fergus. "Last Year in Jerusalem: The Commemoration of the Jewish War in Rome." In *Flavius Josephus and Flavian Rome*, edited by J. Edmondson, S. Mason, and J. Rives, 101–128. Oxford: Oxford University Press, 2005.

———. "Transformations of Judaism under Graeco-Roman Rule: Responses to Seth Schwartz's 'Imperialism and Jewish Society.'" *Journal of Jewish Studies* 57, no. 1 (Spring 2006): 139–158.

Miller, J. Maxwell, and John H. Hayes, *A History of Ancient Israel and Judah*. Philadelphia: The Westminster Press, 1986.

Minh-Ha, Trinh T. *When the Moon Waxes Red: Representation, Gender, and Cultural Politics*. New York: Routledge, 1991.

Mintz, Alan. *Ḥurban: Responses to Catastrophe in Hebrew Literature*. New York: Columbia University Press, 1984.

Mitchell, David T., and Sharon L. Snyder. *Narrative Prosthesis: Disability and the Dependencies of Discourse*. Ann Arbor: University of Michigan Press, 2000.

———. "Re-engaging the Body: Disability Studies and the Resistance to Embodiment." *Public Culture* 13, no. 3 (2001): 367–389.

Mokhtarian, Jason Sion. *Rabbis, Sorcerers, Kings, and Priests: The Culture of the Talmud in Ancient Iran*. Berkeley: University of California Press, 2015.

Morgenstern, M., and M. Segal. "XHev/SePhylactery." In *Miscellaneous Texts from the Judaean Desert*, edited by James Charlesworth et al. Discoveries in the Judaean Desert Series, vol. 38, 183–191. Oxford: Oxford University Press, 2000.

Morrison, Daniel R., and Monica J. Casper. "Intersections of Disability Studies and Critical Trauma Studies: A Provocation." *Disability Studies Quarterly* 32, no. 2 (2012). http://dx.doi.org/10.18061/dsq.v32i2.3189.

Moss, Candida R. "Heavenly Healing: Eschatological Cleansing and the Resurrection of the Dead in the Early Church." *Journal of the American Academy of Religion* 79, no. 4 (2011): 991–1017.

———. "Resisting Empire in Early Christian Martyrdom Literature." In *Reactions to Empire: Sacred Texts in their Socio-Political Contexts*, edited by John Anthony Dunne and Dan Batovici, 147–162. Tübingen: Mohr Siebeck, 2014.

Nadich, Judah. *Legends of the Rabbis: Jewish Legends of the Second Commonwealth*. Northvale, NJ: Jason Aronson, 1994.

Nasrallah, Laura. *Christian Responses to Roman Art and Architecture: The Second-Century Church Amid the Spaces of Empire*. New York: Cambridge University Press, 2010.

Neusner, Jacob. *Development of a Legend: Studies on the Traditions Concerning Yohanan ben Zakkai*. Binghamton: Global Publications, 1960.

———. *A Life of Rabban Yohanan Ben Zakkai, ca. 1–80 CE*. Leiden: Brill, 1962.

———. "Judaism in a Time of Crisis: Four Responses to the Destruction of the Second Temple." *Judaism* 21 (1972): 313–327.

Nixon, Rob. *Slow Violence and the Environmentalism of the Poor*. Cambridge, MA: Harvard University Press, 2011.

Novak, David. "Jewish Marriage: Nature, Covenant, and Contract." In *Marriage, Sex, and Family in Judaism*, edited by Michael J. Broyde and Michael Ausubel, 61–87. Lanham, MD: Rowman & Littlefield, 2005.

Olyan, Saul. *Disability in the Hebrew Bible: Interpreting Mental and Physical Differences*. New York: Cambridge University Press, 2008.

———. "The Ascription of Physical Disability as a Stigmatizing Strategy in Biblical Iconic Polemics." *Journal of Hebrew Scriptures* 9, no. 14 (2009): 2–15.

Oswalt, John. *The Book of Isaiah, Chapters 1–39*. Grand Rapids: William B. Eerdmans Publishing Company, 1986.

Patton, Kimberley. *Religion of the Gods: Ritual, Paradox, and Reflexivity*. New York: Oxford University Press, 2009.

Peskowitz, Miriam. *Spinning Fantasies: Rabbis, Gender, and History*. Berkeley: University of California Press, 1997.

Pham, Xuan Huong Thi. *Mourning in the Ancient Near East and the Hebrew Bible*. Sheffield, UK: Sheffield Academic Press, 1999.

Pilz, Sonja K. *Food and Fear: Metaphors of Bodies and Spaces in the Stories of Destruction*. Würzburg: Ergon Verlag, 2016.

Plaskow, Judith. "Preaching Against the Text." In *The Coming of Lilith: Essays on Feminism, Judaism, and Sexual Ethics, 1972–2003*, edited by Donna Berman, 152–156. Boston: Beacon Press, 2005.

Price, Simon. "From Noble Funerals to Divine Cult: The Consecration of Roman Emperors." In *Rituals of Royalty: Power and Ceremonial in Traditional Societies,* edited by David Cannadine and Simon Price, 56–105. New York: Cambridge University Press, 1987.

Puar, Jasbir. "Coda: The Cost of Getting Better: Suicide, Sensation, Switchpoints." *GLQ: A Journal of Lesbian and Gay Studies* 18, no. 1 (2012): 149–158.

Raphael, Rebecca. *Biblical Corpora: Representations of Disability in Hebrew Biblical Literature.* New York: T&T Clark, 2008.

Richman, Aviva. "Sexual Coercion and Consent and the Development of Legal Subjectivity in Rabbinic Literature." Paper presented at the Society for Jewish Ethics Annual Meeting, Toronto, January 8, 2016.

Rosen-Zvi, Ishay. "The Body and the Book: The List of Blemishes in Mishnah Tractate Bekhorot and the Place of the Temple and Its Worship in the Tannaitic Beit Ha-Midrash" [Hebrew]. *Mada'ei Hayahadut* 43 (2005/6): 49–87.

———. *Demonic Desires: "Yetzer Hara" and the Problem of Evil in Late Antiquity.* Philadelphia: University of Pennsylvania Press, 2011.

———. "The Rise and Fall of Rabbinic Masculinity." *Jewish Studies, an Internet Journal* 12 (2013): 1–22.

———. "In What Sense Were the Rabbis Roman?" *Marginalia,* August 13, 2015. http:// marginalia.lareviewofbooks.org/ishay-rosen-zvi-on-rabbis-as-romans-by-hayim-lapin/.

Rosenblum, Jordan. *Food and Identity in Early Rabbinic Judaism.* New York: Cambridge University Press, 2010.

Rosenfeld, Ben-Zion. *Torah Centers and Rabbinic Activity in Palestine, 70–400 CE: History and Geographic Distribution.* Leiden: Brill, 2010.

Rosenthal, Judah M. "The Talmud on Trial: The Disputation of Paris in the Year 1240." *Jewish Quarterly Review* 47 (1956–1957): 58–76, 145–169.

Rubenstein, Jeffrey. *Talmudic Stories: Narrative Art, Composition, and Culture.* Baltimore: Johns Hopkins University Press, 1999.

———. *The Culture of the Babylonian Talmud.* Baltimore: Johns Hopkins University Press, 2003.

Sage, Michael M. *The Republican Roman Army: A Sourcebook.* New York: Routledge, 2008.

Saldarini, Anthony J. "Johanan ben Zakkai's Escape from Jerusalem: Origin and Development of a Rabbinic Story." *Journal for the Study of Judaism* 6 (1975): 189–220.

———. "Varieties of Rabbinic Response to the Destruction of the Temple." *Society of Biblical Literature Seminar Papers* 21 (1982): 437–458.

———. "Good from Evil: The Rabbinic Response." In *The First Jewish Revolt: Archeology, History, Ideology,* edited by Andrea M. Berlin and J. Andrew Overman, 221–236. New York: Routledge, 2002.

Saperstein, Marc. "Halevi's West Wind." *Prooftexts* 1, no. 3 (September 1981): 306–311.

Sarna, Nahum. *JPS Torah Commentary: Exodus*. Philadelphia: Jewish Publication Society, 1991.

Satlow, Michael. *Tasting the Dish: Rabbinic Rhetorics of Sexuality*. Atlanta: Scholar's Press, 1995.

———. *Jewish Marriage in Antiquity*. Princeton: Princeton University Press, 2001.

Schäfer, Peter. "Die Flucht Yoḥanan b. Zakkais aus Jerusalem und die Gründung des 'Lehrhauses' in Jabne." *Aufstieg und Niedergang der römischen Welt* 2.19.2 (1979): 43–101.

———. *Der Bar-Kokhba-Aufstand: Studien zum zweiten jüdischen Krieg gegen Rom*. Tübingen: Mohr Siebeck, 1981.

———. *Jesus in the Talmud*. Princeton: Princeton University Press, 2007.

Scheidel, Walter. "Quantifying the Sources of Slaves in the Early Roman Empire." *Journal of Roman Studies* 87 (1997): 156–169.

Schipper, Jeremy. *Disability Studies and the Hebrew Bible: Figuring Mephibosheth in the David Story*. New York: T&T Clark, 2006.

———. *Disability and Isaiah's Suffering Servant*. New York: Oxford University Press, 2011.

Schipper, Jeremy, and Jeffrey Stackert. "Blemishes, Camouflage, and Sanctuary Service: The Priestly Deity and His Attendants." *Hebrew Bible and Ancient Israel* 2, no. 4 (December 2013): 458–478.

Schofer, Jonathan. "Protest or Pedagogy? Trivial Sin and Divine Justice in Rabbinic Narrative." *Hebrew Union College Annual* 74 (2003): 243–278.

Schofer, Jonathan Wyn. *Confronting Vulnerability: The Body and the Divine in Rabbinic Ethics*. Chicago: University of Chicago Press, 2003.

Schremer, Adiel. *Brothers Estranged: Heresy, Christianity, and Jewish Identity in Late Antiquity*. New York: Oxford University Press, 2010.

Schwartz, Seth. *Imperialism and Jewish Society, 200 B.C.E. to 640 C.E.* Princeton: Princeton University Press, 2001.

———. "Was There a 'Common Judaism' after the Destruction?" In *Envisioning Judaism: Studies in Honor of Peter Schäfer on the Occasion of his Seventieth Birthday*, edited by Raʿanan S. Boustan et al., 3–21. Tübingen: Mohr Siebeck, 2003.

———. "Political, Social, and Economic Life in the Land of Israel, 66–c.235." In *The Cambridge History of Judaism, Volume 4*, edited by Steven T. Katz, 23–52. New York: Cambridge University Press, 2006.

Scott, James C. *Domination and the Arts of Resistance: Hidden Transcripts*. New Haven, CT: Yale University Press, 1990.

Secunda, Shai. "Talmudic Text and Iranian Context: On the Development of Two Talmudic Narratives." *AJS Review* 33, no. 1 (2009): 45–69.

———. *The Iranian Talmud: Reading the Bavli in Its Sasanian Context*. Philadelphia: University of Pennsylvania Press, 2013.

Segal, Eliezer. "Anthological Dimensions of the Babylonian Talmud." In *The Anthology in Jewish Literature*, edited by David Stern, 81–107. New York: Oxford University Press, 2004.

Septimus, Zvi. "Trigger Words and Simultexts: The Experience of Reading the Bavli." In *Wisdom of Bat Sheva: In Memory of Beth Samuels*, edited by Barry Scott Wimpfheimer, 163–184. Jersey City, NJ: Ktav, 2009.

Setel, T. Drorah. "Prophets and Pornography: Female Sexual Imagery in Hosea." In *Feminist Interpretation of the Bible*, edited by Letty M. Russell, 86–95. Philadelphia: Westminster John Knox Press, 1985.

Sharpley-Whiting, T. Denean. *Frantz Fanon: Conflicts and Feminisms*. Lanham, MD: Rowman & Littlefield, 1998.

Siebers, Tobin. *Disability Aesthetics*. Ann Arbor: University of Michigan Press, 2010.

Siegal, Michal Bar-Asher. *Early Christian Monastic Literature and the Babylonian Talmud*. New York: Cambridge University Press, 2013.

Smallwood, E. Mary. *The Jews under Roman Rule: From Pompey to Dioclecian: A Study in Political Relations*. 1976. Reprint, Leiden: Brill, 2001.

Smith, Andrea. *Conquest: Sexual Violence and American Indian Genocide*. Cambridge, MA: South End Press, 2005.

Sokoloff, Michael. *A Dictionary of Jewish Babylonian Aramaic*. Baltimore: Johns Hopkins University Press, 2002.

Sperber, Daniel. *Roman Palestine 200–400: Money and Prices*, 2nd ed. Ramat-Gan: Bar-Ilan University Press, 1991.

Stathakopoulos, Dionysius Ch. *Famine and Pestilence in the Late Roman and Early Byzantine Empire: A Systematic Survey of Subsistence Crises and Epidemics*. Burlington, VT: Ashgate Publishing House, 2004.

Stemberger, Günter. "Yom Kippur in Mishnah Yoma." In *The Day of Atonement: Its Interpretations in Early Jewish and Christian Traditions*, edited by Thomas Hieke and Tobias Nicklas, 121–138. Leiden: Brill, 2011.

Stern, David. *Parables in Midrash: Narrative and Exegesis in Rabbinic Literature*. Cambridge, MA: Harvard University Press, 1991.

———. "The Captive Woman: Hellenization, Greco-Roman Erotic Narrative, and Rabbinic Literature." *Poetics Today* 19, no. 1 (1998): 91–127.

———, ed. *The Anthology in Jewish Literature*. New York: Oxford University Press, 2004.

Stevens, Maurice E. "Trauma's Essential Bodies." In *Corpus: An Interdisciplinary Reader on Bodies and Knowledge*, edited by Monica J. Casper and Paisley Currah, 171–186. New York: Palgrave Macmillan, 2011.

Stoler, Ann Laura. "Reason Aside: Reflections on Enlightenment and Empire." In *The Oxford Handbook of Postcolonial Studies*, edited by Graham Huggan, 39–66. New York: Oxford University Press, 2013.

———, ed. *Imperial Debris: On Ruins and Ruination*. Durham: Duke University Press, 2013.

Stone, Michael. "Reactions to Destructions of the Second Temple." *Journal for the Study of Judaism* 12 (1981): 195–204.

Stowe, David W. "History, Memory, and Forgetting in Psalm 137." In *The Bible in the Public Sphere: Its Enduring Influence in American Life*, edited by Mark A.

Chancey, Carol Meyers, and Eric M. Meyers, 137–157. Atlanta: Society of Biblical Literature, 2014.

Strack, Hermann L., and Günter Stemberger. *Introduction to the Talmud and Midrash*. Translated by Markus Bockmuehl. Edinburgh: T&T Clark, 1991.

Stratton, Kimberly. *Naming the Witch: Magic, Ideology, and Stereotype in the Ancient World*. New York: Columbia University Press, 2007.

Stumpp, Bettina Eva. *Prostitution in der römischen Antike*. Berlin: Akademie-Verlag, 2001.

Swartz, Michael D. "Jewish Magic in Late Antiquity." In *Cambridge History of Judaism, Volume 4*, edited by Steven T. Katz, 699–720. New York: Cambridge University Press, 2006.

Sweeney, Marvin. *Isaiah 1–4 and the Post-Exilic Understanding of the Isaianic Tradition*. Berlin: Walter de Gruyter, 1988.

Szobel, Ilana. *A Poetics of Trauma: The Work of Dahlia Ravikovitch*. Waltham: Brandeis University Press, 2013.

Tovar, Sofía Torallas. "Violence in the Process of Arrest and Imprisonment in Late Antique Egypt." In *Violence in Late Antiquity: Perceptions and Practices*, edited by Harold Allen Drake, 103–112. Burlington, VT: Ashgate Publishing, 2006.

Tropper, Amram. "Yohanan ben Zakkai, *Amicus Caesaris*: A Jewish Hero in Rabbinic Eyes." *Jewish Studies, an Internet Journal* 4 (2005): 133–149.

Ulmer, Rivka. *Egyptian Cultural Icons in Midrash*. Berlin: Walter de Gruyter, 2009.

Upson-Saia, Kristi. "Resurrecting Deformity: Augustine on the Scarred, Marked, and Deformed Bodies of the Heavenly Realm." In *Disability in Judaism, Christianity and Islam: Sacred Texts, Historical Traditions and Social Analysis*, edited by Darla Schumm and Michael Stoltzfus, 93–122. New York: Palgrave Macmillan, 2011.

Valler, Shulamit. *Sorrow and Distress in the Babylonian Talmud*. Boston: Academic Studies Press, 2011.

Visotzky, Burton. "Most Tender and Fairest of Women: A Study in the Transmission of Aggada." *Harvard Theological Review* 76, no. 4 (October 1983): 403–418.

Weems, Renita J. *Battered Love: Marriage, Sex, and Violence in the Hebrew Prophets*. Minneapolis: Fortress Press, 1995.

Wegner, Judith Romney. *Chattel or Person? The Status of Women in the Mishnah*. New York: Oxford University Press, 1988.

Weiss, Abraham. *Studies in the Literature of the Amoraim* [Hebrew]. New York: Horeb, 1962.

Wiesehöfer, Josef. *Ancient Persia from 550 BC to 650 AD*. London: Tauris, 1996.

Williams, Craig Arthur. *Roman Homosexuality: Ideologies of Masculinity in Classical Antiquity*. New York: Oxford University Press, 1999.

Williamson, Hugh. *Isaiah 1–5: A Critical and Exegetical Commentary*. New York: T&T Clark, 2006.

Wilson, Brittany E. *Unmanly Men: Refigurations of Masculinity in Luke-Acts*. New York: Oxford University Press, 2015.

Wimbush, Vincent. "Reading Darkness, Reading Scriptures." In *African Americans and the Bible: Sacred Texts and Social Structures*, edited by Vincent Wimbush, 1–43. New York: Continuum International, 2000.

Winter, Bruce W. *Roman Wives, Roman Widows: The Appearance of New Women and the Pauline Communities*. Grand Rapids: William B. Eerdmans, 2003.

Wire, Antionette Clarke. *Holy Lives, Holy Deaths: A Close Hearing of Early Jewish Storytellers*. Atlanta: Society of Biblical Literature, 2002.

Yassif, Eli. "The Cycle of Tales in Rabbinic Literature [Hebrew]." *Jerusalem Studies in Hebrew Literature* 12 (1990): 103–146.

———. *The Hebrew Folktale: History, Genre, Meaning*. Bloomington: Indiana University Press, 1999.

Yisraeli-Taran, Anat. *Aggadot ha-Ḥurban: Mesorot ha-Ḥurban be-Sifrut ha-Talmudit*. Tel Aviv: Hakibbutz Hame'uḥad, 1997.

Yoder, Christine Roy. *Proverbs*. Abingdon Old Testament Commentaries. Nashville: Abingdon Press, 2009.

Yuval, Israel. *Two Nations in Your Womb: Perceptions of Jews and Christians in Late Antiquity and the Middle Ages*. Berkeley: University of California Press, 2008.

Zeev, Miriam Pucci Ben. *Jewish Rights in the Roman World*. Tübingen: Mohr Siebeck, 1998.

Zellentin, Holger M. "Jerusalem Fell after Betar: The Christian Josephus and Rabbinic Memory." In *Envisioning Judaism: Studies in Honor of Peter Schäfer on the Occasion of his Seventieth Birthday*, edited by Ra'anan S. Boustan et al., 319–367. Tübingen: Mohr Siebeck, 2003.

———. *Rabbinic Parodies of Jewish and Christian Literature*. Tübingen: Mohr Siebeck, 2011.

General Index

Index of Ancient Sources

CPSIA information can be obtained
at www.ICGtesting.com
Printed in the USA
BVHW072308120720
582861BV00004B/23